Fodor's New Zealand

New
FIFTH EDITION

The complete guide, thoroughly up-to-date

Packed with details that will make your trip

The must-see sights, off and on the beaten path

What to see, what to skip

Mix-and-match vacation itineraries

City strolls, countryside adventures

Smart lodging and dining options

Essential local do's and taboos

Transportation tips, distances and directions

Key contacts, savvy travel tips

When to go, what to pack

Clear, accurate, easy-to-use maps

Books to read, videos to watch, background essays

Fodor's Travel Publications, Inc.
New York • Toronto • London • Sydney • Auckland
www.fodors.com

Fodor's New Zealand

EDITOR: Stephen Wolf

Contributors: Steven Amsterdam, Bob Blake, Barbara Blechman, David Brown, Stu Freeman, Helayne Schiff, M. T. Schwartzman (Gold Guide editor), Mere Wetere

Editorial Production: Tom Holton

Maps: David Lindroth, *cartographer*; Steven Amsterdam and Robert Blake, *map editors*

Design: Fabrizio La Rocca, *creative director*; Guido Caroti, *associate art director*; Jolie Novak, *photo editor*

Production/Manufacturing: Rebecca Zeiler

Cover Photograph: Larry Ulrich/Tony Stone Images

Copyright

Special Sales

Fodor's Travel Publications are available at special discounts for bulk purchases for sales promotions or premiums. Special editions, including personalized covers, excerpts of existing guides, and corporate imprints, can be created in large quantities for special needs. For more information, contact your local bookseller or write to Special Markets, Fodor's Travel Publications, 201 East 50th Street, New York, NY 10022. Inquiries from Canada should be directed to your local Canadian bookseller or sent to Random House of Canada, Ltd., Marketing Department, 2775 Matheson Boulevard East, Mississauga, Ontario L4W 4P7. Inquiries from the United Kingdom should be sent to Fodor's Travel Publications, 20 Vauxhall Bridge Road, London SW1V 2SA, England.

PRINTED IN THE UNITED STATES OF AMERICA

10 9 8 7 6 5 4 3 2 1

CONTENTS

ON THE ROAD WITH FODOR'S

WHEN I PLAN A VACATION, the first thing I do is cast around among my friends and colleagues to find someone who's just been where I'm going. That's because there's no substitute for a recommendation from a good friend who knows your tastes, your budget, and your circumstances, someone who's just been there. Unfortunately, such friends are few and far between. So it's nice to know that there's *New Zealand*.

In the first place, this book won't stay home when you hit the road. It will accompany you every step of the way, steering you away from wrong turns and wrong choices and never expecting a thing in return. Most important of all, it's written and assiduously updated by the kind of people you *would* hit up for travel tips if you knew them. They're as choosy as your pickiest friend, except they've probably seen a lot more of New Zealand. In these pages, they don't send you chasing down every town and sight in the country but have instead selected the best ones, the ones that are worthy of your time and money. To make it easy for you to put it all together in the time you have, they've created short, medium, and long itineraries and, in cities, neighborhood walks that you can mix and match in a snap. Will this be the vacation of your dreams? We hope so.

About Our Writers

Our success in helping to make your trip the best of all possible vacations is a credit to the hard work of our extraordinary writers and editors.

Michael Gebicki wrote the first edition of this book. British by birth, American by education, and Australian since 1979—after a stint living in New Zealand in his youth—he now works as a freelance travel writer and photographer based in Sydney. Dashing articles about his global wanderings appear regularly in travel publications in North America, Europe, and Asia.

This year's man on the islands, **Stu Freeman,** like most Kiwis, loves to get out into the bush on a regular basis, watch rugby, toss back a pint every now and then. He escaped the life of a daily newspaper journalist in the early 80s, threw a pack on his back, and tramped through Asia and Europe. Since then he's been freelance writing about New Zealand and the South Pacific.

Painter, garden designer, and passionate traveler **Barbara Blechman** took her expertise halfway around the world on reports that New Zealand is one of the finest places for growing just about anything. She found it to be a gardener's paradise, which accounts for the horticultural shock she experienced on returning to the island of Manhattan, where she lives, plants, and dreams of antipodean flora.

Mere Wetere's stamina as an updater is the stuff of legend—she added a raft of new sights, activities, hotels, and inns to our South Island chapters. She also brought to her work the perspective of her Maori heritage, and we are very pleased to make that a part of our *New Zealand*. Mere lives outside of Nelson at the top end of South Island, where she has reported for the *Nelson Mail* and worked as an employment consultant for single-parent women.

Vic Williams is all over the New Zealand food and wine map—author of the popular annual *Penguin Good New Zealand Wine Guide*, cuisine editor for *Fashion Quarterly* magazine, wine columnist for the *Evening Post,* and wine and food presenter for the television shows *Weekend* and *5:30 Live*. His pen and his superb taste are behind all of our restaurant and winery selections.

We'd also like to thank John Swinburn of the New Zealand Tourism Board as well as Tourism Christchurch for their assistance with Fodor's South Island travel arrangements.

Connections

We're pleased that the American Society of Travel Agents continues to endorse Fodor's as its guidebook of choice. ASTA is the world's largest and most influential travel trade association, operating in more than 170 countries, with 27,000 members pledged to adhere to a strict code of ethics reflecting the Society's motto, "Integrity in Travel." ASTA shares Fodor's devotion to providing smart, honest travel information and advice to travelers, and we've long recommended that our readers—even those who have guidebooks and traveling friends—consult ASTA member agents for the experience and professionalism they bring to your vacation planning.

On Fodor's Web site (www.fodors.com), check out the new Resource Center, an online companion to the Gold Guide chapter of this book, complete with useful hot links to related sites. In our forums, you can also get lively advice from other travelers and more great tips from Fodor's experts worldwide.

How to Use This Book

Organization

Up front is the **Gold Guide,** an easy-to-use section arranged alphabetically by topic. Under each listing you'll find tips and information that will help you accomplish what you need to in New Zealand. You'll also find addresses and telephone numbers of organizations and companies that offer destination-related services and detailed information and publications.

The first chapter in the guide, Destination: New Zealand helps get you in the mood for your trip. New and Noteworthy cues you in on trends and happenings, What's Where gets you oriented, Pleasures and Pastimes describes the activities and sights that make the country unique, Fodor's Choice showcases our top picks, and Festivals and Seasonal Events alerts you to special events you'll want to seek out.

Chapters in New Zealand are arranged geographically from the top of the country moving down, with two covering North Island and two covering South Island. Each regional chapter is divided by geographical area; within each area, cities and towns are covered in logical geographical order, and attractive stretches of road and minor points of interest between them are indicated by the designation *En Route*. And within town sections, all restaurants and lodgings are grouped together.

To help you decide what to visit in the time you have, all chapters begin with our recommended itineraries. The A to Z section

that ends all chapters covers getting there and getting around. It also provides helpful contacts and resources.

We also have a chapter called Adventure Vacations, which covers a number of outdoor activities and tour guides that can help you get the most out of them while you're in New Zealand. The advantage of using local guides is that they know the territory very well, and they will educate you about animals and plants you're seeing, which can be very exotic. They can also be quite entertaining. So don't pass up Chapter 6.

At the end of the book you'll find Portraits, essays about New Zealand's history and its fascinating flora and fauna, followed by suggestions for pretrip research, from recommended reading to movies on tape that use New Zealand as a backdrop.

Icons and Symbols

★ Our special recommendations
✕ Restaurant
🏠 Lodging establishment
✕🏠 Lodging establishment whose restaurant warrants a special trip
🐥 Good for kids (rubber duck)
☞ Sends you to another section of the guide for more information
✉ Address
☎ Telephone number
🕐 Opening and closing times
💲 Admission prices in New Zealand dollars (those we give apply to adults; substantially reduced fees are almost always available for children, students, and senior citizens)

Numbers in white and black circles (e.g., ③ ❸) that appear on the maps, in the margins, and within the tours correspond to one another.

Dining and Lodging

The restaurants and lodgings we list are the cream of the crop in each price range. Price categories are as follows:

For restaurants:

CATEGORY	COST*
$$$$	over $45
$$$	$35–$45
$$	$25–$35
$	under $25

*per person, excluding drinks, service, and general sales tax (GST, 12.5%)

For hotels:

CATEGORY	COST*
$$$$	over $200
$$$	$125–$200
$$	$80–$125
$	under $80

All prices are for a standard double room, excluding general sales tax (GST, 12.5%).

Hotel Facilities

We always list the facilities that are available—but we don't specify whether you'll be charged extra to use them: When pricing accommodations, always ask what's included. All rooms have private baths unless noted otherwise. In addition, when you book a room, be sure to mention if you have a disability or are traveling with children, if you prefer a private bath or a certain type of bed, or if you have specific dietary needs or other concerns.

Assume that hotels operate on the **European Plan** (with no meals) unless we mention that breakfast is included in rates (BP indicates **Breakfast Plan**), which many lodges (as opposed to hotels) do.

Restaurant Reservations and Dress Codes

Reservations are always a good idea; we mention them only when they're essential or are not accepted. Book as far ahead as you can, and reconfirm as soon as you arrive. Unless otherwise noted, the restaurants listed are open daily for lunch and dinner. We mention dress only when men are required to wear a jacket or a jacket and tie. Look for an overview of local dining-out habits in the Gold Guide and in the Pleasures and Pastimes section that follows each chapter introduction.

Credit Cards

The following abbreviations are used: **AE**, American Express; **DC**, Diners Club; **MC**, MasterCard; and **V**, Visa.

Don't Forget to Write

You can use this book in the confidence that all prices and opening times are based on information supplied to us at press time; Fodor's cannot accept responsibility for any errors. Time inevitably brings changes, so always confirm information when it matters—especially if you're making a detour to visit a specific place.

Were the restaurants we recommended as described? Did our hotel picks exceed your expectations? Did you find a museum we recommended a waste of time? Keeping a travel guide fresh and up-to-date is a big job, and we welcome your feedback, positive *and* negative. If you have complaints, we'll look into them and revise our entries when the facts warrant it. If you've discovered a special place that we haven't included, we'll pass the information along to our correspondents and have them check it out. So send us your thoughts via E-mail at editors@fodors.com (specifying the name of the book on the subject line) or on paper in care of the New Zealand editor at Fodor's, 201 East 50th Street, New York, New York 10022. In the meantime, have a wonderful trip!

Karen Cure
Editorial Director

North Island

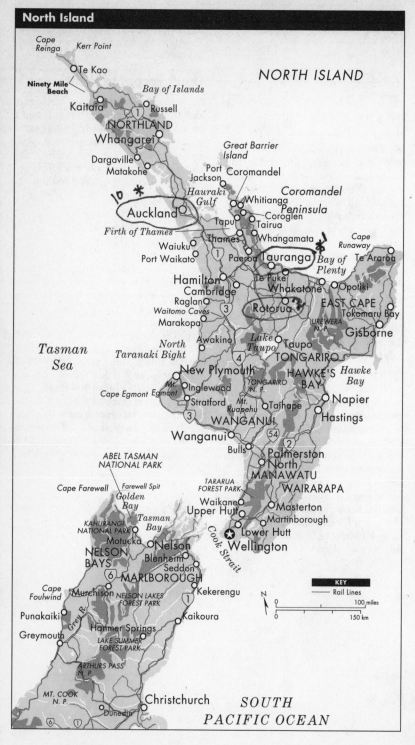

NORTH ISLAND

Cape Reinga
Kerr Point
Te Kao
Ninety Mile Beach
Bay of Islands
Kaitaia
Russell
NORTHLAND
Whangarei
Dargaville
Matakohe
Great Barrier Island
Port Jackson
Coromandel
Coromandel Peninsula
Hauraki Gulf
Whitianga
Coroglen
Auckland
Tapu
Tairua
Firth of Thames
Thames
Whangamata
Cape Runaway
Waiuku
Paeroa
Tauranga
Bay of Plenty
Te Araroa
Port Waikato
Te Puke
Hamilton
Whakatane
Opotiki
Cambridge
EAST CAPE
Raglan
Rotorua
Tokomaru Bay
Waitomo Caves
UREWERA N.P.
Gisborne
Marakopa
Awakino
Lake Taupo
Tasman Sea
North Taranaki Bight
Taupo
TONGARIRO
New Plymouth
TONGARIRO N.P.
HAWKE'S BAY
Hawke Bay
Mt. Egmont
Inglewood
Cape Egmont
Stratford
Mt. Ruapehu
Taihape
Napier
WANGANUI
Hastings
Wanganui
Bulls
Palmerston North
MANAWATU
WAIRARAPA
ABEL TASMAN NATIONAL PARK
TARARUA FOREST PARK
Cape Farewell
Farewell Spit
Golden Bay
Waikanae
Masterton
Upper Hutt
Martinborough
KAHURANGI NATIONAL PARK
Tasman Bay
Cook Strait
Lower Hutt
Motueka
Nelson
Wellington
NELSON BAYS
Blenheim
Seddon
MARLBOROUGH
Cape Foulwind
Murchison
NELSON LAKES FOREST PARK
Kekerengu
Punakaiki
Grey R.
Kaikoura
Greymouth
Hanmer Springs
LAKE SUMNER FOREST PARK
ARTHURS PASS N.P.
MT. COOK N.P.
Christchurch
SOUTH PACIFIC OCEAN
Dunedin

KEY
— Rail Lines
0   100 miles
0   150 km

South Island

Inglewood
Mt. Egmont Stratford
Cape Egmont
③
Wanganui

ABEL TASMAN
NATIONAL PARK

TARARUA
FOREST PARK

Cape Farewell Farewell Spit
Golden
Bay
Waikane
Upper Hutt
Wellington

SOUTH ISLAND

KAHURANGI
NATIONAL PARK
Tasman
Bay

Motueka
Nelson

NELSON
BAYS
Blenheim
Seddon

MARLBOROUGH

Murchison
Cape
Foulwind
NELSON LAKES
FOREST PARK

①
Kekerengu

Punakaiki
Grey R.
Kaikoura

Greymouth
LAKE SUMMER
FOREST PARK
Hanmer
Springs

WEST
COAST
Hawarden

Hokitika
ARTHURS PASS
N. P.

CANTERBURY
Christchurch

Franz Josef
Ashburton
Okains Bay

Fox
Glacier
MT. COOK
N. P.
Akaroa

Mt. Cook Village
Lake Tekapo

Lake Moeraki
⑥
Southern Alps
Lake
Pukaki
⑧
Fairlie

Haast
Haast River
AORANGI
Timaru

Mt. Aspiring
Lake
Wanaka

Milford Sound
Wanaka
Arrowtown
Oamaru

Doubtful
Sound
Lake
Wakatipu
Queenstown

Lake
Te Anau
OTAGO
COASTAL
NORTH

Te Anau
⑧
OTAGO

Lake
Manapouri
Lumsden
Dunedin

SOUTHLAND
SOUTH
PACIFIC OCEAN

⑥
①
Balclutha

FIORDLAND
N. P.
Invercargill

Foveaux St

Halfmoon Bay

Muttonbird
Islands
Stewart
Island

KEY
—— Rail Lines
N
0   100 miles
0   150 km

THE GOLD GUIDE / SMART TRAVEL TIPS

SMART TRAVEL TIPS A TO Z

*Basic Information on Traveling in New Zealand,
Savvy Tips to Make Your Trip a Breeze, and
Companies and Organizations to Contact*

AIR TRAVEL

BOOKING YOUR FLIGHT

Price is just one factor to consider when booking a flight: frequency of service and even a carrier's safety record are often just as important. Major airlines offer the greatest number of departures. Smaller airlines—including regional and no-frills airlines—usually have a limited number of flights daily. On the other hand, so-called low-cost airlines usually are cheaper, and their fares impose fewer restrictions, such as advance-purchase requirements. Safety-wise, low-cost carriers as a group have a good history—about equal to that of major carriers.

When you book, **look for nonstop flights** and **remember that "direct" flights stop at least once.** Try to **avoid connecting flights,** which require a change of plane. Two airlines may jointly operate a connecting flight, so ask if your airline operates every segment—you may find that your preferred carrier flies you only part of the way. International flights on a country's flag carrier are almost always nonstop; U.S. airlines often fly direct.

Ask your airline if it offers electronic ticketing, which eliminates all paperwork. There's no ticket to pick up or misplace. You go directly to the gate and give the agent your confirmation number. There's no worry about waiting in line at the airport while precious minutes tick by.

CARRIERS

When flying internationally, you must usually choose between a domestic carrier, the national flag carrier of the country you are visiting, and a foreign carrier from a third country. You may, for example, choose to fly Air New Zealand to New Zealand. National flag carriers have the greatest

number of nonstops. Domestic carriers may have better connections to your home town and serve a greater number of gateway cities. Third-party carriers may have a price advantage.

➤ MAJOR AIRLINES: **Air New Zealand** (☎ 310/615–1111 or 800/262–1234 in the U.S., 800/663–5494 in Canada) and **Qantas** (☎ 800/227–4500 in the U.S. and Canada) fly from Los Angeles to New Zealand, nonstop and direct. **United** (☎ 800/241–6522) and **Air Canada** (☎ 800/776–3000) connect from points in North America with flights of their own out of L.A. Air New Zealand is the only carrier with direct flights from North America to Christchurch as well as Auckland.

➤ FROM THE U.K.: **British Airways** (☎ 0345/222–111), **Cathay Pacific** (☎ 0171/747–8888), **Japan Airlines** (☎ 0345/747–700), **Qantas** (☎ 0345/747–767), and **Singapore Airlines** (☎ 0171/439–8111) operate between London and Auckland, with a stopover in Asia. **Air New Zealand** (☎ 0181/741–2299) and **United** (☎ 0181/990–9900) operate between London and Auckland by way of the United States.

➤ DOMESTIC AIRLINES: **Air New Zealand** (☎ 09/357–3000) and **Ansett New Zealand** (☎ 0800/267–388 in N.Z.) compete on intercity trunk routes. **Mount Cook Airline** (☎ 0800/800–737 in N.Z.) is an Air New Zealand affiliate that flies between a few North Island and a number of South Island cities, including resort and adventure activity areas.

CONSOLIDATORS

Consolidators buy tickets for scheduled international flights at reduced rates from the airlines, then sell them at prices that beat the best fare available directly from the airlines, usually without restrictions. Sometimes you can even get your money back if you need to return the ticket. Carefully read the fine print detailing penalties for changes and cancellations, and **confirm your consolidator reservation with the airline.**

➤ CONSOLIDATORS: **Cheap Tickets** (☎ 800/377–1000). **Up & Away Travel** (☎ 212/889–2345). **Discount Travel Network** (☎ 800/576–1600). **Unitravel** (☎ 800/325–2222). **World Travel Network** (☎ 800/409–6753).

COURIERS

When you fly as a courier, you trade your checked-luggage space for a ticket deeply subsidized by a courier service. It's all perfectly legitimate, but there are restrictions: You can usually book your flight only a week or two in advance, your length of stay may be set for a certain number of days, and you probably won't be able to book a companion on the same flight.

CUTTING COSTS

The least-expensive airfares to New Zealand are priced for round-trip travel and usually must be purchased in advance. It's smart to **call a number of airlines, and when you are quoted a good price, book it on the spot**—the same fare may not be available the next day. Airlines generally allow you to change your return date for a fee. If you don't use your ticket, you can apply the cost toward the purchase of a new ticket, again for a small charge. However, most low-fare tickets are nonrefundable. To get the lowest airfare, **check different routings.** Compare prices of flights to and from different airports if your destination or home city has more than one gateway. Also price off-peak flights, which may be significantly less expensive.

Travel agents, especially those who specialize in finding the lowest fares (☞ Discounts & Deals, *below*), can be especially helpful when booking a plane ticket. When you're quoted a price, **ask your agent if the price is likely to get any lower.** Good agents know the seasonal fluctuations of airfares and can usually anticipate a sale or fare war. However, waiting can be risky: The fare could go *up* as seats become scarce, and you may wait so long that your preferred flight sells out. A wait-and-see strategy works best if your plans are flexible. If you must arrive and depart on certain dates, don't delay.

DISCOUNT PASSES

Economy-price air travel is expensive compared with the cost of bus or train travel, but you can save a substantial amount of money if you buy multi-trip tickets. **Ansett New Zealand** (☞ Carriers, *above*) has a **New Zealand Airpass** entitling you to fly between three and eight sectors (i.e., point-to-point flights) starting from $450 for a three-sector pass and costing $150 for each additional sector. The pass is valid for the duration of your stay in New Zealand and should be purchased prior to arrival to avoid New Zealand sales tax. Also inquire about Ansett's 4-in-1 Inter-City New Zealand Travelpass. **Air New Zealand** and **Mount Cook** offer similar discount tickets, available through travel agents.

CHECK IN & BOARDING

Airlines routinely overbook planes, assuming that not everyone with a ticket will show up, but sometimes everyone does. When that happens, airlines ask for volunteers to give up their seats. In return these volunteers usually get a certificate for a free flight and are rebooked on the next flight out. If there are not enough volunteers, the airline must choose who will be denied boarding. The first to get bumped are passengers who checked in late and those flying on discounted tickets, so **get to the gate and check in as early as possible,** especially during peak periods.

Although the trend on international flights is to drop reconfirmation requirements, many airlines still ask you to reconfirm each leg of your international itinerary. Failure to do so may result in your reservation being canceled.

Always **bring a government-issued photo ID to the airport.** You may be asked to show it before you are allowed to check in.

ENJOYING THE FLIGHT

For more legroom, **request an emergency-aisle seat.** Don't sit in the row in front of the emergency aisle or in front of a bulkhead, where seats may not recline.

If you don't like airline food, **ask for special meals when booking.** These can be vegetarian, low-cholesterol, or kosher, for example.

When flying internationally, try to maintain a normal routine, to help fight jet-lag. At night, **get some sleep. By day, eat light meals, drink water (not alcohol), and move around the cabin** to stretch your legs.

Many carriers have prohibited smoking on all of their international flights; others allow smoking only on certain routes or certain departures, so **contact your carrier regarding its smoking policy.**

FLYING TIMES

From New York to Auckland (via Los Angeles) it takes about 19 hours; from Chicago, about 17 hours; from Los Angeles to Auckland (nonstop), about 12 hours. From the U.S. and Canada, you will have to connect to a New Zealand–bound flight in L.A.

Flights from London to Auckland take about 24 hours, either via the U.S. or via Southeast Asia. These are all actual air hours and do not include ground time.

HOW TO COMPLAIN

If your baggage goes astray or your flight goes awry, complain right away. Most carriers require that you **file a claim immediately.**

➤ AIRLINE COMPLAINTS: U.S. Department of Transportation **Aviation Consumer Protection Division** (✉ C-75, Room 4107, Washington, DC 20590, ☎ 202/366–2220). **Federal Aviation Administration Consumer Hotline** (☎ 800/322–7873).

AIRPORTS

The major airport is **Auckland International Airport** (☎ 09/275–0789).

BIKE TRAVEL

New Zealand is a sensational place to take cycling tours. For information on multi-day trips throughout the country, ☞ Adventure Vacations, Chapter 6.

BIKES IN FLIGHT

Most airlines will accommodate bikes as luggage, provided they are dismantled and put into a box. Call to see if your airline sells bike boxes (about $5; bike bags are at least $100) although you can often pick them up free at bike shops. International travelers can sometimes substitute a bike for a piece of checked luggage for free; otherwise, it will cost about $100. Domestic and Canadian airlines charge a $25–$50 fee.

BUS TRAVEL

New Zealand is served by an extensive bus network; for many travelers, buses offer the optimal combination of cost and convenience.

➤ BUS LINES: **InterCity** (☎ 09/639–0500) is a major bus line, and connects with the railroad system. The other major operators in North Island are **Newmans** (☎ 09/309–9738) and **Mount Cook Landline** (☎ 310/640–2823 or 800/468–2665 in the U.S.; 800/999–9306 in Canada; 0181/741–5652 in the U.K.; 0800/800–287 in N.Z.).

DISCOUNT PASSES

The InterCity Travelpass allows unlimited travel on all InterCity buses and trains and on the InterIslander ferries that link the North and South Islands (☞ Train Travel, below).

BUSINESS HOURS

Banks are open weekdays 9–4:30, but trading in foreign currencies ceases at 3. Shops are generally open Monday–Thursday 9–5:30, Friday 9–9, and Saturday 9–noon. Sunday trading is becoming more common but still varies greatly from place to place. Most Auckland shopping centers are open at least Sunday mornings.

CAMERAS & COMPUTERS

EQUIPMENT PRECAUTIONS

Always **keep your film, tape, or computer disks out of the sun.** Carry an extra supply of batteries, and **be prepared to turn on your camera, camcorder, or laptop** to prove to security personnel that the device is real. Always **ask for hand inspection of film,** which becomes clouded after successive exposure to airport X-ray machines, and **keep videotapes and computer disks away from metal detectors.**

TRAVEL PHOTOGRAPHY

➤ PHOTO HELP: **Kodak Information Center** (☎ 800/242–2424). *Kodak Guide to Shooting Great Travel Pictures,* available in bookstores or from Fodor's Travel Publications (☎ 800/533–6478; $16.50 plus $4 shipping).

CAR RENTAL

Rates in New Zealand begin at $48 a day and $298 a week for an economy car with unlimited mileage. This does not include tax on car rentals, which is 12.5%.

➤ MAJOR AGENCIES: **Avis** (☎ 800/331–1084, 800/879–2847 in Canada, 008/225–533 in Australia). **Budget** (☎ 800/527–0700, 0800/181181 in the U.K.). **Dollar** (☎ 800/800–4000; 0990/565656 in the U.K., where it is known as Eurodollar). **Hertz** (☎ 800/654–3001, 800/263–0600 in Canada, 0345/555888 in the U.K., 03/9222–2523 in Australia, 03/358–6777 in New Zealand). **National InterRent** (☎ 800/227–3876; 0345/222525 in the U.K., where it is known as Europcar InterRent).

➤ LOCAL AGENCIES: **Mauitours** (☎ 800/351–2323 in the U.S.; 800/663–2002 in Canada; 01737/843242 in the U.K.; 09/275–3013 in New Zealand) rents cars as well as the popular campervans.

CROSS-ISLAND RENTALS

Most major international companies have a convenient service if you are taking the ferry between North and South islands and want to continue your rental contract. You simply drop off the car in Wellington and on the same contract pick up a new car in Picton, or vice-versa. It saves you from paying the considerable fare for taking a car across on the ferry (and it's easier for the company to keep track of its rental fleet). Your rental contract is terminated only at the far end of your trip, wherever you end up. In this system, there is no drop-off charge for one-way rentals, making an Auckland–Queenstown rental as easy as it could be.

CUTTING COSTS

To get the best deal, **book through a travel agent who is willing to shop around.** Also **ask your travel agent about a company's customer-service record.** How has the company responded to late plane arrivals and vehicle mishaps? Are there often lines at the rental counter? If you're traveling during a holiday period, does a confirmed reservation guarantee you a car?

Be sure to **look into wholesalers,** companies that do not own fleets but rent in bulk from those that do and often offer better rates than traditional car-rental operations. Prices are best during off-peak periods. Rentals booked through wholesalers must be paid for before you leave the United States.

➤ RENTAL WHOLESALERS: **Auto Europe** (☎ 207/842–2000 or 800/223–5555, FAX 800–235–6321). **Kemwel Holiday Autos** (☎ 914/835–5555 or 800/678–0678, FAX 914/835–5126).

INSURANCE

When driving a rented car you are generally responsible for any damage to or loss of the vehicle. You also are liable for any property damage or personal injury that you may cause while driving. Before you rent, **see what coverage you already have** under the terms of your personal auto-insurance policy and credit cards.

In New Zealand, deductibles are very high with the most basic coverage, so you may want to opt for total coverage. Be sure to get all of the details from the rental agent before you decide.

REQUIREMENTS

In New Zealand your own driver's license is acceptable. An International Driver's Permit is a good idea; it's available from the American or Canadian automobile association, and, in the United Kingdom, from the Automobile Association or Royal Automobile Club. These international permits are universally recognized, and having one in your wallet may save you a problem with the local authorities.

THE GOLD GUIDE / SMART TRAVEL TIPS

SURCHARGES

Before you pick up a car in one city and leave it in another, **ask about drop-off charges or one-way service fees,** which can be substantial. Rates are often better if you pick-up in the south and drop off in the north—for example: start in Queenstown, and finish in Christchurch. This tends to be against the normal flow of tourism traffic, so rental car companies are often keen to get their vehicles back to northern points. Note, too, that some rental agencies charge extra if you return the car before the time specified in your contract. To avoid a hefty refueling fee, **fill the tank just before you turn in the car,** but be aware that gas stations near the rental outlet may overcharge.

CAR TRAVEL

Nothing beats the freedom and mobility of a car for exploring. Even for those nervous about driving on the "wrong" side of the road, motoring here is relatively easy. Roads are well maintained and generally uncrowded, though signposting, even on major highways, is often poor. Because traffic in New Zealand is relatively light, there has been little need to create major highways, and there are few places where you get straight stretches for very long. So don't plan on averaging 100 km per hour in too many areas. Most of the roads pass through beautiful scenery—so much in fact that you may be constantly agog at what you're seeing. The temptation is strong to look at everything, but keep your eyes on the road. Rest areas, many in positions with great views, are plentiful. Some are incredibly windy; others, like the road from Wanaka to Arrowtown outside of Queenstown, are off limits for rental cars. Ask your rental company in advance where you can and cannot drive if you plan to go off the beaten path.

Finally, remember this simple axiom: drive left, look right. That means keep to the left lane, and when turning right or left from a stop sign, the closest lane of traffic will be coming from the right, so look in that direction first. By the same token, pedestrians should look right before crossing the street. Americans and Canadians, you can blindly step into the path of an oncoming car by looking left as you do when crossing streets at home. So repeat this several times: drive left, look right.

You'll find yourself in a constant comedy of errors when you go to use directional signals and windshield wipers—in Kiwi cars it's the reverse of what you're used to. You won't be able to count how many times those wipers start flapping back and forth when you go to signal a turn (it'll happen in reverse when you get back home). You can be sure it's time to call it a day when you reach over your left shoulder for the seat belt and grab a handful of air.

AUTO CLUBS

➤ IN AUSTRALIA: **Australian Automobile Association** (☎ 06/247–7311).

➤ IN CANADA: **Canadian Automobile Association** (CAA, ☎ 613/247–0117).

➤ IN NEW ZEALAND: **New Zealand Automobile Association** (☎ 09/377–4660).

➤ IN THE U.K.: **Automobile Association** (AA, ☎ 0990/500–600), **Royal Automobile Club** (RAC, ☎ 0990/722–722 for membership, 0345/121–345 for insurance).

➤ IN THE U.S.: **American Automobile Association** (☎ 800/564–6222).

RULES OF THE ROAD

The speed limit is 100 kilometers per hour (62 mph) on the open road and 50 kph (31 mph) in towns and cities. A circular sign with the letters LSZ (Limited Speed Zone) means speed should be governed by prevailing road conditions, but still not exceed 100 kph.

When driving in rural New Zealand, cross one-lane bridges with caution—there are plenty of them. A yellow sign on the left will usually warn that you are approaching a one-lane bridge, and another sign will tell you whether you have the right-of-way. A rectangular blue sign means you have the right-of-way, and a circular sign with a red border means you must pull over to the left and wait to cross until oncoming traffic has passed. Even when you have the right-of-way, slow down and take care. Some one-lane bridges in South Island are used by trains as well as cars. Trains always have the right-of-way.

CHILDREN & TRAVEL

CHILDREN IN NEW ZEALAND

Be sure to plan ahead and **involve your youngsters** as you outline your trip. When packing, include things to keep them busy en route. On sightseeing days try to schedule activities of special interest to your children. If you are renting a car don't forget to **arrange for a car seat** when you reserve.

Baby products such as disposable diapers (ask for napkins or nappies), formula, and baby food can be found in chemists' shops. They are less expensive in supermarkets.

➤ BABY-SITTING: Most hotels and resorts have baby-sitters available at a charge of around $10 to $15 per hour. Baby-sitting services are also listed in the yellow pages of city telephone directories.

➤ STROLLER AND BASSINET RENTAL: **Royal New Zealand Plunket Society** (✉ 5 Alexis Ave., Mt. Albert, Auckland, ☎ 09/849–5652).

DINING

New Zealanders are genuinely fond of and considerate toward children, and their own children are included in most of their parents' social activities. Children are welcome in all restaurants throughout the country. However, they are rarely seen in those restaurants that appear in Fodor's very expensive (**$$$$**) and expensive (**$$$**) price categories. These restaurants may not have high chairs or be prepared to make special children's meals.

FLYING

If your children are two or older, **ask about children's airfares.** As a general rule, infants under two not occupying a seat fly at greatly reduced fares or even for free.

In general the adult baggage allowance applies to children paying half or more of the adult fare. When booking, **ask about carry-on allowances for those traveling with infants.** In general, for babies charged 10% of the adult fare you are allowed one carry-on bag and a collapsible stroller, which may have to be checked; you may be limited to less if the flight is full.

Experts agree that it's a good idea to use safety seats aloft for children weighing less than 40 pounds. Airlines, however, can set their own policies: U.S. carriers allow FAA-approved models but usually require that you buy a ticket, even if your child would otherwise ride free, since the seats must be strapped into regular seats. Airline rules vary, so it's important to **check your airline's policy about using safety seats during takeoff and landing.** Safety seats cannot obstruct the movement of other passengers in the row, so get an appropriate seat assignment as early as possible.

When making your reservation, **request children's meals or a free-standing bassinet** if you need them; the latter are available only to those seated at the bulkhead, where there's enough legroom. Remember, however, that bulkhead seats may not have their own overhead bins, and there's no storage space in front of you—a major inconvenience.

GROUP TRAVEL

When planning to take your kids on a tour, look for companies that specialize in family travel.

➤ FAMILY-FRIENDLY TOUR OPERATORS: **Rascals in Paradise** (✉ 650 5th St., Suite 505, San Francisco, CA 94107, ☎ 415/978–9800 or 800/872–7225, FAX 415/442–0289).

HOTELS

In hotels, roll-away beds are usually free, and children under 12 sharing a hotel room with adults either stay free or receive a discount rate. Few hotels have separate facilities for children.

Home hosting provides an ideal opportunity for visitors to stay with a local family, either in town or on a working farm. For information on home and farm stays, home exchange, and apartment rentals, see Lodging, *below.*

THE GOLD GUIDE / SMART TRAVEL TIPS

CONSUMER PROTECTION

Whenever possible, **pay with a major credit card** so you can cancel payment or get reimbursed if there's a problem, provided that you can provide documentation. This is the best way to pay, whether you're buying travel arrangements before your trip or shopping at your destination.

If you're doing business with a particular company for the first time, **contact your local Better Business Bureau and the attorney general's offices** in your state and the company's home state, as well. Have any complaints been filed?

Finally, if you're buying a package or tour, always **consider travel insurance** that includes default coverage (☞ Insurance, *below*).

➤ LOCAL BBBs: **Council of Better Business Bureaus** (✉ 4200 Wilson Blvd., Suite 800, Arlington, VA 22203, ☎ 703/276–0100, FAX 703/525–8277).

CUSTOMS & DUTIES

When shopping, **keep receipts** for all of your purchases. Upon reentering the country, **be ready to show customs officials what you've bought.** If you feel a duty is incorrect, appeal the assessment. If you object to the way your clearance was handled, get the inspector's badge number. In either case, first ask to see a supervisor, then write to the appropriate authorities, beginning with the port director at your point of entry.

IN NEW ZEALAND

New Zealand has stringent regulations governing the import of weapons, foodstuffs, and certain plant and animal material. Anti-drug laws are strict and penalties severe. In addition to personal effects, nonresidents over 17 years of age may bring in, duty-free, 200 cigarettes or 250 grams of tobacco or 50 cigars, 4.5 liters of wine, one bottle containing not more than 1,125 milliliters of spirits or liqueur, and personal purchases and gifts up to the value of US$440 (NZ$700).

Don't stash any fruit in your carry-on to take into the country. The agricultural quarantine is serious business.

So if you've been hiking recently and are bringing your boots with you, clean them before you pack. The authorities for very good reason don't want any non-native seeds haplessly transported into the country. It's a small and fragile ecosystem, and Kiwis rightfully want to protect it.

IN AUSTRALIA

Australia residents who are 18 or older may bring back $A400 worth of souvenirs and gifts (including jewelry), 250 cigarettes or 250 grams of tobacco, and 1,125 ml of alcohol (including wine, beer, and spirits). Residents under 18 may bring back $A200 worth of goods.

➤ INFORMATION: **Australian Customs Service** (Regional Director, ✉ Box 8, Sydney, NSW 2001, ☎ 02/9213–2000, FAX 02/9213–4000).

IN CANADA

Canadian residents who have been out of Canada for at least 7 days may bring in C$500 worth of goods duty-free. If you've been away less than 7 days but more than 48 hours, the duty-free allowance drops to C$200; if your trip lasts 24–48 hours, the allowance is C$50. You may not pool allowances with family members. Goods claimed under the C$500 exemption may follow you by mail; those claimed under the lesser exemptions must accompany you. Alcohol and tobacco products may be included in the 7-day and 48-hour exemptions but not in the 24-hour exemption. If you meet the age requirements of the province or territory through which you reenter Canada, you may bring in, duty-free, 1.14 liters (40 imperial ounces) of wine or liquor *or* 24 12-ounce cans or bottles of beer or ale. If you are 16 or older you may bring in, duty-free, 200 cigarettes and 50 cigars.

You may send an unlimited number of gifts worth up to C$60 each duty-free to Canada. Label the package UNSOLICITED GIFT—VALUE UNDER $60. Alcohol and tobacco are excluded.

➤ INFORMATION: **Revenue Canada** (✉ 2265 St. Laurent Blvd. S, Ottawa, Ontario K1G 4K3, ☎ 613/993–0534, 800/461–9999 in Canada).

IN THE U.K.

From countries outside the EU, including New Zealand, you may import, duty-free, 200 cigarettes or 50 cigars; 1 liter of spirits or 2 liters of fortified or sparkling wine or liqueurs; 2 liters of still table wine; 60 milliliters of perfume; 250 milliliters of toilet water; plus £136 worth of other goods, including gifts and souvenirs.

➤ INFORMATION: **HM Customs and Excise** (✉ Dorset House, Stamford St., London SE1 9NG, ☎ 0171/202–4227).

IN THE U.S.

U.S. residents may bring home $400 worth of foreign goods duty-free if they've been out of the country for at least 48 hours (and if they haven't used the $400 allowance or any part of it in the past 30 days).

U.S. residents 21 and older may bring back 1 liter of alcohol duty-free. In addition, regardless of your age, you are allowed 200 cigarettes and 100 non-Cuban cigars. Antiques, which the U.S. Customs Service defines as objects more than 100 years old, enter duty-free, as do original works of art done entirely by hand, including paintings, drawings, and sculptures.

You may also send packages home duty-free: up to $200 worth of goods for personal use, with a limit of one parcel per addressee per day (and no alcohol or tobacco products or perfume worth more than $5); label the package PERSONAL USE, and attach a list of its contents and their retail value. Do not label the package UNSOLICITED GIFT, or your duty-free exemption will drop to $100. Mailed items do not affect your duty-free allowance on your return.

➤ INFORMATION: **U.S. Customs Service** (Inquiries, ✉ Box 7407, Washington, DC 20044, ☎ 202/927–6724; complaints, Office of Regulations and Rulings, ✉ 1301 Constitution Ave. NW, Washington, DC 20229; registration of equipment, Resource Management, ✉ 1301 Constitution Ave. NW, Washington, DC 20229, ☎ 202/927–0540).

DINING

Some restaurants offer a fixed-price dinner, but the majority are à la carte. It's wise to make a reservation and inquire if the restaurant has a liquor license or is "BYOB" or "BYO" (Bring Your Own Bottle). Attire country-wide is pretty casual; unless you're planning to dine at the finest of places, men won't need to bring a jacket and tie. At the same time, the most common dinner attire is usually one level above jeans and sports shirts.

DISABILITIES & ACCESSIBILITY

ACCESS IN NEW ZEALAND

The **New Zealand Tourism Board** (☎ 04/472–8860) publishes *Access: A Guide for the Less Mobile Traveller,* listing accommodations, attractions, restaurants, and thermal pools with special facilities. In New Zealand, all accommodations are required by law to provide at least one room with facilities for guests with disabilities.

AIR TRAVEL

In addition to making arrangements for wheelchair-using passengers, both **Qantas** and **Ansett Airlines** accommodate trained dogs accompanying passengers with sight- and hearing-impairments. On **Air New Zealand**, wheelchairs for in-flight mobility are standard equipment; seat-belt extensions, quadriplegic harnesses, and padded leg rests are also available. Ask for the company's brochure "Air Travel for People with Disabilities." *See* ☞ Air Travel, *above.*

CAR RENTAL

Only **Budget** offers cars fitted with hand controls, but these are limited. **Hertz** will fit hand-held controls onto standard cars in some cities. *See* ☞ Car Rental, *above.*

LODGING

The major hotel chains (such as **Parkroyal**) provide three or four rooms with facilities for guests with disabilities in most of their properties. Even independent lodgings with more than eight rooms should provide at least one room with such facilities.

MAKING RESERVATIONS

New Zealand is at the forefront in providing facilities for people with disabilities. Still, when discussing accessibility with an operator or reservations agent, **ask hard questions.** Are there any stairs, inside *or* out? Are there grab bars next to the toilet *and* in the shower/tub? How wide is the doorway to the room? To the bathroom? For the most extensive facilities meeting the latest legal specifications, **opt for newer accommodations,** which are more likely to have been designed with access in mind. Older buildings or ships may have more limited facilities. Be sure to **discuss your needs before booking.**

TAXIS

Companies have recently introduced vans equipped with hoists and floor clamps, but these should be booked several hours in advance if possible; contact the **Plunket Society** (☞ Children & Travel, *above*) for more information.

TRAIN TRAVEL

Passengers on mainline passenger trains in New Zealand can request collapsible wheelchairs to negotiate narrow interior corridors. However, compact toilet areas and platform access problems make long-distance train travel difficult.

TRANSPORTATION

➤ COMPLAINTS: **Disability Rights Section** (✉ U.S. Department of Justice, Civil Rights Division, Box 66738, Washington, DC 20035–6738, ☎ 202/514–0301 or 800/514–0301, TTY 202/514–0383 or 800/514–0383, FAX 202/307–1198) for general complaints. **Aviation Consumer Protection Division** (☞ Air Travel, *above*) for airline-related problems. **Civil Rights Office** (✉ U.S. Department of Transportation, Departmental Office of Civil Rights, S-30, 400 7th St. SW, Room 10215, Washington, DC, 20590, ☎ 202/366–4648, FAX 202/366–9371) for problems with surface transportation.

TRAVEL AGENCIES & TOUR OPERATORS

As a whole, the travel industry has become more aware of the needs of travelers with disabilities. In the U.S., the Americans with Disabilities Act requires that travel firms serve the needs of all travelers. Note, though, that some agencies and operators specialize in making travel arrangements for individuals and groups with disabilities.

➤ TRAVELERS WITH MOBILITY PROBLEMS: **Access Adventures** (✉ 206 Chestnut Ridge Rd., Rochester, NY 14624, ☎ 716/889–9096), run by a former physical-rehabilitation counselor. **Accessible Journeys** (✉ 35 W. Sellers Ave., Ridley Park, PA 19078, ☎ 610/521–0339 or 800/846–4537, FAX 610/521–6959), for escorted tours exclusively for travelers with mobility impairments. **Flying Wheels Travel** (✉ 143 W. Bridge St., Box 382, Owatonna, MN 55060, ☎ 507/451–5005 or 800/535–6790, FAX 507/451–1685), a travel agency specializing in customized tours and itineraries worldwide. **Hinsdale Travel Service** (✉ 201 E. Ogden Ave., Suite 100, Hinsdale, IL 60521, ☎ 630/325–1335), a travel agency that benefits from the advice of wheelchair traveler Janice Perkins.

DISCOUNTS & DEALS

Be a smart shopper and **compare all your options** before making any choice. A plane ticket bought with a promotional coupon may not be cheaper than the least expensive fare from a discount ticket agency. For high-price travel purchases, such as packages or tours, keep in mind that what you get is just as important as what you save. Just because something is cheap doesn't mean it's a bargain.

CLUBS & COUPONS

Many companies sell discounts in the form of travel clubs and coupon books, but these cost money. You must use participating advertisers to get a deal, and only after you recoup the initial membership cost or book price do you begin to save. If you plan to use the club or coupons frequently, you may save considerably. Before signing up, find out what discounts you get for free.

➤ DISCOUNT CLUBS: **Entertainment Travel Editions** (✉ 2125 Butterfield Rd., Troy, MI 48084, ☎ 800/445–

4137; $20–$51, depending on destination). **Great American Traveler**
(✉ Box 27965, Salt Lake City, UT
84127, ☎ 801/974–3033 or 800/
548–2812; $49.95 per year). **Mo-
ment's Notice Discount Travel Club**
(✉ 7301 New Utrecht Ave., Brooklyn, NY 11204, ☎ 718/234–6295;
$25 per year, single or family). **Privi-
lege Card International** (✉ 237 E.
Front St., Youngstown, OH 44503,
☎ 330/746–5211 or 800/236–9732;
$74.95 per year). **Sears's Mature
Outlook** (✉ Box 9390, Des Moines,
IA 50306, ☎ 800/336–6330; $19.95
per year). **Travelers Advantage** (✉
CUC Travel Service, 3033 S. Parker
Rd., Suite 1000, Aurora, CO 80014,
☎ 800/548–1116 or 800/648–4037;
$59.95 per year, single or family).
Worldwide Discount Travel Club
(✉ 1674 Meridian Ave., Miami
Beach, FL 33139, ☎ 305/534–2082;
$50 per year family, $40 single).

CREDIT-CARD BENEFITS

When you use your credit card to
make travel purchases you may get
free travel-accident insurance, colli-
sion-damage insurance, and medical
or legal assistance, depending on the
card and the bank that issued it.
American Express, MasterCard, and
Visa provide one or more of these
services, so **get a copy of your credit
card's travel-benefits policy.** If you are
a member of an auto club, always **ask
hotel and car-rental reservations
agents about auto-club discounts.**
Some clubs offer additional discounts
on tours, cruises, and admission to
attractions.

DISCOUNT RESERVATIONS

To save money, **look into discount-
reservations services** with toll-free
numbers, which use their buying
power to get a better price on hotels,
airline tickets, even car rentals. When
booking a room, always **call the
hotel's local toll-free number** (if one is
available) rather than the central
reservations number—you'll often get
a better price. Always ask about
special packages or corporate rates.

When shopping for the best deal on
hotels and car rentals, **look for guar-
anteed exchange rates,** which protect
you against a falling dollar. With your

rate locked in, you won't pay more,
even if the price goes up in the local
currency.

➤ AIRLINE TICKETS: ☎ **800/FLY–4–
LESS.**

➤ HOTEL ROOMS: **Travel Interlink**
(☎ 800/888–5898). **VacationLand**
(☎ 800/245–0050).

PACKAGE DEALS

Packages and guided tours can save
you money, but don't confuse the
two. When you buy a package, your
travel remains independent, just as
though you had planned and booked
the trip yourself. Fly/drive packages,
which combine airfare and car rental,
are often a good deal.

ELECTRICITY

To use your U.S.-purchased electric-
powered equipment, **bring a converter
and adapter.** The electrical current in
New Zealand is 240 volts, 50 cycles
alternating current (AC); wall outlets
take slanted three-prong plugs (but
not the U.K. three-prong) and plugs
with two flat prongs set at a "V"
angle.

If your appliances are dual-voltage,
you'll need only an adapter. Don't use
110-volt outlets, marked FOR SHAVERS
ONLY, for high-wattage appliances
such as blow-dryers. Most laptops
operate equally well on 110 and 220
volts and so require only an adapter.

GAY & LESBIAN TRAVEL

➤ GAY- AND LESBIAN-FRIENDLY TRAVEL
AGENCIES: **Corniche Travel** (✉ 8721
Sunset Blvd., Suite 200, West Holly-
wood, CA 90069, ☎ 310/854–6000
or 800/429–8747, FAX 310/659–
7441). **Islanders Kennedy Travel**
(✉ 183 W. 10th St., New York, NY
10014, ☎ 212/242–3222 or 800/
988–1181, FAX 212/929–8530). **Now
Voyager** (✉ 4406 18th St., San Fran-
cisco, CA 94114, ☎ 415/626–1169
or 800/255–6951, FAX 415/626–
8626). **Yellowbrick Road** (✉ 1500 W.
Balmoral Ave., Chicago, IL 60640,
☎ 773/561–1800 or 800/642–2488,
FAX 773/561–4497). **Skylink Travel
and Tour** (✉ 3577 Moorland Ave.,
Santa Rosa, CA 95407, ☎ 707/585–
8355 or 800/225–5759, FAX 707/
584–5637), serving lesbian travelers.

HEALTH

DIVERS' ALERT

Do not fly within 24 hours after scuba diving.

MEDICAL PLANS

No one plans to get sick while traveling, but it happens, so **consider signing up with a medical-assistance company.** Members get doctor referrals, emergency evacuation or repatriation, 24-hour telephone hot lines for medical consultation, cash for emergencies, and other personal and legal assistance. Coverage varies by plan, so **review the benefits of each carefully.**

➤ MEDICAL-ASSISTANCE COMPANIES: **International SOS Assistance** (✉ 8 Neshaminy Interplex, Suite 207, Trevose, PA 19053, ☎ 215/245–4707 or 800/523–6586, FAX 215/244–9617; ✉ 12 Chemin Riantbosson, 1217 Meyrin 1, Geneva, Switzerland, ☎ 4122/785–6464, FAX 4122/785–6424; ✉ 10 Anson Rd., 14-07/08 International Plaza, Singapore, 079903, ☎ 65/226–3936, FAX 65/226–3937).

STAYING WELL

Nutrition and general health standards in New Zealand are high, and it would be hard to find a more pristine natural environment. There are no venomous snakes, and the only poisonous spider, the katipo, is a rarity. There is one surprising health hazard: don't drink the water in New Zealand's outdoors. While the country's alpine lakes might look like backdrops for mineral-water ads, some in South Island harbor a tiny organism that can cause "duck itch," a temporary but intense skin irritation. The organism is found only on the shallow lake margins, so the chances of infection are greatly reduced if you stick to deeper water. Streams can be infected by giardia, a water-borne protozoal parasite that can cause gastrointestinal disorders, including acute diarrhea. Giardia is most likely contracted when drinking from streams that pass through an area inhabited by mammals (such as cattle or possums). There is no risk of infection if you drink from streams above the tree line.

The major health hazard in New Zealand is sunburn or sunstroke. Even people who are not normally bothered by strong sun should cover up with a long-sleeve shirt, a hat, and long pants or a beach wrap. Keep in mind that at higher altitudes you will burn more easily. Apply sunscreen liberally before you go out—even for a half-hour—and wear a visored cap or sunglasses.

Dehydration is another serious danger that can be easily avoided, so be sure to carry water and drink often. Above all, limit the amount of time you spend in the sun for the first few days until you are acclimatized, and always avoid sunbathing in the middle of the day.

One New Zealander you will come to loathe is the tiny black sandfly, common to the western half of South Island, which inflicts a painful bite that can itch for several days (some call it the state bird). In other parts of the country, especially around rivers and lakes, you may be pestered by mosquitoes. Be sure to use insect repellent, readily available throughout the country.

INSURANCE

Travel insurance is the best way to **protect yourself against financial loss.** The most useful plan is a comprehensive policy that includes coverage for trip cancellation and interruption, default, trip delay, and medical expenses (with a waiver for preexisting conditions).

Without insurance, you will lose all or most of your money if you cancel your trip, regardless of the reason. Default insurance covers you if your tour operator, airline, or cruise line goes out of business. Trip-delay covers unforeseen expenses that you may incur due to bad weather or mechanical delays. It's important to compare the fine print regarding trip-delay coverage when comparing policies.

For overseas travel, one of the most important components of travel insurance is its medical coverage. Supplemental health insurance will pick up the cost of your medical bills should you get sick or injured while traveling. U.S. residents should note that Medicare generally does not cover health-care costs outside the United States, nor do many privately issued policies. Residents of the United Kingdom can buy an annual travel-insurance policy valid for most vacations taken during the year in which the coverage is purchased. If you are pregnant or have a pre-existing condition, make sure you're covered. British citizens should buy extra medical coverage when traveling overseas, according to the Association of British Insurers. Australian travelers should buy travel insurance, including extra medical coverage, whenever they go abroad, according to the Insurance Council of Australia.

Always **buy travel insurance directly from the insurance company**; if you buy it from a cruise line, airline, or tour operator that goes out of business you probably will not be covered for the agency or operator's default, a major risk. Before you make any purchase, **review your existing health and home-owner's policies** to find out whether they cover expenses incurred while traveling.

➤ TRAVEL INSURERS: In the U.S., **Access America** (✉ 6600 W. Broad St., Richmond, VA 23230, ☎ 804/285–3300 or 800/284–8300). **Travel Guard International** (✉ 1145 Clark St., Stevens Point, WI 54481, ☎ 715/345–0505 or 800/826–1300). In Canada, **Mutual of Omaha** (✉ Travel Division, 500 University Ave., Toronto, Ontario M5G 1V8, ☎ 416/598–4083, 800/268–8825 in Canada).

➤ INSURANCE INFORMATION: In the U.K., **Association of British Insurers** (✉ 51 Gresham St., London EC2V 7HQ, ☎ 0171/600–3333). In Australia, the **Insurance Council of Australia** (☎ 613/9614–1077, FAX 613/9614–7924).

LANGUAGE

To an outsider's ear, Kiwi English can be mystifying. Even more so, the Maori (pronounced *moh*-ree) language has added to the New Zealand lexicon words that can seem utterly unpronounceable. It is still spoken by many New Zealanders of Polynesian descent, but English is the everyday language for all people. A number of Maori words have found their way into common usage, most noticeably in place names, which often refer to peculiar features of the local geography or food supply. The Maori word for New Zealand, Aotearoa, means "land of the long white cloud." The South Island town of Kaikoura is famous for its crayfish—the word means "to eat crayfish." Whangapiro (fang-ah-pee-ro), the Maori name for the Government Gardens in Rotorua, means "an evil-smelling place," and if you visit the town you'll find out why. A Polynesian word you'll sometimes come across in Maori churches is tapu—"sacred"—which has entered the English language as the word taboo. Another Maori word you will frequently encounter is pakeha, which means you, the non-Maori. The Maori greeting is kia ora, which can also mean "goodbye," "good health," or "good luck."

A Personal Kiwi-Yankee Dictionary, by Louis S. Leland, Jr., is an amusing and informative guide to New Zealand idioms.

LODGING

The **New Zealand Tourism Board** (☞ Visitor Information, *below*) publishes an annual Where to Stay directory listing more than 1,000 properties.

APARTMENT & VILLA RENTALS

If you want a home base that's roomy enough for a family and comes with cooking facilities, **consider a furnished rental.** These can save you money, especially if you're traveling with a large group of people. Home-exchange directories list rentals (often second homes owned by prospective house swappers), and some services search for a house or apartment for you (even a castle if that's your fancy) and handle the paperwork. Some send an illustrated catalog; others send photographs only of specific properties, sometimes at a charge. Up-front registration fees may apply.

➤ RENTAL AGENTS: **Europa-Let/Tropical Inn-Let** (✉ 92 N. Main St., Ashland, OR 97520, ☎ 541/482–5806 or 800/462–4486, FAX 541/482–0660). **Hideaways International** (✉ 767 Islington St., Portsmouth, NH 03801,

SMART TRAVEL TIPS / THE GOLD GUIDE

☎ 603/430–4433 or 800/843–4433, FAX 603/430–4444; membership $99) is a club for travelers who arrange rentals among themselves.

B&BS

➤ RESERVATION SERVICES: **Hospitality Plus** (⊠ PO Box 56-175, Auckland 3, ☎ 09/8109–175, FAX 09/8109–445) is a one-number booking system for bed and breakfasts, as well as homestays and farmstays, around New Zealand. The company has about 300 places on its books. Once in New Zealand you will find the **New Zealand Bed and Breakfast Book** in most major bookstores. It lists about 1,000 bed and breakfasts, but be aware that the editorial copy in the book has been provided by the property owners themselves, rather than providing independent assessments as this Fodor's guide does.

CAMPING

There are almost 900 backcountry huts in New Zealand. They provide basic shelter but few frills. Huts are usually placed about four hours apart, although in isolated areas it can take a full day to get from one hut to the next. They are graded 1 to 4, and cost varies from nothing to $14 per person per night. Category 1 huts (the $14 ones) have cooking equipment and fuel, bunks or sleeping platforms with mattresses, toilets, washing facilities, and a supply of water. At the other end of the scale, Category 4 huts (the free ones) are simple shelters without bunks or other facilities. Pay for huts with coupons, available in books from Department of Conservation offices. If you plan to make extensive use of huts, an annual pass giving access to all Category 2 and 3 huts for one year is available for $58.

HOME AND FARM STAYS

Home and farm stays, which are very popular with visitors to New Zealand, offer not only comfortable accommodations but a chance to get to know the lands and their people—a great thing to do because Kiwis are so naturally friendly. Most operate on a bed-and-breakfast basis, though some also offer an evening meal. Farm accommodations vary from modest shearers' cabins to elegant homesteads. Guests can join in farm activities or explore the countryside. Some hosts offer day trips, as well as horseback riding, hiking, and fishing. For two people, the average cost is $90–$150 per night, including all meals. Home stays, the urban equivalent of farm stays, are less expensive. Most New Zealanders seem to have vacation homes, called baches on North Island, cribs on South Island, and these are frequently available for rent.

➤ RESERVATIONS & INFORMATION: **New Zealand Farm Holidays Ltd.** (⊠ Box 256, Silverdale, Auckland, ☎ 09/307–2024) or **Homestay Ltd. Farmstay Ltd.** (⊠ Box 25–115, Auckland, ☎ 09/575–9977). **Baches and Holiday Homes to Rent,** by Mark and Elizabeth Greening ($14.95; ⊠ Box 3017, Richmond, Nelson, New Zealand, ☎ FAX 03/544–5799), lists 430 self-contained holiday homes.

HOSTELS

No matter what your age, you can **save on lodging costs by staying at hostels.** In some 5,000 locations in more than 70 countries around the world, Hostelling International (HI), the umbrella group for a number of national youth hostel associations, offers single-sex, dorm-style beds and, at many hostels, "couples" rooms and family accommodations. Membership in any HI national hostel association, open to travelers of all ages, allows you to stay in HI-affiliated hostels at member rates (one-year membership is about $25 for adults; hostels run about $10–$25 per night). Members also have priority if the hostel is full; they're eligible for discounts around the world, even on rail and bus travel in some countries.

In addition to the International Youth Hostels, a network of low-cost, independent backpacker hostels operates in New Zealand. They can be found in nearly every city and tourist spot, and they offer clean, twin- and small-dormitory–style accommodations and self-catering kitchens, similar to those of the Youth Hostel Association (or YHA, the Australian version of IYH), with no membership required.

➤ HOSTEL ORGANIZATIONS: **Hostelling International—American Youth Hostels** (✉ 733 15th St. NW, Suite 840, Washington, DC 20005, ☎ 202/783–6161, FAX 202/783–6171). **Hostelling International—Canada** (✉ 400-205 Catherine St., Ottawa, Ontario K2P 1C3, ☎ 613/237–7884, FAX 613/237–7868). **Youth Hostel Association of England and Wales** (✉ Trevelyan House, 8 St. Stephen's Hill, St. Albans, Hertfordshire AL1 2DY, ☎ 01727/855215 or 01727/845047, FAX 01727/844126); membership in the U.S. $25, in Canada C$26.75, in the U.K. £9.30).

In New Zealand, hostelling information and registration are available at **YHA Travel Centres** (✉ 36 Customs St. East or Box 1687, Auckland, ☎ 09/379–4224; ✉ corner of Gloucester and Manchester Sts., Christchurch, ☎ 03/379–8046). To find out about backpacker hostels, contact **Budget Backpackers Hostels NZ, Ltd.** (✉ Rainbow Lodge, 99 Titiraupenga St., Taupo, ☎ 07/378–5754; or ✉ Foley Towers, 208 Kilgore St., Christchurch, ☎ 03/366–9720).

MOTELS

Motels are by far the most common accommodations, and most offer comfortable rooms for $60–$90 per night. Some motels have two-bedroom suites for families. All motel rooms come equipped with tea- and coffee-making equipment, many have toasters or electric frying pans, and full kitchen facilities are not uncommon.

SPORTING LODGES

At the high end of the price scale, a growing number of luxury sporting lodges offer the best of country life, fine dining, and superb accommodations. Fishing is a specialty at many of them, but there is usually a range of outdoor activities for nonanglers. Tariffs run about $350–$800 per day for two people; meals are generally included.

TOURIST CABINS AND FLATS

The least expensive accommodations in the country are the tourist cabins and flats in most of the country's 400 motor camps. Tourist cabins offer basic accommodation and shared cooking, laundry, and bathroom facilities. Bedding and towels are not provided. A notch higher up the comfort scale, tourist flats usually provide bedding, fully equipped kitchens, and private bathrooms. Overnight rates run about $6–$20 for cabins and $25–$70 for flats.

MAIL

POSTAL RATES

Post offices are open weekdays 9–5. The cost of mailing a letter within New Zealand is 40¢ standard post, 80¢ fast post. Sending a standard size letter by air mail costs $1.50 to North America, $1.80 to Europe, and $1 to Australia. Aerogrammes and postcards are $1 to any overseas destination.

RECEIVING MAIL

If you wish to receive correspondence, have mail sent to New Zealand held for you for up to one month at the central post office in any town or city if it is addressed to you "c/o Poste Restante, CPO," followed by the name of the town. This service is free.

MONEY

COSTS

For most travelers, New Zealand is not an expensive destination. The cost of meals, accommodation, and travel is slightly higher than in the United States but considerably less than in Western Europe. At about $1 per liter—equal to about US$2.10 per gallon—premium-grade gasoline is expensive by North American standards, but not by European ones.

Inflation, which reached a peak of almost 20% in the late 1980s, has now been reduced to less than 5%.

The following are sample costs in New Zealand at press time:

Cup of coffee $2.50; glass of beer in a bar $2.50–$4; take-out ham sandwich or meat pie $2.50; hamburger in a café $5–$8; room-service sandwich in a hotel $12; a 2-kilometer (1¼-mile) taxi ride $5.

CREDIT & DEBIT CARDS

Should you use a credit card or a debit card when traveling? Both have benefits. A credit card allows you to delay payment and gives you certain rights as a consumer (☞ Consumer Protection, *above*). A debit card, also known as a check card, deducts funds directly from your checking account and helps you stay within your budget. When you want to rent a car, though, you may still need an old-fashioned credit card. Although you can always *pay* for your car with a debit card, some agencies will not allow you to *reserve* a car with a debit card.

Otherwise, the two types of plastic are virtually the same. Both will get you cash advances at ATMs worldwide if your card is properly programmed with your personal identification number (PIN). **(To use an ATM in New Zealand, your PIN must be four digits long.)** Both offer excellent, wholesale exchange rates. And both protect you against unauthorized use if the card is lost or stolen. Your liability is limited to $50, as long as you report the card missing.

➤ ATM LOCATIONS: **Cirrus** (☎ 800/424–7787). **Plus** (☎ 800/843–7587) for locations in the U.S. and Canada, or visit your local bank.

CURRENCY

All prices quoted in this guide are in New Zealand dollars.

New Zealand's unit of currency is the dollar, divided into 100 cents. Bills are in $100, $50, $10, and $5 denominations. Coins are $2, $1, 50¢, 20¢, 10¢, and 5¢. At press time the rate of exchange was NZ$1.97 to the U.S. dollar, NZ$1.30 to the Canadian dollar, NZ$3.00 to the pound sterling, and NZ$1.20 to the Australian dollar. Exchange rates change on a daily basis.

EXCHANGING MONEY

For the most favorable rates, **change money through banks.** Although fees charged for ATM transactions may be higher abroad than at home, Cirrus and Plus exchange rates are excellent, because they are based on wholesale rates offered only by major banks. You won't do as well at exchange booths in airports or rail and bus stations, in hotels, in restaurants, or in stores, although you may find their hours more convenient. To avoid lines at airport exchange booths, **get a bit**

of local currency before you leave home.

➤ EXCHANGE SERVICES: **Chase Currency To Go** (☎ 800/935–9935; 935–9935 in NY, NJ, and CT). **International Currency Express** (☎ 888/842–0880 on the East Coast, 888/278–6628 on the West Coast). **Thomas Cook Currency Services** (☎ 800/287–7362 for telephone orders and retail locations).

TRAVELER'S CHECKS

Do you need traveler's checks? It depends on where you're headed. If you're going to rural areas and small towns, go with cash; traveler's checks are best used in cities. Lost or stolen checks can usually be replaced within 24 hours. To ensure a speedy refund, buy your own traveler's checks—don't let someone else pay for them: irregularities like this can cause delays. The person who bought the checks should make the call to request a refund.

OUTDOOR ACTIVITIES & SPORTS

For information on guided bicycling, canoeing and sea-kayaking, cross-country skiing, diving, fishing, hiking, horseback riding, rafting, and sailing tours and tour operators, ☞ Chapter 6.

FISHING

Wherever you fish, and whatever you fish for, you will profit immensely from the services of a local guide. On Lake Taupo or Rotorua, a boat with a guide plus all equipment will cost around $130 for two hours. In South Island, a top fishing guide who can supply all equipment and a four-wheel-drive vehicle will charge about $400 per day for two people. In the Bay of Islands region, an evening fishing trip aboard a small boat can cost as little as $35. For a big-game fishing boat, expect to pay between $600 and $1,000 per day. There are also several specialist lodges that provide guides and transport to wilderness streams sometimes accessible only by helicopter.

Fishing licenses are available from fishing-tackle and sports shops for daily, weekly, monthly, or seasonal periods. Costs range from $10.50 for a single day to $53 for the season, and licenses are valid for the entire country, with the exception of Lake Taupo, for which a separate permit is required. For anyone who plans to fish extensively, the best buy is a tourist fishing license—available from Visitor Information Centres in all major cities—which, for $56.26, permits fishing anywhere in New Zealand for one month.

GOLF

Generally speaking, clubs can be rented, but you'll need your own shoes. Greens fees range from $5 at country courses to $60 at exclusive city courses. The better urban courses also offer resident professionals and golf carts for hire.

For more information, contact the Executive Director, **NZ Golf Association** (✉ Box 11–842, Wellington).

HIKING

The traditional way to hike in New Zealand is freedom walking. Freedom walkers carry their own provisions, sleeping bags, food, and cooking gear, and sleep in basic huts. A more refined alternative—usually available only on more popular trails—is the guided walk, on which you trek with just a light day pack, guides do the cooking, and you sleep in heated lodges. If you prefer your wilderness served with hot showers and an eiderdown on your bed, the guided walk is for you.

If you plan to walk the spectacular Milford or Routeburn Tracks in December or January, book at least six months in advance. At other times, three months is usually sufficient. (If you arrive without a booking, there may be last-minute cancellations, and parties of one or two can often be accommodated.) The Milford Track is closed due to snowfall from the end of April to early September.

Plan your clothing and footwear carefully. Even at the height of summer weather can change quickly, and hikers must be prepared—especially for the rainstorms that regularly drench the Southern Alps. (The Milford Sound region, with its average annual rainfall of 160 inches, is one of the wettest places on earth.) The most cost-effective rain gear you can buy is the U.S. Army poncho.

Wear a hat and sunglasses and put on sun block to protect your skin against the sun. Keep in mind that at higher altitudes, where the air is thinner, you will burn more easily. Sun reflected off of snow, sand, or water can be especially strong. Apply sunscreen liberally before you go out—even if only for a half-hour—and wear a visored cap or sunglasses.

Also, be careful about heatstroke. Symptoms include headache, dizziness, and fatigue, which can turn into convulsions, unconsciousness, and can lead to death. If someone in your party develops any of these conditions, have one person seek emergency help while others move the victim into the shade, wrap him or her in wet clothing (is a stream or lake nearby?) to cool him or her down.

Temperatures can vary widely from day to night. Be sure to bring enough warm clothing for hiking and camping, along with wet weather gear. Exposure to the degree that body temperature dips below 95°F (35°C) produces the following symptoms: chills, tiredness, then uncontrollable shivering and irrational behavior, with the victim not always recognizing that he or she is cold. If someone in your party is suffering from any of this, wrap him or her in blankets and/or a warm sleeping bag immediately and try to keep him or her awake. The fastest way to raise body temperature is through skin-to-skin contact in a sleeping bag. Drinking warm liquids also helps.

Avoid drinking from streams or lakes, no matter how clear they may be. Giardia organisms can turn your stomach inside out. And in South Island a tiny organism found on the shallow margins of lakes can cause "duck itch," a temporary but intense skin irritation. The easiest way to purify water is to dissolve a water purification tablet in it. Camping equipment stores also carry purification pumps. Boiling water for 15 minutes is always a reliable method, if time- and fuel-consuming.

For information on camping, *see* Lodging, *above*.

PACKING

LUGGAGE

How many carry-on bags you can bring with you is up to the airline. Most allow two, but the limit is often reduced to one on certain flights. Gate agents will take excess baggage—including bags they deem oversize—from you as you board and add it to checked luggage. To avoid this situation, make sure that everything you carry aboard will fit under your seat. Also, get to the gate early, and request a seat at the back of the plane; you'll probably board first, while the overhead bins are still empty. Since big, bulky baggage attracts the attention of gate agents and flight attendants on a busy flight, make sure your carry-on is really a carry-on. Finally, a carry-on that's long and narrow is more likely to remain unnoticed than one that's wide and squarish.

If you are flying internationally, note that baggage allowances may be determined not by piece but by weight—generally 88 pounds (40 kilograms) in first class, 66 pounds (30 kilograms) in business class, and 44 pounds (20 kilograms) in economy.

Airline liability for baggage is limited to $1,250 per person on flights within the United States. On international flights it amounts to $9.07 per pound or $20 per kilogram for checked baggage (roughly $640 per 70-pound bag) and $400 per passenger for unchecked baggage. You can buy additional coverage at check-in for about $10 per $1,000 of coverage, but it excludes a rather extensive list of items, shown on your airline ticket.

Before departure, **itemize your bags' contents** and their worth, and label the bags with your name, address, and phone number. (If you use your home address, cover it so that potential thieves can't see it readily.) Inside each bag, **pack a copy of your itinerary.** At check-in, **make sure that each bag is correctly tagged** with the destination airport's three-letter code. If your bags arrive damaged or fail to arrive at all, file a written report with the airline before leaving the airport.

PACKING LIST

In New Zealand, be prepared for temperatures varying from day to night and weather that can turn suddenly, particularly at the change of seasons. The wisest approach to dressing is to wear layered outfits. You'll appreciate being able to remove or put on a jacket. Take along a light raincoat and umbrella, but remember that plastic raincoats and nonbreathing polyester are uncomfortable in the tropics. Don't wear lotions or perfume in the tropics either, since they attract mosquitoes and other bugs; carry insect repellent. Bring a hat with a brim to provide protection from the strong sunlight (☞ Health, *above*). You'll need warm clothing for South Island.

Dress is casual in most cities, though top resorts and restaurants may require a jacket and tie. In autumn, a light wool sweater and/or a jacket will suffice for evenings in coastal cities, but winter demands a heavier coat—a raincoat with a zip-out wool lining is ideal. Comfortable walking shoes are a must. You should have a pair of running shoes or the equivalent if you're planning to trek, and rubber-sole sandals or canvas shoes are needed for walking on reef coral.

In your carry-on luggage **bring an extra pair of eyeglasses or contact lenses** and **enough of any medication you take** to last the entire trip. You may also want your doctor to write a spare prescription using the drug's generic name, since brand names may vary from country to country. **Never put prescription drugs or valuables in luggage to be checked.** To avoid customs delays, carry medications in their original packaging. And don't forget to copy down and carry addresses of offices that handle refunds of lost traveler's checks.

PASSPORTS & VISAS

When traveling internationally, **carry a passport even if you don't need one** (it's always the best form of I.D.), and make **two photocopies of the data page** (one for someone at home and another for you, carried separately from your passport). If you lose your passport, promptly call the nearest embassy or consulate and the local police.

ENTERING NEW ZEALAND

U.S., Canadian, and U.K. citizens need only a valid passport to enter New Zealand for stays of up to 90 days.

PASSPORT OFFICES

The best time to apply for a passport or to renew is during the fall and winter. Before any trip, be sure to check your passport's expiration date and, if necessary, renew it as soon as possible. (Some countries won't allow you to enter on a passport that's due to expire in six months or less.)

➤ AUSTRALIAN CITIZENS: **Australian Passport Office** (☎ 131–232).

➤ CANADIAN CITIZENS: **Passport Office** (☎ 819/994–3500 or 800/567–6868).

➤ U.K. CITIZENS: **London Passport Office** (☎ 0990/21010), for fees and documentation requirements and to request an emergency passport.

➤ U.S. CITIZENS: **National Passport Information Center** (☎ 900/225–5674; calls are charged at 35¢ per minute for automated service, $1.05 per minute for operator service).

SENIOR-CITIZEN TRAVEL

To qualify for age-related discounts, **mention your senior-citizen status up front** when booking hotel reservations (not when checking out) and before you're seated in restaurants (not when paying the bill). Note that discounts may be limited to certain menus, days, or hours. When renting a car, **ask about promotional car-rental discounts,** which can be cheaper than senior-citizen rates.

➤ EDUCATIONAL PROGRAMS: **Elderhostel** (⊠ 75 Federal St., 3rd floor, Boston, MA 02110, ☎ 617/426–8056). **Interhostel** (⊠ University of New Hampshire, 6 Garrison Ave., Durham, NH 03824, ☎ 603/862–1147 or 800/733–9753, FAX 603/862–1113). **Folkways Institute** (⊠ 14600 Southeast Aldridge Rd., Portland, OR 97236-6518, ☎ 503/658–6600 or 800/225–4666, FAX 503/658–8672).

STUDENT TRAVEL

TRAVEL AGENCIES

To save money, **look into deals available through student-oriented travel agencies.** To qualify you'll need a bona fide student I.D. card. Members of international student groups are also eligible.

➤ STUDENT I.D.s & SERVICES: **Council on International Educational Exchange** (⊠ CIEE, 205 E. 42nd St., 14th floor, New York, NY 10017, ☎ 212/822–2600 or 888/268–6245, FAX 212/822–2699), for mail orders only, in the United States. **Travel Cuts** (⊠ 187 College St., Toronto, Ontario M5T 1P7, ☎ 416/979–2406 or 800/667–2887) in Canada.

➤ STUDENT TOURS: **Contiki Holidays** (⊠ 300 Plaza Alicante, Suite 900, Garden Grove, CA 92840, ☎ 714/740–0808 or 800/266–8454, FAX 714/740–2034).

TAXES

AIRPORT

Visitors exiting New Zealand must pay a departure tax of $20.

VALUE-ADDED TAX (V.A.T.)

A goods and services tax (GST) of 12.5% is levied throughout New Zealand. It's usually incorporated into the cost of an item, but in hotels and some restaurants it is added to the bill.

TELEPHONES

COUNTRY CODES

The country code for New Zealand is 64. When dialing from abroad, drop the initial 0 from the local area code.

INTERNATIONAL CALLS

AT&T, MCI, and Sprint international access codes make calling the United States relatively convenient, but you may find the local access number blocked in many hotel rooms. First ask the hotel operator to connect you. If the hotel operator balks, ask for an international operator, or dial the international operator yourself. One way to improve your odds of getting connected to your long-distance carrier is to travel with more than one company's calling card (a hotel may block Sprint, for example, but not MCI). If all else fails, call from a pay phone in the hotel lobby.

➤ ACCESS CODES: **AT&T Direct** (☎ 000–911). **MCI WorldPhone** (☎ 000–912). **Sprint International Access** (☎ 000–913).

PUBLIC PHONES

Most pay phones now accept PhoneCards or major credit cards rather than coins. PhoneCards, available in denominations of $5, $10, $20, or $50, are sold at shops displaying the green PhoneCard symbol. To use a PhoneCard, lift the receiver, put the card in the slot in the front of the phone, and dial. The cost of the call is automatically deducted from your card; the display on the telephone tells you how much credit you have left at the end of the call. A local call from a public phone costs 20¢ per minute. Don't forget to take your PhoneCard with you when you finish your call. You may end up making some very expensive calls by leaving it behind.

TIME

Trying to figure out just what time it is in New Zealand can get dizzying, especially because of cross-hemisphere daylight savings times and multi-time-zone countries. Without daylight savings times, Auckland is 17 hours ahead of New York; 18 hours ahead of Chicago and Dallas; 20 hours ahead (or count back four hours and add a day) from Los Angeles; and 12 hours ahead of London.

From Canada and the States, **call New Zealand after 5 PM.** From the U.K. or Europe, it isn't quite as complicated: call early in the morning or very late at night. **When faxing,** it's usually not a problem to ring discreet fax numbers at any time of day.

TIPPING

Tipping is not widely practiced in New Zealand. Only in the better city restaurants and international hotels will you be expected to show your appreciation for good service with a 10% tip.

TOUR OPERATORS

Buying a prepackaged tour or independent vacation can make your trip to New Zealand less expensive and more hassle-free. Because everything is prearranged, you'll spend less time planning.

Operators that handle several hundred thousand travelers per year can use their purchasing power to give you a good price. Their high volume may also indicate financial stability. But some small companies provide more personalized service; because they tend to specialize, they may also be more knowledgeable about a given area.

BOOKING WITH AN AGENT

Travel agents are excellent resources. In fact, large operators accept bookings made only through travel agents. But it's a good idea to **collect brochures from several agencies,** because some agents' suggestions may be influenced by relationships with tour and package firms that reward them for volume sales. If you have a special interest, **find an agent with expertise in that area**; ASTA (☞ Travel Agencies, *below*) has a database of specialists worldwide.

Make sure your travel agent knows the accommodations and other services. Ask about the hotel's location, room size, beds, and whether it has a pool, room service, or programs for children, if you care about these. Has your agent been there in person or sent others you can contact?

Do some homework on your own, too: Local tourism boards can provide information about lesser-known and small-niche operators, some of which may sell only direct.

BUYER BEWARE

Each year consumers are stranded or lose their money when tour operators—even very large ones with excellent reputations—go out of business. So **check out the operator.** Find out how long the company has been in business, and ask several travel agents about its reputation. If the package or tour you are considering is priced lower than in your wildest dreams, **be skeptical.** Try to **book with a company that has a consumer-protection program.** If the operator has such a program, you'll find information about it in the company's brochure. If the operator you are considering does not offer some kind of consumer protection, then ask for references from satisfied customers.

In the U.S., members of the National Tour Association and United States Tour Operators Association are required to set aside funds to cover your payments and travel arrangements in case the company defaults. It's also a good idea to choose a company that participates in the American Society of Travel Agent's Tour Operator Program (TOP). This gives you a forum if there are any disputes between you and your tour operator; ASTA will act as mediator.

➤ TOUR-OPERATOR RECOMMENDA-TIONS: **American Society of Travel Agents** (☞ Travel Agencies, *below*). **National Tour Association** (⊠ NTA, 546 E. Main St., Lexington, KY 40508, ☎ 606/226–4444 or 800/755–8687). **United States Tour Operators Association** (⊠ USTOA, 342 Madison Ave., Suite 1522, New York, NY 10173, ☎ 212/599–6599 or 800/468–7862, ℻ 212/599–6744).

COSTS

The more your package or tour includes, the better you can predict the ultimate cost of your vacation. Make sure you know exactly what is covered, and **beware of hidden costs.** Are taxes, tips, and service charges included? Transfers and baggage handling? Entertainment and excursions? These can add up.

Prices for packages and tours are usually quoted per person, based on two sharing a room. If traveling solo, you may be required to pay the full double-occupancy rate. Some operators eliminate this surcharge if you agree to be matched with a roommate of the same sex, even if one is not found by departure time.

GROUP TOURS

Among companies that sell tours to New Zealand, the following are nationally known, have a proven reputation, and offer plenty of options. The classifications used below represent different price categories, and you'll probably encounter these

terms when talking to a travel agent or tour operator. The key difference is usually in accommodations, which run from budget to better, and better-yet to best.

➤ SUPER-DELUXE: **Abercrombie & Kent** (⊠ 1520 Kensington Rd., Oak Brook, IL 60521-2141, ☎ 630/954–2944 or 800/323–7308, ℻ 630/954–3324). **Travcoa** (⊠ Box 2630, 2350 S.E. Bristol St., Newport Beach, CA 92660, ☎ 714/476–2800 or 800/992–2003, ℻ 714/476–2538).

➤ DELUXE: **Globus** (⊠ 5301 S. Federal Circle, Littleton, CO 80123-2980, ☎ 303/797–2800 or 800/221–0090, ℻ 303/347–2080). **Maupintour** (⊠ 1515 St. Andrews Dr., Lawrence, KS 66047, ☎ 785/843–1211 or 800/255–4266, ℻ 785/843–8351). **Tauck Tours** (⊠ Box 5027, 276 Post Rd. W, Westport, CT 06881-5027, ☎ 203/226–6911 or 800/468–2825, ℻ 203/221–6866).

➤ FIRST-CLASS: **AAT King's Australian Tours** (⊠ 9430 Topanga Canyon Blvd., #207, Chatsworth, CA 91311, ☎ 800/353–4525, ℻ 818/700–2647). **ATS Tours** (⊠ 2381 Rosencrans Ave., #325, El Segundo, CA 90245, ☎ 310/643–0044 or 800/423–2880). **Brendan Tours** (⊠ 15137 Califa St., Van Nuys, CA 91411, ☎ 818/785–9696 or 800/421–8446, ℻ 818/902–9876). **Collette Tours** (⊠ 162 Middle St., Pawtucket, RI 02860, ☎ 401/728–3805 or 800/340–5158, ℻ 401/728–4745). **Gadabout Tours** (⊠ 700 E. Tahquitz Canyon Way, Palm Springs, CA 92262–6767, ☎ 619/325–5556 or 800/952–5068). **Newmans South Pacific Vacations** (⊠ 6033 W. Century Blvd., Ste. 1270, Los Angeles, CA 90045, ☎ 310/348–8282 or 800/421–3326, ℻ 310/215–9705). **South Pacific Your Way** (⊠ 2819 1st Ave., #280, Seattle, WA 98121-1113, ☎ 206/441–8682 or 800/426–3610, ℻ 206/441–8862). **Swain Australia Tours** (⊠ 6 W. Lancaster Ave., Ardmore, PA 19003, ☎ 610/896–9595 or 800/227–9246, ℻ 610/896–9592).

➤ BUDGET: **Cosmos** (☞ Globus, *above*).

PACKAGES

Like group tours, independent vacation packages are available from major tour operators and airlines. The companies listed below offer vacation packages in a broad price range.

➤ AIR/HOTEL: Qantas Vacations (✉ 300 N. Continental Blvd., #610, El Segundo, CA 90245, ☎ 800/641-8772, 800/268-7525 in Canada, FAX 310/535-1057). United Vacations (☎ 800/328-6877).

➤ CUSTOMIZED PACKAGES: Australia/New Zealand Down Under Travel (✉ 4962 El Camino Real, Ste. 107, Los Altos, CA 94022, ☎ 650/969-2153 or 800/886-2153, FAX 650/969-3215). Down Under Connections (✉ 6640 Roswell Rd. NE, Atlanta, GA 30328, ☎ 404/255-1922 or 800/937-7878). Islands in the Sun (✉ 2381 Rosencrans Ave., #325, El Segundo, CA 90245, ☎ 310/536-0051 or 800/828-6877, FAX 310/536-6266). Pacific Experience (✉ 63 Mill St., Newport, RI 02840, ☎ 401/849-6258 or 800/279-3639).

➤ FROM THE U.K.: Kuoni Travel (✉ Kuoni House, Dorking, Surrey RH5 4AZ, ☎ 01306/740-500). Qantas Holidays (✉ Sovereign House, 361 King St., Hammersmith, London W6 9NA, ☎ 0990/673-464). Virgin Holidays Ltd. (✉ The Galleria, Station Rd., Crawley, West Sussex RH10 1WW, ☎ 01293/617-181).

THEME TRIPS

➤ ADVENTURE: Adventure Center (✉ 1311 63rd St., #200, Emeryville, CA 94608, ☎ 510/654-1879 or 800/227-8747, FAX 510/654-4200). Safaricentre (✉ 3201 N. Sepulveda Blvd., Manhattan Beach, CA 90266, ☎ 310/546-4411 or 800/223-6046, FAX 310/546-3188). Wilderness Travel (✉ 1102 Ninth St., Berkeley, CA 94710, ☎ 510/558-2488 or 800/368-2794).

➤ BICYCLING: Backroads (✉ 801 Cedar St., Berkeley, CA 94710-1800, ☎ 510/527-1555 or 800/462-2848, FAX 510-527-1444). Butterfield & Robinson (✉ 70 Bond St., Toronto, Ontario, Canada M5B 1X3, ☎ 416/864-1354 or 800/678-1147, FAX 416/864-0541). Down Under Answers (✉ 12727 NE 20th St., Ste. 5, Bellevue, WA 98005, ☎ 425/895-0895 or 800/788-6685, FAX 425/895-8929). Vermont Bicycle Touring (✉ Box 711, Bristol, VT, 05443-0711, ☎ 800/245-3868 or 802/453-4811, FAX 802/453-4806).

➤ FISHING: Anglers Travel (✉ 1280 Terminal Way, #30, Reno, NV 89502, ☎ 702/324-0580 or 800/624-8429, FAX 702/324-0583). Fishing International (✉ Box 2132, Santa Rosa, CA 95405, ☎ 707/539-3366 or 800/950-4242, FAX 707/539-1320). Rod & Reel Adventures (✉ 566 Thomson Ln., Copperopolis, CA 95228, ☎ 209/785-0444, FAX 209/785-0447).

➤ GOLF: Australia/New Zealand Down Under Travel (☞ Customized Packages, *above*). ITC Golf Tours (✉ 4134 Atlantic Ave., #205, Long Beach, CA 90807, ☎ 310/595-6905 or 800/257-4981).

➤ HOMES AND GARDENS: Coopersmith's England (✉ Box 900, Inverness, CA 94937, ☎ 415/669-1914, FAX 415/669-1942).

➤ HORSEBACK RIDING: Equitour FITS Equestrian (✉ Box 807, Dubois, WY 82513, ☎ 307/455-3363 or 800/545-0019, FAX 307/455-2354).

➤ LEARNING: Earthwatch (✉ Box 9104, 680 Mount Auburn St., Watertown, MA 02272, ☎ 617/926-8200 or 800/776-0188, FAX 617/926-8532) for research expeditions. Natural Habitat Adventures (✉ 2945 Center Green Ct., Boulder, CO 80301, ☎ 303/449-3711 or 800/543-8917, FAX 303/449-3712). Nature Expeditions International (✉ 6400 El Dorado Circle, Suite 210, Tucson, AZ 85715, ☎ 520/721-6712 or 800/869-0639, FAX 520/721-6719). Questers (✉ 381 Park Ave. S, New York, NY 10016, ☎ 212/251-0444 or 800/468-8668, FAX 212/251-0890). Victor Emanuel Nature Tours (✉ Box 33008, Austin, TX 78764, ☎ 512/328-5221 or 800/328-8368, FAX 512/328-2919).

➤ MOTORCYCLE: Beach's Motorcycle Adventures (✉ 2763 W. River Pkwy., Grand Island, NY 14072-2053, ☎ 716/773-4960, FAX 716/773-5227). Edelweiss Bike Travel (✉ Hartford

Holidays Travel, 129 Hillside Ave., Williston Park, NY 11596, ☎ 516/ 746–6761 or 800/877–2784, FAX 516/746–6690).

➤ PHOTOGRAPHY: **Joseph Van Os Photo Safaris** (✉ Box 655, Vashen, WA 98070, ☎ 206/463–5383, FAX 206/463–5484).

➤ SINGLES AND YOUNG ADULTS: **Contiki Holidays** (✉ 300 Plaza Alicante, #900, Garden Grove, CA 92840, ☎ 714/740–0808 or 800/266–8454, FAX 714/740–0818).

➤ SPORTS: **Championship Tennis Tours** (✉ 8040 E. Morgan Trail #12, Scottsdale, AZ 85258, ☎ 602/443– 9499 or 800/468–3664, FAX 602/ 443–8982).

➤ WALKING/HIKING: **Butterfield & Robinson** (☞ Bicycling, *above*). **Country Walkers** (✉ Box 180, Waterbury, VT 05676-0180, ☎ 802/244– 1387 or 800/464–9255, FAX 802/ 244–5661). **Walking the World** (✉ Box 1186, Fort Collins, CO 80522, ☎ 970/498–0500 or 800/340–9255, FAX 970/498–9100) specializes in tours for ages 50 and older.

➤ YACHT CHARTERS: **Huntley Yacht Vacations** (✉ 210 Preston Rd., Wernersville, PA 19565, ☎ 610/678–2628 or 800/322–9224, FAX 610/670– 1767). **The Moorings** (✉ 19345 U.S. Hwy. 19 N, 4th floor, Clearwater, FL 34624-3193, ☎ 813/530–5424 or 800/535–7289, FAX 813/530–9474).

TRAIN TRAVEL

Trains in New Zealand's InterCity network usually cost the same as buses and are marginally quicker, but they run far less frequently. The country's most notable rail journey is the Tranz-Alpine Express, a spectacular scenic ride across Arthur's Pass and the mountainous spine of South Island between Greymouth and Christchurch.

➤ INFORMATION & SCHEDULES: **InterCity** ☎ 09/357–8400).

DISCOUNT PASSES

To save money, **look into rail passes.** But be aware that if you don't plan to cover many miles, you may come out ahead by buying individual tickets.

Travelers can purchase an InterCity Travelpass for unlimited travel by train, bus, and InterIsland ferry. The pass allows 5 days of travel within a 10-day period (NZ$360), 8 days within 21-days (NZ$485), 15 days of travel within 32 days (NZ$610), or 22 days of travel within 56 days (NZ$710). Children ages 5 to 14 pay 67% of the adult fare. The 4-in-1 New Zealand Travelpass, available for purchase outside New Zealand only, includes one flight sector on Ansett New Zealand between assigned city pairs. The flight may be at any time after the date of issue of the Travelpass and up to seven days after expiration of the Travelpass. The pass entitles the visitor to 5 days of travel in 10 days (NZ$615), 8 days of travel in 21 days (NZ$740), 15 days of travel in 32 days (NZ$865), or 22 days of travel in 56 days (NZ$965). Children ages 5 to 14 pay 67% of the adult fare. Two additional flight sectors may be purchased at NZ$255 per sector. For Youth Hostel Association members, the InterCity Youth Hostel Travel Card ($75 for 14 days, $99 for 28 days) gives a 50% discount on most train service, all InterCity coach service, and on InterIsland ferries. Students with an International Student Identity Card (ISIC) get a 20% discount.

Contact **InterCity Travel Centres** (☎ 09/639–0500) in Auckland, 03/379– 9020 in Christchurch, 04/472–5111 in Wellington) for ticket information. In the United States, contact **ATS Tours** (☎ 818/841–1030) or **Austravel Inc.** (☎ 800/633–3404).

➤ BUYING PASSES: **InterCity Travel Centres** (☎ 09/639–0500 in Auckland, 03/379–9020 in Christchurch, 04/472–5111 in Wellington). In the United States, **ATS Tours** ☎ 818/ 841–1030) or **Austravel Inc.** (☎ 800/ 633–3404).

TRAVEL AGENCIES

A good travel agent puts your needs first. Look for an agency that has been in business at least five years, emphasizes customer service, and has someone on staff who specializes in your destination. In addition, **make sure the agency belongs to a profes-**

sional trade organization, such as ASTA in the United States. If your travel agency is also acting as your tour operator, *see* Buyer Beware in Tour Operators, *above*).

➤ LOCAL AGENT REFERRALS: **American Society of Travel Agents (ASTA, ☎ 800/965–2782 24-hr hot line, FAX 703/684–8319). Association of Canadian Travel Agents (✉ Suite 201, 1729 Bank St., Ottawa, Ontario K1V 7Z5, ☎ 613/521–0474, FAX 613/ 521–0805). Association of British Travel Agents (✉ 55–57 Newman St., London W1P 4AH, ☎ 0171/ 637–2444, FAX 0171/637–0713). Australian Federation of Travel Agents (☎ 02/9264–3299). Travel Agents' Association of New Zealand (☎ 04/499–0104).**

TRAVEL GEAR

Travel catalogs specialize in useful items, such as compact alarm clocks and travel irons, that can **save space when packing.** They also offer dual-voltage appliances, currency converters, and foreign-language phrase books.

➤ CATALOGS: **Magellan's (☎ 800/ 962–4943, FAX 805/568–5406). Orvis Travel (☎ 800/541–3541, FAX 540/ 343–7053). TravelSmith (☎ 800/ 950–1600, FAX 800/950–1656).**

U.S. GOVERNMENT

Government agencies can be an excellent source of inexpensive travel information. When planning your trip, **find out what government materials are available.**

➤ ADVISORIES: **U.S. Department of State** (✉ Overseas Citizens Services Office, Room 4811 N.S., Washington, DC 20520; ☎ 202/647–5225 or FAX 202/647–3000 for interactive hot line; ☎ 301/946–4400 for computer bulletin board); enclose a self-addressed, stamped, business-size envelope.

➤ PAMPHLETS: **Consumer Information Center** (✉ Consumer Information Catalogue, Pueblo, CO 81009, ☎ 719/948–3334 or 888/878–3256) for a free catalog that includes travel titles.

TRIP PLANNING

The difficulty with planning a trip to New Zealand is exquisite agony—nearly every square kilometer of the country is spectacular. And nearly everyone who comes back from the country wishes he or she had planned to spend more time there. Yet if you try to see too much, you may end up feeling like you haven't seen anything at all. So give yourself time to really savor two or three areas and get to know them and meet a few locals. Four days to a week per locale will leave you feeling that you have actually been somewhere. It's no exaggeration that time in New Zealand will feel like time spent in paradise.

VISITOR INFORMATION

➤ NEW ZEALAND TOURISM BOARD: In the U.S.: ✉ 501 Santa Monica Blvd., Los Angeles, CA 90401, ☎ 310/395–7480 or 800/388–5494, FAX 310/ 395–5454. In Canada: ✉ 888 Dunsmuir St., Suite 1200, Vancouver, BC V6C 3K4, ☎ 800/888–5494, FAX 604/ 684–1265. In the U.K.: ✉ New Zealand House, Haymarket, London, SW1Y 4TQ, ☎ 0171/930–1662, FAX 0171/839–8929.

WHEN TO GO

New Zealand is in the Southern Hemisphere, which means that seasons are reversed—it's winter down under during the American and European summer. The ideal months for comfortable all-round travel are October–April, especially if you want to participate in adventure activities. Avoid school holidays, when highways may be congested and accommodation is likely to be scarce and more expensive. Summer school holidays (the busiest) fall between mid-December and the end of January; other holiday periods are mid-May to the end of May, early July to mid-July, and late August to mid-September.

CLIMATE

Climate in New Zealand varies from subtropical in the north to temperate in the south. Summer (December–March) is generally warm, with an average of seven to eight hours of sunshine per day throughout the country. Winter (June–September) is mild at lower altitudes in South Island, but heavy snowfalls are common in South Island, particularly on the peaks of the Southern Alps. Rain can pour at any time of the year. (Some areas on the west coast of South Island receive an annual rainfall of more than 100 inches.)

The following are average daily maximum and minimum temperatures for some major cities in New Zealand.

AUCKLAND

Jan.	74F	23C	May	63F	17C	Sept.	61F	16C
	61	16		52	11		49	9
Feb.	74F	23C	June	58F	14C	Oct.	63F	17C
	61	16		49	9		52	11
Mar.	72F	22C	July	56F	13C	Nov.	67F	19C
	59	15		47	8		54	12
Apr.	67F	19C	Aug.	58F	14C	Dec.	70F	21C
	56	13		47	8		58	14

CHRISTCHURCH

Jan.	70F	21C	May	56F	13C	Sept.	58F	14C
	54	12		40	4		40	4
Feb.	70F	21C	June	52F	11C	Oct.	63F	17C
	54	12		36	2		45	7
Mar.	67F	19C	July	50F	10C	Nov.	67F	19C
	50	10		36	2		47	8
Apr.	63F	17C	Aug.	52F	11C	Dec.	70F	21C
	45	7		36	2		52	11

QUEENSTOWN

Jan.	72F	22C	May	52F	11C	Sept.	56F	13C
	49	9		36	2		38	3
Feb.	70F	21C	June	47F	8C	Oct.	61F	16C
	50	10		34	1		41	5
Mar.	67F	19C	July	46F	8C	Nov.	65F	18C
	47	8		34	– 1		45	7
Apr.	61F	16C	Aug.	50F	10C	Dec.	70F	21C
	43	6		34	1		49	9

➤ FORECASTS: **Weather Channel Connection** (☎ 900/932–8437), 95¢ per minute from a Touch-Tone phone.

1 Destination: New Zealand

THE EDEN DOWN UNDER

FIRST LAID EYES on New Zealand in 1967, near the end of an ocean voyage from Los Angeles to Australia. For a long morning, we skirted the New Zealand coastline north of Auckland, slipping past a land of impossibly green hills that seemed to be populated entirely by sheep. When the ship berthed in Auckland, I saw parked along the quay a museum-quality collection of vintage British automobiles, the newest of which was probably 15 years old. The explanation was simple enough: The alternative would be new imports, and imports were taxed at an enormous rate. But to a teenager fresh from the U.S.A., it seemed as though we had entered a time warp. When we took a day tour into the hills, the bus driver kept stopping for chats with other drivers; in those days it seemed possible to know everyone in New Zealand.

Since then, Auckland has caught up with the rest of the world. Its cars, its cellular-phone-toting execs, its waterfront restaurants with sushi and French mineral water all exist, unmistakably, in the 1990s. Yet the countryside still belongs to a greener, cleaner, friendlier time. Nostalgia is a strong suit in New Zealand's deck—second, of course, to its incomparable scenery. You'll still find people clinging sentimentally to their Morris Minors, Wolseley 1300s, VW Beetles, or Austin Cambridges—even though inexpensive used Japanese imports have flooded the market in recent years. So if you travel in search of glamorous shopping, sophisticated nightlife, and gourmet pleasures, this may not be the place for you. For some of New Zealand's most notable cultural achievements have been made in conjunction with nature—in the spectacular displays of its gardens, the growing reputation of its wineries, the fascinating lives and artifacts of the Maori (pronounced *moh*-ree), even the respect for nature shown in its current eco-tourism boom. Auckland, Christchurch, and Wellington may never rival New York, Paris, or Rome, but that's probably not why you're considering a trip to New Zealand. And when you are in the cities,

you're likely to find just as much warmth, calm, and graciousness as you will in rural areas.

Humanity was a late arrival to New Zealand. Its first settlers were Polynesians who reached its shores about AD 850, followed by a second wave of Polynesian migrants in the 14th century. These were not carefree, grass-skirted islanders living in a palmy utopia, but a fierce, martial people who made their homes in hilltop fortresses, where they existed in an almost continual state of warfare with neighboring tribes. That fierceness turned out to ensure them more respect from—the *Pakeha*—the Maori word for Europeans—than that received by many other native groups around the world in their encounters with colonial powers. The first Europeans to come across New Zealand were on board the Dutch ships of explorer Abel Tasman, which anchored in Golden Bay atop South Island on December 16, 1642. Miscommunication with a local Maori group the next day resulted in the death of four Europeans. The famous Captain James Cook was the next to explore New Zealand, in the 18th century, but it wasn't until the 1840s that European settlers, primarily from England, arrived in numbers.

Compared with other modern immigrant societies such as the United States and Australia, New Zealand is overwhelmingly British—in its love of gardens, its architecture, its political system, and its food. Even so, changes are afoot. Momentum is gathering toward New Zealand becoming a republic, though it would undoubtedly remain within the British Commonwealth. In 1993, the country held a referendum that threw out the "first past the post" electoral system inherited from Westminster, adopting instead a mixed-member proportional election, the first of which was held in 1996. This means that each voter now casts two votes, one for a local representative and the other for the party of his or her choice. To govern, a party (or combination of parties) must have at least 50% of the actual vote—not just 50% of parliamentary seats. So rather than being dominated by just two strong parties, with various minor political entities filling out the numbers, New Zealand is now governed by party coalitions. Currently it has a National/New Zealand First party coalition and its prime minister is Jenny Shipley, the country's first woman PM.

The Maori remain an assertive minority of 9%, a dignified, robust people whose oral tradition and art bears witness to a rich culture of legends and dreams. That culture comes dramatically to life in performances of songs and dances, including the *haka,* or war dance, which was calculated to intimidate and demoralize the enemy. It's little wonder that the national rugby team performs a haka as a prelude to its games. It would be a mistake, however, to feel that the Maori people's place in New Zealand is confined to history and cultural performances for tourists. They are having considerable impact in a modern political sense, reclaiming lost rights to land, fisheries, and other resources. Deputy Prime Minister and Treasurer Winston Peters is a Maori, as are several other government ministers. You'll see Maori who are prominent television newscasters, literary figures, and major athletes, at the same time keeping their cultural traditions alive.

The New Zealand landmass consists of two principal islands, with other outlying islands as well. Most of the country's 3.42 million people live on North Island, while South Island has the lion's share of the national parks (more than one-tenth of the total area has been set aside as park land). In a country about the size of Colorado—or just slightly larger than Great Britain—nature has assembled active volcanoes, subtropical rain forests, geysers, streams now filled with some of the finest trout on earth, fjords, beaches, glaciers, and some two dozen peaks that soar to more than 10,000 ft. The country has spectacular scenery from top to bottom, but while North Island often resembles a pristine, if radically hilly, golf course, South Island is wild, majestic, and exhilarating.

Experiencing these wonders is painless. New Zealand has a well-developed infrastructure of hotels, motels, and tour operators—but the best the country has to offer can't be seen through the windows of a tour bus. A trip here is a hands-on experience: hike, boat, fish, hunt, cycle, raft, and breathe some of the freshest air on earth. If these adventures sound a little too intrepid for you, the sheer beauty of the landscape and the clarity of the air will give you muscles you never knew you had.

—Michael Gebicki

WHAT'S WHERE

Geography and Population

New Zealand consists of three main islands: North Island (44,197 square mi), South Island (58,170 square mi), and Stewart Island (676 square mi). There are also Antarctic islands and the Chatham Islands, some 800 km (500 mi) east of Christchurch in the South Pacific. If New Zealand were stretched out along the west coast of the United States, the country would extend from Los Angeles to Seattle. No point is more than 112 km (70 mi) from the sea, and owing to the narrow, hilly nature of the country, rivers tend to be short, swift, and broad.

About 3,550,000 people live on the islands of New Zealand, and population density is very low. It is less than half that of the United States (with all of its open land in the west), and about 5% of the United Kingdom. New Zealanders are very friendly people—they seem to go out of their way to be hospitable. Some would argue that the low population takes away many of the stresses that people in more densely occupied areas experience. True or not, you're likely to be charmed by Kiwi hospitality.

More than 70% of the total population lives on North Island, where industry and government are concentrated. South Island is dominated by the Southern Alps, a spine of mountains running almost two-thirds the length of the island close to the West Coast.

North Island

The mighty 1,200-year-old *kauri* (cow-ree) trees, ferny subtropical forests, and miles of island-strewn coastline of Northland and the Coromandel Peninsula are a perfect foil for Auckland, New Zealand's largest city, and its neighborhood bustle and sprawl. Mid-island, Sulphuric Rotorua bubbles and oozes with surreal volcanic activity. It is one of the population centers of New Zealand's pre-European inhabitants, the Maori—try dining at one of their *hangi* (a traditional feast). Great hiking abounds in a variety of national parks, glorious gardens grow in the rich soil of the Taranaki Province, and charming, Art Deco Napier and the nation's capital in Wellington are friendly counterpoints to the countryside.

South Island

Natural wonders never cease—not on South Island. Nor do the opportunities for adventure: sea-kayaking, glacier hiking, trekking, fishing, mountain biking, rafting, and rock climbing. If you'd rather have an easier feast for your senses, fly over brilliant glaciers and snowy peaks, watch whales from on deck, and taste some of Marlborough's delicious wine. South of urbane Christchurch you'll head straight into picture-postcard New Zealand, where the country's tallest mountains are reflected in crystal-clear lakes and sheer rock faces tower above the fjords. The choice of activity is yours. You can enjoy some of the world's most dramatic views in complete peace and quiet, or leap—literally, if you'd like—from one adrenaline rush to the next. Take the four-day Milford Track walk or the less ambitious Kaikoura Track, with its splendidly isolated and warmly rustic overnight cottages. Or opt for the remote isolation of pristine Stewart Island. Add New Zealand hospitality to all of that, and you can't go wrong.

PLEASURES AND PASTIMES

As much as or more than any other countries, New Zealanders love sports—professional, amateur, and any variety of weekend sports. You'll see a number of them listed below. If you are interested in a particular adventure activity, be sure to consult Chapter 6 for specific guided trips. If you want to do it yourself, Chapter 6 can also point out desirable regions where you can strike out on your own.

Beaches

The list of unique and outstanding New Zealand beaches is almost endless—including the dramatic Karekare Beach in West Auckland shown in Jane Campion's film *The Piano*. There are no private beaches and no risks from pollution. The greatest danger is sunburn.

Most New Zealanders prefer beaches along the east coast of North Island, where the combination of gentle seas and balmy summers is a powerful attraction during January holidays. Sand on the west coast of North Island is black as a result of volcanic activity.

South Island beaches are no less spectacular, particularly those in the northwest in Abel Tasman National Park and down the West Coast. In summer popular beaches close to cities and in major holiday areas are patrolled by lifeguards. Swim with caution on unpatrolled beaches.

You'll find the best surfing conditions at Auckland's west coast beaches—Piha is recommended—and at Whangamata, Waihi, and Mount Manganui in the Coromandel and coastal Bay of Plenty regions. Taranaki beaches in the North island and areas around Dunedin in the south are also worthy.

Bicycling

Despite its often precipitous topography, New Zealand is great for biking. A temperate climate, excellent roads with relatively little traffic, and scenic variety make it a delight for anyone who is reasonably fit and has time to travel slowly. The most common problem for cyclists is buckled wheel rims: Narrow, lightweight alloy rims won't stand up long to the rigors of the road. A wide-rimmed hybrid or mountain bike with road tires is a better bet for extensive touring.

If two-wheel touring sounds appealing but pedaling a heavily laden bicycle doesn't, consider a guided cycle tour. Tours last from 2 to 18 days; bikes are supplied, and your gear is loaded on a bus or trailer that follows the riders. And you have the option of busing in the "sag wagon" when your legs give out.

Boating: Sailing, Rafting, and Sea-Kayaking

The country's premier cruising regions are the Bay of Islands, Marlborough Sounds, and the coast around Abel Tasman National Park, near the northern tips of North and South Islands, respectively. Both areas have sheltered waters, marvelous scenery, and secluded beaches. The Bay of Islands enjoys warmer summer temperatures, while Marlborough Sounds has a wild, untamed quality. Both areas have opportunities for sea-kayaking as well.

In Auckland, City of Sails, it is easy to rent a yacht and go out bareboat for the day, or to hire a skipper along with the vessel. Keen and experienced "yachties" could even try turning up at a yacht club along Westhaven Drive and asking if anyone is looking for crew that day. If you want a less active role, there are ferries and cruise boats with half- and full-day trips around Auckland's Hauraki Gulf and its islands.

The Wanganui River, flowing from the western slopes of Mt. Tongariro on North Island to meet the sea at the west coast town of Wanganui, is New Zealand's premier canoeing river. The longest navigable waterway in the country, this captivating river winds through native bushland with occasional rapids, cascades, and gorges. The most popular canoe trip begins at Taumarunui, taking four to five days to get downstream to Pipriki. Do this in warmer months, between November and March.

For thrills and spills, white-water rafting on the Shotover River near Queenstown is hard to beat. For something challenging in North Island, the Kaituna River near Rotorua has the highest commercially rafted waterfall in the southern hemisphere.

Country Life

In New Zealand rural settings are never far away from even the largest cities. To really get a taste of Kiwi life, don't confine your stay to tourist spots, towns, and cities. Many farms are open to visitors, either for a day visit or an overnight stay. You are usually welcome to try your hand at milking a cow or taking part in other activities. *See* the Gold Guide for information on farmstays.

Another way to get insight into the rural scene is to attend an agricultural and pastoral (A and P) fair. These are held at various times of the year by communities large and small, but the best time to see them is during summer. Check at information centers to find out where the nearest show is being held during your stay.

These events are an opportunity for farmers to bring their chickens, cattle, goats, sheep, and other stock into town and compete for ribbons. The farmers are only too happy to chat about their live exhibits to anyone who will ask. A and P shows are great for kids, who are usually welcome to pat and stroke the animals. Other favorites include wood-chopping contests, sheep shearing, and crafts displays. One tip: Many of these shows go on for two or three days, one of which is declared a local holiday so that families in the area can attend. If possible, avoid such times and go on quieter days.

Dining

Old New Zealand, new New Zealand— what you'll find culinarily on your trip spans the 20th century, from farmers' fare of yore to very contemporary preparations. Auckland, Wellington, Christchurch, and Dunedin offer cosmopolitan dining, and there is an expanding coterie of restaurateurs city and country who are serving clean, contemporary cuisine on both major islands. That said, much country cooking still follows the meat-and-two-veg school of English cuisine.

The waters around New Zealand are some of the cleanest in the world, and their produce is sensational. The New Zealand crayfish, essentially a clawless lobster, is delicious, and succulent white-shelled Bluff oysters, available from March to about July, are rated highly by aficionados. Watch for orange roughy, a delicate white-fleshed fish best served with a light sauce. And don't miss *pipis* (clams), scallops (with delicious roe in spring), green-lipped mussels, *paua* (abalone) with their iridescent shells, the small seasonal fish called whitebait, usually served in fritters, and very fine freshwater eel.

Back on land, lamb and venison are widely available, and many chefs are preparing exciting dishes using cervena, a leaner, lighter deer raised on farms. Other foods: Capsicum is red or green bell pepper; courgettes are zucchini. The *kumara* (koomer-ah) is a tasty, white-fleshed sweet potato that the Maori brought with them from Polynesia. It grows in warmer North Island soil. Don't confuse entrées with main courses—entrées are part of the appetizer course that comes before the main course. Pudding generally speaking is dessert, and one New Zealand favorite is pavlova, also called pav, a white meringue pie named after ballerina Anna Pavlova.

A native specialty is the *hangi,* a Maori feast of steamed meat and vegetables. Tour operators can take you to a hangi at a Maori *marae* (meeting house). Several hotels in Rotorua offer a hangi, usually combined with an evening of Maori song and dance. Unfortunately, these days it's often unlikely that food will be cooked by steaming it in the traditional earthen oven.

For inexpensive lunches, the standard take-aways are meat pies and fish-and-chips. But keep in mind that there are more and more contemporary cafés and ethnic restaurants opening up in unexpected places. Occasionally, you'll also find good vegetarian restaurants. Most country pubs serve reasonable cooked lunches and sometimes a selection of salads. In season, stock up on fruit from roadside stalls that are scattered throughout the country's fruit-growing areas.

Fishing

Considering that trout were introduced from California little more than a hundred years ago, today's population of these fish in New Zealand's lakes and rivers is phenomenal. One reason for this is that commercial trout fishing is illegal, which means you won't find trout on restaurant menus. You can, however, bring your own catch for a chef to prepare.

Getting back to fishing, the average summer rainbow trout taken from Lake Tarawera, near Rotorua, weighs 5 pounds, and 8- to 10-pound fish are not unusual. In the lakes of North Island, fingerlings often reach a weight of 4 pounds nine months after they are released. Trout do not reach maturity until they grow to 14 inches, and all trout below that length must be returned to the water.

Trout fishing has a distinctly different character on the two islands. In the Rotorua-Taupo region of North Island, the main quarry is rainbow trout, which are usually taken from the lakes with wet flies or spinners. Trolling is also popular and productive. On South Island, where brown trout predominate, there is outstanding dry-fly fishing. It's best in the Nelson region and in the Southern Lakes district, at the top and bottom ends of South Island, respectively. Trout season lasts from October through April in most areas, though Lakes Taupo and Rotorua are open all year.

Salmon are found in rivers that drain the eastern slopes of the Southern Alps, especially those that reach the sea between Christchurch and Dunedin. Salmon season runs from October to April, reaching its peak from January to March.

The seas off the east coast of North Island are among the world's finest big-game fishing waters. The quarry is mako, hammerhead, tiger shark, and marlin—especially striped marlin, which average around 250 pounds. For light tackle fishing, bonito and skipjack tuna and *kahawai* (sea trout) offer excellent sport. Many anglers maintain that kahawai are better fighters, pound for pound, than freshwater trout. Bases for big-game fishing are the towns of Paihia and Russell, which have a number of established charter operators. The season runs from January to April, although smaller game fishing is good all year.

Glorious Gardens

New Zealand is rapidly becoming a major destination for garden lovers on vacation. Since the first British settlers arrived with seeds from their homeland, Kiwis have looked toward Great Britain for horticultural inspiration. However, as in other parts of the world, gardeners here are discovering the unique beauty of their native plants and are gradually welcoming them into their gardens, successfully mixing them with exotics and creating a look that couldn't be achieved elsewhere else.

So while northern hemisphere gardens are lying fast asleep for the winter, head to New Zealand to see nature in full bloom. The climate couldn't be more accommodating to the plant life, with cool summers, mild winters, and abundant rainfall. The rich, spongy, alluvial soil readily absorbs the rain, courtesy of countless volcanic eruptions over time. With few stresses, plants respond by growing to enormous proportions. Trees are taller, flowers more abundant, perfumes stronger.

Equally delightful are the gardeners themselves—a large part of the population that appears to include all economic and social groups. Being New Zealanders, they are enthusiastic, hospitable, and only too glad to show off their hearts' delights. As a result, hundreds of private gardens, in addition to public gardens, are open to visitors. With the foresight of a phone call, not only can a beautiful garden be visited, but a passion can be shared—an exchange that makes the world feel like a smaller, friendlier place.

Golf

You will find courses of an extremely high standard, such as Titirangi, Formosa, Gulf Harbour, and Millbrook. However, keen golfers should also take the time to enjoy a country course, where the main hazards include sheep droppings and friendly locals who will keep you chatting until the sun goes down if you let them. You can play year-round; winter is the major season. Most of New Zealand's 400 courses welcome visitors.

Hiking

If you want to see the best of what New Zealand has to offer, put on a pair of hiking boots and head for the bush—the Kiwi word for the great outdoors. Range upon range of mountains, deep, ice-carved valleys, wilderness areas that have never been farmed, logged, or grazed, and a first-class network of marked trails and tramping huts are just some of the reasons that bushwalking (read: hiking) is a national addiction.

The traditional way to hike in New Zealand is freedom walking. Freedom walkers carry their own provisions, sleeping bags, food, and cooking gear and sleep in basic huts. A more refined alternative—usually available only on more popular trails—is the guided walk, on which you trek with just a light day pack, guides do the cooking, and you sleep in heated lodges. If you prefer your wilderness served with hot showers and an eiderdown on your bed, the guided walk is for you.

The most popular walks are in the Southern Alps, where South Island's postcard views of mountains, wild rivers, mossy beech forests, and fjords issue a challenge to the legs that is hard to resist. Trekking season in the mountains usually lasts from October to mid-April. The best known of all New Zealand's trails is the Milford Track, a four-day walk through breathtaking scenery to the edge of Milford Sound. Its main drawback is its popularity. This is the only track in New Zealand on which numbers are controlled: You

are required to obtain a permit and to begin walking on the day specified (to ensure that the overnight huts along the track don't become impossibly crowded).

Although the Milford gets the lion's share of publicity, many other walks offer a similar—some would say better—combination of scenery and exercise. The Routeburn Track is a three-day walk that rises through beech forests, traverses a mountain face across a high pass, and descends through a glacial valley. The Kepler and the Hollyford are both exceptional, and the Abel Tasman, at the northern end of South Island, is a spectacular three- to four-day coastal track that can be walked year-round.

By all means don't rule out tramping on North Island, which has plenty of wonders of its own. The Coromandel Peninsula has tremendous forests of gigantic, 1,200-year-old kauri trees, 80-ft-tall tree ferns, a gorgeous coastline, and a Coromandel Track scheduled to open soon. You can hike among active volcanic peaks in Tongariro National Park. And on a nub of the west coast formed by volcanic activity hundreds of years ago, the majestic, Fuji-like Mt. Taranaki, also known as Mt. Egmont, is positively mystifying as it alternately dons cloaks of mist and exposes its brilliant, sunlit, snowy cap. In fact, there are few areas in the North or South islands that don't have their own intriguing geological eccentricities worth exploring on foot.

If time is short, at least put aside a few hours for trekking in the Waitakerei Ranges, just a short drive from Auckland city.

Kiwi English

There are a few Kiwi expressions that you should know about to avoid eliciting occasional puzzled looks or embarrassment. In a restaurant, don't ask for a napkin unless your baby needs a diaper, as in nappies—ask for a **serviette**. A bathroom is where you actually bathe, so ask for a **toilet** (or **loo**) if you have to go—in fact, New Zealand may be the easiest country in the world to find a public toilet, especially on the road: They're signposted in even the smallest of hamlets.

Keep in mind that **tea** isn't just the beverage, it also generally means dinner. **Devonshire tea** is served morning and afternoon: cream tea with scones. If someone offers you a **cuppa,** say whether you'd like a cuppa tea or a cuppa coffee; the word refers to both. If you've stopped at a pub to **sink a few** and the local you start talking with offers to **shout,** tell him what you're drinking and consider shouting a round later to return the favor.

There are two terms for vacation houses: In North Island it's **bach** (baches plural, pronounced batch and batches); in South Island it's **crib. En suites** are bathrooms attached to your hotel or B&B room. The great outdoors is called the **bush,** through which you **tramp** (hike). When you go tramping, bring along insect repellent for the **mozzies** (mosquitoes). And don't call your waist pack a fanny pack—if you do, you'll shock Kiwis, for whom fanny refers to women's privates.

And when you're driving your car on the left—on a **sealed** (paved) road, **metal** (gravel), or dirt—for God's sake don't get yourself into a **prang** (accident).

Maori Language

Even if you have a natural facility for picking up languages, the Maori words that you'll find all over New Zealand can be baffling. The West Coast town of Punakaiki (pronounced poon-ah-*kye*-kee) is relatively straightforward, but when you get to places like Whangamata, the going gets tricky—the opening *wh* is pronounced like an *f,* and the accent is placed on the last syllable: "fahng-ah-ma-*ta.*" Sometimes it is the mere length of words that makes them difficult, as in the case of Waitakaruru (why-ta-ka-ru-ru) or Whakarewarewa (fa-ka-*re*-wa-*re*-wa). You'll notice that the ends of both of these have repeats—of "ru" and "rewa"—, which is something to look out for to make longer words more manageable. Town names like Waikanea (*why*-can-eye) you'll just have to repeat to yourself a few times before saying them without pause.

A few more points: the Maori *r* is rolled so that it sounds a little like a *d.* Thus the Northland town of Whangarei is pronounced "fang-ah-day," and the word *Maori* is pronounced "mo-dee," with the *o* sounding like it does in the word mould, and a rolled *r.* All of this is a little too complicated for some pakeha (pahk-eh-ha), the Maori word for descendents of European settlers, who choose not to bother with Maori pronunciations. So in some places,

if you say you've just driven over from "fahng-ah-ma-*ta,*" the reply might be: "You mean 'wang-ah-*ma*-tuh.'" "You can pronounce these words either way, but more and more Kiwis are saying Maori words as the Maori do.

There are some key Maori words that you should know. *Kia ora* (kee-ah oar-ah) means hello or good luck. *Haere mai* (ha-air-ay my) means welcome, *haere ra* means good-bye if you are the one staying, and *e noho ra* if you are leaving. Thank you is *ka pai* (kah pie). And a *hoa* is a friend.

The Maori word *tapu* is the origin of the Western word taboo, which has its roots in sacredness. Other words you'll encounter are *hangi* (hahng-ee), both the traditional feast and the oven in which the feast is cooked. *Manu* means bird, *ika* is fish. *Moku* is the Maori facial tattoo. *Motu* means island, *puke* is hill, *rangi* is the sky, and *whanga* means harbor. A *pa* is a fortified Maori village, often atop a hill, and a *whare* (fah-ray) is a house. Some of these words occur in place names.

Shopping

New Zealand produces several unique souvenirs, but don't expect to find many bargains. Sheepskins and quality woolens are widely available. Bowls hewn from native timber and polished to a lustrous finish are distinctive souvenirs, but a fine example will cost several hundred dollars. Greenstone, a type of jade once prized by the Maori, is now used for ornaments and jewelry—especially the figurines known as *tiki,* often worn as pendants. The two major areas for crafts are the Coromandel Peninsula close to Auckland and the environs of Nelson at the northern tip of South Island; those areas also have local potters. Kerikeri in Northland and Katikati on coastal Bay of Plenty are also emerging as arts and crafts centers. The Parnell area of Auckland and the Galleria in the Christchurch Arts Centre are the places to shop for souvenirs. In Nelson, Craft Habitat brings together some of the finest local arts and crafts under one roof.

Skiing

New Zealand has 27 peaks that top the 10,000-ft mark, and the June–October ski season is the reason many skiers head "down under" when the snow melts in the northern hemisphere. South Island has most of the country's 13 commercial ski areas, and the outstanding runs are at Treble Cone and Cardrona, near the town of Wanaka, and Coronet Peak and the Remarkables, close to Queenstown. North Island has two commercial ski areas, Whakapapa and Turoa, both near Lake Taupo on the slopes of Mount Ruapehu.

What New Zealand ski fields lack is sophistication. By international standards they are comparatively small, and slopes lack the extensive interlocking lift systems that are a feature of European skiing. So there are no lift-side accommodations. You'll have to stay in nearby subalpine towns.

Heli-skiing is very popular. Harris Mountains Heliski, the second-largest heli-ski operation in the world, gives access from the town of Wanaka to more than 200 runs on more than 100 peaks accessible to skiers by no other means. The ultimate heli-ski adventure is the 13-km (8-mi) run down Tasman Glacier.

Swimming with Marine Life

Dolphins and seals are plentiful off many parts of New Zealand, and you're likely to spot them from regular cruises and ferry trips. It's not unusual to see dolphins or even orcas (killer whales) on a cruise in and beyond Auckland's Hauraki Gulf.

If you want to get even closer, a number of operators now have swim-with-dolphins—or-seals—tours. The best places from which to access these are Pahia in Northland, Tauranga and Whakatane in the coastal Bay of Plenty, and Kaikoura in South Island. Most tours run daily, and gear is included in the price. Many of them also guarantee at least a sighting of marine mammals and offer a free trip the next day if the animals are not spotted. Check on these details before you hand over your money.

To swim or snorkel with large numbers of fish at no cost, go to Goat Island, an hour and a half's drive north of Auckland.

Wine

New Zealand is one of the wine world's latest upstarts, and Kiwi grapes and vignerons are producing first-class wine. Sauvignon blanc was the first New Zealand varietal to win an international award—that was Hunter's 1985 vintage, from the Marlborough region. Dry Rieslings and rich chardonnays are also excellent, and some *méthode champenoise* sparkling wines are coming into their own as well. As for reds, pinot noir tends to be the most refined. Cabernets, merlots, and blends are perhaps best appreciated with food.

New Zealand wine makers more often than not have food in mind when they create their wine, and you should plan to try sauvignon blanc alongside scallops or crayfish, chardonnay with salmon, or some of the bold reds with lamb or venison. You'll discover just how well those audacious flavors work with local cuisine.

You won't have to go out of your way to try New Zealand wine—licensed restaurants are extremely loyal to Kiwi wineries—but you might want to. If you've come from Australia or the United Kingdom, chances are you've seen more Kiwi wine back home. Not so for Americans: the California wine industry has acted as a barrier to the importation of New Zealand wine, and New Zealand's production isn't high enough to allow mass distribution in the U.S. market.

Of the major Kiwi wine routes, we cover four: Hawke's Bay and its well-known chardonnay, cabernet sauvignon, cabernet franc, and merlot grapes; Gisborne–East Cape, often overshadowed by nearby Hawke's Bay but arguably stronger in the chardonnay category; Wairarapa-Martinborough, with it's esteemed pinot noir; and Marlborough, where sauvignon blanc reigns supreme, but you'll also find very good sparkling whites, Rieslings, chardonnays, even Muller-Thurgau, and a host of reds. We also cover a couple of Waiheke Island wineries, near Auckland.

If you aren't familiar with New Zealand wine, you're sure to find plenty of wine that isn't available at your local vintner. Bring back as much as you can—sauvignon blanc to drink soon, chardonnay to let stand for a year or two, and the red of choice to age longer.

FODOR'S CHOICE

Special Moments

North Island

★ Digging out your own thermal bath at Hot Water Beach, Coromandel Peninsula

⭐ Listening to the Maori choir, St. Faith's Church, Rotorua

⭐ Biting into a crisp, juicy apple just picked from an orchard in Hawke's Bay

⭐ Your first glimpse of Mt. Taranaki, be it in sunshine or cloud

⭐ Experiencing a simulated earthquake or a bungee jump at Te Papa, Museum of New Zealand, Wellington

South Island

⭐ Kayaking with dolphins off of Abel Tasman National Park

⭐ Marveling at blue-ice formations on Franz Josef or Fox Glacier, West Coast

⭐ Sailing on a fjord, just taking in the wonder of it all, Fiordland National Park

⭐ Hurtling along Shotover River in a jet boat, Queenstown

National Parks and Natural Wonders

North Island

⭐ *The Piano*'s Karekare Beach, West Auckland

⭐ Taking one of Kiwi Dundee's wilderness hikes on the Coromandel Peninsula

⭐ Stands of giant native kauri and tree ferns, Coromandel Peninsula

⭐ Gurgling, slopping, bubbling volcanic activity in Rotorua

⭐ Fishing in the lakes and rivers around Rotorua and Taupo

⭐ The wild landscapes of volcanic Tongariro National Park

⭐ Remote landscapes of the East Cape

⭐ Lake Waikaremoana, Urewera National Park

⭐ The Pinnacles, Wairarapa

South Island

⭐ Dipping a line into a backcountry river in Nelson Lakes National Park

⭐ Glaciers grinding down 12,000-ft peaks into the rain forests of the West Coast

⭐ Mt. Cook and Tasman Glacier in Mount Cook National Park

⭐ The Remarkables viewed as a backdrop to Lake Wakatipu, Queenstown

⭐ Fiordland National Park's Milford Track, Mitre Peak, and Milford Sound

⭐ The isolation and night skies of southernmost Stewart Island

Wildlife Viewing

North Island

⭐ Diving in the Bay of Islands

⭐ Birding in Tongariro National Park

⭐ The gannet colony at Cape Kidnapper, south of Napier

⭐ Swimming with dolphins at Whakatane

South Island

⭐ Dolphins off Abel Tasman National Park

⭐ Cruising with sperm whales off Kaikoura

⭐ Fiordland crested penguins and fur seals at Wilderness Lodge Lake Moeraki, West Coast

⭐ The royal albatrosses, Taiaroa Head, Otago Peninsula

⭐ Night watch for kiwis on Stewart Island

Dining

North Island

⭐ Antoine's, Auckland ($$$$)

⭐ Cin Cin on Quay, Auckland ($$$)

⭐ You & Me, Rotorua ($$$)

⭐ Bayswater Bistro, Napier ($$$)

⭐ The Mountain House, Stratford, Taranaki ($$$)

⭐ Boulcott Street Bistro, Wellington ($$$)

⭐ Logan Brown, Wellington ($$$$)

South Island

⭐ Walnut Café, Richmond, Nelson ($$$)

⭐ Crayfish shacks around Kaikoura ($$)

⭐ Thornley's, Christchurch ($$$$)

⭐ Espresso 124, Christchurch ($$)

⭐ Main Street Café, Christchurch ($)

⭐ Bellpepper Blues, Dunedin ($$$)

City Lodging

North Island

★ Stamford Plaza, Auckland (*$$$$*)

★ Peace and Plenty Inn, Devonport, Auckland (*$$$$*)

★ Devonport Villa, Devonport, Auckland (*$$*)

★ County Hotel, Napier (*$$$*)

★ Parkroyal, Wellington (*$$$$*)

South Island

★ Hotel d'Urville, Blenheim (*$$$$*)

★ Charlotte Jane, Christchurch (*$$$$*)

★ Riverview Lodge, Christchurch (*$$*)

Country Lodging

North Island

★ Huka Lodge, Lake Taupo (*$$$$*)

★ Acton Estate, Gisborne (*$$$$*)

★ Martinborough Hotel, Wairarapa (*$$$*)

★ Wharekauhau, Palliser Bay, Wairarapa (*$$$$*)

South Island

★ Timara Lodge, Blenheim, Marlborough (*$$$$*)

★ Lake Brunner Sporting Lodge, near Greymouth (*$$$$*)

★ Wilderness Lodge Lake Moeraki, West Coast (*$$$*)

★ Willow Cottage, near Wanaka (*$$$*)

★ Millbrook Resort, near Queenstown (*$$$$*)

FESTIVALS AND SEASONAL EVENTS

Sport features heavily in New Zealand's festival calendar. Horse and boat races, triathlons, and fishing competitions are far more prominent than celebrations of the arts. Just about every town holds a yearly agricultural and pastoral (A and P) show, and these proud displays of local crafts, produce, livestock, and wood-chopping and sheep-shearing prowess provide a memorable look at rural New Zealand. An annual calendar, *New Zealand Special Events,* is available from government tourist offices.

SUMMER

➤ Dec. 25–26: On **Christmas Day** and **Boxing Day** the country virtually closes down.

➤ Jan. 1: **New Year's Day** is a nationwide holiday.

➤ Jan. 25: For the **Auckland Anniversary Day Regatta,** Auckland's birthday party, the City of Sails takes to the water. ☎ 09/579–0923.

➤ Feb. 3–14: The **Festival of Romance** is held in Christchurch—the city where lovers can stroll through an old English garden and enjoy a punt ride on the Avon River. ☎ 03/379–9629.

➤ Feb. 5–6: **Speights Coast to Coast** is the ultimate iron-man challenge—a two-day, 238-km (148-mi) marathon of cycling, running, and kayaking that crosses

South Island from west to east. *Information: Robin Judkins,* ☎ 03/326–5493.

➤ Feb. 6: **Waitangi Day,** New Zealand's national day, commemorates the signing of the Treaty of Waitangi between Europeans and Maori in 1840. The focus of the celebration is, naturally enough, the town of Waitangi in the Bay of Islands.

➤ Feb. 14–22: Christchurch's **Garden City Festival of Flowers,** the country's largest flower show, finds the city bursting with blossoms and activity, with plenty of related events, displays, and exhibitions.

➤ Feb. 22–24: **The Devonport Food and Wine Festival** showcases some of the country's best restaurants and is easily reached by a ferry trip from Auckland city.

➤ Feb. 26: The **Aotearoa WOMAD Pacific Festival** highlights the many Pacific Island cultures found in Auckland with plenty of color, music, and dance. The main activity is at Western Springs lakeside, near the Auckland Zoo. ☎ 09/307–5075, ext. 8063.

➤ 1st Thurs.–Sat. of Mar.: **Golden Shears International Shearing Championship** is a three-day event that pits men armed with shears against the fleecy sheep in Masterton, just north of Wellington. *Information:* ✉ *Masterton Visitor Information Centre, 5 Dixon St.,* ☎ 06/378–7373.

➤ Mar. 21: Auckland's **Round the Bays Run** is one of the world's largest

10-km (6.25-mi) fun runs. A few people take it seriously, but thousands of others jog, walk, or ride about the course in their own time. The run starts in the city, follows Tamaki Drive around the waterfront, and finishes in the plush suburb of St. Heliers. ☎ 09/525–2166.

AUTUMN

➤ Mar. 31–Apr. 3: The **Easter** holiday weekend lasts from Good Friday through Easter Monday. The Royal Easter Show is held in Auckland over the holiday.

➤ Apr. 25: **Anzac Day** honors the soldiers, sailors, and airmen and women who fought and died for the country.

➤ Early May: The **Fletcher Marathon** around Lake Rotorua is New Zealand's premier long-distance event.

➤ 1st Mon. in June: The **Queen's Birthday** is celebrated nationwide.

WINTER

➤ Early to mid-July: At the **Queenstown Winter Festival,** the winter-sports capital hits the slopes for a week of competition by day and entertainment by night.

➤ Late July: **Mad, Mad Mid-Winter Festival** is a

mixture of sporting events
held in Rotorua, from
outrigger canoeing to
nighttime mountain
biking to a mountain-
rafting championship
contest.

SPRING

➤ OCT. 15–22: **Dunedin
Rhododendron Festival**
opens the city's gardens
for tours and offers lec-
tures and plant sales.
☎ 03/474–3300.

➤ OCT. 23: **Labour Day** is
observed throughout the
country.

➤ NOV. 1–10: **Taranaki
Rhododendron Festival** in
and around New Ply-
mouth is a major event.
One hundred–plus pri-
vate gardens are open to
the public, there are
lectures, and the vast
Pukeiti Rhododendron
Trust holds a series of
cultural events and festivi-
ties. ☎ 06/752–4141.

➤ MID- TO LATE NOV.:
Ellerslie Flower Show in
Auckland is one of the
headline events on New
Zealand's gardening
calendar. It is modeled on
London's Chelsea Flower
Show.

➤ 2ND WEEK IN NOV.:
**Canterbury Agricultural
and Pastoral Show** spot-
lights the farmers and

graziers of the rich countryside surrounding
Christchurch. *Informa-
tion:* ✉ *Canterbury Visitor Information Centre,
Worcester St. and Oxford
Terr., Christchurch,* ☎ *03/
379–9629.*

➤ 2ND WEEKEND IN NOV.:
The city of Blenheim's
Garden Marlborough has
local garden tours and a
fête with products for
sale. The festival follows
Auckland's Ellerslie
Flower Show, which gives
the international experts
who attended the Auck-
land event time to get to
South Island and give
excellent lectures and
workshops. ☎ 03/572–
8707.

2 Auckland and the North

The mighty 1,200-year-old kauri trees, ferny semitropical forests, and miles of island-strewn coastline of Northland and the Coromandel Peninsula are the perfect counterpoint to Auckland, New Zealand's largest city, and its neighborhood bustle and sprawl.

AS YOU FLY INTO AUCKLAND, New Zealand's gateway city, you might wonder where the city is. Most people arriving for the first time, and even New Zealanders coming home, are impressed by the sea views and the green forest that dominate the view on the approach to the airport.

By Michael Gebicki and Stu Freeman

The drive from the airport—with scenery commanded by some of the city's 46 volcanic hills, their grass kept closely cropped by those four-legged lawnmowers known as sheep—does little to dispel the clean, green image so many people have of the country. And reading the highway signs will begin to give you a taste of the unusual and sometimes baffling Maori place-names around the country.

Yet a couple of days in this city of about 1 million will reveal a level of development and sophistication that belies first impressions. In the past 10 years Auckland has grown up in more ways than one. Many shops are open seven days, central bars and nightclubs welcome patrons well into the night and early morning, and a cosmopolitan mix of Polynesians, Asians, and Europeans all contribute to the cultural milieu. Literally topping things off is the 1,082-ft Sky Tower, dwarfing everything around it and acting as a beacon for the casino, hotel, and restaurant complex that opened early in 1996. This is the newest, if least pervasive, face of modern New Zealand.

In the midst of the city's activity, you'll see knots of cyclists and joggers. Like all other New Zealanders, Aucklanders are addicted to the outdoors—especially the water. There are some 70,000 powerboats and sailing craft in the Greater Auckland area—about one for every four households. And a total of 102 beaches lies within an hour's drive of the city center. The city is currently working to enhance its greatest asset, Waitemata Harbour—a Maori name meaning "Sea of Sparkling Waters." The city will stage its first defense of the America's Cup in the year 2000, and the regatta has been acting as a catalyst for major redevelopment of the waterfront.

Auckland is not easy to explore. Made up of a sprawling array of neighborhoods (Kiwis call them suburbs), the city spreads out on both shores of Stanley Bay and Waitemata Harbour. It's best to have a car for getting around between neighborhoods, and even between some city center sights. One good introduction to the city, particularly if you arrive at the end of a long flight and time is limited, is the commuter ferry that crosses the harbor to the village of Devonport, where you can soak up the charming suburb's atmosphere in a leisurely stroll, at a local café or bookstore, or munching on fish-and-chips on the town green.

As you put Auckland behind you, and with it the signs of overdevelopment, you'll find yourself in the midst of some of the great open space that so defines New Zealand. North of the city, the Bay of Islands is both beautiful—for its lush forests, splendid beaches, and shimmering harbors—and historic—as the place where westernized New Zealand came into being with the signing of the Treaty of Waitangi in 1840. South and east of the city is the rugged and exhilarating Coromandel Peninsula, with mountains stretching the length of its middle and a Pacific coastline afloat with picturesque islands.

Note: For more information on bicycling, diving, deep-sea fishing, hiking, and sailing in Auckland and the north, *see* Chapter 6.

Pleasures and Pastimes

Beaches

When the sun comes out, Aucklanders head to the beach. With seas both to the west and the east, few people in the city live more than a 15-minute drive from the coast. Generally speaking the best surfing is at the black-sand beaches on the west coast, and the safest swimming is on the east coast. Beaches that do have a reputation for large waves and rips are patrolled in the summer, so play it safe and swim between the flags. The only other danger is from the sun itself. The ozone layer is weak above New Zealand, so slap on the sunscreen and resist the temptation to bake.

Boating

Auckland is dubbed City of Sails for good reason. The population is crazy about boating and any other recreation associated with the sea. A variety of ferries and high-speed catamarans operate on Waitemata Harbor. Even better, go for a sail on the *Pride of Auckland*. Northland and the ravishing Bay of Islands also have a diverse choice of boat and sailing trips, and taking a small boat out to Cathedral Cove on the Coromandel Peninsula is a great way to see its stunning coastline.

Dining

Auckland's culinary revolution is in full swing—and that's good news for foodies. It is one of the great dining cities of the Pacific Rim—a cosmopolitan mix of cafés, restaurants, brasseries, and bars. The local style leans to the Mediterranean, but its strong sideways glance toward Asia is a signature element. Daily seafood specials abound—don't miss such delicacies as Bluff or Nelson Bay oysters, New Zealand green-shell mussels, scallops, and crayfish (clawless lobster).

The top restaurant strips are Ponsonby and Parnell roads, suburbs a 10-minute bus or cab ride from the city center. Dominion and Mount Eden roads in the city, as well as Hurstmere Road in the North Shore suburb of Takapuna, are also worth exploring. The mix is eclectic—Indian, Chinese, and Thai eateries sit comfortably alongside supercasual taverns, pizzerias, and high-end restaurants. At hole-in-the-wall spots in and around the city center, a few dollars will buy you anything from fish-and-chips to nachos, noodles, or nan bread. Ponsonby Road leads the field in street-side dining.

As you put Auckland behind you, the choice of fare reduces sharply, though there are increasing numbers of enlightened cooks in countryside nooks. That said, tradition does have its place when cutting-edge cuisine palls. At least once, give old-style roast lamb and veggies a try—if you don't like New Zealand lamb, chances are you won't like it anywhere.

For price ranges, *see* the price chart *in* On the Road with Fodor's.

Lodging

Around Auckland and the north, a great variety of accommodation is available, from flashy downtown hotels to comfortable B&Bs to mom-and-pop motels. Because Kiwis are so naturally hospitable, it's hard not to recommend lodgings where you have a chance to talk with your hosts—unless you prefer anonymity. For price ranges, *see* the price chart *in* On the Road with Fodor's.

Volcanoes and Vistas

Auckland is built on and around 48 volcanoes, and the tops of many of them provide sweeping views of the city. Mt. Eden is probably the most popular, and several bus tours include this central site. Rangitoto Island has an even better vista. This volcano emerged from the sea just

600 years ago, no doubt much to the wonder of the Maori people living next door on Motutapu Island. Take a ferry to the island, then either a short ride or an hour's walk to the top will give you a 360-degree view of the city and the Hauraki Gulf islands.

Walking and Hiking

There is superb bushwalking around Auckland, Northland, and the Coromandel Peninsula. New Zealand's largest city is fringed by bush to the west, and the Waitakere Ranges are an ideal way to experience the country's flora if you have limited time. The Northland and Coromandel bush is full of impressive ancient kauri trees and interesting birds, such as tuis (*too*-ees), fantails, and wood pigeons.

Exploring Auckland and the North

Northland and the Coromandel Peninsula have beautiful countryside, coasts, and mountains—some of the finest in North Island. Auckland is a thoroughly modern, car-oriented metropolis, with interesting restaurants and a handful of suburbs to poke around. But it isn't the easiest place to figure out in a couple of days, the way you can get a sense of the character of other New Zealand cities. Auckland has built out, rather than up, and the sprawl makes the city close to impossible to explore on foot. What might look like reasonable walking distances on maps can turn out to be 20- to 30-minute treks, and stringing a few of those together can get frustrating. If you only want to see the city center close to the harbor, Devonport, and Parnell, you can get around by busing and ferrying between places.

Interestingly enough, Aucklanders seem to talk as much about what surrounds the city as what's in it: beaches, the Waitakere Ranges, and Waiheke Island and its vineyards. To get to most of these and to happening suburbs like Ponsonby, you will need a car, which you can then use to go farther afield to Northland and the Coromandel Peninsula.

Great Itineraries

Numbers in the text correspond to numbers in the margin and on the Auckland, Northland and the Bay of Islands, and Coromandel Peninsula maps.

IF YOU HAVE 2 DAYS

Explore central Auckland by starting at the **Civic Theatre** ① and walking down to the **Ferry Building** ⑩. Then spend the best part of the day on the harbor. Take a boat to **Devonport** for some shopping and a streetside lunch. On returning to the city side, visit **Kelly Tarlton's Underwater World and Antarctic Encounter** ⑫ and follow that with some seafood in a nearby restaurant. The next day, visit the **Auckland Domain** ④ for a peaceful stroll and the **Auckland Institute Museum** ⑤ for a look into Maori history and culture. Then head to **Parnell Village** ⑧ for some of Auckland's best shopping and dining and the **Parnell Rose Gardens** ⑨. Any spare time in the afternoon could be spent back in the city at the **National Maritime Museum** ⑪, which houses historical and current exhibits with plenty of hands-on opportunities.

If you're not in an urban mood, spend a day on Auckland's beaches, at the vineyards of **Waiheke Island,** or hiking in the **Waitakere Ranges,** or you can just chuck it all and go to the **Coromandel Peninsula** for two glorious days in the bush and on the beach. Just two hours from Auckland by car, the Coromandel is a great, unspoiled getaway.

IF YOU HAVE 5 OR MORE DAYS

Spend the first day or two looking around metropolitan Auckland, then head west to the Waitakere Ranges and explore the bush or west coast beaches with their volcanic black sand. Or visit a few of Auckland's vineyards instead. Then head either to the popular Bay of Islands or the less trodden Coromandel Peninsula. With more than a week, you could see both, but the drive connecting the two is more than six hours, making it more sensible to choose one of the two places. Heading north to the Bay of Islands, stop in **Warkworth** ⑮ for a look at some great old kauri trees or a hillside garden. **Whangarei** ⑯ is also on the way—a good place for lunch, perhaps a picnic by the harbor or at the waterfall. This area is steeped in history and has superb coastal scenery. Continue north and spend a couple of days exploring **Paihia and Waitangi** ⑰, with the nearby **Waitangi Treaty House,** and the charming town of **Russell** ⑱. When you return south, take the western route to **Waipoua State Forest** ㉑, and stop farther down at the **Matakohe Kauri Museum** ㉒ to learn about the area's incredible native trees. If you want to stay off the main road dropping back into Auckland, go past the scenic Kaipara Harbour, then through Helensville.

The Coromandel Peninsula is an easy two-hour drive south and east of Auckland. **Thames** ㉓ is a logical first stop, then wind your way up the Firth of Thames coast to the town of **Coromandel** ㉔, a good base for exploring the upper peninsula. Then turn to the east coast, where you'll find some of the best Coromandel beaches. **Hot Water Beach** ㉗ is a combination of thermal activity and surf—dig a hole in the sand, and you've got a hot bath!—and you can overnight in nearby **Tairua** ㉘. A range of mountains runs in a line up the Coromandel, and from just about any point you can head into the hills for great hiking through lush ferny forests. To the south are the popular surf beaches of **Whangamata** ㉙ and Wahi. If you have extra time, you could linger here or even head toward the coastal **Bay of Plenty.**

When to Tour Auckland and the North

Snow doesn't fall on this part of New Zealand, and the weather doesn't exactly get frigid. Still, to see these areas at their finest, mid-November through mid-April are the beautiful months, with December through March being the highest season for tourism. If you plan to come around the Christmas holidays, reserve well in advance, especially in seaside places. The Bay of Islands is a summertime hot spot for vacationing Kiwis, and the Coromandel town of Whangamata, for example, gets overrun by surfer dudes around the New Year.

AUCKLAND

City Center

❸ **Albert Park.** These 15 acres of formal gardens, fountains, and statue-studded lawns are a favorite for Aucklanders who pour out of nearby office blocks and the university and polytechnic to eat lunch on a sunny day. The park is built on the site of a garrison from the 1840s and 1850s that was used to protect settlers from neighboring Maori tribes. There are still remnants of its stone walls (with rifle slits) behind university buildings on the east side of the park. ⊠ *Wellesley St. W, Kitchener St., Waterloo Quad.*

❷ **Auckland City Art Gallery.** The country's finest collection of contemporary art as well as paintings of New Zealand dating back to the time of Captain Cook hang here. Look for works by Frances Hodgkins, New Zealand's best-known artist. The gallery expanded with the opening of what is known as the **New Art Gallery** in 1995; historic items of interest are to be found in the older **Heritage Art Gallery.** In winter the museum presents jazz and classical music concerts some Sunday af-

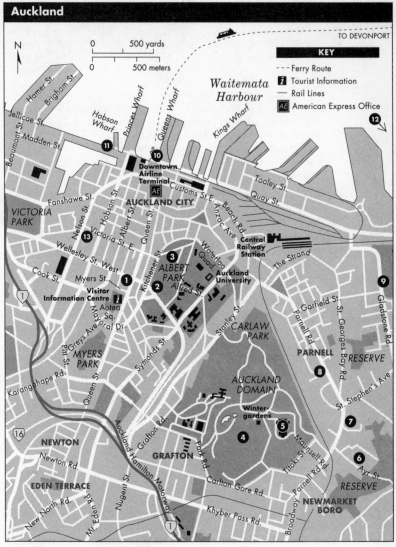

Auckland

Albert Park, **3**

Auckland City Art
Gallery, **2**

Auckland Institute
Museum, **5**

Cathedral Church of
St. Mary, **7**

Civic Theatre, **1**

Ewelme Cottage, **6**

Ferry Building, **10**

Kelly Tarlton's
Underwater World
and Antarctic
Encounter, **12**

National Maritime
Museum, **11**

Parnell Rose
Gardens, **9**

Parnell Village, **8**

Sky City, **13**

ternoons. ⊠ *Kitchener St. and Wellesley St. E,* ☎ *09/307–7700,* FAX
09/302–1096. ☎ *Free.* ⊙ *Daily 10–5.*

❹ Auckland Domain. Sunday picnickers and morning runners are two types
of Aucklanders who take advantage of the rolling, 340-acre Domain.
Watch the local paper for free summer weekend evening concerts, which
usually include opera and fireworks displays. Take a bottle of wine and
a basketful of something tasty and join in with the locals—up to 300,000
of them per show. Within the Domain near the **Auckland Institute Museum,** the domed **Wintergardens** house a collection of tropical plants
and palms and seasonally displayed hothouse plants. The gardens aren't
really worth going out of your way for, unless you're missing your house-
plants. ⊠ *Entrances at Stanley St., Park Rd., Carlton Gore Rd., and
Maunsell Rd.* ☎ *Free.* ⊙ *Wintergardens daily 10–4.*

❺ Auckland Institute Museum. Dominating the Domain atop a hill, the
Greek Revival Institute is known especially for its Maori artifacts, the
largest collection of its kind. Portraits of Maori chiefs by C. F. Goldie
are splendid character studies of a fiercely martial people. Other exhibits in the museum are dedicated to natural history, geology, and a
reconstructed streetscape of early Auckland. Although entrance remains
free, the museum is combating a local image of becoming tired and dusty
by putting on special exhibits and charging a nominal fee for these.
The best of the lot is **Weird and Wonderful,** an interactive display for
kids of all ages. ⊠ *Auckland Domain,* ☎ *09/309–0443 or 09/306–
7069,* FAX *09/379–9956.* ☎ *Free.* ⊙ *Daily 10–5.*

❼ Cathedral Church of St. Mary. Gothic Revival wooden churches don't
get much finer than this one, which was built in 1886. It is one of a
number of churches commissioned by the early Anglican missionary
Bishop Selwyn. The craftsmanship inside the church is remarkable, as
is the story of its relocation. St. Mary's originally stood on the other
side of Parnell Road, and in 1982 the entire structure was moved
across the street. Photographs inside show the progress of the work.
The church now forms part of the Cathedral of Holy Trinity. ⊠
Parnell Rd. and St. Stephen's Ave. ⊙ *Daily 8–6.*

❶ Civic Theatre. This extravagant Art Nouveau movie theater was the talk
of the town when it opened in 1929, but just nine months later the
owner, Thomas O'Brien, went bust and fled, taking with him the
week's revenues and an usherette. During World War II a cabaret
show in the basement was popular with Allied servicemen in transit
to the battlefields of the Pacific. One of the entertainers, Freda Stark,
is said to have appeared regularly wearing nothing more than a coat
of gold paint. To see the best of the building, don't restrict your visit
to standing outside. Sit down to a movie, look up to the ceiling, and
you will see a simulated night sky. The theater is close to the Visitor
Information Centre (☞ Visitor Information *in* Auckland A to Z,
below). ⊠ *Queen and Wellesley Sts.,* ☎ *09/377–3315.*

❻ Ewelme Cottage. Built by the Reverend Vicesimus Lush and inhabited
by his descendants for more than a century, the cottage stands behind
a picket fence. The house was constructed of kauri, a resilient timber
highly prized by the Maori for their war canoes and later by Europeans
for ship masts. Kauri became the basic building material for Western
settlers, and most of the great old trees were cut down. All kauri are
now protected by law, but only a few examples of majestic mature trees
remain in forests. Ewelme Cottage contains much of the original furniture and personal effects of the Lush family. ⊠ *14 Ayr St.,* ☎ *09/
379–0202.* ☎ *$3.* ⊙ *Wed.–Sun. 10:30–noon and 1–4:30.*

⑩ **Ferry Building.** Boats leave here for Devonport weekdays on the hour between 10 and 3, and at half-hour intervals during the morning and evening commuter periods; on Saturday they leave every hour from 6:15 AM until 1 AM, on Sunday from 7 AM to 11 PM. On Friday and Saturday after 7 PM, the regular Devonport boat is replaced by the MV *Kestrel,* a turn-of-the-century ferry, with its wood and brass restored, which is fitted with a bar and a jazz band. This is also the place to catch ferries to the Hauraki Gulf Islands: Waiheke, Rangitoto, and Motutapu. ⊠ *Quay St.* 🚢 *Round-trip $7.*

☙ ⑫ **Kelly Tarlton's Underwater World and Antarctic Encounter.** The creation of New Zealand's most celebrated undersea explorer and treasure hunter, this harborside marine park offers a fish-eye view of the sea. A submerged transparent tunnel, 120 yards long, makes a circuit past moray eels, lobsters, sharks, and stingrays. In Antarctic Encounter, you enter a replica of Scott's Hut at McMurdo Sound, then circle around a deep-freeze environment aboard a heated Snow-Cat that winds through a penguin colony and an aquarium exhibiting marine life of the polar sea, emerging at Scott Base 2000 for a glimpse of the next century's Antarctic research and exploration. ⊠ *Orakei Wharf, Tamaki Dr.,* ☎ *09/528–0603.* 🚢 *$16.* ⊙ *Daily 9–9, last admission 8* PM.

☙ ⑪ **National Maritime Museum.** New Zealand's rich seafaring history is on display in a marina complex on Auckland Harbour. You can experience what it was like to travel steerage class in the 1800s, and there are detailed exhibits on early whaling, a collection of outboard motors, yachts, ship models, Polynesian outriggers, a replica of a shipping office from the turn of the century, and a scow that conducts short trips on the harbor, among other exhibits. The museum also hosts workshops, where traditional boatbuilding, sail making, and rigging skills are kept alive. The pride of the museum is the *KZ1,* the 133-ft racing sloop built for the America's Cup challenge in 1988. ⊠ *Eastern Viaduct, Quay St.,* ☎ *09/358–3010.* 🚢 *$10.* ⊙ *Oct.–Easter, daily 9–6, Easter–Sept., daily 9–5.*

⑨ **Parnell Rose Gardens.** When you tire of boutiques and cafés, take a 10-minute stroll to gaze upon and sniff this collection of some 5,000 rosebushes. The main beds contain mostly modern hybrids, with new introductions being planted regularly. The adjacent **Nancy Steen Garden** is the place to admire the antique varieties. And don't miss the garden's incredible trees. There is a 200-year-old pohutukawa (puh-hoo-too-*ka*-wa) whose weighty branches touch the ground and rise up again and a kanuka (*leptospermum pricoides*) that is one of Auckland's oldest trees, dating from when the area was called Maryland. The Rose Garden Restaurant serves lunch (open Sunday–Friday and public holidays noon–2). ⊠ *Gladstone and Judges Bay Rds.,* ☎ *09/302–1252.* 🚢 *Free.* ⊙ *Daily dawn–dusk.*

⑧ **Parnell Village.** The pretty Victorian timber villas along the slope of Parnell Road have been transformed into antiques shops, designer boutiques, street cafés, and restaurants. Parnell Village is the creation of Les Harvey, who saw the potential of the quaint but run-down shops and houses and almost single-handedly snatched them from the jaws of the developers' bulldozers by buying them, renovating them, and leasing them out. Harvey's vision has paid handsome dividends, and today this village of trim pink-and-white timber facades is a delightful part of the city. At night its restaurants, pubs, and discos attract Auckland's smart set. Parnell's shops are open Sunday. ⊠ *Parnell Rd. between St. Stephen's Ave. and Augustus Rd.*

⓭ **Sky City.** The joke among Auckland residents is that your property value rises if you *can't* see the **Sky Tower,** the 1,082-ft beacon to the Sky City complex. Yet it's also the first place Aucklanders take friends and relatives visiting from overseas in order to give them a view of the city. Up at the main observation level, the most outrageous thing is the glass floor panels—looking down at your feet, you see the street hundreds of yards below. Adults usually step gingerly onto the glass, while kids delight in jumping up and down on it. More educational are the audio guides to Auckland, live weather feeds, and touch-screen computers that you'll find on the deck. There is also an outdoor observation level, where you'll feel the wind on your face as you see the sights. Sky City also includes New Zealand's largest casino, but you needn't walk through the gambling den to get to the tower. ✉ *Victoria and Federal Sts.,* ☎ *09/912–6000.* ✉ *Sky Tower $15.* ☉ *Sun.–Fri. 8:30 AM–11 PM (last lift 10:30 PM), Sat. 8:30 AM–midnight (last lift 11:30 PM).*

Devonport

The 20-minute ferry to Devonport across **Waitemata Harbour** provides one of the finest views of Auckland. The first harbor ferry service began with whaleboats in 1854. Later in the century the Devonport Steam Ferry Co. began operations, and ferries scuttled back and forth across the harbor until the Harbour Bridge opened in 1959. The bridge now carries the bulk of the commuter traffic, but the ferry still has a small, devoted clientele.

Originally known as Flagstaff, after the signal station on the summit of Mt. Victoria, Devonport was the first settlement on the north side of the harbor. Later the area drew some of the city's wealthiest traders, who built their homes where they could watch their sailing ships arriving with cargoes from Europe. These days, Aucklanders have fixed up and repopulated its great old houses, laying claim to the suburb's relaxed, seaside atmosphere.

The **Esplanade Hotel** is one of the first things you'll see as you leave the ferry terminal. It stands at the harbor end of **Victoria Road,** a pleasant street for taking a stroll, stopping at a shop, a bookstore, or a café, or for picking up some fish-and-chips to bite into next to the giant Moreton Bay fig tree across the street on the green.

Long before the era of European settlement, the ancient volcano now called **Mt. Victoria** was the site of a Maori *pa* (fortified village) of the local Kawerau tribe. On the northern and eastern flanks of the hill you can still see traces of the terraces once protected by palisades of sharpened stakes. Don't be put off by its name—this is more molehill than mountain, and the climb isn't much. ✉ *Kerr St. off Victoria Rd.*

New Zealand's navy is hardly a menacing global force, but the small **Naval Museum** has interesting exhibits on the early exploration of the country and information on its involvement in various conflicts. The museum is five blocks west of Victoria Wharf along Queens Parade. ✉ *Queens Parade.* ✉ *Small donation.* ☉ *Daily 10–4.*

North Head is an ancient Maori defense site, and its position jutting out from Devonport into Auckland's harbor was enough to convince the European settlers that they, too, should use the head for strategic purposes. Rumor has it that veteran aircraft are still stored in the dark, twisting tunnels under North Head, but plenty of willing explorers have not found any. You can still get into most tunnels, climb all over the abandoned antiaircraft guns, and get great views of Auckland and the islands to the east. North Head is a 20-minute walk east of the ferry terminal on King Edward Parade, then Cheltenham Street, then out Takarunga Road. ✉ *Takarunga Rd.*

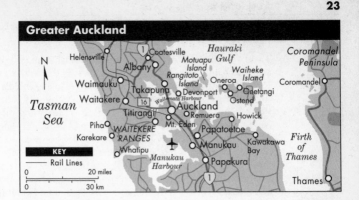

Greater Auckland

Around Auckland

★ **Beaches.** Auckland's beaches are commonly categorized by area—East, West, or North. The ones closest to the city are the east coast beaches along Tamaki Drive on the south side of the harbor, which do not have heavy surf. **Judge's Bay** and **Mission Bay** are particularly recommended for their settings. The best swimming is at high tide.

Black-sand west coast beaches are popular in summer, but the sea is often rough, and sudden rips and holes can trap the unwary. The most visited of these is **Piha,** some 40 km (25 mi) from Auckland, which has pounding surf as well as a sheltered lagoon dominated by the reclining mass of Lion Rock. **Whatipu,** south of Piha, is a broad sweep of sand offering safe bathing behind the sandbar that guards Manukau Harbour. **Bethells,** to the north, often has heavy surf. In the vicinity, **Karekare** is the beach where the dramatic opening scenes of Jane Campion's *The Piano* were shot. Across Waitemata Harbour from the city, a chain of magnificent beaches stretches north as far as the Whangaparaoa Peninsula, 40 km (25 mi) from Auckland.

☉ **Museum of Transport and Technology.** This fascinating collection of aircraft, telephones, cameras, locomotives, steam engines, and farm equipment is a tribute to Kiwi ingenuity. One of the most intriguing exhibits is the remains of an aircraft built by Robert Pearse, who made a successful powered flight barely three months after the Wright brothers first took to the skies. The flight ended inauspiciously when his plane crashed into a hedge, but Pearse, considered a wild eccentric by his farming neighbors, is recognized today as a mechanical genius. ⊠ *Great North Rd. (off North-Western Motorway, Rte. 16), Western Springs,* ☎ *09/846–0199.* 🎫 *$10.* ☉ *Daily 10–5.*

Waiheke Island. Once a sleepy suburb of Auckland, Waiheke was mainly used as a weekend and summer holiday retreat, with beach houses dotting its edges. Since the late 1980s more people have moved to the island as a lifestyle choice, commuting each day by ferry to the city. The island is also earning an international reputation for its vineyards, and local cafés sometimes stock wines that aren't available on the mainland—vintners make them purely for island enjoyment. Buses meet ferries at the terminal and make a loop around the island.

The ferry lands at **Matiatia Wharf.** The walk to the small town of **Oneroa** is five minutes, where you'll find the excellend Mudbrick Vineyard and Restaurant (⊠ Church Bay Rd., ☎ 09/372–9050). Another minute's walk gets you to **Oneroa Beach,** one of the island's finest and most accessible beaches. The bus that meets the ferry can also take you to Oneroa. Another great beach on Waiheke is **Onetangi,** on the north side of the island, 20 minutes from Matiatia by bus. **Whakanewha Re-**

gional Park is on the south of the island and has bushwalk and picnic options.

There are close to 20 vineyards on Waiheke Island, but only a handful are producing wine. First to plant grapes (and olives) were Kim and Jeanette Goldwater, whose eponymous wines have earned a reputation for excellence. The **Goldwater Estate** (⊠ 18 Causeway Rd., Putiki Bay, ☎ 09/372–7493, FAX 09/372–6827) cabernet sauvignon–merlot–cabernet franc blend is outstanding, and the chardonnay—made, oddly enough, at the other end of the country in Marlborough—is thoroughly pleasant. Stephen White's **Stonyridge Vineyard** (⊠ 80 Onetangi Rd., Ostend, ☎ 09/372–8822) has the island's highest profile, and his Larose red, made from the classic Bordeaux varieties, is world class—and priced accordingly. Steven calls for faxed orders months before release and is usually sold out hours later. Across a grass airstrip from Stonyridge is **Waiheke Vineyards** (⊠ 76 Onetangi Rd., ☎ 09/486–3859, FAX 09/486–2341), which produces a highly rated red called Te Motu.

If you're planning on going farther afield on the island, you can purchase an all-day bus pass from **Fullers Auckland** (☎ 09/367–9111). The $30 pass includes the ferry trip and bus travel on regular services to Oneroa, Palm Beach, Onetangi, and Rocky Bay. To use the pass, you need to take the 8:15, 10, or noon ferry. Return time is optional. Additional organised trips are available, too. The **Island Explorer Tour and Ferry** (☎ 09/367–9111) costs $34 and stops at Onetangi Beach on the trip. The **Waiheke Vineyard Explorer Tour** takes 5½ hours and costs $55, ferry included. The **Beyond and Back Tour** takes you to the more remote east side of Waiheke, also stopping at Onetangi Beach, for $40, ferry included. Bookings are essential in summer. You can also take a shuttle to beaches or vineyards; **Waiheke Island Shuttles** (☎ 09/372–7756) has reliable service. The best way to get to Whakanewha Regional Park is by shuttle.

Waitakere Ranges. This scenic mountain range west of Auckland is a favorite walking and picnic spot for locals. The 20-minute **Arataki Nature Trail** is a great introduction to kauri, a species of pine, and other native trees. The highlight of the **Auckland City Walk** is Cascade Falls. The **Arataki Visitors Centre** displays modern Maori carvings and has information on the Waitakeres and other Auckland Parks. To get to the Waitakeres, head along the northwestern motorway, Route 16, from central Auckland, take the Waterview turnoff, and keep heading west to the small village of Titirangi, the gateway to the Waitakeres. A sculpture depicting fungal growths tells you you're heading in the right direction. From here the best route to follow is the Scenic Drive, with spectacular views of Auckland and its two harbors. The visitors center is 5 km (3 mi) along the drive.

Dining

Harborside

$$$–$$$$ ✕ **Kermadec.** With harborside views and suitable Pacific-theme decor, this complex's two restaurants—one of them more casual—both put a major emphasis on seafood. Start with a tian of tuna and salmon with avocado, drizzled with a passion-fruit and poppy-seed vinaigrette, then move to a main course of crispy skinned fillet of snapper on a mussel and pine-nut risotto with a watercress and olive oil emulsion sauce. Or share a seafood platter and try sashimi, smoked salmon, scallops, prawns, mussels, smoked eel, scampi, John Dory, and snapper. Desserts are equally imaginative. ⊠ *1st floor, Viaduct Quay, Quay and Lower Hobson Sts.,* ☎ *09/309–0413 brasserie, 09/309–0412 restaurant. AE, DC, MC, V.*

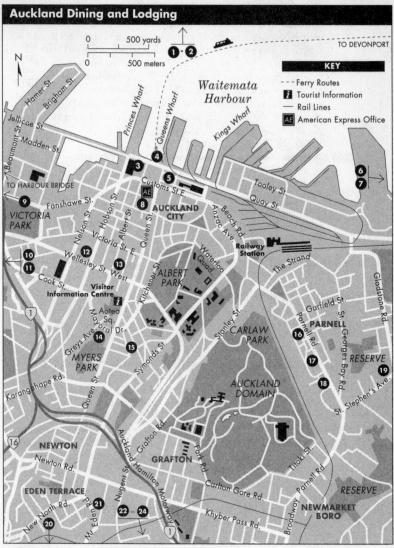

Auckland Dining and Lodging

Dining
Antik's, **20**
Antoine's, **18**
Bolero, **9**
Burger Wisconsin, **10**
Cin Cin on Quay, **4**
Galbraith's Ale
House, **21**
Harbourside Seafood
Bar and Grill, **5**
Iguaçú, **17**

Kermadec, **3**
Non Solo Pizza, **16**
Saint's Waterfront
Brasserie, **6**
Sun World, **15**
Vinnie's, **11**

Lodging
Albion Hotel, **12**
Ascot Parnell, **19**
Brooklands Country
Estate, **22**
Carlton, **14**
Centra, **13**
Devonport Villa, **1**
Florida Motel, **7**
Hotel du Vin, **23**

Peace and
Plenty Inn, **2**
Sedgwick-Kent
Lodge, **24**
Stamford Plaza, **8**

$$$ ✕ **Cin Cin on Quay.** Auckland's first California-style brasserie is still
★   one of the city's best. Look for innovative pizzas (try tandoori chicken
     with avocado-mango chutney and red onion) and clever entrée and main
     selections like paddle-crab pot stickers (think wontons) with cucum-
     ber salad and Thai curry sauce, or spit-roasted lamb racks with pigs'
     feet and coffee-barbecue sauce. The wine list includes several vintages
     of local vinous icons like Kumeu River Chardonnay or Stonyridge Larose,
     a power-packed cabernet-based blend from Waiheke Island. If you're
     in town on the weekend, book an outside table overlooking the har-
     bor for the good-value breakfast. ✉ *Auckland Ferry Bldg., 99 Quay
     St.,* ☎ *09/307–6966. AE, DC, MC, V.*

$$$ ✕ **Harbourside Seafood Bar and Grill.** Overlooking the water from the
     upper level of the restored ferry building (above Cin Cin), this vast,
     modish seafood restaurant is a fine choice for warm-weather dining.
     Some of the finest New Zealand fish and shellfish, including tuna, salmon,
     and snapper, appear on a menu with a fashionably Mediterranean ac-
     cent. Lobster fresh from the tank is a house specialty and is one rea-
     son the restaurant is a favorite with Japanese tourists. Non-fish-eaters
     have their choice of venison, lamb, and poultry. On warm nights,
     book ahead and request a table outside on the deck. ✉ *Auckland Ferry
     Bldg., 99 Quay St.,* ☎ *09/307–0486. AE, DC, MC, V.*

Parnell and City Center

$$$$ ✕ **Antoine's.** Owners Tony and Beth Astle have run this stately Par-
★   nell institution for more than 21 years, and the food today is better
     than ever. Tony is still at the stove, and his current menu reads as if it
     were designed by a chef half his age. The classics are there—oxtail casse-
     role, braised lamb shanks, and creamy tripe are still big sellers—but
     they are joined by the likes of pork fillet on a white bean puree, grilled
     salmon with mashed potatoes, and a terrine of goat cheese and veg-
     etables. The wine list is extensive and international at this must for se-
     rious foodies. ✉ *333 Parnell Rd.,* ☎ *09/379–8756. AE, DC, MC, V.*

$$$ ✕ **Antik's.** The decor is eccentric at this pioneer café in an area set to
     be the city's newest foodie strip—wall ornaments include antique skis,
     a pair of crutches, and a grocer's bicycle. And owner Tim Holman han-
     dles the place with panache and humor: Glasses (sponsored by a local
     optician) and a torch (flashlight) are offered to anyone finding the menu
     hard to read—or a magnifying glass if the glasses aren't strong enough.
     The menu is eclectic, with such dishes as *hangi*-marinated chicken, seared
     tuna with a honey-based sauce, and cervena (farm-raised venison)
     stuffed with aged feta. The wine list is reasonably extensive, and you
     are welcome to bring your own as an alternative. ✉ *248A Dominion
     Rd.,* ☎ *09/638–6254. AE, DC, MC, V. Licensed & BYOB.*

$$–$$$ ✕ **Non Solo Pizza.** The name means "not only pizza," and that tells it
★   like it is. This uncompromisingly Italian eatery offers pasta as a single
     serving or in table-sharing bowls that feed four or more. Try the
     aubergine (eggplant), panfried and layered with mozzarella, tomato,
     basil, and Parmesan, or look for spaghetti with fresh cockles. And there's
     always pizza with traditional toppings followed by a masterfully pre-
     pared green salad. The same team runs Toto, on the other side of town,
     so if you can't get a seat here, ask if the sister restaurant is also full.
     ✉ *259 Parnell Rd.,* ☎ *09/379–5358. AE, DC, MC, V.*

$$ ✕ **Iguaçú.** With flares blazing near the entrance, dappled red ocher walls,
     enormous mirrors in Mexican metalwork frames, a glass ceiling, and
     a pair of chandeliers made from copper tubing festooning the interior,
     the decor strives as much for cultural cacophony as do dishes like wok-
     seared garlic prawns with peanut-lime noodles and lemongrass beurre
     blanc, or braised lamb shanks with Shanghai noodles and Asian greens.
     Befitting its fashionable status, the restaurant is generally full of pa-

trons who come to see and be seen as much as to enjoy the food. ⊠ *269 Parnell Rd.,* ☎ *09/309–4124. AE, DC, MC, V.*

$–$$ ✕ **Sun World.** In the last five years, Auckland has absorbed a huge num-
★ ber of immigrants from Hong Kong and Taiwan, and the standard of Chinese restaurants has improved dramatically as a result. Sun World is the place to go for *yum char* (dim sum), that admirable institution that allows you to choose from a variety of dishes that are carried past your table. It's on every day from 11 AM, and it is enthusiastically sup-ported by Asian family groups—you'll think you're in Kowloon or Taipei, you'll have a great time, and you'll eat really cheaply. Choose a well-priced bottle of wine from the reasonable list or save cash by sticking to complimentary fragrant tea. ⊠ *56 Wakefield St.,* ☎ *09/373–5335. AE, DC, MC, V.*

Ponsonby

$ ✕ **Burger Wisconsin.** Consistently rated the best burger joint in town, Wisconsin offers such bunned delights as chicken breast with cream cheese and apricot sauce, Malaysian satay, bacon and beef with may-onnaise, and even a vegetarian burger bulging with a soy and sesame-seed patty. There's not much seating, but you can order your burger to go and enjoy it in nearby Western Park, if the weather's fine. ⊠ *168 Ponsonby Rd.,* ☎ *09/360–1894. AE, DC, MC, V.*

Other Suburbs

$$$ ✕ **Bolero.** Maria Tieni is a mercurial character who ruled the stoves
★ at several city-side high-flyers before moving to the North Shore, where she might just have finally settled down. Bolero is bright, breezy, and close to the sea, and Maria's fitting style is influenced by the Mediter-ranean, very much in her own way. Tuna is cooked rare, scattered with pomegranate seeds, and drizzled with extra virgin olive oil; poussin is pot-roasted with bacon and grapes; and local fresh fish is panfried with sage, tomato, olives, and tahini. Many dishes are served in huge plates or bowls, but thankfully—unless you're exceptionally hungry—they're not usually full. ⊠ *129–155 Hurstmere Rd., Takapuna,* ☎ *09/489–3104. Reservations not accepted. AE, DC, MC, V.*

$$$ ✕ **Saint's Waterfront Brasserie.** On any warm weekend, this stylish brasserie, a 15-minute drive east of the city, is the perfect place to enjoy the City of Sails sunny-side up along with good, modern New Zealand fare. Try the Hereford prime beef-eye fillet with mashed potatoes in winter or any of the seafood dishes in summer. The weekend brunch menu includes healthy combinations of fresh fruit plates with yogurt, bagels, croissants, fruit whips, and muesli. The gray carpet and white tablecloths under glass create a smart, clean atmosphere, accented by art deco motifs. Big concertina doors frame an impressive sea view dom-inated by the cone of Rangitoto Island. ⊠ *425 Tamaki Dr., St. Heliers,* ☎ *09/575–5210. AE, DC, MC, V.*

$$$ ✕ **Vinnie's.** The decor is Paris bistro, but the food leans more toward
★ the gutsy styles of Provence and southern Italy at this shop-front restaurant in suburban Herne Bay, west of the city center. Chinese five-spice duck confit with pineapple-sherry vinegar dressing and wild greens, red-braised lamb tongues with bok choy and shiitake mush-rooms, and roasted lamb rack with sticky rice cake, summer vegeta-bles, and Vietnamese dressing are typical selections from a menu that also includes imaginative desserts. ⊠ *166 Jervois Rd., Herne Bay,* ☎ *09/376–5597. AE, DC, MC, V. No lunch Jan.–Nov.*

$ ✕ **Galbraith's Ale House.** Brew lovers and Brits craving a taste of home, head straight for Keith Galbraith's traditionally decorated ale-house. The English-style ales are made on the premises and served at proper cellar temperature. Keith learned the art of brewing in the U.K., and he sticks religiously to the style—his ales are likely the most

English in the land. Order a half or handle with well-priced dishes such as chili beef or vegetarian burritos, smoked chicken fettuccine, or pea-pie-pud—a traditional British dish that tops a steak pie with potato mash, minted green peas, and gravy. ✉ *2 Mount Eden Rd., Grafton,* ☎ *09/379–3557. AE, DC, MC, V.*

Lodging

City Center

$$$$ 🏨 **Carlton.** Its proximity to the Aotea Centre and downtown makes the Carlton a favorite with business travelers. Guest rooms are spacious and elegantly furnished, and bathrooms are particularly well equipped. The best views are from the rooms that overlook the parklands and the harbor to the east. Polished granite and warm, earthy tones have been used liberally throughout the building. The hotel's restaurants have occasional food festivals and cooking classes. ✉ *Mayoral Dr.,* ☎ *09/366–3000,* 🖷 *09/366–0121. 286 rooms with bath. 2 restaurants, 2 bars, coffee shop, tennis court. AE, DC, MC, V.*

$$$$ 🏨 **Stamford Plaza.** This midcity hotel brought a dash of style to Auck-
★   land when it opened as a Regent in the mid-'80s, and despite some energetic competitors, its service, sophistication, and attention to detail keep it on top. Standard rooms are large and furnished extensively with natural fabrics and native woods in an updated Art Deco style. The marble bathrooms are luxuriously appointed. The best rooms are on the harbor side—the higher the better. ✉ *Albert St.,* ☎ *09/309–8888,* 🖷 *09/379–6445. 332 rooms with bath. 3 restaurants, bar, pool. AE, DC, MC, V.*

$$$ 🏨 **Centra.** Rooms at this city landmark are equal to those in just about any of Auckland's leading hotels, but cutting down on facilities and glossy public areas has reduced prices substantially. Rooms have a standard, functional layout, and each has its own iron and ironing board. Accommodations begin on the 16th floor, and every room has a view. The suites on the 28th floor have great views and bigger bathrooms for just a slightly higher price. The hotel opened in 1991 and is aimed primarily at business travelers. Service is keen and professional. ✉ *128 Albert St.,* ☎ *09/302–1111,* 🖷 *09/302–3111. 252 rooms with bath. Restaurant, bar, exercise room. AE, DC, MC, V.*

$$ 🏨 **Ascot Parnell.** Accommodations and facilities in this sprawling guest house are comfortable and functional, but space and character have been sacrificed to provide rooms with en-suite facilities or private bathrooms at a reasonable price. The room with the attached sunroom at the back of the house is small but pleasant. The house stands on a relatively busy street, within easy walking distance of the shops and nightlife of Parnell Village. Smoking is not permitted inside. ✉ *36 St. Stephens Ave., Parnell,* ☎ *09/309–9012,* 🖷 *09/309–3729. 9 rooms with bath. BP. AE, MC, V.*

$ 🏨 **Albion Hotel.** If you'd like comfortable, modern accommodations in the heart of the city and outstanding value, look no farther. Rooms are modest in size and have no views, but all are neat and well kept. The best room in the house, the Hobson Suite, is equipped with a water bed and Jacuzzi and costs only slightly more than a standard room. Despite the busy corner location, the area is quiet after 6 PM. However, rooms on the lower floors can be affected by noise from the ground-floor pub, which is especially busy on Friday night. The Aotea Centre and the shops of Queen Street are only a few blocks away. ✉ *Hobson and Wellesley Sts.,* ☎ *09/379–4900,* 🖷 *09/379–4901. 20 rooms with bath. Brasserie, pub. AE, DC, MC, V.*

Devonport

$$$$ 🏨 **Peace and Plenty Inn.** Devonport's neighborhoody atmosphere makes
★   for a pleasant alternative to staying in central Auckland, and Carol and

Graham Ward's beautiful Victorian B&B is one of the treats of the town. In guest rooms, milk-painted walls, country antiques, thoughtfully combined decorative objects, cushy duvets, and abundant flowers create a feeling of earthy sophistication. Two rooms have small private verandas, and one garden-level room has its own entrance. On the main floor, there is a spacious lounge where you can make coffee, tea, or pour yourself a glass of sherry or port. Breakfasts are an all-out display of culinary finesse and Kiwi hospitality. ✉ *6 Flagstaff Terr., Devonport,* ☎ *09/445–2925,* 𝔽𝔸𝕏 *09/445–2901. 4 rooms with bath. BP. AE, MC, V.*

$$ 🔲 **Devonport Villa.** This gracious timber villa combines tranquil, historic surroundings and fresh sea air, a 20-minute ferry ride from the
★ city. Rooms are individually decorated and have handmade quilts, queen-size beds with Edwardian-style headboards, lace curtains, and colonial furniture. Cheltenham Beach, which offers safe swimming, is a two-minute walk away, and the picture-book village of Devonport is a short walk. Arriving guests can be collected from the Devonport ferry terminal. ✉ *46 Tainui Rd., Devonport,* ☎ *09/445–8397,* 𝔽𝔸𝕏 *09/445–9766. 4 rooms with bath. Lounge. BP. AE, V.*

Other Suburbs and Auckland Environs

$$$$ 🔲 **Brooklands Country Estate.** A fine alternative in the country only a 90-minute drive south of Auckland, Brooklands is ideal if you are short of time and want some rural hospitality. The turn-of-the-last-century homestead is set among gardens and surrounded by a 2,000-acre sheep, cattle, and deer station. Drink in the homey atmosphere in the library and lounge, where you will find plenty of timber, leather furnishings, and books from the owner's family. A open fire is the centerpiece of the dining room in cooler months, while in summer dinner is often served outside by the pool. The watercolors around the lodge were painted by the owner's father, Robert Gower. Antique oak furniture and Persian rugs on the old Kauri floors give rooms a pleasant country atmosphere. For something slightly unusual, the attic room has slanting ceilings. ✉ *R.D. 1, Ngaruawahia,* ☎ *07/825–4756,* 𝔽𝔸𝕏 *07/825–4873. 10 rooms with shower. Pool, tennis court, croquet, billiards, helipad. AE, DC, MC, V.*

$$$$ 🔲 **Hotel du Vin.** There can be no finer introduction to New Zealand
★ than to head south from the Auckland International Airport to this smart, luxurious hotel, set on the floor of a valley and surrounded by native forests and the grapevines of the de Redcliffe estate. Standard rooms are palatial, and the newer rooms at the far end of the resort are the best. The decor is crisp and modern, and the central restaurant and reception areas glow with honey-color wood and rough stone fireplaces. The restaurant has an excellent reputation, though prices are high. The hotel is 64 km (40 mi) from Auckland, a 45-minute drive from both Auckland airport and the city via the motorway. Casual visitors are welcome to taste the wines or stop for an evening meal—a pleasant way to break the journey between Auckland and the Coromandel region. ✉ *Lyons Rd., Mangatawhiri Valley,* ☎ *09/233–6314,* 𝔽𝔸𝕏 *09/233–6215. 46 rooms with bath. Restaurant, bar, indoor pool, spa, tennis courts, exercise room, bicycles. AE, DC, MC, V.*

$$–$$$$ 🔲 **Sedgwick-Kent Lodge.** On a quiet street in the suburb of Remuera,
★ between the airport and downtown, the single-story Edwardian villa where Wort and Helma van der Lans carry on a tradition of taking good care of guests is a wonderful retreat from the city. Entering through a garden courtyard, you immediately sense the lodge's graceful style. Inside, native timber trims intriguing doorways—appropriate transitions to rooms fitted with writing desks and luxuriously appointed antique bedsteads. Some rooms open onto elevated verandas. Decorative touches everywhere indicate excellent taste. The hosts' breakfasts are delightful, whether you give in and ask for a sumptu-

ous hot dish or restrain yourself and stick with freshly squeezed orange juice, muffins, fruit, and homemade muesli and yogurt. ⊠ *65 Lucerne Rd., Remuera,* ☎ *09/524–5219,* FAX *09/520–4825. 5 rooms with TV and bath, 1 apartment with kitchen. BP. AE, DC, MC, V.*

$$ 🏨 **Florida Motel.** In a harborside suburb a 15-minute drive east of the city center (and close to a major bus route into the city), this motel offers exceptional value. Rooms come in three versions: studios or one- or two-bedroom units. The units have a lounge room separate from the bedroom, and the two-bedroom units are particularly good for families. All rooms have separate, fully equipped kitchens and a few nice touches, such as wall-mounted hair dryers, French-press coffeemakers, and ironing boards with irons. As the motel is immaculately maintained and extremely popular, rooms must be booked several months in advance. ⊠ *11 Speight Rd., Kohimarama,* ☎ *09/521–4660,* FAX *09/ 521–4662. 8 rooms with bath. AE, DC, MC, V.*

Nightlife and the Arts

The Arts

For a current listing of plays, opera, dance, and musical events in Auckland, a brochure called *Auckland Alive* is available from the **Visitor Information Centre** (⊠ 299 Queen St., at Aotea Sq., ☎ 09/366– 6888) and the Aotea Centre. For current films, check the entertainment pages of the daily newspapers.

For tickets, **Ticketek** (☎ 09/307–5000) is the central agency for all theater, music, and dance performances, as well as major sporting events.

MUSIC AND OPERA

Aotea Centre. Auckland's main venue for music and the performing arts hosts musical and dramatic performances throughout the year. For general inquiries there is an information desk in the Owens Foyer, Level 2 of the complex. The **Auckland Philharmonia Orchestra** performs regularly at the center, and the **New Zealand Symphony Orchestra** performs both at the Town Hall and at the Aotea Centre. ⊠ *Aotea Sq., Queen and Myers Sts.,* ☎ *09/309–2678 or 09/307–5060.*

Dame Kiri Te Kanawa often performs at the Aotea Centre on return visits to her homeland. Tickets are usually sold out months in advance.

Nightlife

After sunset the liveliest area of the city is Parnell, which has several restaurants, bars, and nightclubs. For a late-night café scene, head to Ponsonby Road, southwest of the city center off Karangahape Road, where you will find street-side dining, small dessert-only restaurants, and intimate bars. For a walk on the seedier side of the city, wander along Karangahape Road itself (it crosses Queen Street just north of Highway 1), or downtown in Fort Street. Auckland tends to have three or four lively nightclubs running at any one time, but they are transient animals with names and addresses changing as young Aucklanders follow the trend of the day. For the latest information on nightclubs check with the information center (☞ *Visitor Information in* Auckland A to Z, *below*).

BARS AND LOUNGES

Civic Tavern. At the heart of the city center, this unremarkable building houses the **London Bar,** which has a vast selection of beer and an impressive variety of Scotch whiskey. ⊠ *1 Wellesley St.,* ☎ *09/373– 3684.* ☉ *Mon.–Thurs. 11 AM–midnight, Fri.–Sat. 11 AM–2 AM.*

Loaded Hog. This popular brewery and bistro with indoor or outdoor dining and drinking can get crowded late in the week, so try to arrive early. Part of the Hobson's Wharf development, the tavern has a vaguely nautical feel. Jazz musicians perform most evenings. ✉ *104 Quay St.,* ☎ *09/366–6491.* ☉ *Daily 11 AM–late.*

Shakespeare Tavern. The beer in this atmospheric city-center brewpub goes by colorful names like Willpower Stout and Falstaff's Real Ale. There are several bars inside. ✉ *Albert and Wyndham Sts.,* ☎ *09/ 373–5396.* ☉ *Mon.–Wed. 11:30–10, Thurs.–Fri. 11:30 AM–midnight, Sat. noon—midnight, Sun. 2 PM–10 PM.*

Outdoor Activities and Sports

Biking

Auckland is good for cycling, especially around the waterfront. **Penny Farthing Cycle Shop** rents mountain bikes for $25 per day or $100 per week. ✉ *Symonds St. and Khyber Pass Rd.,* ☎ *09/379–2524.* ☉ *Mon.–Thurs. 8:30–5:30, Fri. 8:30 AM–9 PM, weekends 10–4.*

Golf

Chamberlain Park Golf Course is an 18-hole public course in a parkland setting a five-minute drive from the city. The club shop rents clubs and carts. Greens fees are $16 weekdays, $20 weekends. ✉ *Linwood Ave. (off North-Western Motorway, Rte. 16), Western Springs,* ☎ *09/ 846–6758.*

Titirangi Golf Course, a 15-minute drive south of the city, is one of the country's finest 18-hole courses. Nonmembers are welcome to play provided they contact the professional in advance and show evidence of membership at an overseas club. Clubs and golf carts can be rented; the greens fee is $75. ✉ *Links Rd., New Lynn,* ☎ *09/827–5749.*

Running

Auckland's favorite running track is **Tamaki Drive,** a 10-km (6-mi) route that heads east from the city along the south shore of Waitemata Harbour and ends at St. Heliers Bay. The **Auckland Domain** (☞ City Center, *above*) is popular with executive lunchtime runners.

Swimming

The **Tepid Baths,** near the heart of Auckland, has a large indoor swimming pool, a whirlpool, saunas, and a steam room. ✉ *102 Customs St. W,* ☎ *09/379–4794.* ☑ *$5.50; pool only $3.50.* ☉ *Weekdays 6 AM–9 PM, weekends 7–7.*

Tennis

ASB Tennis Centre has 12 hard courts indoors and outdoors, 1 km (½ mi) east of the city center. ✉ *72 Stanley St.,* ☎ *09/373–3623.* ☑ *Outdoor court $10 per person singles, $6 per person doubles per hr; indoor court $18 per person singles, $10 per person doubles per hr.* ☉ *Weekdays 7–11, weekends 8–8.*

Spectator Sports

Eden Park is the city's major stadium for sporting events. This is the best place in winter to see New Zealand's sporting icon, the rugby team All Blacks, consistently among the world's top three teams. Cricket is played in summer. For information on sporting events, *Auckland Alive* is a quarterly guide available from the Visitor Information Centre. Tickets can be booked through **Ticketek** (☎ 09/307–5000).

Shopping

Department Store

Smith and Caughey Ltd. ✉ *253–261 Queen St.,* ☎ *09/377–4770.* ☉ *Mon.–Thurs. 9–5:30, Fri. 9–8, Sat. 10–5.*

Shopping Districts

Auckland's main shopping precinct for clothes, outdoor gear, duty-free goods, greenstone jewelry, and souvenirs is **Queen Street. Ponsonby,** about 1½ km (1 mi) west of the city center, is known for its antiques shops and fashion boutiques.

Street Markets

Victoria Park Market. Auckland's main bazaar consists of 2½ acres of clothing, footwear, sportswear, furniture, souvenirs, and crafts at knockdown prices. It's housed in the city's former garbage incinerator. ⊠ *Victoria and Wellesley Sts.,* ☎ *09/309–6911.* ☉ *Daily 9–6.*

Specialty Stores

BOOKS AND MAPS

Legendary Hard to Find (but worth the effort) Quality Second-hand Books, Ltd. With a name like that, what's more to say—except that it's probably the biggest for second-hand in the country and a local favorite. Its smaller sister in Devonport, **Hard to Find North Shore** (⊠ 81A Victoria St., ☎ 09/446–0300), is a great spot to stop into for a browse. ⊠ *171–175 The Mall, Onehunga,* ☎ *09/634–4340.* ☉ *Mon.–Thurs. 9:30–5, Fri. 9:30–7:30, Sat.–Sun. 10–4.*

Unity Books. This general bookstore specializes in travel, fiction, science, biography, and New Zealand–related books. ⊠ *19 High St.,* ☎ *09/307–0731.* ☉ *Mon.–Thurs. 8:30–7, Fri. 8:30 AM–9 PM, Sat. 9:30–9, Sun. 11–5.*

CLOTHES

Outdoor Heritage. This nationwide chain of stores sells high-quality outdoor clothing. ⊠ *75 Queen St.,* ☎ *09/309–6571.* ☉ *Mon.–Thurs. 9:30–6:30, Fri. 9:30–8, Sat. 10–5, Sun. 10–4.*

SOUVENIRS

Elephant House. Follow elephant footprints down an alley in Parnell Village for an extensive collection of souvenirs, many unavailable elsewhere. ⊠ *237 Parnell Rd.,* ☎ *09/309–8740.* ☉ *Weekdays 9:30–5:30, weekends 9:30–5.*

Wild Places. Proceeds from posters, T-shirts, books, and cards on the themes of whales, rain forests, and native birds all go to conservation projects in New Zealand and the Pacific. ⊠ *28 Lorne St.,* ☎ *09/358–0795.* ☉ *Mon.–Thurs. 9–5:30, Fri. 9–7:30, Sat. 10–4.*

SPORTS AND HIKING

Kathmandu. If you haven't brought your own, Kathmandu sells quality New Zealand–made clothing and equipment for the outdoor enthusiast. ⊠ *350 Queen St.,* ☎ *09/309–4615.* ☉ *Mon.–Thurs. 9–5:30, Fri. 9–9, Sat. 10–4.*

Tisdall's Sports. The extensive range of outdoor gear, especially boots and clothing, is made especially for New Zealand conditions. ⊠ *176 Queen St.,* ☎ *09/379–0254,* FAX *09/303–4321.* ☉ *Mon.–Thurs. 9–5:30, Fri. 9–8, Sat. 9:30–2.*

WINE

Accent on Wine. If you've circled New Zealand without picking up a few bottles of wine to take home with you, stop in Parnell to stock up. At the very least bring home some sauvignon blanc—Cloudy Bay if you can get it. ⊠ *347 Parnell Rd., Parnell,* ☎ *09/358–2552.*

Auckland A to Z

Arriving and Departing

BY BUS

The terminal for **InterCity Coaches** (☎ 0800/802–802) is the Auckland Central Railway Station (☞ *below*). **Newmans Coaches** (☎ 09/309–9738) arrive and depart from the Downtown Airline Terminal (✉ Quay and Albert Sts.).

BY CAR

By the standards of most cities, Auckland traffic is moderate, parking space is inexpensive and readily available, and motorways pass close to the heart of the city. Getting used to driving on the left, if you'll be traveling by car, can be especially difficult when trying to figure out where to get onto highways. Taking a close look at a city map before you set out is a good idea.

BY PLANE

Auckland International Airport lies 21 km (13 mi) southwest of the city center. The **Visitor Information Centre,** open daily 5 AM–2 AM in the terminal, provides free maps and brochures as well as a booking service for tours and accommodations. There are two **currency exchange booths**: one in the gate area and one near rental car booths outside the customs area.

A free **Interterminal Bus** links the international and domestic terminals, with frequent departures in each direction 6 AM–10 PM. Otherwise, the walk between the two terminals takes about 10 minutes along a signposted walkway. Luggage for flights aboard the two major domestic airlines, Air New Zealand and Ansett New Zealand, can be checked at the international terminal.

Major international carriers serving Auckland include **Air New Zealand** (☎ 09/357–3000), **Canadian Airlines International** (☎ 09/309–0735), **Cathay Pacific** (☎ 09/379–0861), **Qantas** (☎ 09/357–8900), **Singapore Airlines** (☎ 09/379–3209), and **United Airlines** (☎ 09/379–3800).

Domestic carriers with services to Auckland are **Air New Zealand** (☎ 09/357–3000), **Air Nelson** (☎ 09/379–3510), **Ansett New Zealand** (☎ 09/302–2146), and **Mount Cook Airlines** (☎ 0800/80–0737).

Airport to City Center. The journey between the airport and the city center takes about 30 minutes.

The **Airbus** (☎ 09/275–9396) costs $9 and leaves the international terminal every 20 minutes between 6:20 AM and 8:20 PM. The fixed route between the airport and the Downtown Airline Terminal, on the corner of Quay Street and Albert Road, includes a stop at the railway station and, on request, at any bus stop, hotel, or motel along the way. Returning from the city, the bus leaves the Downtown Airline Terminal at 20-minute intervals between 6:20 AM and 9 PM. Travel time is 35–45 minutes.

Hallmark Limousines and Tours (☎ 09/629–0940) operates Ford LTD limousines between the airport and the city for approximately $65.

Johnston's Shuttle Link (☎ 09/275–1234) operates a minibus service between the airport and any address in the city center. The cost is $14 for a single traveler, $10 per person for two traveling together. The service meets all incoming flights.

Taxi fare to the city is approximately $35.

The terminal for all InterCity train services is **Auckland Central Railway Station** (☎ 0800/802–802) on Beach Road, about 1½ km (1 mi) east of the city center. A booking office is inside the **Auckland Visitor Information Centre** (✉ Aotea Sq., Queen and Meyer Sts., ☎ 09/366–6888).

Getting Around

BY BUS

Auckland's public bus system, the **Yellow Bus Company,** operates Monday–Saturday 6 AM–11:30 PM, Sunday 9–5. The main terminal for public buses is the **Municipal Transport Station,** between Commerce Street and Britomart Place near the Central Post Office. The bus network is divided into zones; fares are calculated according to the number of zones traveled. For travel within the inner city, the fare is 50¢ for adults. **Bus-About passes,** which allow unlimited travel on all buses after 9 AM daily, are available from bus drivers for $8.40. For timetables, bus routes, fares, and lost property, stop by the **Bus Place** (✉ Hobson and Victoria Sts.), which is open weekdays 8:15–5, or call **Buz A Bus** (☎ 09/366–6400), open Monday–Saturday 7–7.

BY FERRY

Various companies serve Waitemata Harbour; one of the best and least expensive is the **Devonport commuter ferry.** The ferry terminal is on the harbor side of the Ferry Building on Quay Street, near the corner of Albert Street. Ferries depart Monday–Thursday 6:15 AM–11 PM, Friday and Saturday 6:15 AM–1 AM, and Sunday 7 AM–11 PM. Ferries also make the 35-minute run to Waiheke Island approximately every two hours, beginning at 6:30 AM. They cost $23 round-trip. Return ferries leave about every two hours on odd-numbered hours. ☎ 09/367–9118. ⌾ Round-trip $7.

BY TAXI

Taxis can be hailed in the street but are more readily available from taxi ranks throughout the city. Auckland taxi rates vary with the company, but the fare and flag fall are listed on the driver's door. Most taxis will accept major credit cards. **Alert Taxis** (☎ 09/309–2000), **Auckland Cooperative Taxi Service** (☎ 09/300–3000), and **Eastern Taxis** (☎ 09/527–7077) are reliable operators with radio-controlled fleets.

Contacts and Resources

CAR RENTAL

Avis, Budget, and **Hertz** have offices inside the Auckland International Airport (☞ Car Rental *in* the Gold Guide).

CONSULATES

U.S. Consulate. ✉ *General Assurance Bldg., Shortland and O'Connell Sts.,* ☎ *09/303–2724.* ⊙ *Weekdays 9:30–12:30.*
British Consulate. ✉ *Fay Richwhite Bldg., 151 Queen St.,* ☎ *09/303–2971.* ⊙ *Weekdays 9:30–12:20.*
Canadian Consulate. ✉ *Jetset Centre, 48 Emily Pl.,* ☎ *09/309–3690.* ⊙ *Weekdays 8:30–4:30.*
Australian Consulate. ✉ *Union House, 32–38 Quay St.,* ☎ *09/303–2429.* ⊙ *Weekdays 8:30–4:45.*

CURRENCY EXCHANGE

Two **Bank of New Zealand** branches inside the international terminal of Auckland International Airport are open for all arriving and departing flights. In the city, there are several currency-exchange agencies on Queen Street between Victoria and Customs streets offering the same rate as banks (open weekdays 9–5 and Saturday 9–1). Foreign currency may also be exchanged daily 8–4 at the cashier's office above Celebrity Walk at the Drake Street entrance of **Victoria Park Market** (☎ 09/309–6911). A 24-hour exchange machine outside the **Downtown Airline Terminal** on Quay Street will change notes of any major currency into New Zealand dollars, but the rate is significantly less than that offered by banks.

EMERGENCIES

Dial 111 for **fire, police, or ambulance** services.

Auckland Hospital. ⊠ *Park Rd., Grafton,* ☎ *09/379–7440.*

Southern Cross Central. ⊠ *122 Remuera Rd., Remuera,* ☎ *09/524–5943 or 09/524–7906.*

St. John's Ambulance. St. John's can refer you to the nearest dentist on duty. ☎ *09/579–9099.*

GUIDED TOURS

The **Antipodean Explorer** (☎ 09/302–2400) offers a minibus tour of the wineries, coast, and native forests of the Waitakere Ranges west of Auckland, including a visit to a gannet colony. It costs $65 and departs daily at 9:30 AM, with pickups from your accommodation. The company also offers specialist tours from one to four weeks duration.

Fullers Cruise Centre (☎ 09/367–9111) has a variety of cruises around the harbor and to the islands of Hauraki Gulf. The two-hour coffee cruise ($22) departs daily at 9:30, 11:30, and 2:30, with an extra afternoon cruise from late December to April. The Jetraider cruise ($50) to Great Barrier Island, the most distant of the Hauraki Gulf Islands, is a popular day trip for Aucklanders; however, the voyage can be canceled due to rough seas. You may want to take a guided bus tour of the island ($17). The cruise departs Tuesday, Thursday, Friday, and weekends at 9, returning to Auckland at about 6. Reservations are essential.

The **Pride of Auckland Company** sails for lunch and dinner on the inner harbor. The 1½-hour lunch cruise departs at 11 and 1, and the three-hour dinner cruise departs at 6. An Experience Sailing trip departs at 3. Boats leave from the wharf opposite the Downtown Airline Terminal on the corner of Quay and Albert streets. ☎ *09/373–4557.* 🖃 *Experience Sailing $30, lunch cruise $39, dinner cruise $75.*

Scenic Tours (☎ 09/634–0189) operates a three-hour City Highlights guided bus tour, which takes in the main attractions in the city and Parnell and the view from the lookout on Mt. Eden. Tours leave at 9:30 and 2, and tickets are $35. The **Gray Line** (☎ 09/377–0904) runs a Morning Highlights tour, which includes admission to Kelly Tarlton's Underwater World. This tour departs daily from the Downtown Airline Terminal on Quay Street at 9 and costs $51.

United Airlines Explorer Bus (☎ 09/360–0033) is a convenient introduction to Auckland. The blue-and-gray double-decker bus travels in a circuit, stopping at eight of the city's major attractions; you can leave at any stop and reboard any following Explorer bus. The loop begins at the Downtown Airline Terminal every hour between 9 and 4 daily; tickets are available from the driver. 🖃 *1-day pass $15, 2-day pass $25.*

LATE-NIGHT PHARMACY

The Late-Night Pharmacy. ⊠ *60 Broadway,* ☎ *09/520–6634.* ☉ *Weekdays 5:30 PM–7 AM, weekends 9 AM–7 AM.*

TRAVEL AGENCIES

American Express Travel Service. ⊠ *101 Queen St.,* ☎ *09/379–8243.*

Thomas Cook. ⊠ *107 Queen St.,* ☎ *09/379–3924.*

VISITOR INFORMATION

The Thursday *Auckland Tourist Times* is a free newspaper with the latest information on tours, exhibitions, and shopping. The paper is available from hotels and from the Visitor Information Centre.

Auckland Visitor Information Centre. ⊠ *Aotea Sq., Queen and Meyer Sts.,* ☎ *09/366–6888.* ⊙ *Mon.–Fri. 8:30–5:30, weekends 9–5.*

NORTHLAND AND THE BAY OF ISLANDS

Beyond Auckland, North Island stretches a long arm into the South Pacific. This is Northland, an undulating region of farms, forests, and marvelous beaches. The Bay of Islands is the main attraction, an is-land-littered seascape with a mild, subtropical climate and some of the finest game-fishing waters in the country—witness its record catches of marlin and mako shark. Big-game fishing is expensive, but small fish-ing boats can take you out for an evening of trawling for under $50.

It was on the Bay of Islands that the first European settlement was es-tablished and where modern New Zealand became a nation with the signing of the Treaty of Waitangi in 1840. The main town is Paihia, a strip of motels and restaurants along the waterfront. If you plan to spend more than a day in the area, the town of Russell, just a short ferry trip away, makes for a more atmospheric and attractive base.

You can explore Northland in an easy loop from Auckland, driving up Highway 1 and returning on Highway 12 with little revisiting of sights on the way back. Bay of Islands is a favorite vacation spot for Kiwis, particularly from mid-December to the end of January, when accommodations are often filled months in advance.

Albany

⑭ *12 km (7 mi) north of Auckland.*

Albany is a small village north of Auckland, the first town north after the northern motorway narrows. In December the pohutukawa trees along the roadside blossom for the Kiwi Christmas by erupting in a blaze of scarlet, hence their Pakeha (European) name—the New Zealand Christmas tree. To the Maori, the flowers had another meaning: the beginning of shellfish season. The spiky-leaved plants that grow in clumps by the roadside are New Zealand flax. The fibers of this plant, the raw material for linen, were woven into clothing by the Maori. The huge tree ferns—common throughout the forests of North Island, where they can grow as high as 30 ft—are known locally as pungas.

Warkworth

⑮ *47 km (29 mi) north of Albany.*

One of the great natural features of the north half of North Island is one native pine species, the kauri tree. Two giants stand near the **Warkworth Museum.** The larger one, the **McKinney Kauri,** measures almost 25 ft around its base, yet this 800-year-old colossus is a mere adoles-cent by kauri standards. Kauri trees, once prolific in this part of the North Island, were highly prized by Maori canoe builders, because a canoe capable of carrying a hundred warriors could be made from a single trunk. Unfortunately these same characteristics—strength, size, and durability—made kauri timber ideal for ships, furniture, and hous-ing, and the kauri forests were rapidly depleted by early European set-tlers. Today the trees are protected by law, and infant kauri are

Northland and the Bay of Islands

Doubtless Bay

Mangonui

CAPE REINGA & 90-MILE BEACH

Kaeo

10

Takou Bay

1

Mangamuka

Mount Bledisloe

Kerikeri 19

Bay of Islands

Paihia and Waitangi 17

18 **Russell**

Moerewa

Opua

Kawakawa

1

Rawene

12

Kaikohe

Towai

Waiotu

Otonga

Matapouri

20 **Opononi**

Awarua

NORTHLAND

Poor Knights Islands

SOUTH PACIFIC OCEAN

21 **Waipoua State Forest**

Whangarei

16

Clapham's Clock Museum

12

Titoki

Maungatapere

Portland

Whangarei Harbour

Kaihu River

14

Bream Bay

Parry Channel

Hen and Chickens Group

Waiotira

Dargaville

Taipuga

Te Kopuru

12

Paparoa

22

Matakohe Kauri Museum

Waipu Cove

Bellvue

Maungaturoto

Jellicoe Channel

Little Barrier Island

Poutu

Tapora

Kaipara

1

Wellsford

15 **Warkworth**

Tasman Sea

Harbour

Ahuroa

16

Shelly Beach

1

Kawau Island

Orewa

Hauraki Gulf

Helensville

Coatesville

Albany 14

Rangitoto Island

Waiheke Island

Waimauku

Takapuna

Waitakere

Auckland

N

Manukau Harbour

Papatoetoe

Manukau

Papakura

Pukekohe

2

Waiuku

1

KEY

— Rail Lines

0 ——— 40 miles

0 ——— 60 km

NEW ZEALAND

appearing in the forests of North Island, although their growth rate is painfully slow. The museum contains a collection of Maori artifacts and farming and domestic implements from the pioneering days of the Warkworth district. The museum also has a souvenir shop with kauri bowls and other wooden items. ⊠ *Tudor Collins Dr.,* ☎ *09/425–7093.* 🖅 *$3.* ⊙ *Daily 9–4.*

En Route   Even if you aren't a hortomaniac, come to Daniel and Vivian Papich's **Bellvue** for its spectacular views of the Pacific Ocean. The Hen and Chickens Islands lie right off the coast, and on clear days you can even see the Poor Knights Islands, a good 70 km (45 mi) away. This hillside garden has been designed on several levels to take advantage of its topography. The bold foliage of agaves, bromeliads, succulents, and puka trees is abundant, setting off the more delicate exotics and adding year-round interest. Vivian's container plantings—300 at last count—are everywhere, even hanging from the trees. Conceived as a way to keep more demanding plants from struggling in the hard clay soil here, the containers have evolved into an art form. They are often composed of unconventional materials and used in inventive seasonal displays. Birders, keep your eyes and ears open for the fantails, whiteyes, and tuis that frequent the garden. The distance from Warkworth to Waipu and the garden is 55 km (34 mi). ⊠ *Coastal Hwy., Langs Beach, southeast of Waipu,* ☎ *09/432–0465.* 🖅 *Small entry fee.* ⊙ *By appointment.*

For a glimpse of what the New Zealand coast must have been like 200 years ago, take a trip to the **Goat Island** marine reserve. Fishing is prohibited here, and marine life has returned in abundance, with prominent species including blue maomao, snapper, and cod. You can put on a snorkel and easily glide around the island, just a little way offshore. You can rent mask, snorkel, and flippers ($8) at the beach from Maria Anthoni of **Seafriends** (☎ 09/422–6212). **Habitat Explorer** (☎ 09/422–6334) has a glass-bottom boat that runs around the island ($15). But you needn't get even this serious to see plenty of fish. Just walk into the water up to your waist and look around you. To drum up more action, throw some bread or noodles into the sea and watch the fish congregate just inches from you. The beach area is good for a picnic as well.

To get to Goat Island head toward Leigh, 21 km (13 mi) northeast of Warkworth. From Leigh, once you have reached that small township, take a left turn and follow the signs for a couple of miles. The area can get crowded, but if you arrive by 10 AM or earlier, you should avoid the masses. Department of Conservation leaflets detailing Goat Island can be obtained from the Warkworth Visitor Information Centre (☞ Contacts and Resources *in* Northland and the Bay of Islands A to Z, *below*).

Whangarei

🖸 *127 km (79 mi) north of Warkworth, 196 km (123 mi) north of Auckland.*

Many people on the way to the Bay of Islands bypass Whangarei (*fahng*-ar-ay), but it is well worth taking the turnoff from the main highway, especially since the area known as the **Whangarei Town Basin** has been improved. Here you will find a **Museum of Fishes**, which in New Zealand means looking at exhibits of species that you wouldn't see back home. Also at the basin is **Ahipupu Maori and Pacific Arts and Crafts**, where you will find both traditional and contemporary works.

Claphams Clock Museum is another Town Basin site. Just about every conceivable method of telling time is represented in this collection of more than 1,400 clocks, from primitive water clocks to ships' chronometers to ornate masterworks from Paris and Vienna. Some of the most intriguing examples were made by the late Mr. Clapham himself, like his World War II air force clock that automatically changed the position of aircraft over a map. Ironically, the one thing you won't find here is the correct time. If all the bells, chimes, gongs, and cuckoos went off together, the noise would be deafening, so the clocks are set to different times. ⊠ *Quay-side Whangarei,* ☎ *09/438–3993.* ▣ *$3.50.* ☼ *Daily 10–4.*

The oldest kauri villa in Whangarei, **Historical Reyburn House** contains the Northland Society of Arts exhibition gallery, which hosts a free exhibition each month. It is separated from the Town Basin by a playground. ⊠ *Lower Quay St.,* ☎ *09/438–3074.* ☼ *Tues.–Sun. 10–4.*

The town also has a lovely picnic spot at **Whangarei Falls.** There are viewing platforms atop the falls and a short trail through the local bush. ⊠ *Ngunguru Rd., 5 km (3 mi) northeast of town.*

Early settlers anxious to farm the rich volcanic land around Whangarei found their efforts constantly thwarted by an abundance of rock in the soil. To make use of the stuff they dug up, they built walls—miles of walls. The current settlers at **Greagh,** Kathleen and Clark Abbot, have carried on this tradition, giving their gardens the Celtic name for "land among the stone." It comes as no surprise then that the hardscape here first catches the eye, forming a handsome framework for perennials and roses. Plantings emphasize the beauty and strength of the stone on terraces and in five separate walled gardens. ⊠ *Three Mile Bush Rd., Whangarei,* ☎ *09/435–1980.* ▣ *Small entry fee.* ☼ *Oct.–mid-Dec., daily 10–4; mid-Dec.–Apr. by appointment.*

Lodging

$$ 🏠 **Parua House.** On the edge of Parua Bay, 17 km (11 mi) from central Whangarei, this is a great base from which to explore the towering Whangarei Heads that enclose the bay. Parua House dates from 1882, though it has gone through considerable changes since. Owners Pat and Peter Heaslip—solid practitioners of Kiwi hospitality—who lived in England for more than 20 years before purchasing the house a few years ago. They've given it back much of its colonial charm, which now includes a French oak table brought from England and two sideboards in the dining room, one of which is some 300 years old. Furnishings and decorations in guest rooms also have touches of old England. You can take a walk through the nearby bush or even help milk their cow. ⊠ *Whangarei Heads Rd., R.D. 4, Parua Bay,* ☎ *09/436–5855,* FAX *09/436–5855. 2 rooms with shower. Hot tub. BP. No credit cards.*

Paihia and Waitangi

⓱ *69 km (43 mi) north of Whangarei.*

As the main holiday base for the Bay of Islands, Paihia is an unremarkable stretch of motels at odds with the quiet beauty of the island-studded seascape and the rounded green hills that form a backdrop to the town, yet nearby Waitangi is one of the country's most important historic sites. It was near here that the Treaty of Waitangi, the founding document for modern New Zealand, was signed.

Waitangi National Reserve is at the northern end of Paihia. Inside the visitor center, a 23-minute video, shown every hour on the hour, sketches the events that led to the Treaty of Waitangi. The center also displays Maori artifacts and weapons, including a musket that belonged to Hone Heke Pokai, the first Maori chief to sign the treaty. After his initial display of enthusiasm for British rule, Hone Heke was quickly disillusioned, and less than five years later he attacked the British in their stronghold at Russell. From the visitor center, follow a short track through the forest to **Nga Toki Matawhaorua** (ng-ga to-ki ma-ta-*fa*-oh-*roo*-ah), a Maori war canoe. This huge kauri canoe, capable of carrying 150 warriors, is named after the vessel in which Kupe, the Polynesian navigator, is said to have discovered New Zealand.

Treaty House in Waitangi National Reserve is a simple white timber cottage, which has a remarkable air of dignity despite its size. The interior is fascinating, especially the back, where exposed walls demonstrate the difficulties that early administrators faced—such as an acute shortage of bricks (since an insufficient number had been shipped from New South Wales) with which to finish the walls.

The Treaty House was prefabricated in New South Wales for the British Resident James Busby, who arrived in New Zealand in 1832. Busby had been appointed to protect British commerce and put an end to the brutalities of the whaling captains against the Maori, but Busby lacked either the judicial authority or the force of arms necessary to impose peace. On one occasion, unable to resolve a dispute between Maori tribes, Busby was forced to shelter the wounded of one side in his house. While tattooed headhunters screamed war chants outside the windows, one of the warriors sheltered Busby's infant daughter, Sarah, in his cape.

The real significance of the Treaty House lies in the events that took place here on February 6, 1840, the day that the **Treaty of Waitangi** was signed by Maori chiefs and Captain William Hobson, representing the British crown. Under the treaty, the chiefs agreed to accept the authority of the crown; in return, the British recognized the Maori as the legitimate landowners and granted them all the rights and privileges of British subjects. The treaty also confirmed the status of New Zealand as a British colony, forestalling French overtures in the area, and legitimized—at least according to European law—the transfer of land from Maori to European hands. In recent years the Maori have used the treaty successfully to reclaim land that they maintain was misappropriated by white settlers.

The Treaty House has not always received the care its significance merits. When Lord Bledisloe bought the house and presented it to the nation in 1932, it was being used as a shelter for sheep.

Whare Runanga (fah-ray roo-nang-ah) is a Maori meeting house with an elaborately carved interior. Inside, an audio show briefly outlines traditional Maori society. The house is on the northern boundary of Waitangi National Reserve. ⊠ *Waitangi Rd., Waitangi,* ☎ *09/402-7437.* ☜ *$5.* ☼ *Daily 9–5.*

☞ The *Tui,* high and dry on the banks of the Waitangi River, is a historic kauri sailing vessel that was built to carry sugar to a refinery in Auckland. Below decks is an exhibition of artifacts recovered from shipwrecks by the famous New Zealand salvage diver Kelly Tarlton. In addition to the brass telescopes, sextants, and diving helmets that you can try on for size, there is an exquisite collection of jewelry that belonged to Isidore Jonah Rothschild (of the famous banking family), which was lost when the SS *Tasmania* sank in 1897. Rothschild was on a sales trip to New Zealand at the time. ⊠ *Waitangi Bridge, Paihia,* ☎ *09/402-7018.* ☜ *$5.* ☼ *Daily 10–5.*

Mount Bledisloe offers a splendid view across Paihia and the Bay of Islands. The handsome ceramic marker at the top showing the distances to major world cities was made by Doulton in London and presented by Lord Bledisloe in 1934 during his term as governor-general of New Zealand. The mount is 3 km (2 mi) from the Treaty House, on the other side of the Waitangi Golf Course. From a small parking area on the right of Waitangi Road, a short track rises above a pine forest to the summit.

Dining and Lodging

$$ ✕ **Saltwater Café.** Fresh ingredients, mostly local, are prepared here with innovation and style. Try the Orongo Bay oysters with mango and chili salsa and charred lemon. Buy from the wine list or bring your own bottle. ✉ *Kings Rd., Paihia,* ☎ *09/402–7783. Reservations not accepted. DC, MC, V.*

$$$ ⊡ **Copthorne Resort Waitangi.** The biggest hotel north of Auckland and a favorite with coach tour groups, this complex sprawls along a peninsula within walking distance of the Treaty House. Resort-style units face the sea, while garden-facing rooms are decorated in a French provincial style, with yellows and blues and wrought-iron light fixtures. ✉ *Waitangi Rd., Waitangi,* ☎ *09/402–7411, ℻ 09/402–8200. 138 rooms with bath. 3 restaurants, 2 bars, pool, coin laundry. AE, DC, MC, V.*

$$ ⊡ **Austria Motel.** The large, double-bed rooms here are typical of motel accommodations in the area—clean and moderately comfortable but almost totally devoid of charm. Each has a kitchenette. The motel also has a family unit on the ground level of the two-story wing. The shops and waterfront at Paihia are a two-minute walk away. ✉ *36 Selwyn Rd.,* ☎ ℻ *09/402–7480. 7 rooms with bath. AE, DC, MC, V.*

Outdoor Activities and Sports

BOATING

Moorings Yacht Charters (☎ 09/402–7821) has charter boats for sailors of various abilities. A catamaran operated by **Straycat Day Sailing Charters** (✉ Doves Bay Rd., Kerikeri, ☎ 09/407–7342 or 025/96–9944) makes one-day sailing trips in the Bay of Islands from Russell and Paihia at $60 per person.

DIVING

The Bay of Islands has some of the finest scuba diving in the country, particularly around Cape Brett, where the marine life includes moray eels, stingrays, and grouper. The wreck of the Greenpeace vessel *Rainbow Warrior,* sunk by French agents, is another Bay of Islands underwater highlight. Water temperature at the surface varies from 62°F in July to 71°F in January. From September through November, underwater visibility can be affected by a plankton bloom. **Paihia Dive Hire and Charter** (✉ Box 210, Paihia, ☎ 09/402–7551) offers complete equipment hire and regular boat trips for accredited divers for about $135 per day.

FISHING

The Bay of Islands is one of the world's premier game-fishing grounds for marlin and several species of shark. **NZ Billfish Charters** (✉ Box 416, Paihia, ☎ 09/402–8380) goes for the big ones. A far less expensive alternative is to fish for snapper, kingfish, and John Dory in the inshore waters of the bay. **Skipper Jim** (☎ 09/402–7355) and **MV Arline** (☎ 09/402–8511) offer a half day of fishing, including bait and rods, for about $50 per person.

Russell

⓮ *4 km (2½ mi) east of Paihia by ferry, 13 km (8 mi) by road.*

Russell is regarded as the "second" town in the Bay of Islands, but it is far more interesting than Paihia. Hard as it is to believe these days, sleepy little Russell was once dubbed the Hellhole of the Pacific. Early last century (when it was still known by its Maori name, Kororareka) it was a swashbuckling frontier town, a haven for sealers and for whalers who found the east coast of New Zealand to be one of the richest whaling grounds on earth. Tales of debauchery were probably exaggerated, but British administrators in New South Wales (as Australia was known at the time) were sufficiently concerned to dispatch a British Resident in 1832 to impose law and order. After the Treaty of Waitangi, Russell was the national capital, until in 1844 the Maori chief Hone Heke attacked the British garrison and most of the town burned to the ground. Hone Heke was finally defeated in 1846, but Russell never recovered its former prominence, and the seat of government was shifted first to Auckland, then to Wellington. Today Russell is a delightful town of timber houses and big trees that hang low over the seafront, framing the yachts and game-fishing boats in the harbor. The atmosphere can best be absorbed in a stroll along the Strand, the path along the waterfront.

Pompallier House, at the southern end of the Strand, was named after the first Catholic bishop of the South Pacific. Marist missionaries built the original structure out of rammed earth (mud mixed with dung or straw—a technique known as *pise* in their native France), since they lacked the funds to buy timber. For several years the priests and brothers operated a press here, printing Bibles in the Maori language. The original building forms the core of the elegant timber house that now stands on the site. ⊠ *The Strand, Russell,* ☎ *09/403–7861.* ⊠ *$5.* ☉ *Daily 9–5.*

The **Russell Museum** houses a collection of Maori tools and weapons and some fine portraits. The pride of its display is a ⅕-scale replica of Captain Cook's ship, HMS *Endeavour,* which entered the bay in 1769. The museum was previously known as the Captain Cook Memorial Museum, and some locals still refer to it by that name. The museum is set back slightly from the waterfront, some 50 yards north of Pompallier House. ⊠ *York St., Russell,* ☎ *09/403–7701.* ⊠ *$2.50.* ☉ *Daily 10–5.*

Christ Church is the oldest church in the country. One of the donors to its erection in 1835 was Charles Darwin, at that time a wealthy but unknown young man making his way around the globe on board the HMS *Beagle.* Behind the white picket fence that borders the churchyard, gravestones tell a fascinating and brutal story of life in the early days of the colony. Several graves belong to sailors from the HMS *Hazard* who were killed in this churchyard by Hone Heke's warriors in 1845. Another headstone marks the grave of a Nantucket sailor from the whaler *Mohawk.* As you walk around the church, look for the musket holes made when Hone Heke besieged the church. The interior is simple and charming—embroidered cushions on the pews are examples of a folk-art tradition that is still very much alive. ⊠ *Church and Robertson Sts., Russell.* ☉ *Daily 8–5.*

You can drive between Russell and Paihia, but the quickest and most convenient route is by ferry. Three passenger boats make the crossing between Paihia and Russell, with departures at least every 30 minutes in each direction from 7:30 AM to 11 PM. The one-way fare is $1.50. The car ferry is at Opua, about 5 km (3 mi) south of Paihia. This ferry operates from 6:40 AM to 8:50 PM (Friday until 9:50 PM), with departures at approximately 20-minute intervals from either shore. The last boat leaves from Russell at 8:50 (Friday 9:50), from Opua at 9 (Friday 10). The one-way fare is $7 for car and driver plus $1 for each adult passenger.

Dining and Lodging

$$ ✕ **The Quarterdeck.** The specialty of this seafront restaurant is fish al-fresco—crayfish (clawless lobster), tarakihi, flounder, scallops, and snapper, all served with chips and salad—and though the prices are rather steep for less than glamorous dining, the outdoor tables overlooking the lively harbor are a pleasant spot on a warm evening. The Quarterdeck is popular with families. ⊠ *The Strand, Russell,* ☎ *09/403–7761. AE, DC, MC, V. BYOB. No lunch weekdays fall–spring.*

$$ ✕ **Swordy's.** Overlooking Kororareka Bay in a pretty cream-and-white timber building, the restaurant of the Bay of Islands Swordfish Club is dedicated to fish and fish people, from the decor to the menu to the conversation. First courses make good use of green-shell mussels and fresh local oysters; main courses include panfried scallops, asparagus with oyster sauce, and even roast lamb for the landlubber among your party. Request a table at the window and begin the evening with a drink in the friendly bar upstairs—where, in the summer holiday period, you may have to wait for a table anyway. Officially visitors must be signed in by a member of the club, but provided you look sober, neat, and capable of enthusing over marlin fishing, the barman will request a club member to countersign the visitor's book for you (after which it would be diplomatic to treat the member to a drink). ⊠ *The Strand, Russell,* ☎ *09/403–7652. AE, MC, V. No lunch.*

$$$$ ✕🏠 **Kimberley Lodge.** The most luxurious accommodation in the Bay
★   of Islands, this splendid white timber mansion occupies a commanding position overlooking Russell and Kororareka Bay. The house has been designed with big windows and sunny verandas to take maximum advantage of its location. Below, terraced gardens fall away down a steep hillside to the sea. The house is opulently furnished in contemporary style, and the en-suite bathrooms are very well equipped. Only one bedroom at the rear of the house—Pompallier—lacks impressive views. The best room in the house is the Kimberley Suite, which costs more than the standard suites. Dinner is available by arrangement. Smoking is not allowed indoors. ⊠ *Pitt St.,* ☎ *09/403–7090,* ℻ *09/403–7239. 4 rooms with bath. Pool. BP. AE, DC, MC, V.*

$$$$ 🏠 **Okiato Lodge.** Okiato is high up on Okiato Point—hence its name—and has views of Opua, Paihia, and other Bay of Islands locales. If you happen to be sipping predinner drinks on the lawn on a Wednesday evening, you'll even see the local yacht club sailing by in the harbor below. Spacious rooms with step-down lounge areas, high vaulted ceilings, plenty of timber furnishings, and large windows allowing great views add up to a high standard of comfort. The lodge's hosts have in-depth knowledge of the surrounding area and are happy to help with arranging activities and sightseeing. Most guests do some fishing or golf, but the most exhilarating thing might be a day visiting 90 Mile Beach and Cape Reinga at the northern tip of North Island. ⊠ *Okiato Point, R.D. 1, Russell,* ☎ *09/403–7948,* ℻ *09/403–7515. 8 rooms with bath. Bar, dining room, lounge, hot tub. AE, DC, MC, V.*

$$ 🏠 **Duke of Marlborough Hotel.** This historic hotel is a favorite with the yachting fraternity, for whom ready access to the harbor and the bar downstairs is the most important consideration. Rooms are clean and tidy enough, and all have en-suite facilities, but they have no memorable character despite the hotel's long and colorful history. The front rooms with harbor views are the most expensive but also the ones most likely to be affected by noise from the spirited crowd in the bar, especially on weekends. ⊠ *The Strand,* ☎ *09/403–7829,* ℻ *09/403–7760. 29 rooms with bath. Restaurant, bar. DC, MC, V.*

$ 🏠 **Russell Lodge.** Surrounded by quiet gardens two streets back from the waterfront, this lodge—owned and operated by the Salvation Army—offers neat, clean rooms in several configurations. Family units have a separate bedroom with two single beds and either a double or a single bed in the main room. The largest room is Unit 15, a two-bedroom flat with a kitchen, which will sleep six. Backpacker-style accommodations are also available in rooms for four; towels and sheets are not provided in these rooms but may be rented. All rooms have en-suite bathrooms, and five have kitchen facilities. ✉ *Chapel and Beresford Sts., Russell,* ☎ *09/403–7640,* fax *09/403–7641. 24 rooms with bath. Pool, coin laundry. AE, MC, V.*

Outdoor Activities and Sports

FISHING

Bay of Islands Sportsfishing (✉ Box 78, Russell, ☎ 09/403–7008) represents several operators who can meet most sport-fishing requirements. **Dudley Smith** (✉ Box 203, Russell, ☎ 09/403–7200) and **Nighthawk** (✉ Russell, ☎ 09/407–8999) are two outfitters.

Kerikeri

⑲ *20 km (12 mi) north of Paihia.*

Kerikeri is often referred to as the cradle of a nation because so much of New Zealand's earliest history, especially in terms of interaction between Maori and European, took place here. The main town itself is a small but pleasant enough shopping center.

The **Historic Kerikeri Basin,** just north of the modern town, is where most of the interest lies. Missionaries arrived in this area in 1819, having been invited to Kerikeri by its most famous historical figure, the great Maori chief Hongi Hika. The chief visited England in 1820, where he was showered with gifts. On his way back to New Zealand, during a stop in Sydney, he traded many of these presents for muskets. Having the advantage of these prized weapons, he set in motion plans to conquer other Maori tribes, enemies of his own Ngapuhi people. The return of his raiding parties over five years, with many slaves and gruesome trophies of conquest, put considerable strain between Hongi Hika and the missionaries. Eventually his warring ways were Hongi's undoing. He was shot in 1927 and died as a result of complications from the wound a year later.

The **Stone Store** is Kerikeri's most picturesque attraction and is the most striking building in the historic basin. Built between 1832 and 1836, it is New Zealand's oldest existing stone building. It was part of the Kerikeri Mission Station and was built to hold stores for the whole New Zealand mission of the time. In November 1998, after a three-year-long renovation, it opened in what is close to its original state. ✉ *Kerikeri Historic Basin, Kerikeri Rd.,* ☎ *09/407–9236.* ✉ *Donations suggested.* ☉ *Nov.–Apr., daily 10–5; May–Oct., Sat.–Wed. 10–5.*

Adjacent to the Stone Store, the 1821 **Kemp House** is otherwise known as Mission House. It has gone through many changes since then, but ironically a major flood in 1981 has helped in its "authentic" restoration. The flood washed away the garden and damaged the lower floor, and during repair much information about the structure of the house was revealed. As a result, its ground floor is more like it was in its earliest years. The upper floor remained unharmed and is still presented in its Victorian decoration. The present garden is based on what was planted in early missionary days. ✉ *Kerikeri Historic Basin, Kerikeri Rd.,* ☎ *09/407–9236.* ✉ *$5.* ☉ *Nov.–Apr., daily 10–5; May–Oct., Sat.–Wed. 10–5.*

Across the road from the Stone Store is a path leading to the historic site of **Kororipo Pa,** the fortified headquarters of Chief Hongi Hika.

Untrained eyes will have a bit of difficulty working out exactly where the *pa* (hilltop fortification) was, as there are no structures left. Information boards and drawings aid the imagination. The pa was built on a steep-sided promontory between the Kerikeri River and the Wairoa Stream. You'll still get a fine view over both.

Rewi's Village depicts times before and during the earliest settlement of Europeans (it was actually built in 1969). The community wanted to save the area from threatened urban development. The result is a reconstructed *kainga* (unfortified fishing village), the kind where the people who originally occupied the area would have lived, taking refuge in nearby Kororipo Pa when threatened by enemy tribes. A video plays near the entrance, with an interesting history of Chief Hongi Hika. In the village itself are the chief's house, the weapons store, the family enclosure, two original canoes dug up from local swamps, and original hangi stones (used to cook traditional Maori feasts) found on the site. ⊠ *Kerikeri Historic Basin, Kerikeri Rd.,* ☎ *09/407–6454.* ☞ *$2.50.* ☉ *Nov.–Apr., daily 9–5; May–Oct., daily 10–4.*

Lodging

$$ ☖ **Kauri Park.** This small cluster of chalets is a notch above the usual, with modern decor and an excellent setting among fruit trees adjacent to farmland. Owners Alexander Gramse and Helene Henriksen have also combined a touch of European hospitality—a free drink on arrival, a guest lounge—to the usual Kiwi hospitality. Each unit has a veranda, and the furnishings are colorful. It is a little bit out of town, which gives it a rural feeling, but it's still only a few minutes' drive from the historic sights. ⊠ *Kerikeri Rd. (south end),* ☎ *09/407–7629. 5 rooms with showers. Lounge, coin laundry. AE, DC, MC, V.*

Opononi

⓴ *85 km (53 mi) west of Paihia.*

Opononi is a small town near the mouth of the Hokianga Harbour. It is the place where Opi, a tame dolphin, came to play with swimmers in the mid-1950s, putting the town on the national map for the first and only time in its history. There is a statue in front of the pub commemorating the much-loved creature.

㉑ **Waipoua State Forest** contains the largest remnant of the kauri forests that once covered this part of the country, along with some delicious forest air. A short path leads from the parking area through the forest to **Tane Mahuta**, "Lord of the Forest," standing nearly 173 ft high and measuring 43 ft around its base. The largest tree in New Zealand, it's said to be 1,200 years old. There are other trees of note in the forest, among them the **Four Sisters**, four trees together in an interesting formation.

Matakohe

95 km (59 mi) south of Opononi.

㉒ **Matakohe Kauri Museum** is one of the most intriguing museums in the country. Its vast collection of artifacts, tools, photographs, documents, and memorabilia tells the story of the pioneers who settled this part of the country in the second half of the 19th century—a story interwoven with the kauri forests. Here you'll find superb examples of craftsmanship: furniture and a complete kauri house, as well as an early example of an American-built Caterpillar bulldozer, which was used to drag logs from the forest. One of the most fascinating displays is the room of kauri gum, the transparent lumps of resin that form when the sticky sap of the kauri tree hardens. This gum, which was used to make varnish, can be polished to a warm, lustrous finish that looks remarkably like amber—right down to the insects that are sometimes trapped and preserved inside. At one time collecting this gum was an important rural industry. **Volunteers Hall** contains a huge kauri slab running from one end of the hall to the other, and there is also a Women in the Bush display, a replica of a cabinetmaker's shop, and an exhibition dedicated to fishing in Kaipara Harbour. ⊠ *Church Rd., Matakohe,* ☎ *09/431–7417.* ▨ *$5.* ⊙ *Daily 9–5.*

Northland and the Bay of Islands A to Z

Arriving and Departing

BY BUS

Northliner Express (☎ 09/307–5873), **InterCity** (☎ 09/358–4085), and **Newmans** (☎ 09/309–9738) run several times daily between Auckland and Paihia.

BY CAR

The main route from Auckland is Highway 1. Leave the city by the Harbour Bridge and follow signs to Whangarei. Driving time for the 250-km (150-mi) journey to Paihia is about four hours.

Contacts and Resources

EMERGENCIES

Dial 111 for **fire, police, or ambulance** services.

GUIDED TOURS

Fullers Northland has one-, two-, and three-day tours from Auckland to the Bay of Islands. Its three-day Bay Explorer includes a tour of the historic Waitangi Treaty House, a trip to Cape Reinga, a swim with dolphins, a voyage around the bay aboard a schooner, and accommodations in Russell. ⊠ *Bay of Islands Travel Centre, Shop 2, Downtown Shopping Centre, Customs St., Auckland,* ☎ *09/358–0259.* ▨ *$459.*

Fullers Northland runs cruises in the Bay of Islands itself, departing from both Paihia and Russell. The most popular is the half-day catamaran cruise to Cape Brett, at the eastern extremity of the bay. This includes a journey through a large hole in Motukako Island, known naturally enough as "the hole in the rock." The Cream Trip is an enjoyable six-hour cruise that stops in at many of the bay islands. ⊠ *Maritime Bldg., Paihia,* ☎ *09/402–7421.* ▨ *Cape Brett $52, Cream Trip $65.* ⊙ *Cape Brett Cruise departs Paihia daily 9 and 1:30. Cream Trip departs Paihia Oct.–May, daily 10; June–Sept., Mon., Wed., Thurs., and Sat. 10.*

The **4x4 Dune-Rider** is a novel way to get to Cape Reinga—via the vast strip of 90 Mile Beach. The company uses four-wheel-drive vehicles for small groups and makes slightly unusual stops, such as a visit to the "world-famous" Mangonui fish-and-chips shop. The drive gives you a chance to dig for the shellfish known as tuatua and goes to the dramatically set Cape Reinga Lighthouse. ⊠ *Box 164, Paihia,* ☎ *09/402–8681.* ▨ *$75.* ⊙ *Departs daily Paihia 7:30, Kerikeri 8:15.*

Russell Mini Tours' one-hour tours of the historic sights of Russell depart from the Fullers office, opposite the wharf. ⊠ *Box 70, Russell,* ☎ *09/403–7891.* ▨ *$12.* ⊙ *Tour daily at 11, 1, 2, and 3:30.*

VISITOR INFORMATION

Bay of Islands Visitor Information Centre Paihia. ⊠ *Maritime Reserve, Paihia,* ☎ *09/402–7426.* ⊙ *Nov.–Mar., daily 7:30–7:30; Apr.–Oct., daily 8–5.*

Bay of Islands Visitor Information Centre Russell. ⊠ *The Strand, Russell,* ☎ *09/403–7866.* ⊙ *Daily 8–4:30.*

Warkworth Visitor Information Centre. ⊠ *1 Baxter St., Warkworth,* ☎ *09/425–9081,* 𝖥𝖠𝖷 *09/425–7584.* ⊙ *Daily 9–5.*

THE COROMANDEL PENINSULA

New Zealand has countless pockets of beauty that are not included in standard itineraries. One of the most accessible is the Coromandel Peninsula, which juts out like a hitchhiker's thumb east of Auckland. As with so many lands "discovered" by Europeans, the peninsula was looted for its valuable resources: kauri trees, then gum digging, and finally gold in the 1870s. Relative quiet since the 1930s has allowed the region to recover a little, and without question natural beauty abounds.

The center of the peninsula is dominated by a craggy spine of volcanic peaks that rise sharply to a height of almost 3,000 ft. The west coast cradles the Firth of Thames, while along the east coast the Pacific has carved out a succession of beaches and inlets separated by rearing headlands. Due to its rich volcanic soil, the peninsula has many spectacular gardens, several of which are open to the public. From the town of Thames, the gateway to the region, Highway 25 and the 309 Road circle the lower two-thirds of the peninsula—an exhilarating drive with the sea on one side and great forested peaks on the other. Hiking in the peninsula's lush forest is also exhilarating, and the east coast beaches are spectacular. Especially considering the Coromandel's proximity to Auckland, it would be difficult to find a finer introduction to the wonders of New Zealand.

Thames

🟤 *120 km (75 mi) southeast of Auckland.*

Thames is a historic town in the southwest corner of the peninsula about an hour and a half from Auckland. Since the 1920s the city has changed from a center for the once-active gold-mining industry to one for local agriculture. The mineral history remains, and at the rock lover's **Mineralogical Museum** (⊠ Brown and Cochrane Sts.) and the **Historical Museum** (⊠ Pollen and Cochrane Sts.) you can look into earlier ways of life in the town. If you want to learn even more about early gold-mining efforts in the Coromandel, stop in at the **stamper battery,** north on the way out of town, and take a brief underground tour of the old Golden Crown Claim, which was first worked in 1868. Five hundred feet below this site, the Caledonia strike was one of the richest in the world. A guide will describe the geological and historical interest of the mine. ⊠ *State Hwy. 25, north of Waiotahi Creek Rd.,* ☎ *07/868–7448.* 🎫 *$2 each museum.* ⊙ *Historical Museum daily 1–4, Mineralogical Museum Tues.–Sun. 11–4.*

While in Thames, take a quick look into **St. George's Anglican Church.** The interior is unpainted, and the kauri wood used to build it is gorgeous. ⊠ *Willoughby and MacKay Sts.*

Meonstoke is probably New Zealand's most unusual garden, and nothing printed here will quite prepare you for it. For more than 35 years, Pam Gwynne has been working every square inch of her quarter-acre lot. Numerous paths wind through a junglelike space, where the world appears before you as it did in childhood. There are no lookouts or vistas to distract you from closing in on the magic around you. Pam is a collector, not only of top horticultural specimens, but of found objects as well, which she ingeniously incorporates with plants in sur

The Coromandel Peninsula

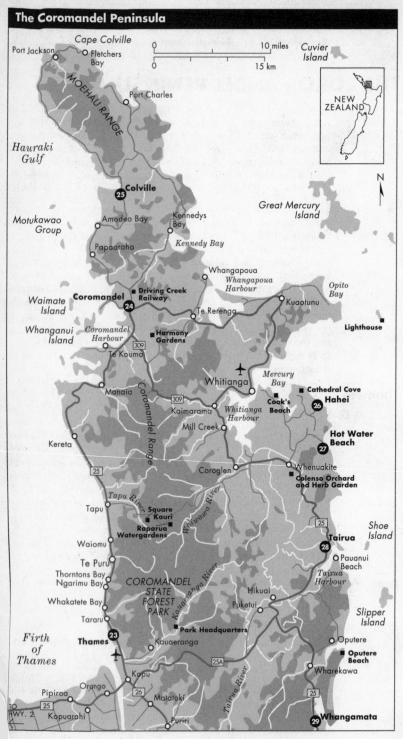

real and often humorous vignettes. On one path, a row of a ceramic pitchers is suspended from a rod (to collect rainwater?), while an overflowing bird feeder serves two hungry porcelain doves. Elsewhere, tiny winking porcelain Chinamen festoon Bonsai plants, and an old black tricycle looks as if a knickered young boy has just left it there. Although the garden is small, allow yourself plenty of time. There are hundreds of delights, many of which you'll miss the first time around. Pam's passion continues indoors, and if you are interested in dolls, ask to see her collection—unbelievable! Remember that this is a private home, and visitors are welcome only by appointment. The small entry fee goes to local charities. ☎ *07/868–6560 or 07/868–6850.*

Lodging

$–$$ ☒ **Te Kouma Harbour Farmstay.** A little off the beaten track, this set of single-story wooden chalets set on a deer farm is excellent for families, with outdoor options like kayaking, nearby bushwalking, and a soccer field, petanque (the French game *boules*), and pool on site—enough to keep you busy for a couple of days. Large, bright multiroom cabins have contemporary furniture and kitchen areas with cooking facilities. Breakfast is available by arrangement, but most guests cook for themselves. There are also barbecue areas on the grounds. The cabins are down a long drive that is well signposted from Highway 25 north out of Thames. ☒ *Te Kouma Harbour,* ☎ *07/866–8747. 6 rooms with shower. Picnic area, pool, recreation room, boating. AE, DC, MC, V.*

Hiking

Coromandel State Forest Park has more than 30 walking trails, which offer anything from a 30-minute stroll to a three-day trek, overnighting in huts equipped with bunks. The most accessible starting point is the delightful Kauaeranga Valley Road, where the Coromandel Forest Park Headquarters provides maps and information (☎ 07/868–6381). The office is open weekdays 8–4. Camping is also available. Keep in mind that the park can be very busy from late December to mid-January. If you're traveling then, plan to visit the park midweek. To reach the Kauaeranga Valley, head south from Thames and on the outskirts of the town turn left on Banks Street, then right on Parawai Road, which becomes Kauaeranga Valley Road.

En Route The Coromandel Ranges drop right down to the seafront Highway 25 as it winds up the west coast of the peninsula. Turn upon turn makes each view seem more spectacular than the last, and when you top the hills north of Kereta on the way to Coromandel, mountains, pastures, and islands in the Firth of Thames open out before you—spectacular.

Tapu

25 km (16 mi) north of Thames.

The earthen **Tapu-Coroglen Road** turns off Highway 25 in the hamlet of Tapu to wind into the mountains. It's a breathtaking route, where 80-ft tree ferns grow out of the roadside hills. About 5 km (3 mi) from Tapu, pull over to climb 178 steps up to the 1,200-year-old **Square Kauri,** so named for the shape that a cross section of its trunk would have. This elder was spared the ax by a gentlemen's agreement—ironic considering that local forests were otherwise zealously toppled in the 19th century. At 133 ft tall and 30 ft around, this is only the 15th-largest kauri in New Zealand. From a tree-side platform there is a splendid view across the valley to Mau Mau Paki, one of the Coromandel Ranges peaks. Continuing east, the road passes **Raparua Watergardens** on its way across the peninsula through forests and sheep paddocks—a mythically beautiful ride in sun or mist.

Raparua Watergardens, full of native and exotic flowering species, has been sculpted from the wilderness in a 65-acre sheltered valley in the Coromandel Ranges. Raparua (running water) is a wonderful place to witness the role water plays in New Zealand gardens and the tranquillity that can result. In the garden's various streams, waterfalls, fountains, and 14 ponds, fish and ducks swim among colorful water lilies and other bog plants while songbirds lilt overhead. Paths wind among the waters through collections of grasses, flaxes, gunneras, rhododendrons, and camellias. Giant tree ferns and rimu, rata, and kauri trees form a lush canopy overhead. The combination of delicacy and rugged grandeur may have moved the hardworking gardener to philosophy, which you'll find painted on signs, as in KEEP YOUR VALUES IN BALANCE AND YOU WILL ALWAYS FIND HAPPINESS. Note that organic gardening practices have fostered all of this beauty. Be sure to take the easy 10-minute walk to the cascading falls known as Seven Steps to Heaven, especially if you aren't planning on spending much time in the native bush. Raparua has a tearoom and a crafts shop with work by Coromandel artisans. ⊠ *Tapu-Coroglen Rd., 6 km (4 mi) east of Tapu,* ☎ ℻ *07/ 868–4821.* 🖼 *$6.* ⊙ *Daily 10–5.*

Coromandel

㉔ *60 km (38 mi) north of Thames, 29 km (18 mi) northwest of Whitianga.*

Coromandel became the site of New Zealand's first gold strike in 1852 when sawmiller Charles Ring found gold-bearing quartz at Driving Creek, just north of town. The find was important for New Zealand, since the country's manpower had been severely depleted by the gold rushes in California and Australia. Ring hurried to Auckland to claim the reward that had been offered to anyone finding "payable" gold. The town's population soared, but the reef gold could be mined only by heavy and expensive machinery, and within a few months Coromandel resumed its former sleepy existence as a timber town—and Charles Ring was refused the reward.

Driving Creek Railway is one man's magnificent folly. Barry Brickell is a local potter who discovered that clay on his land was perfect for his work. The problem was that the deposit lay in a remote area at the top of a steep slope; so he hacked a path through the forest and built his own miniature railroad to haul the stuff. Visitors to his studio began asking if they could go along for a ride, and Brickell now takes passengers on daily tours aboard his toy train. The route that the diesel-powered, narrow-gauge locomotive follows incorporates a cutting, a double-decker bridge, two tunnels, a spiral, and a switchback. The round-trip takes about 50 minutes. The "station" is 3 km (2 mi) north of Coromandel township. ⊠ *410 Kennedy's Bay Rd., Coromandel,* ☎ *07/ 866–8703.* 🖼 *$9.* ⊙ *Late Oct.–Apr., daily at 2, 4, and 10:30.*

Dining and Lodging

$–$$ ✗ **Pepper Tree Restaurant and Bar.** Coromandel seafood takes precedence on the menu of this pleasant local eatery. Locally farmed oysters are served simply on the half shell, and green-shell mussels are turned into fritters and offered with a dipping sauce. Organically farmed meat is used in mostly simple ways, which is all for the better. Nachos, potato wedges, and other easygoing nibbles dominate the all-day menu, but things get more serious after sundown. ⊠ *Kapanga Rd., Coromandel,* ☎ *07/866–8211. AE, MC, V.*

$$$$ ✗▤ **Buffalo Lodge.** Perched on a hillside and surrounded by bush just
★   out of Coromandel town, the lodge looks across the Hauraki Gulf toward Auckland. And owners Raouf and Yvelyne Siegrist-Huang have made

sure that all rooms, the dining room, and lounge area have great scenic backdrops. They've added personal touches as well—their own artwork adorns walls at the lodge's entrance and in guest rooms. Raouf confesses to a love of wood, which is used in the ceilings, floors, and furnishings. In the evening the restaurant is popular with guests and others staying in town. A three-course meal costs $65, and specialties include New Zealand king salmon, venison, lamb fillet, and fish fresh from waters around the Coromandel. With a limit of six people staying at any one time, you'll never feel crowded. ⊠ *Buffalo Rd.,* ☎ *07/ 866–8960,* 𝔽𝔸𝕏 *07/866–8960. 3 rooms with shower, 1 deluxe suite with shower and bath. BP. AE, DC, MC, V. Closed July–Sept.*

$$ 🏠 **Coromandel Colonial Cottages.** These eight immaculate timber cottages offer spacious and comfortable self-contained accommodations
★ for about the same price as a standard motel room. Six of the units have two bedrooms, a lounge room with convertible beds, a large, well-equipped kitchen, and a dining area. The two newer units have only one bedroom but still feel spacious. Arranged with military precision in two ranks, the cottages face each other across a tailored lawn surrounded by green hills on the northern outskirts of Coromandel. For vacation periods book several months in advance. ⊠ *Rings Rd., Coromandel,* ☎ *07/866–8857. 8 cottages. Pool, hot tub, miniature golf, croquet, coin laundry. AE, DC, MC, V.*

Colville and Beyond

㉕ *30 km (19 mi) north of Coromandel.*

If you find yourself possessed with the urge to reach land's end on the wilds of the peninsula—with more rugged coastline, beautiful coves, beaches, and pasturelands—follow the sealed road up to Colville. Beyond that, a gravel road will take you to the **Mt. Moehau** trail that climbs to the peninsula's highest point (2,923 ft); to the sands at **Port Jackson**; or all the way to the tip, at **Fletcher's Bay** (60 km, or 38 mi, from Coromandel). Colville's classic counterculture **General Store** (☎ 07/866–6805) sells foodstuffs, wine, and gasoline and has a café with vegetarian meals. It is the northernmost supplier on the peninsula, so don't forget to fill up before you move on.

En Route On your way south from Coromandel, **Harmony Gardens** is delightful, tranquil, noted for its rhododendrons, and filled with the sounds of birds and running water. From Coromandel, drive down Highway 25 for about 4 km (2½ mi) and turn inland where a sign points to WHITIANGA—309 ROAD. After about 2 km (1 mi), this road passes the gardens. ☎ *07/866–8487.* 🎟 *$4.* ☉ *Spring–fall, daily 10–4.*

Hahei

㉖ *14 km (9 mi) northeast of Whenuakite on Hahei Beach Rd.*

The beaches and seaside land formations in and around Hahei make for a great day of exploring—or lounging. **Te Pare Historic Reserve** is the site of a Maori *pa* (fortified village), though no trace remains of the defensive terraces and wooden spikes that ringed the hill. A much larger pa was on the hilltop overlooking this site. At high tide, the blowhole at the foot of the cliffs will add its booming bass note to the sound of waves and the sighing of the wind in the grass. The reserve is past Hahei on Pa Road. To reach the pa, follow the red arrow down the hill from the parking area. After some 50 yards take the right fork through a grove of giant pohutukawa trees, then through a gate and across an open, grassy hillside. The track is steep in places and becomes increasingly overgrown as you climb, but persist until you reach the summit, then head toward more pohutukawas off to your right at the south end of the headland.

Cathedral Cove is a beautiful white-sand crescent with a great rock arch. It is only accessible at low tide, about a 45-minute walk each way. To get there, travel along Hahei Beach Road, turn right toward town and the sea, and then, just past the shops, turn left into Grange Road and follow the signs. From the carpark you will get excellent views over Mahurangi Island, a marine reserve.

Cook's Beach lies along Mercury Bay, so named for Captain James Cook's observation of the transit of the planet Mercury in November 1769. The beach is notable because of the captain's landfall here—it was the first by a European, and it is commemorated by a beachside plaque. The beach itself is one of the less attractive ones in the area.

★ ㉗ The popular **Hot Water Beach** is a delightful thermal oddity. A warm spring seeps beneath the beach, and by scooping a shallow hole in the sand, you can create a pool of warm water; the deeper you dig, the hotter the water becomes, but the phenomenon occurs only at low to midtide, so time your trip accordingly. For a swim without the spa treatment, nearby is one of the finest well-protected coves on the coast, with sands tinted pink from crushed shells. It is at the end of Hahei Beach Road. Hot Water Beach is well signposted off of Hahei Beach Road from Whenuakite (fen-oo-ah-*kye*-tee).

NEED A
BREAK?
Colenso Orchard and Herb Garden, on Highway 25 just south of the Hahei turnoff, is a relaxed cottage café that you might find yourself wishing would franchise across rural New Zealand. Set in a garden full of lavender and kitchen herbs, Colenso serves fresh juices (from their own orchards), daily soups, focaccia sandwiches, those addictive chocolate fudge biscuits (also called slices) that are a real Kiwi treat, and Devonshire teas—simple, wholesome fare that goes with the droning of bees and the sound of wind chimes. Before getting back on the road, buy a bag of their freshly harvested fruit at the roadside stand. ⊠ Main Rd., Whenuakite, ☎ 07/866-3725. ☺ Sept.-July, daily 10-5.

En Route   Between Tairua and Whangamata you'll pass the mountainous wilderness around the second branch of the Tairua River, which is the remarkable domain of Doug Johansen. Over the past 20 years he has cut his own trails in the valley's lush rain forest—not that you could find them even if you were walking on one. Their minimal invasiveness is uncanny. Heading into the woods with a knowledgeable, and in this case entertaining, guide to point out native plants and their uses can make later hikes on your own even more rewarding. *See* Kiwi Dundee Adventures *in* Coromandel A to Z, *below.*

Tairua

㉘   *28 km (18 mi) south of Hahei, 37 km (23 mi) north of Whangamata.*

A town that you'll actually notice when you pass through it, Tairua is a harborside center where you can find food stores and a seafood joint or two. The twin volcanic peaks of Paku rise up beside the harbor.

Dining and Lodging

$$$$ ✗▨ **Puka Park Resort.** This stylish hillside hideaway, which attracts a largely European clientele, lies immersed in native bushland on Pauanui Beach, at the seaward end of Tairua Harbour on the east coast of the peninsula. Timber chalets are smartly furnished with black cane tables and wooden Venetian blinds. Sliding glass doors lead to a balcony perched among the treetops. Bathrooms are well equipped but

small. The lodge offers a full range of activities for those who want to take advantage of the splendor of the surrounding beaches and forests. Rates are comparatively low for accommodations of this standard. Food and service in the international restaurant are outstanding. The turnoff from Highway 25 is about 6 km (4 mi) south of Tairua. ✉ *Private Bag, Pauanui Beach,* ☎ *07/864–8088,* 𝐅𝐀𝐗 *07/864–8112. 48 rooms with bath. Restaurant, bar, pool, tennis court, bicycles. AE, DC, MC, V.*

$$$ ✕▦ **Pacific Harbour Motor Lodge.** Clustered between the road and an ocean inlet, these stand-alone cottages here are attractively designed in a Fijian style, with shell paths between them. Peak-ceilinged interiors are trimmed with New Zealand rimu (a local timber), and furnishings are pleasant and tasteful. All units have fully equipped kitchenettes. The motor lodge has its own bar and restaurant, with local seafood on the menu, and there is a helpful local activities list available at the front desk. ✉ *Hwy. 25, Box 5, Tairua,* ☎ 𝐅𝐀𝐗 *07/864–8581. 25 suites. Restaurant, bar, hot tub. AE, DC, MC, V.*

$$$ ▦ **Pauanui Pines.** This modern motor lodge provides a less expensive but still comfortable alternative to Puka Park. Owners Ian and Sue Wilkinson have gone for light, bright decor to suit a beach holiday, and even the designs on the crockery closely match the colors of the furniture. The units here are self-contained, with French-press coffeemakers a nice extra. Portable gas barbecues are even available. Continental breakfast is available by arrangement, but for other meals guests cook their own or wander to the nearby Pauanui township, where there are a restaurant and café. ✉ *168 Vista Paku, Pauanui Beach,* ☎ *07/864–8086,* 𝐅𝐀𝐗 *07/864–7122. 15 1-bedroom units, 3 2-bedroom units, all with shower. AE, DC, MC, V.*

En Route On the road between Tairua and Whangamata, stop at Oputere Beach and the Wharekawa (fah-ray-*ka*-wa) Wildlife Refuge for a 15-minute stroll through the forest to another great stretch of white sand. The long beach is bounded at either end by headlands, and there are stunning views of Slipper Island. An estuary nearby the parking lot is a breeding ground for shorebirds. In the late afternoon waterfowl are often present as the sun slants across the Coromandel Ranges to the west. A handsome bridge arches over the river to the forest walk.

Whangamata

㉙ *37 km (23 mi) south of Tairua, 60 km (38 mi) east of Thames.*

Whangamata (fahng-a-ma-*ta*) is another harborside village backed by the Coromandel Ranges. The town of 4,000 is a local seat, but the modest houses and main strip won't exactly bowl you over. Its harbor, surf beaches, mangroves, and coastal islands, however, are glorious. It is a great spot for deep-sea fishing, and its bar break brings in some of the best waves in New Zealand. Around the Christmas holidays and into January, it's a favorite for throngs of surfers.

Dining and Lodging

$ ✕ **Ginger's Health Shop & Cafe.** If you need breakfast or a sandwich
★ to take to the beach, you're sure to find something at this mostly vegetarian haven. The sandwiches, savory and sweet scones (ooh, those date scones), apricot-muesli bars, and other treats here may make Ginger's your favorite local spot for fueling up. A full range of alternative health products, including homeopathics, is available, too. ✉ *601 Port Rd., Whangamata,* ☎ *07/865–7265. No credit cards.* ☉ *Summer, daily 6–5; shorter hrs in winter.*

$$$ ▦ **Brenton Lodge.** Looking out over suburblike Whangamata and the
★ islands in its harbor from your hillside suite, you'll have no trouble settling into an almost luxurious mood. Fresh flowers and a welcom-

ing tray of fruit and muffins greet you on arrival, as do cheerful furnishings: a couch, breakfast table and chairs (for a private breakfast),
a wonderfully comfortable bed, terry-cloth robes, and coffee- and tea-
making paraphernalia. The lodge's only rooms are two suites on the
second floors of attractive outbuildings. Stroll around the garden,
peep at the birds in the aviary, and in spring breathe in the scent of
orange and jasmine blossoms. ⊠ *Box 216, Whangamata,* ☎ *07/865–
8400. 2 suites. BP. AE, MC, V.*

$$ ☷ **The Sands.** Giving a new meaning to beachfront accommodation,
you literally step out of the door of this B&B and on to the sand. Each
guest room has a private deck with great views across the sea. The Sands
is just a few yards south of the Whangamata Surf Club and a few min-
utes' walk from the nearest restaurant and bar. Rates include break-
fast; smoking inside is not permitted. ⊠ *106 Seaview Rd., Whangamata,*
☎ *07/865–8314. 3 double rooms with shower. No credit cards.*

The Bay of Plenty—En Route to Rotorua

Katikati is the gateway to the Bay of Plenty. In its early days, this area
was heavily populated by Maori, and many pa (fortified village) sites
have been found—an indication of frequent tribal warfare. These days,
kiwi- and other fruit growing keeps the economy afloat. Katikati's most
noticeable features are the 26 murals that locals have painted on build-
ings around town. Look for the Returned Servicemen's Association's
Those Who Served murals, and those that depict the arrival of the Maori
by *waka* (canoe).

Waihi Beach, 19 km (12 mi) north of Katikati is ideal for swimming
and surfing and has access to numerous walkways. At low tide, peo-
ple bent over digging in the sand are looking for tuatua and pipi—shell-
fish that are delicious after you boil them in a pot until they open.

The population center of the Bay of Plenty, **Tauranga** is a pleasant town—
one of North Island's fastest growing, thanks to retirees escaping the
bustle of Auckland. At the popular **Historic Village Museum,** volun-
teers, mainly from Tauranga's elderly community, bring their living his-
tory to the village's 91 mostly original colonial buildings. ⊠ *17th Ave.
W,* ☎ *07/578–1302,* ℻ *07/578–1822.* ☞ *$6.* ⊙ *Daily 9–5.*

Tauranga is also one of the places in New Zealand to swim with dol-
phins. **Dolphin Seafaris** (⊠ Coronation Pier, Tauranga, ☎ ℻ 07/577–
1061 or 0800/326–8747) will take you out to frolic with these delightful
creatures. Wet suits, dive gear, and towels are included in the $80 price
tag. Trips depart daily at 8, check-in is at 7:30.

The formerly volcanic **Mt. Maunganui** is the geological talisman of the
region, with its conical, rocky outline rising 761 ft above sea level. Re-
garded as one of the best beach areas in New Zealand, the Mount gets
crowded around Christmas and New Year's Eve. To see it at its best,
come in November, early December, or between mid-January and late
March. A system of tracks and paths around Mauao—the Mount's local
Maori name—include an easy walk around its base and the more
strenuous Summit Road from the campground by the Pilot Bay boat
ramp.

For yet another chance to laze on the beach, **Whakatane** (fah-kah-*tah*-
nee), southeast of Tauranga, claims to be North Island's sunniest town.
This was landfall on New Zealand for the first migratory Maori ca-
noes, and the fertile hinterland was the first part of the country to be
farmed. Whakatane is also known as a base from which to explore **White
Island,** where you can deep-sea fish or swim with dolphins. The island
is an active volcano, and whether you see it by plane, boat, or on foot,

its billowing steam makes for a typically awesome Pacific Rim geothermal experience.

The least expensive way to get to White Island is by boat. Options include tours on the **Te Kahurangi,** a 37-ft SuperCat vessel. The vessel only carries small groups; the cost is $85. **Vulcan Helicopters** has a nine-seat helicopter; pilot-owner Robert Fleming is an authority on the island. Two-hour flights cost $275 and include a landing. **East Bay Flight Centre** and **Bell Air** each have fixed-wing aircraft that fly over the island's crater; 50-minute trips cost $95.

For more close aqueous encounters of the mammalian kind, **Dolphins Down Under** (⊠ 19 Quay St., Whakatane, ☎ 07/308–4636 or 0800/354–7737, 𝔽𝔸𝕏 07/308–0359) has four-hour cruises during which you can swim with or simply view dolphins. Wet suits, masks, snorkels, and fins are provided. Cruises leave at 7:30 AM and cost $85 per person.

Dining and Lodging
In Katikati, stay at ✕🏨 **Fantail Lodge** (⊠ Rea Rd., ☎ 07/549–1581, 𝔽𝔸𝕏 07/549–1417; AE, DC, MC, V, $$$$), with its Bavarian touches and enveloping orchards. Its restaurant serves local produce; the lodge itself has 16 rooms and a pool and tennis court. Also in Katikati, 🏨 **Moanui Hills** (⊠ 287 Lunds Rd., R.D. 2, ☎ 07/549–2237; $$) is a B&B on an emu farmlet with spectacular views over the sea and mountain ranges. There is only one guest room.

Forty kilometers (25 miles) outside **Tauranga,** ✕🏨 **Cassimir** (⊠ 20 Williams Rd, Pyes pa, R.D. 3, ☎ 07/543–2000, 𝔽𝔸𝕏 07/543–1999; AE, DC, MC, V; $$$$) is a grand colonial country villa, the original core of which was built in 1890. Stunning rural scenery is all around, and owner Reg Turner is a well-known character in New Zealand lodge circles—his enthusiasm is infectious. The lodge has four rooms.

Getting Around
Katikati is 62 km (39 mi) southeast of Thames on Highway 2. Tauranga is 35 km (22 mi) southeast of Katikati and 86 km (54 mi) north of Rotorua. Whakatane is 100 km (62 mi) southeast of Tauranga.

Coromandel A to Z

Arriving and Departing
BY BUS
InterCity (☎ 07/8687251) links Whitianga, Thames, and Auckland daily.

The **Coromandel Bus Plan** is the cheapest and most flexible way to travel around the region by bus. It is valid for three months, and you can get on and off where you wish. A rate of $49 covers the Thames–Coromandel–Whitianga–Tairua–Thames loop, and you can take round-trips to Hahei, Hot Water Beach, and Whangamata. ⊠ *Thames Information Centre, 405 Queen St.,* ☎ *07/868–7284.*

BY CAR
From Auckland take the Southern Motorway, following signs to Hamilton. Just past the narrowing of the motorway, turn left onto Highway 2 and follow the signs to Thames. Allow 1- to 2½-hours for the 118-km (73-mi) journey.

Contacts and Resources
EMERGENCIES
Dial 111 for **fire, police, or ambulance** services.

GUIDED TOURS
Kiwi Dundee Adventures. A trip to New Zealand really wouldn't be complete without a day or more with Doug Johansen and Jan Poole

or one of their expert associate guides. Their humorous tricks and total enthusiasm for the region inevitably rub off on anyone who takes a Kiwi Dundee tour. There are one- to five-day or longer experiences of the majesty of the Coromandel, or all of New Zealand if you'd like. Spectacular coastline, ferny rain forests, mountains, and gorges; glow-worm caves, old gold mines, thermal springs, native flora and fauna—natural phenomena that they know intimately and respect deeply—and odd bits of history and bush lore are all rolled into their hikes and walks. They have a great time as conservationists and guides, and you're sure to have one with them in their beautiful neck of the woods. ⊠ *Box 198, Whangamata,* ☎ FAX *07/865–8809.*

Mercury Bay Safaris has a swim-with-the-dolphins program, plus a glass-bottom boat trip and a journey around islands in the area. Departures from Whitianga Wharf are subject to weather conditions. ⊠ *Whitianga Information Centre, Whitianga,* ☎ *07/866–5555,* FAX *07/866–2205.* ☏ *Dolphin Quest $75, glass-bottom boat $30, Seven Island Safari $70.*

VISITOR INFORMATION

Thames Visitor Information Centre. ⊠ *Old Railway Station, Queen St., Thames,* ☎ *07/868–7284,* FAX *07/808–7584.* ☉ *Weekdays 8:30–5, weekends 9–4.*

Whitianga Visitor Information Centre. ⊠ *66 Albert St.,* ☎ *07/866–5555.* ☉ *Spring–fall, weekdays 9–5, weekends 10–1; summer, daily 9–5.*

3 Rotorua to Wellington

Sulphuric Rotorua bubbles and oozes with surreal volcanic activity. It is one of the population centers of New Zealand's pre-European inhabitants, the Maori—try dining at a traditional hangi *feast. Great hiking abounds in a variety of national parks, glorious gardens grow in the rich soil of the Taranaki Province, and charming, Art Deco Napier and the nation's capital in Wellington are friendly urban counterpoints to the countryside.*

NORTH AND SOUTH ISLANDS have different sorts of natural beauty. South Island's better-known heroic landscapes are generally flat or precipitous. North Island's rolling pasturelands have a more human scale—some think of Scotland, not only because of the sheep paddocks. Parts of North Island do break the rhythm of these verdant contours: the majestic, Fuji-like Mt. Taranaki, also called Mt. Egmont, the rugged wilderness areas of Urewera and Tongariro national parks, the rocky forms in the Wairarapa district northeast of Wellington, and the bizarre geological plumbing around Rotorua.

Rotorua is the midisland's population center, and it has been heavily touristed since Europeans first heard of the healing qualities of local hot springs and pools. All around, nature has crafted a gallery of surreal wonders that include limestone caverns, volcanic wastelands, steaming geysers, and hissing ponds. From the shores of Lake Taupo—the country's largest lake and the geographic bull's-eye of North Island—Mt. Ruapehu, the island's tallest peak, is plainly visible. Site of New Zealand's largest ski area, the mountain is the dominant feature of Tongariro National Park, a haunting landscape of craters, volcanoes, and lava flows that ran with molten rock as recently as 1988 and were throwing up some threatening clouds in 1996.

Southeast of Lake Taupo, on the shores of Hawke Bay, the town of Napier has an interesting aggregation of Art Deco architecture. Around Napier, the Hawke's Bay region is one of the country's major wine routes. A diversion to the north will take you to relatively isolated Gisborne and Eastland, which are often overlooked but extremely rewarding. The largely agricultural East Cape juts out above Gisborne, coursing with trout-rich streams and ringed with beaches and coves made even more beautiful by their isolation.

The lush Taranaki region literally sprang from the ocean floor in a series of volcanic blasts, forming that odd hump down the west coast of North Island. The now-dormant cone of Mt. Taranaki is the breathtaking symbol of the province. Because of the mountain's proximity to the coast, you can easily climb its sides in the morning and come back down for an afternoon swim on the shores of the Tasman Sea. Agriculture thrives in the area's volcanic soil, and Taranaki's gardens are some of the country's most spectacular, from a massive rhododendron trust to smaller private gardens. It almost goes without saying that the Maori were the province's first settlers, and their local mythology and historical sites deepen any experience of the area.

More and more people are finding their way to Wellington by choice rather than necessity. The city is gaining a reputation for fostering the arts and preserving its culture in a way that the more brash Auckland to the north does not. Because it is perched at the southern tip of North Island, Wellington is the jumping-off point for the ferry south—but don't jump south too quickly. If you delay your departure even for a day, you'll find that Wellington is a charming, sociable city. Small enough to explore easily on foot, it is arguably the country's most cosmopolitan city, with an excellent arts complex, the popular new Te Papa Museum, cafés, contemporary clothing designers, and music of all kinds. Also consider taking a side trip to the Wairarapa, another coastal area with a range of outdoor activities and some of the country's finest wineries.

Note: For more information on bicycling, fishing, hiking, and rafting in central North Island, *see* Chapter 6.

Pleasures and Pastimes

Dining

Between Rotorua and Wellington, you'll come across a number of small towns with little more than a country-style pub to satisfy the appetite. Don't avoid these places, as what they lack in sophistication they more than make up for with friendliness and good home cooking.

Rotorua is the best place to try the unique Maori hangi (feast). Traditionally, meat and vegetables placed in flax baskets were gently steamed in an earth oven lined with heated stones and wet leaves—lamb, pork, and seafood along with pumpkin and kumara (sweet potato), a staple of the Maori diet. Nowadays, the food may well be prepared above ground, but it doesn't lose much in the translation. Almost without exception, a Rotorua hangi will be followed by a Maori concert, usually a commercialized but entertaining performance of traditional songs and dances—with much audience participation.

In central North Island, try to arrange a taste of freshly hooked trout. Laws prohibit trout being sold commercially, so you may have to catch it yourself (or know someone who has), then ask your host or a local chef to cook it. (Not long ago, an enterprising restaurateur tried to bypass the law by offering the trout free and charging $28 for the sauce. Nice try, but he didn't get away with it!) Also try game food such as wild boar, venison, and hare—with a Hawke's Bay merlot or a Martinborough pinot noir.

For price ranges, *see* the price chart *in* On the Road with Fodor's.

Fishing

Central North Island is trout country. You can get out on any of the designated lakes and waterways if you have your own gear and a fishing license. It is worthwhile, however, to engage a local guide to take you to the right spots. On the lakes around Rotorua, and perhaps even more on Lake Taupo, few people leave disappointed. For extensive information on central North Island fishing, *see* Chapter 6.

Lodging

New Zealand lodges are often small and exclusive, set in places of great beauty. Some of the best are in central North Island, the most famous being Huka Lodge just outside Taupo and Solitaire near Rotorua. They tend to attract people keen on fishing, hunting, or other outdoor activities, and the area's best guides are always nearby. The wine and food available at lodges is another point of appeal. If your budget allows, even one night at one of these lodges will be an experience you won't soon forget.

The up and down fortunes of New Zealand's rural communities over the last decade or so have persuaded farming families to supplement their incomes by offering farmstay accommodations. Farmstays usually aren't luxurious, but the best provide hands-on involvement with the working life of the farm. And the New Zealanders whom you meet often have the pioneering spirit of those who work the land for a living. Standards can vary, as the hosts have often not had extensive hospitality training, but you will be safe sticking to farmstays recommended in this book. Or ask for guidance at the nearest information center.

In Rotorua there are many more hotel beds than visitors for much of the year, and a number of hotels and motels offer significant discounts on their standard rates. The exception is school holidays, for which you should book well in advance. For price ranges, *see* the price chart *in* On the Road with Fodor's.

Soaking

In Rotorua and Taupo, thermal springs are literally on tap. You can soak in your own thermal bath in even the cheapest hotels in Rotorua, or take advantage of public facilities such as Polynesian Spa. Many Taupo motels and hotels also have their own thermal baths or pools. Lying on your back and closing your eyes is a great way to relax. You'll be amazed how relaxed you feel afterward.

Tramping and Walking

Central North Island doesn't have the famous walking tracks of South Island, but it does have equally serious bushwalking and plenty of pleasant walking trails. Excellent longer tracks circle Mt. Taranaki or climb through the alpine areas in Tongariro National Park. Some of the most rugged bush in the country is in Urewera National Park southeast of Rotorua, and hiking opportunities abound around Rotorua, Taupo, and the Wairarapa.

Exploring Central North Island and Wellington

You could easily spend a month traveling between Auckland and Wellington and still touch on only the major sights. Realistically, you're most likely to travel either straight through the middle or down the east or west coasts. The difficulty comes in deciding which coast and which smaller areas to explore. If you're interested in the bizarre thermal activity of Rotorua, start there. If you're a garden lover, starting in Taranaki to the west and stopping at other spots on the way to Wellington is the way to go. If wine routes are more appealing, you can take in three on the east coast: Gisborne, Hawke's Bay, and Wairarapa. If you want to get into some astonishing backcountry, Tongariro and Urewera national parks are unbeatable, as are parts of the Wairarapa. And Wellington is a pleasant city for refreshing yourself for a couple of days before hopping over to South Island.

There are, in other words, a great many activities listed in this chapter. Allow yourself time to get a good sense of where you are by spending three to four days minimum in each area, and plan for more travel time than you might expect—this island is larger than it looks.

Great Itineraries

Numbers in the text correspond to numbers in the margin and on the Central North Island, Napier, Wellington, and Greater Wellington and Wairarapa maps.

IF YOU HAVE 3 DAYS

Three days will only allow you to see one of the major areas covered in the chapter or to scratch the surface of two—especially taking travel time into account. If you do have only three days, spend all of them in ⊞ **Rotorua** taking in its sights and smells, popping over to **Waitomo Caves** ② for the glowworm spectacle and spending all or part of a day fishing; or take three in ⊞ **Napier** ⑰–㉗, with a day in the city and two days in the surrounding wine country and natural beauty; or ⊞ **Wellington** ㊶–㊻, taking a day or two in the city and the rest in the ⊞ **Wairarapa,** visiting wineries, hiking, or seeing rare native animals. You would have to fly in and out of New Plymouth for spending three days in ⊞ **Taranaki**'s gardens and walking on the slopes of Mt. Egmont. If surface treatment will do, you could take a day in Rotorua before dropping down the next morning to Napier for the rest of the time. Fly from there to your next stop.

IF YOU HAVE 6 DAYS

With almost a week to spend covering central and southern North Island, you can put together a more diverse experience of a couple of

Central North Island

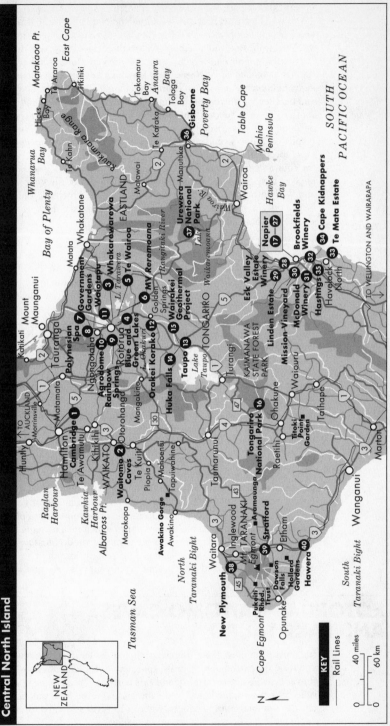

NEW ZEALAND

KEY

Rail Lines

0   40 miles
0   60 km

N

SOUTH
PACIFIC OCEAN

Bay of Plenty

Poverty Bay

Hawke Bay

Tasman Sea

regions. Pick a path for moving from north to south and leave a half day or more for travel between Rotorua and Napier or Taranaki, then another half day plus for the trip down to Wellington if you have a car. Start in ☒ **Rotorua,** spending two to three days in the bubble and ooze, fishing, going to a hangi at night; then continue either east to the Art Deco city of ☒ **Napier and Hawke's Bay** and the surrounding wine country, or west to ☒ **Taranaki** for gardens, mountain walks, and beaches for the rest of the time. Or from Rotorua you could head south to ☒ **Lake Taupo** ⑬ and **Tongariro National Park** ⑯ for serious outdoor activities: fishing, canoeing, rafting, and hiking. Going to Napier or Taupo would set you up for a stop in the ☒ **Wairarapa** for more spectacular countryside, including rugged coastal scenery, one of the country's finest wildlife parks, and a wine tour in ☒ **Martinborough** ㊗ In six days you could also combine Taranaki, the Wairarapa, and Wellington, with one day each in the last two. Or chuck it all and head straight for ☒ **Gisborne and Eastland** for six days of New Zealand's finest off-the-beaten-path travel.

IF YOU HAVE 9 DAYS

You might think that you can see it all in nine days, but try not to get too ambitious—always allow more time in each place to absorb the local atmosphere. In this case, the more you take on, the more travel time you'll have between places. One more word of caution: The small mountain roads on a Napier to Taranaki crossing will run you ragged, so don't try them. Allow one day of the nine for time on the road. So then, the two-day-in-each surface treatment options for nine-day stays are **Rotorua–Napier–Wairarapa–Wellington,** or **Rotorua–Taranaki–Wairarapa–Wellington.** To give yourself a better sense of place, each of the five following combinations will provide in-depth experiences of the delights of central and southern North Island: **Taranaki** (4 days)–**Wairarapa** (2 days)–**Wellington** (2 days); *or* **Eastland** (5 days)–**Napier** (3 days); *or* **Napier** (3 days)–**Wairarapa** (3 days)–**Wellington** (2 days); *or* **Rotorua and Taupo** (5 days)–**Wairarapa** (3 days); *or* **Rotorua and Taupo** (4 days)–**Taranaki** (4 days). Pick one!

When to Tour Central North Island and Wellington

The months from December through mid-April are the best for central and southern North Island. The weather is glorious, and everything is open. Except for the late-spring to early autumn months, rainy days can get chilly. Some say that Taranaki's Rhododendron Festival nearly always gets rained on, the answer to which is to skip the festival and go in late November for more than just rhodo blossoms. Of course if you want to do some skiing, August is the month to hit Tongariro National Park and Mt. Egmont to put your tips into some white stuff.

ROTORUA, WAITOMO CAVES, AND LAKE TAUPO

It's one of the most extraordinary sights in the country. Everywhere you turn, the earth bubbles, boils, spits, and oozes. Drainpipes steam, flower beds hiss, rings tarnish, and cars corrode. The rotten-egg smell of hydrogen sulphide hangs in the air, and even the local golf course has its own mud-pool hot spots, where a lost ball stays lost forever.

New Zealand's most famous tourist attraction, Rotorua (ro-to-*roo*-ah) sits smack on top of the most violent segment of the Taupo Volcanic Zone, which runs in a broad belt from White Island in the Bay of Plenty to Tongariro National Park, south of Lake Taupo. These spurting geysers and sulphur springs have spawned an unashamedly touristy town—

with a Motel Alley of more than 100 motels—that can be taken in easily in one day. The city has tidied up its act considerably in the past few years, particularly by making the lakefront into a pleasant park setting where you can sit and watch the lake activity. Even so, if somebody else's idea of fun and the air in "Sulphur City" doesn't appeal, drive outside the city limits, and you'll find yourself in magnificent, untamed country, where spring-fed streams sprint through native forests into lakes that are an abundant source of some of the largest rainbow trout on earth. Anglers regularly pull 10-pounders from Lake Tarawera.

Rotorua has a well-established Maori community tracing its ancestry back through the Te Arawa tribe to the great Polynesian migration of the 14th century. Maori culture is stamped indelibly on the town. For more intimate contact with their culture, attend a hangi followed by a Maori concert.

Cambridge

❶ *150 km (94 mi) southeast of Auckland, 85 km (53 mi) northwest of Rotorua.*

A small town in the district of Waikato, Cambridge is a place most visitors drive through in a hurry to get to Rotorua from Auckland—and are left wishing they hadn't. Even a quick glance reveals that this is a charming town, with its historic buildings, tree-lined streets, and rural English atmosphere. Rotorua is an hour or so away, which gives you plenty of time for a stopover on your way down from the north.

Cambridge has grappled with its image a bit, calling itself variously the town of trees and a center for crafts and antiques. The best way to find both is simply to leave your car and take a walk along Victoria, Empire, and Commerce streets. Cambridge is also regarded as New Zealand's Kentucky, and, in fact, the Thoroughbred industry has become the most prominent local feature.

Ⓒ **Horse Magic** at Cambridge Thoroughbred Lodge is a must for anyone interested in horse racing or the Thoroughbred industry. Experienced presenters tailor shows for each audience, easily moving from expert-level information to antics for any kids that might be in the group. A two-year-old Thoroughbred is shown off in full racing gear; other horses are led out in costume as well. If you do come with children, they can go for a short ride while you take a cup of coffee and muffins. Auctions, which are interesting to drop in on if you're in the area, are held in March, May, August, and November. ⊠ *State Hwy. 1, 6 km (4 mi) south of town,* ☎ *07/827–8118,* ℻ *827–8005.* ⊡ *$12.* ☉ *Tour and show daily at 10:30, 1:30 tour by arrangement only.*

Dining

Cambridge has a number of restaurants to choose from, most casual and café style. Fran's (☞ *below*), a slice of everyday New Zealand, is a good place to stop in for a bite on the way south.

$$$ ✕ **Souter House.** In summer sit on the covered veranda of this restored Edwardian villa. Indoors, surroundings are stately in a way that's hard to find in today's café-crazy society. The menu has a few classics, and there's plenty of innovation in dishes like smoked lamb "waterfall," which drapes the lamb over salad greens adorned with a creamy balsamic-mint dressing and red onion marmalade, or a snapper fillet crusted with herbs before being baked and served with a sauce based on oranges and green peppercorns. The wine list is far-, and high-, reaching. ⊠ *19 Victoria St., Cambridge,* ☎ *07/827–3610. AE, DC, MC, V.*

$ ✕ **Fran's Café and Continental Cake Kitchen.** A clutch of tables in the
main room, a few on the patio behind out back—line up inside at an
old wooden counter at the back for a hot dish or pick out a sandwich
from the self-serve counter on the side; all the food is homemade. You
might feel yourself slipping back a couple of decades as you sit down
with ladies lunching, a mother and her children, or a group of local
businesspeople. Don't forget to order a cuppa (Kiwi coffee or tea—
Fran's doesn't have a license to sell wine) and a piece of cake. The food
is tasty, the servings generous, and the staff takes obvious pride in it.
⊠ *62 Victoria St., Cambridge,* ☎ *07/827–3946.*

Shopping
Cambridge Country Store, in a brightly painted old church, is the first
building you'll notice as you come into town from the north. The em-
porium is chockablock with New Zealand–made goods: from wool
scarves, throw rugs, and hand-knit sweaters to wine and food products (but not lunch). ⊠ *92 Victoria St.,* ☎ *07/827–8715.*

Waitomo Caves

❷   *65 km (41 mi) southwest of Cambridge, 150 km (95 mi) west of Rotorua, 190 km (120 mi) north of New Plymouth.*

Waitomo Caves are parts of an ancient seabed that was lifted and then
spectacularly eroded into a surreal landscape of limestone formations
and caves, many of them still unexplored. Only two caves are open to
the public for guided tours: the Aranui and the Waitomo, or Glowworm, Cave. **Waitomo Cave** takes its name from the Maori words *wai*
and *tomo*, water and cave, since the Waitomo River vanishes into the
hillside here. You ride through in a boat. In **Glowworm Grotto,** the
larvae of *Arachnocampa luminosa,* measuring between 1 and 2 inches,
live on cave ceilings. They snare prey by dangling filaments of tiny, sticky
beads, which trap insects attracted to the light the worm emits by a
chemical oxidation process. A single glowworm produces far less light
than any firefly, but when massed in great numbers in the dark, their
effect is a bit like looking at the night sky in miniature.

Aranui Cave, 2 km (1 mi) beyond Glowworm Cave, is a very different experience. Eons of dripping water have sculpted a delicate garden in pink-and-white limestone. The cave is named after a local
Maori, Te Rutuku Aranui, who discovered the cave in 1910 when his
dog disappeared inside in pursuit of a wild pig. Each cave tour lasts
45 minutes. Glowworm Cave is high on the list of every coach tour,
so try to avoid visiting between 11 and 2, when groups arrive from
Auckland. ⊠ *Te Anga Rd.,* ☎ *07/878–8227.* ▣ *Waitomo Cave
$19.50, both caves $27.* ☉ *Glowworm Cave tour Nov.–Easter, daily
every ½ hr 9–5:30; and Easter–Oct., daily every hr 9–5; Aranui Cave
tour daily at 10, 11, 1, 2, and 3.*

In the center of the caves village, the **Museum of Caves** provides an entertaining and informative look at the formation of the caves and the
life cycle of the glowworm, with a number of interactive displays designed especially for children. ⊠ *Waitomo Caves Village,* ☎ *07/878–
7640.* ▣ *$4.* ☉ *Daily 8–5:30.*

The **Waitomo Walkway** is a 5-km (3-mi), 2½-hour walk that begins
across the road from the Museum of Caves and follows the Waitomo
River. The track passes through forests and impressive limestone outcrops, and it may leave you with your fondest memories of Waitomo.
It is relatively easy and highly recommended, but you must walk back
to Waitomo Caves Village on the same path. If you prefer an alternative to the complete walk, take Te Anga Road from the village, turn

left into Tumutumu Road, park at Ruakuri Reserve, and walk the short final section of the track through this delightful reserve.

TE ANGA–MAROKOPA ROAD – This classic dirt road works its way west out of Waitomo toward the coast. It makes for a spectacular detour—or the scenic long way to Taranaki—winding past sheep paddocks and stunning vistas of the hillsides of Waikato and the King Country. Some 26 km (16 mi) out of Waitomo, stop at the **Mangapohue** (mang-ah-po-*hoo*-ay) **Natural Bridge.** From the parking area, there are two approaches to the bridge. One to the right climbs over a hill, dropping into a valley strewn with oyster-fossil rocks that defy description. The natural bridge rises off to the left. The other path follows a stream through a gorge it has carved out. The gorge walls climb ever higher until they meet and form the bridge that closes over the path. The walk takes only 15 to 20 minutes to complete, but you may want to linger longer to take it all in.

About 5 km (3 mi) farther along the road to Marokopa, **Piripiri Caves** beckon with their interesting fossil legacy—the marks of giant oysters that resided here during the area's onetime subaqueous existence. The place is fascinating, but the approach and entrance to the caves are steep and slippery, so wear appropriate shoes or boots, and bring a jacket for the cool air and a powerful torch (flashlight) to cut through the gloom if you really want to see the extensive underground network.

A couple of miles farther still, the 120-ft **Marokopa Falls** are another local wonder. Look at them from a small roadside platform or walk down a trail to get closer. And a few miles beyond the falls, the Maori-run pub at Te Anga is a good place to stop for refreshment before heading back, or onward.

You can continue west on this road to Marokopa, then south on a more difficult stretch for an incredibly scenic route to the Taranaki region. If you're in for the duration, fill up your gas tank before turning off State Highway 1 for Waitomo.

Black-Water Rafting

This is an unusual and entertaining way to see the caves. Participants must first prove themselves with a giant leap into the Huhunoa Stream; the next three hours are spent dressed in wet suits and equipped with cavers' helmets and inflated inner tubes, floating through underground caverns. Although the combination of darkness and freezing water might sound like a refined form of torture, the trip is an exhilarating one that will live vividly in your memory long after the goose bumps have disappeared. The cost is $50 per person. Departure times vary, depending on daily demand. ⊠ *Black Water Rafting, Box 13, Waitomo Caves,* ☎ *07/878–7640.*

Rotorua

85 km (53 mi) south of Cambridge, 200 km (125 mi) southeast of Auckland.

❸ **Whakarewarewa** (*fa*-ka-*ree*-wa-*ree*-wa) is one mouthful of a name—locals just call it Whaka. This is easily the most accessible and popular of Rotorua's thermal areas and also the most varied, as it provides insight into Maori culture. You are free to wander at your own pace, but you'll gain far more from the experience if you take a guided tour from the Arts and Crafts Institute near the ticket office. The trails winding through the complex pass sinister, steaming pools, spitting mud ponds, and smooth silica terraces that appear to be coated in melted candle wax. **Pohutu** (the big splash) is a rather erratic geyser that from time to time shoots to a height of more than 80 ft. You'll also find a reconstructed Maori village with houses, gates, a *marae* (meeting house), and a modern Maori village, where residents cook in the traditional manner by placing meat and vegetables in flax baskets and dunking them in steaming pools at the back of the village. At the village entrance is a graveyard in which the graves are all above ground since it's impossible to dig into the earth. A one-hour Maori concert takes place daily at 12:15 in the Arts and Crafts Institute. Whakarewarewa is 3 km (2 mi) along Fenton Street from the Rotorua Visitor Centre, heading toward Taupo. ⊠ *Hemo Rd.*, ☎ *07/348–9047.* ☞ *$15.50, concert $15.50.* ⊙ *Oct.–Mar., daily 8–5:30; Apr.– Sept., daily 8–5:30.*

❹ **Blue and Green lakes** are on the road to ☞ Te Wairoa (the buried village) and Lake Tarawera. The Green Lake is off-limits except for its viewing area, but the Blue Lake is a popular picnic and swimming area. To get to them, turn right off Fenton Street into Amohau Street (at the McDonald's on the left). The road loops through forests and skirts the edge of the lakes.

❺ At the end of the 19th century, **Te Wairoa** (tay why-*ro*-ah, the buried village) was the starting point for expeditions to the pink-and-white terraces of Rotomahana, on the slopes of Mt. Tarawera. These silica terraces were formed by the mineral-rich water from a geyser. As the water cascaded down the mountainside, it formed a series of baths, which became progressively cooler as they neared the lake. In the latter half of the last century these fabulous terraces were the country's major tourist attraction, but they were completely destroyed when Mt. Tarawera erupted in 1886. The explosion, heard as far away as Auckland, killed 153 people and buried the village of Te Wairoa under a sea of mud and hot ash. The village has been excavated, and a path circles the site. Of special interest is the *whare* (*fah*-ray, hut) of the *tohunga* (priest) Tuhoto Ariki, who predicted the destruction of the village. Eleven days before the eruption, two separate tourist parties saw a Maori war canoe emerge from the mists of Lake Tarawera and disappear again—a vision the tohunga interpreted as a sign of impending disaster. Four days after the eruption, the 100-year-old tohunga was dug out of his buried whare still alive, only to die in the hospital a few days later. The path circles the village, dives down the hill alongside Te Wairoa Falls, then passes through a cave, crosses a bridge, and ascends the moist, fern-covered slope on the far side. The walk is a delight; its lower section is steep and can be slippery in places. ⊠ *Tarawera Rd.*, ☎ *07/362–8287.* ☞ *$9.50.* ⊙ *Fall–spring, daily 9–4:30; summer, daily 8:30–5:30.*

❻ From the shores of Lake Tarawera, the **MV Reremoana,** a restored lake cruiser, makes regular scenic runs. The two-hour cruise is especially recommended; it departs at 11 and stops for 30 minutes at the foot of Mt. Tarawera, where you can picnic, swim, or walk across the isthmus to Lake Rotomahana. Forty-five-minute cruises depart from the landing at one-hour intervals from 1:30 to 4:30. Four kilometers (2½ miles) beyond the village, on Spencer Road, a sign points to LAUNCH CRUISES and the *Reremoana*'s parking lot. ⊠ *Tarawera Launch Cruises,* ☎ *07/362–8595.* ☞ *$22.50.*

★ At the northern end of town on the shores of the lake stands **St. Faith's,** the Anglican church for the Maori village of Ohinemutu. Before the present Tudor-style church was built in 1910, one of the ministers was Seymour Spencer Mills, of Hartford, Connecticut, who preached to the Arawa people for 50 years. He is commemorated in a small window above the organ chancel, preaching to a group of Maori as he holds his habitual umbrella. The interior of the church, which is richly decorated with carvings inset with mother-of-pearl, deserves attention at any time, but it's at its best during Sunday services, when the sonorous, melodic voices of the Maori choir rise in hymns. The service at 8 AM is in the Maori language; the 10 AM service is in both Maori and English. ⊠ *Memorial Dr.*

❼ Government Gardens. The Maori call this area Whangapiro (fang-ah-*pee*-ro, evil-smelling place)—an appropriate name for these bizarre gardens, where sulphur pits bubble and fume behind manicured rose beds. The focus of interest here is the extraordinary neo-Tudor **Bath House.** Built as a spa at the turn of the century, it is now Rotorua's Art and History Museum. One room on the ground floor is devoted to the eruption of Mt. Tarawera. A number of artifacts that were unearthed from the debris and a remarkable collection of photographs show the terraces of Rotomahana before the eruption. Recent digging has revealed remnants of the original bathhouse, which you can walk through. ⊠ *Arawa St.,* ☎ *07/349–8334.* ☞ *$6.* ⊙ *Daily 9:30–5.*

❽ A trip to Rotorua would hardly be complete without a dip in the soothing, naturally heated **Polynesian Spa.** A wide choice of mineral baths is available, from large communal pools to family pools to small, private baths for two. Massage and saunas are also available. The newest addition to the pools is the Lake Spa, set out as four shallow rock pools overlooking Lake Rotorua. There is also a relaxation lounge with drinks and light snacks available. The pools are close to the Government Gardens. ⊠ *Hinemoa St.,* ☎ *07/348–1328.* ☞ *Family or adult pool $8.50, private pool $9 per ½ hr, lake spa $25.* ⊙ *Daily 6:30 AM– 11 PM.*

OFF THE
BEATEN PATH

Heading north out of Rotorua on Fairy Springs Road, stop in at **Hillside Herbs,** a garden that holds demonstrations of various herbal uses: cooking, healing, and making potpourri among them. Wander around the garden or take one of the tours (at 11 and 2, for $8). ⊠ *166 Fairy Springs Rd.,* ☎ *07/347–9535.* ⊙ *Daily 8:30–5:30.*

❾ Leafy **Rainbow Springs** park is home to many species of New Zealand wildlife, including deer, kiwis and other native birds, wild kuni kuni pigs, and most of all, trout. The trout that congregate for feeding sessions at the Rainbow and Fairy springs are the King Kongs of the trout world. On the other side of State Highway 5, Rainbow Farm demonstrates New Zealand farming life. A sheep show takes place daily at 10:30, 11:45, 1, and 2:30. ⊠ *Fairy Springs Rd., 5 km (3 mi) northwest of Rotorua,* ☎ *07/347–9301.* ☞ *Rainbow Springs $10, Rainbow Farm $10, springs and farm $16.50.* ⊙ *Daily 8–5.*

❿ The **Agrodome** is a sprawling complex, part of a 320-acre farm, 10 minutes northwest of Rotorua off State Highway 5. Most of it is dedicated to the four-footed woolly New Zealander. Shows daily at 9:30, 11, and 2:30 demonstrate the different breeds of sheep, shearing techniques, and sheepdogs at work. There are farm buggy tours after the shows, and children can participate by feeding lambs and milking a cow. ⊠ *Riverdale Park, Western Rd., Ngongotaha,* ☎ *07/357–4350.* ☞ *$10, farm tour $12.* ⊙ *Daily 9–4:30.*

⓫ Waiotapu (why-oh-*ta*-pu) is a complete thermal wonderland—a freakish, fantastic landscape of deep, sulphur-crusted pits, jade-color ponds, silica terraces, and a steaming lake edged with red algae and bubbling with tiny beads of carbon dioxide. **Lady Knox Geyser** erupts precisely at 10:15 daily—but not through some miracle of Mother Nature. Five pounds of soap powder poured into the vent of the geyser causes the water to boil, and the vent is then blocked with rags until the pressure builds sufficiently for the geyser to explode. The phenomenon was discovered early this century. Wardens from a nearby prison farm would bring convicts to a pool here to wash their clothes. They found that when the water became soapy, the pool would boil fiercely, and one of the wardens built a rock cairn to serve as a nozzle, concentrating the force of the boiling water and making the geyser rise even higher. To get here, leave Rotorua by Fenton Street, which becomes Highway 5, and follow the signs to Taupo. After 30 km (19 mi), turn left where the sign points to Waiotapu. ⊠ *State Hwy. 5, 30 km (19 mi) southeast of Rotorua,* ☎ *07/366–6333.* ⊡ *$10.* ☉ *Daily 8:30–5.*

⑫   Even if you think you have seen enough bubbling pools and fuming craters to last a lifetime, the captivating thermal valley of **Orakei Korako** is likely to change your mind. Geyser-fed streams hiss and steam as they flow into the waters of the lake, and there is an impressive multicolor silica terrace, believed to be the largest in the world since the destruction of the terraces of Rotomahana. At the bottom of Aladdin's Cave, the vent of an ancient volcano, a jade-green pool was once used exclusively by Maori women as a beauty parlor, which is where the name *Orakei Korako* (a place of adorning) originated. You will find the valley by traveling along Highway 5 toward Taupo. At Kihi Bridge, just past Golden Springs, turn right where the sign points to Orakei Korako, which is reached by jet boat from the shores of Lake Ohakuri. It is 68 km (43 mi) southwest of Rotorua, or 37 km (23 mi) north of Taupo. ☎ *07/378–3131.* ⊡ *$12.50.* ☉ *Spring–fall, daily 8:30–4:30; winter, daily 8:30–4.*

Dining and Lodging

$$$ ✕ **Maori Hangis.** Tamaki Tours' (☎ 07/346–2823) hangi takes place at a Maori village *Te Tawa Ngahere Pa.* A coach picks you up at your hotel, and on the way to the village you get briefed on Maori protocol. Once there, you are formally welcomed and get to see the hangi being raised before consuming its contents. The cost, including pickup, is $52. Hangis at the **Sheraton** (☎ 07/349 5200, $49) and the **Lake Plaza** (☎ 07/348–1174, $43) have long-standing reputations for serving authentic-tasting food and having good concerts. At the Lake Plaza you can watch the food being lifted out of the hangi—usually an hour before the food is served, but call ahead to confirm.

$$$ ✕ **Poppy's Villa Restaurant.** This florid restaurant is Rotorua's big-occasion spot, yet prices are relatively moderate. First courses on the contemporary menu include mussels poached in an Italian-style tomato and basil sauce, and sweetbreads in wine and tarragon sauce served with walnut brioche. Baby lamb rack with a rosemary glaze and fresh salmon with a herbed cream sauce are among the mains. Vegetarians are accommodated with a couple of imaginative dishes. ⊠ *4 Marguerita St., Rotorua,* ☎ *07/347–1700. AE, DC, MC, V. No lunch.*

$$$ ✕ **You and Me.** Kaname Yamamato is one of the most creative chefs not just in Rotorua, but in the whole of New Zealand. Japanese-born and French-trained, he combines both culinary disciplines (and others) with dishes like carpaccio of cervena (venison) with garlic and *shiso* (a Japanese herb) vinaigrette, lamb fillet filled with roasted cashews and sage, served with ginger wine and roasted sesame seeds, and Madras curry scallops with chi-won (fresh Chinese egg-) noodles. This is the only restaurant in Rotorua that can be said to have achieved a notable culinary style. ⊠ *31 Pukuatua St., Rotorua,* ☎ *07/347–6178. AE, DC, MC, V. BYOB. Closed Sun. and Mon. No lunch.*

$$–$$$ ✕ **Copper Crioli.** Cajun food in a town where the ground steams? Seems logical. This kinky eatery is worth visiting just for the decor. A turn-of-the-century bank teller's cage takes pride of place, and the espresso machine is in the center of the room, dramatically plumbed from above with antique copper piping. The food's seriously Cajun, with jambalaya, gumbo, spicy chicken marinated in Coca Cola(!) with piri piri peppers, blackened chicken Rochambeau (filled with brie and pecans), even a Louisiana-style mud cake. ⊠ *1151 Arawa St.,* ☎ *07/348–1333. AE, DC, MC, V.*

$$ ✕ **Zanelli's Italian Cuisine.** Rotorua's favorite Italian restaurant offers a predictable range of dishes—spaghetti Bolognese, lasagna, cannelloni, and fettuccine with various sauces. The food is dated but well flavored, and the service is efficient. The decor—walls lined with split cane, a stone-tile floor, Formica tables—and up-tempo Italian music create a slightly hectic atmosphere. ⊠ *23 Amohia St., Rotorua,* ☎ *07/348–4908. DC, MC, V. Closed Sun. No lunch.*

$ ✕ **The Fat Dog Café and Bar.** The eclectic but homely decorating style attracts young, old, and everyone in-between. Fish tanks, lots of oak, and even a few lounges give it atmosphere, and the food's cheap and cheerful. Think pies—fish, lamb, chicken, beef, or whatever takes the kitchen's fancy. Lasagna and Thai curry are local favorites, and there's a large range of salads. Oh—and the cakes are legendary. ⊠ *69 Arawa St.,* ☎ *07/347–7586. AE, DC, MC, V.*

$$$$ ▥ **Muriaroha Lodge.** Although it lacks trout streams and lake views, when it comes to style, facilities, food, and comfort, this handsome lodge on the outskirts of Rotorua evokes the finest traditions of the luxury sporting lodge—at a much lower rate. Guest rooms are paired in bungalows separate from the main building; to ensure privacy, adjoining rooms are not assigned when one of a pair is occupied. The rooms, gardens, lounge, and dining room all have an English country-house flavor. For the duration of your stay, you are extended complimentary membership at the Arikikapaka Golf Course, just across the road. ⊠ *411 Old Taupo Rd.,* ☎ *07/346–1220,* ℻ *07/346–1338. 8 rooms with bath. Restaurant, pool, bar. AE, DC, MC, V.*

$$$$ ▥ **Solitaire Lodge.** It would be difficult to imagine a finer backdrop than the lakes, forests, and volcanoes that surround this plush retreat. Set high on a peninsula that juts out into Lake Tarawera, the lodge has been designed as a sophisticated hideaway where a few guests at a time can enjoy the scenery in a relaxed, informal atmosphere. All suites are luxuriously equipped, though the bathrooms in the junior suites are modest in size. The best room is the more expensive Tarawera Suite, which has panoramic views. The surroundings are perfect for hiking, boating, and fishing, and the lodge has boats and fishing gear. Smoking is not permitted indoors. Rates include all meals. ⊠ *Ronald Rd., Lake Tarawera,* ☎ *07/362–8208,* ℻ *07/362–8445. 10 rooms with bath. Restaurant, bar, spa, boating, fishing. AE, DC, MC, V.*

$$ ▥ **Cedar Lodge Motel.** These spacious, modern two-story units, about a half mile from the city center, are a good value, especially for families. All have a kitchen and lounge room on the lower floor, a bedroom on the mezzanine floor above, and at least one queen-size and one single bed, while some have a queen-size bed and three singles. Every unit has its own spa pool in the private courtyard at the back. Gray-flecked carpet, smoked-glass tables, and recessed lighting are clean and contemporary. Request a room at the back, away from Fenton Street. ⊠ *296 Fenton St.,* ☎ *07/349–0300,* ℻ *07/349–1115. 15 rooms with shower. Coin laundry. AE, DC, MC, V.*

$$ ▥ **Princes Gate Hotel.** Across the road from the Government Gardens, this ornate timber hotel was built in 1897 on the Coromandel Peninsula. It was brought here in 1917, and efforts have been made to re-create a turn-of-the-century feeling. Rooms are large and comfortable, without the dowdy look they once had. The motel rooms, in a separate wing, are suites with kitchens—good for families. ⊠ *1 Arawa St.,* ☎ *07/348–1179,* ℻ *07/348–6215. 28 hotel rooms, 12 motel units. 2 restaurants, bar, hot tub, mineral baths, tennis court. AE, DC, MC, V.*

$ ▣ **Eaton Hall.** This well-kept, friendly B&B has an outstanding location one street from the heart of Rotorua. Guest rooms are homey and comfortable, maintained to a standard well above that in most guest houses. All rooms have a washbasin, and Room 4, a twin-bedded room with its own shower, is available at no extra charge. A two-course dinner with fresh garden produce is available upon request at an additional charge. ⊠ *39 Hinemaru St.,* ☎ *07/347–0366,* ☏ *07/348–6287. 8 rooms share 2 baths. Hot tub. BP. AE, DC, MC, V.*

Outdoor Activities and Sports

FISHING

The lakes of the Rotorua and Taupo region are some of the few places where tales of the "big one" can actually be believed. If you want to keep the trout of a lifetime from becoming just another fish story, it pays to have a boat with some expert advice on board. Expect to pay about $65 per hour for a fishing guide and a 20-ft cruiser that will take up to six passengers. The minimum charter period is two hours, and fishing gear and bait are included in the price. A one-day fishing license costs $11 per person and is available on board the boat. In Rotorua fishing operators include **Clark Gregor** (☎ 07/347–1730), **Bryan Colman** (☎ 07/348–7766), and **Ray Dodunski** (☎ 07/349–2555). Highly recommended is *Clear Water Pride* (☎ 07/362–8590), a luxury 38-ft launch that operates fishing trips on Lake Tarawera. The cost for up to seven passengers is $95 per hour, including all gear and light refreshments. For 8 to 15 passengers, the cost is $140 per hour and a hostess is provided. *See* Chapter 6 for in-depth fishing information.

RAFTING

The center of North Island has a number of rivers with Grade-3 to Grade-5 rapids that make excellent white-water rafting. For scenic beauty, the Rangitaiki River is recommended. For experienced rafters who want a challenge, the Wairoa River has exhilarating Grade-5 rapids. The climax of a rafting trip on the Kaituna River is the drop over a 21-ft waterfall, among the highest to be rafted by a commercial operator anywhere. With **Kaituna Cascades** (☎ 07/357–5032), transportation, wet suits, and meals are provided. The price of a one-day trip starts at $58 per person, depending on the river. Different rivers are open at different times of year, depending on water levels. Another recommended operator is **River Rats** (⊠ Box 601, ☎ 07/347–6049), which rafts the Kaituna ($59) and the gentler Rangitaiki rivers ($89).

Taupo

⑬   *82 km (51 mi) south of Rotorua, 150 km (94 mi) northwest of Napier, 335 km (210 mi) west of Gisborne.*

The town of Taupo is the base for Lake Taupo, the largest lake in New Zealand. You can take your pick here from a wide range of water sports—sailing, cruising, waterskiing, swimming, but most of all, fishing: Taupo is the rainbow trout capital of the universe. The average Taupo trout weighs in around 4 pounds, and the lake is open year-round. For nonanglers, several sailboats, modern catamarans, and vintage riverboats have sightseeing trips. There are restaurants and lodging in Taupo, if you plan to stay in the area. Otherwise, from Taupo at the top of the lake the drive back to Rotorua takes about 90 minutes.

⑭   At **Huka Falls,** the Waikato River thunders through a narrow chasm and over a 35-ft rock ledge before it pours into Lake Taupo. The view from the footbridge is superb. Turn off to the left just after the Wairakei power station.

Craters of the Moon are just what you'd expect from a place with that name—except that the craters are filled with boiling, bubbling water. The area gets extremely steamy and is worth the stop if you've missed or avoided the commercially run thermal parks in Rotorua. Entrance is by donation, and the craters are up Karapiti Road, across from the road from the Huka Falls turnoffs on Highway 5.

⑮ From the junction of Routes 1 and 5, the **Wairakei Geothermal Project** is visible in the distance, wreathed in swirling clouds of steam. The steam is tapped through underground shafts to drive generators that provide about 5% of New Zealand's electric power. There are no guided tours of the plant, but the Geothermal Information Centre close to the highway has a display on the process by which steam is converted into electricity. ⊠ *State Hwy. 1,* ☎ *07/374–8216.* ⊡ *Free.* ☉ *Daily 9–noon and 1–4.*

Dining and Lodging

$$–$$$ ✕ **Walnut Keep.** Award-winning chef Glen Sando is regarded nationwide as Taupo's best. He's got some great ideas, like filling Indian-style *samosas* with scallops or spiking an onion puree with wasabi and using it as a base for pink-cooked lamb. Locals rave about the duck—a half bird, roasted after being marinated in honey and cumin. The clubby atmosphere encourages leisurely dining, and the port list makes lingering no hardship. ⊠ *77 Spa Rd.,* ☎ *07/378–30777. AE, DC, MC, V. No lunch.*

$ ✕ **The Replete Food Company.** The food is served at the counter from display cabinets, and there's no wine license, but Replete's trump card is its management team—it's owned by cookbook author Greg Heffernan, formerly executive chef at plush Huka Lodge down the road. The regularly changing menu might include a roast vegetable Cajun pizza, smoked fish pie with green salad, tarakihi (a local fish) with dill sauce in phyllo pastry, or a superhearty seafood gumbo. In town for a while? Ask about the cooking classes. ⊠ *45 Heu Heu St.,* ☎ *07/377–3011. AE, DC, MC, V.*

$$$$ ✕▥ **Huka Lodge.** Buried in parklike grounds at the edge of the frisky
★ Waikato River, this superb lodge is the standard by which New Zealand's other sporting lodges are judged. The large, lavish guest rooms, decorated in muted grays and whites, are arranged in blocks of two or three. All have sliding glass doors that open to a view across lawns to the river. In the interest of tranquillity, guest rooms are not equipped with telephones, televisions, or radios. The five-course formal dinners are gourmet affairs served at a communal dining table. The wine list is a showcase of the very best New Zealand has to offer—its stores are housed in a wine cellar with more than 50,000 bottles of wine from New Zealand and around the world. Breakfasts are superb. Rates include breakfast and dinner. ⊠ *Huka Falls Rd., Box 95, Taupo,* ☎ *07/378–5791,* ℻ *07/378–0427. 17 rooms with bath. Restaurant, bar, spa, tennis court, fishing. AE, DC, MC, V.*

$$$ ▥ **Cascades Motor Lodge.** Set on the shores of Lake Taupo, these at-
★ tractive brick-and-timber rooms are large, comfortable, and furnished and decorated in a smart contemporary style. The two-story "luxury" apartments, which sleep up to seven, have a lounge room, bedroom, kitchen, and dining room on the ground floor in an open-plan design, glass doors leading to a large patio, and a second bedroom and bathroom on the upper floor. Studio rooms have one bedroom. All rooms are equipped with a jet bath. Room 1 is closest to the lake and a small beach. ⊠ *Lake Terr.,* ☎ *07/378–3774,* ℻ *07/378–0372. 22 rooms with bath. Pool. AE, DC, MC, V.*

Outdoor Activities and Sports

FISHING

For great fishing in the Taupo area, contact **Richard Staines** (☎ 07/ 378–2736) or **Punch Wilson** (☎ 07/378–5596). At the other end of the scale, a luxury cruiser on Lake Taupo costs about $150 per hour; for more information, contact **Chris Jolly Boats** (✉ Box 1020, Taupo, ☎ 07/378–0623). *See* Chapter 6 for in-depth fishing information.

RAFTING

The Grade-5 Wairoa and Mohaka rivers are accessible from Taupo, as are the Rangitaiki and Tongariro. With **Rapid Descents** (☎ 07/ 377–0419), transportation, wet suits, and meals are provided. The price of a one-day trip is about $75 per person. Different rivers are open at different times of year, depending on water levels.

Tongariro National Park

⑯ *110 km (69 mi) southwest of Taupo.*

Tongariro is the country's first national park, established on sacred land donated by a Maori chief. Southwest of Lake Taupo, the park is dominated by three active volcanic peaks: Tongariro, Ngauruhoe, and Ruapehu, which at 9,175 ft is the highest North Island mountain. Ruapehu last erupted in 1996, spewing forth ash and showers of rocks.

Tongariro's spectacular combination of dense rimu pine forests, crater lakes, barren lava fields, and bird life makes it the most impressive and popular of the island's national parks. It has numerous walking trails, from the 40-minute Ridge Track to the Mt. Tongariro Traverse, which crosses the mountain from one side to the other and is one of the finest walks in the country. The longest hike in the park is the four-day Round the Mountain Track. Wherever you hike, be prepared for rapidly changing weather conditions with warm and waterproof clothing. The Whakapapa ski area, on the north side of Mt. Ruapehu, is New Zealand's largest, with about a 2,400-ft vertical drop. On the south side of the mountain, Turoa is a second ski area, which generally has a longer ski season than Whakapapa's, from June through October.

Highway 1 skirts the east side of the park, but the easiest access is from Highway 47, on the north side. For more information, contact the Department of Conservation Field Centre at Whakapapa Village off Highway 47 (✉ Whakapapa Visitor Centre, Private Bag, Mt. Ruapehu, ☎ 07/892–3729). Accommodations in the village range from the recently refurbished **Grand Chateau Hotel** (✉ Mt. Ruapehu, ☎ 07/ 892–3809), in the $$$$ category, to cabins and campsites in motor camps. The park has nine trailside huts for hikers.

Just east of Tongariro National Park, **Kaimanawa Forest Park** is a less visited wilderness. Trails aren't as frequently marked here, so be sure to pick up a Department of Conservation map at the Taupo Information Centre (✉ Tongariro St.). The park has single-day hikes as well as two- to five-day tramps between overnight huts. However far you go, be prepared for rapidly changing weather conditions by taking waterproof and warm clothing at all times of the year. And be aware that in late March and April the Kaimanawa Ranges are particularly popular with hunters of sika deer. At other times, check hunting activities in the area with the Department of Conservation before setting out.

OFF THE
BEATEN PATH
★

Gordon Collier is one of New Zealand's most visible garden diplomats. Having lectured extensively domestically and overseas, he has helped to develop a true New Zealand garden style. His **Titoki Point Garden and**

Nursery—carved out of the rolling 5,000-acre Wakarua Sheep Station between Lake Taupo and Wellington—is a highly successful marriage of native New Zealand flora with plants collected from around the world. One highlight is what Collier and his wife, Annette, refer to as the damp garden, at the bottom of a gully. One of the best of its kind in the country, it is home to giant gunnera, hosta, bergenia, trillium, native ferns, and primula. Titoki Point also has a towering stand of 70-year-old California redwoods and a lovely avenue of weeping Japanese maples. All of this looks out on the feisty, nearby Mt. Ruapehu volcano. ⊠ *R.D. 1, Bells Junction, 95 km (59 mi) south of bottom of Lake Taupo, 85 km (53 mi) north of State Hwy. 3 in Bulls,* ☎ *06/388–0085.* ☉ *Oct.–Mar. (subject to change), daily 10–4.*

Rotorua, Waitomo Caves, Lake Taupo A to Z

Arriving and Departing

BY BUS

InterCity (☎ 09/358–4085) has four buses daily between Auckland and Rotorua. Buses also run daily between Auckland and Waitomo Caves and between Waitomo Caves and Rotorua. **Newmans** (☎ 09/309–9738) operates twice daily on the Auckland–Rotorua route.

BY CAR

Waitomo Caves and Rotorua are each three hours from Auckland. Take Highway 1 south, following signs to Hamilton, where you will turn south onto Highway 3. For Rotorua, follow Highway 1 south past Hamilton and Cambridge to Tirau, where Highway 5 breaks off to Rotorua. Taupo is four hours from Auckland (take Highway 1 the whole way) and 70 minutes from Rotorua.

BY PLANE

Air New Zealand (☎ 07/346–1001) and **Ansett New Zealand** (☎ 07/347–0146) have daily flights that link Rotorua with Auckland and Wellington, with further connections throughout New Zealand. Rotorua Airport is about 10 km (6 mi) from the city center. Taxi fare to the city is $18.

Contacts and Resources

EMERGENCIES

Dial 111 for **fire, police, and ambulance** services.

GUIDED TOURS

Gray Line (☎ 09/377–0904) has day trips from Auckland to Waitomo ($136 round-trip), plus Auckland–Waitomo–Rotorua links ($144) and Auckland–Rotorua ($118 round-trip).

Mount Tarawera 4WD Tours has a sensational half-day, four-wheel-drive trip to the edge of the Mt. Tarawera crater. Departures are available at 8:30 and 1:30. ⊠ *Box 5157, Rotorua,* ☎ *07/357–4026.* ☞ *$65.*

Tamaki Tours' Volcanic Wilderness Safari is a two-day trip that combines horse trekking in the Rainbow Mountain–Mt. Tarawera area, rafting on the Rangitaiki River, and an introduction to traditional Maori legends and lifestyle. Tours run between November and February. The company is a Maori-owned and -operated venture. ⊠ *Box 1492, Rotorua,* ☎ *07/346–2823.* ☞ *$320.*

Tarawera Helicopters (☎ 07/348–1223) offers a choice of scenic flights, from a short flight over the city and Whakarewarewa Thermal Reserve ($50 per person) to a longer flight over crater lakes and the Waimangu Valley, with a landing on top of Mt. Tarawera ($325 per person).

The **Waimangu Round Trip** is probably the most complete tour of Rotorua. It includes an easy 5-km (3-mi) hike through the Waimangu Thermal Valley to Lake Rotomahana, where a cruiser takes you past steaming cliffs to the narrow isthmus that divides the lake from Lake Tarawera. After crossing the lake on a second cruiser, the tour visits a village that was buried by a volcanic eruption and ends with a dip in the Polynesian Pools in Rotorua. Lunch is included. ⊠ *Reserve at Rotorua Visitor Information Centre,* ☎ *07/347–1199.* 🎫 *$130.*

The **MV** *Wairaka* (☎ 07/374–8338) is a vintage riverboat that cruises from Taupo to Huka Falls daily at 10 and 2. The two-hour cruise costs $18. A barbecue cruise departs at 12:30 and costs $35.

VISITOR INFORMATION

Taupo Visitor Information Centre. ⊠ *13 Tongariro St., Taupo,* ☎ *07/ 378–9000.* ◷ *Daily 8:30–5.*

Tourism Rotorua Visitor Information Centre. In addition to an information office, this modern complex houses a café, a film-processing service, a map shop operated by the Department of Conservation, and a lost-luggage facility. It is also Rotorua's main tour bus stop. ⊠ *67 Fenton St., Rotorua,* ☎ *07/348–5179.* ◷ *Daily 8–5:30.*

Waitomo Caves Visitor Information Centre. ⊠ *Waitomo Museum of Caves,* ☎ *07/878–7640.* ◷ *Daily 9–5:30.*

NAPIER AND HAWKE'S BAY

New Zealand prides itself on natural wonders. By that way of thinking, Napier is an exception. This city of 50,000, situated about two-thirds of the way down the east coast of North Island, is best known for its architecture. After an earthquake devastated Napier in 1931, citizens rebuilt it in the fashionable Art Deco style of the day. Its well-kept uniformity of style makes it a pleasant and comfortable sort of period piece. The mild climate and beaches of Hawke Bay make this a popular vacation area for New Zealanders. (*Hawke* Bay is the body of water; *Hawke's* Bay is the region.) And then there is the wine—the region produces some of New Zealand's best.

Napier

150 km (94 mi) southeast of Taupo, 345 km (215 mi) northeast of Wellington.

The focus of any visit to Napier is its Art Deco buildings—many of which lie between Emerson, Herchell, Dalton, and Browning streets—and the city is a pleasure to tour on foot. Art Deco was born at the 1925 International Exposition of Modern Decorative and Industrial Arts in Paris. Its influences around the Western world are broad: from skyscrapers and diners to toasters and jewelry. The style is bold and geometrical, often using stainless steel to represent the sleekness of the machine age as it was seen in the 1920s, 1930s, and beyond. In some cases, Napier's Art Deco heritage has been spoiled by the addition of garish advertising or unsympathetic alterations to shop fronts. The elements that remain are often found above the ground floor, so any walk will involve looking up frequently. After stretching your legs in the morning, relax on a brief wine-tasting tour for the rest of the day. Another point of interest in Hawke's Bay is the gannet colony at Cape Kidnapper—which you can see only between October and March.

❶ One of Napier's notable buildings is the **ASB Bank,** at the corner of Hastings and Emerson streets. The Maori theme on the lintels above the main entrance is echoed in the ceiling inside the building.

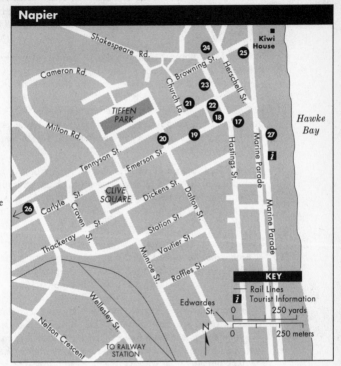

18 The **Criterion Hotel** (⊠ Hastings St.) is typical of the Spanish Mission style, which Napier took on due to its success in Santa Barbara, California, where an earthquake had similarly wreaked havoc just a few **19** years before the New Zealand catastrophe. Along **Emerson Street** and its pedestrian mall, **Hannahs,** the **Bowman's Building, McGruers,** and the **Hawke's Bay Chambers** are among the city's finest Art Deco examples.

20 **Dalton Street** has its treasures as well. South of the intersection with Emerson Street, the pink **Countrywide Bank Building,** with its balcony, is one of Napier's masterpieces. **Hildebrand's,** at Tennyson Street, has an excellent frieze, which is best viewed from across Dalton. Hildebrand was a German who migrated to New Zealand—hence the German flag at one end, the New Zealand at the other, and the wavy lines in the middle to symbolize the sea passage between the two countries.

21 The **Daily Telegraph Building** (⊠ Tennyson St. and Church La.) is another Napier classic. If you can turn back the clock in your mind and **22** imagine the city littered with heaps of rubble, you would see the **Market Reserve Building** (⊠ Tennyson and Hastings Sts.) as the first to rise following the earthquake. You would have seen Hartson's Music Shop survive the quake had you lived through it, and you may have lived to **23** see it turn into **Hartson's Bar** (⊠ Hastings St. between Browning and Tennyson Sts.), the facade of which has changed little since its change in ownership replaced songs with suds.

24 The **Ministry of Works** (⊠ Browning St.), with its decorative lighthouse pillar at the front, takes on the almost Gothic menace that Art Deco architecture sometimes has (like New York's Chrysler Building).

25 Using newspaper reports, photographs, and audiovisuals, the **Hawke's Bay Museum** re-creates the suffering caused by the earthquake. It also houses a unique display of artifacts of the Ngati Kahungunu Maori people of the east coast. ⊠ *65 Marine Parade,* ☎ *06/835–9668.* 🎫 *$4.* ⊘ *Daily 10–4:30.*

㉖ Stop in for a natural counterpoint to the city's architecture at the **Botanical Gardens,** about 1½ km (about 1 mi) from Clive Square. Here you can stroll across lawns, among flower beds, over ornamental bridges, and under shady arbors. Follow Carlyle Street southwest to Chaucer Road. Turn right and continue to Napier Terrace, where the entrance to the gardens is to the left. In the adjacent graveyard, there are some 19th-century headstones. ⊠ *Napier Terr.* 🎫 *Free.* ⊘ *Daily dawn–dusk.*

☾ **㉗** **Hawkes Bay Aquarium** displays sharks, rays, tropical fish, saltwater crocodiles, turtles, and piranha in a drum-shape building on the waterfront. (At press time, the aquarium was to be closed for a period of renovation—phone ahead to see that it's open.) ⊠ *Marine Parade, Napier,* ☎ *06/834–1404.* 🎫 *$9.* ⊘ *Daily 9–5.*

Dining and Lodging

$$$ ✕ **Bayswater Bistro.** Despite this bay-side restaurant's changes in own-
★ ership, it holds onto its status as one of Napier's finest eateries with dishes like green-shell mussels served in a gewürztraminer-and-chive sauce, Waikanae crab paired with a relish of pickled vegetables, and lamb rump marinated, roasted medium-rare, and served with hummus (chick-pea and sesame puree), pickled chilies, and grilled aubergine. The voguish white interior has a faintly art deco feeling and large doors that open to a sparkling sea view. In warm weather request a table on the deck outside, or at least a table at the window. The restaurant can be hard to spot at night—take Marine Parade out of the city center, and it's about 1 km (½ mi) north of the port just after the playground. ⊠ *Harding Rd., Napier,* ☎ *06/835–8517. AE, DC, MC, V.*

$$$ ✕ **Pierre sur le quai.** This smart, modern bistro is the backdrop for
★ Pierre Vuilleumier's robust French provincial cooking. Hawke's Bay scampi (miniature lobsters) are panfried with fresh herbs, tomato, and cognac; green-shell mussels are poached in an onion, leek, and garlic broth. Main courses include beef topped with liver mousse and red wine sauce and—surprisingly—the Middle Eastern classic, couscous, made with chicken and wild goat. This waterfront restaurant may take some finding, but make the effort. ⊠ *62 W. Quay, Ahuriri,* ☎ *06/834–0189. AE, DC, MC, V.*

$$–$$$ ✕ **Casa-Gardini.** Blood-red walls and plush carpet keep you visually warm in this popular Napier eatery. In summer dine on the roof garden and enjoy the view. The menu leans to the Mediterranean, with dishes like a Spanish omelet, chicken breast filled with *bocconcini* on a polenta cake, and lamb rump with rosemary and garlic. Tapas (Spanish-style nibbles) are available from 4:30 PM. ⊠ *Upper Level, 77 Dalton St.,* ☎ *06/835–7788. AE, DC, MC, V. No lunch.*

$$ ✕ **Restaurant Indonesia.** Local wine maker Alan Limmer, who makes
★ the world-beating Stonecroft gewürztraminer (voted best in the show in London 1997 against competitors from Germany and Alsace), holds an annual gewürztraminer dinner at this tiny slice of Indonesia in the Bay. The food is Dutch-Indonesian, and the rijsttafel, which consists of 13 sampling dishes, is the best way to try it. Other favorites: marinated prawn satay, and *babi panggang*—grilled pork loin with a sweet-and-sour sauce based on onions, pineapple, and lemon juice. ⊠ *409 Marine Parade,* ☎ *06/835–8303. AE, DC, MC, V.*

$$ ✕🖭 **Mon Logis Hôtel Privé.** The French owner of this seafront house
★ has modeled his accommodations on the *logis* of his homeland—a refined version of a traditional bed-and-breakfast. Rooms are large and

prettily decorated in a Continental style with eiderdowns and feather pillows. Although they lack the sea view, the two rooms at the back of the house are freer from the noise of the nearby port: Buttes Chaumont has an en-suite bathroom, while Paris's bathroom is off the hall. What most sets this place apart from the standard B&B is the food. In the morning you'll have complimentary coffee and a basket of freshly baked French breads delivered to your room. A four-course dinner, including wine, is available by arrangement for $45. Children are not accommodated. ⊠ *415 Marine Parade, Napier,* ☎ *06/835–2125,* FAX *06/435–2125. 4 rooms with bath. BP. AE, DC, MC, V.*

$$$ 🏨 **The County Hotel.** Built in 1909 as the headquarters of the Hawke's Bay County Council, this is one of the few buildings that survived the 1931 earthquake that all but leveled Napier. You can't help but feel with its refurbishment that you're stepping back in time—high ceilings, brass fittings, wood paneling, and Art Deco–style lights in the rooms are betrayed only by TVs and fax and modem plugs. Each room has a white-tile bathroom with shower, some have a claw-foot tub as well. The original hotel's doors are of native kauri wood, and there are a magnificent rimu stairway and a clubby library off the atrium. As of mid-1998, the hotel's new ownership is planning to add air-conditioning to the bedrooms. ⊠ *12 Browning St., Napier,* ☎ *06/835–7800,* FAX *06/835–7797. 8 rooms with shower, 2 rooms with shower and bath. Restaurant, bar. AE, DC, MC, V.*

$$ 🏨 **Anleigh Heights.** Built in 1900 as a town house for a wealthy sheep rancher, this sprawling hilltop guest house is one of Napier's landmark buildings and a fine example of the city's Victorian timber architecture. Although the patrician character of the house has not been fully translated to the interior, the owners are charming and attentive hosts. The Colenso Suite is recommended. Smoking is not allowed in the house. ⊠ *115 Chaucer Rd., North Napier,* ☎ FAX *06/835–1188. 8 rooms, 5 with bath, 3 with shower. BP. AE, DC, MC, V.*

$$ 🏨 **Edgewater Motor Lodge.** These motel rooms are about average in size, facilities, character, and appearance, but they have a central location and sea views. Rooms on the upper level have balconies, and there are several room styles to suit couples or families. ⊠ *359 Marine Parade, Napier,* ☎ *06/835–1148,* FAX *06/835–6600. 20 rooms with shower. Pool, hot tub, coin laundry. AE, DC, MC, V.*

Hawke's Bay

The natural world provides as vital an experience of Hawke's Bay as the human factor does. The gannet colony on the coast southeast of the city is a beautiful and fascinating spot. Then there is the wine—Napier's surrounding countryside grows some of New Zealand's most highly esteemed grapes, reds being of particular note.

28 **Esk Valley Estate Winery** is terraced on a north-facing hillside, ensuring it full sun and a cherished location for grape growing. Esk Valley produces chardonnay, sauvignon blanc, chenin blanc, merlot, and several variations on the cabernet sauvignon–merlot–cabernet franc–malbec theme, including a rare and expensive red simply called The Terraces. Look for the Reserve version of any varietal to find out what the wine maker has done with the best grapes from given years. The winery is 12 km (8 mi) north of Napier, just north of the town of Bay View before Highways 2 and 5 split. ⊠ *Main Rd., Bay View, Napier,* ☎ *06/836–6411.* ☉ *Nov.–Mar., daily 9–5:30; Apr.–Oct., daily 9:45–5; tour by appointment.*

29 **Linden Estate** is next to a historic church, which manages to look thoroughly at home surrounded by vines. Wine maker Nick Chan makes reliably good sauvignon blanc, chardonnay, and cabernet-merlot blends, all of which have achieved some medal success. His Linden Reserve Chardonnay is served to first-class Air New Zealand passengers. ⊠ *SH5, Napier-Taupo Hwy., Napier,* ☎ *06/836–6806.* ⊘ *Daily 9–5.*

③⓪ The **Mission Vineyard** at Taradale is the oldest in New Zealand, established by Catholic Marist brothers in the late 1850s after an earlier vineyard farther north at Poverty Bay was abandoned. Legend has it that in 1852 one of the brothers made a barrel of sacramental wine and shipped it to Napier; the seamen broached the cargo, drank the wine, and filled the empty cask with seawater. The Jewelstone label is reserved for the top wines, while the Mission Estate label is used for a wide range of well-made varietals including sauvignon blanc, Riesling, pinot gris, and cabernet blends. To reach the vineyard, leave Napier by Kennedy Road, heading southwest from the city center toward Taradale. Just past Anderson Park, turn right into Avenue Road and continue to its end at Church Road. ⊠ *Church Rd., Taradale,* ☎ *06/844–2259.* ⊘ *Mon.–Sat. 8:30–5:30, Sun. 11–4.*

③① The long-established **McDonald Winery** benefited from an injection of capital and expertise when the Montana wine-making group bought it in 1989 in an effort to add a top chardonnay and cabernet sauvignon to its holdings. The resulting Church Road Chardonnay and Cabernet Sauvignon have received rave reviews, particularly the Reserve versions. Free tours run weekdays at 11 and 2, weekends at 11, 1, 2, and 3. ⊠ *150 Church Rd., Taradale,* ☎ *06/844–2053.* ⊘ *Daily 9–5.*

③② **Brookfields Winery** is one of the most attractive wineries in the area, befitting its status as a premier producer. The Reserve Chardonnay and Pinot Gris are usually outstanding, but the showpiece is the gold-label cabernet merlot, with its intense fruit and assertive oak. The winery restaurant (☞ Dining and Lodging, *below*) is superb. From Napier take Marine Parade toward Hastings and turn right on Awatoto Road. Follow it to Brookfields Road and turn left; signs will point to the winery. ⊠ *Brookfields Rd., Meeanee,* ☎ *06/834–4615.* ⊘ *Daily 11–4.*

③③ **Te Mata Estate** is quite simply one of New Zealand's finest wineries, its interesting architectural forms rising out of ground first planted with grapes in the 1890s. Te Mata's Coleraine Cabernet Merlot subtly balances dark fruit and oak flavors and is regarded as the archetypal Hawke's Bay red. Elston Chardonnay and Cape Crest Sauvignon Blanc show similar restraint and balance. From Napier head south on Marine Parade through Clive and turn left at the Mingatere Tree School. Signs from there will lead you to Te Mata Road and the estate. ⊠ *Te Mata Rd., Box 8335, Havelock North,* ☎ *06/877–4399.* ⊘ *Weekdays 9–5, Sat. 10–5, Sun. 11–4; tour Christmas holidays–Jan., daily at 10:30.*

★ **③④** **Cape Kidnappers** was named by Captain James Cook after local Maori tried to kidnap the servant of Cook's Tahitian interpreter. The cape is the site of a large **gannet colony.** The gannet is a large white seabird with black-tipped flight feathers, a golden crown, and wings that can reach a span of 6 ft. When the birds find a shoal of fish, they fold their wings and plunge straight into the sea at tremendous speed. Their migratory pattern ranges from western Australia to the Chatham Islands, about 800 km (500 mi) east of Christchurch, but they generally nest only on remote islands. The colony at Cape Kidnappers is believed to be the only mainland gannet sanctuary in existence. Between October and March, about 15,000 gannets build their nests here, hatch their young, and prepare them for their long migratory flight.

You can walk to the sanctuary along the beach from Clifton, which is about 24 km (15 mi) south of Napier, but not at high tide. The 8-km

(5-mi) walk must begin no earlier than three hours after the high tide mark, and the return journey must begin no later than four hours before the next high tide. Tidal information is available at Clifton. A rest hut with refreshments is available near the colony.

Because of these tidal restrictions, one easy way to get to the colony is to take a **Gannet Beach Adventures** (☎ 06/875–0898) tractor-trailer, which is pulled along the beach starting Clifton Reserve, Clifton Beach. Tractors depart approximately two hours before low tide, and the trip ($18) takes 4–4½ hours. If tides prevent the trip along the beach, the only other access is across private farmland. **Gannet Safaris** (☎ 06/875–0888) runs a four-wheel-drive bus to Cape Kidnappers from Summerlee Station, just past Te Awanga. A minimum of four is required for this tour ($38 each).

③⑤ **Hastings** is Napier's twin city in Hawke's Bay, and it is well worth a visit if you have an extra day in the area. Some of Hawke's Bay's wineries are actually easier to reach if you are based in Hastings, particularly **Vidals Estate Winery** (✉ 913 St. Aubyn St. E, Hastings, ☎ 06/876–8105), a sister winery of Esk Valley Estate that consistently produces some of New Zealand's finest reds, and **Huthlee Estate Winery** (✉ 84 Montana Rd., Bridge Pa, ☎ FAX 06/879–6234).

Stonecroft is best known for a rare and expensive syrah, but Dr. Alan Limmer also produces startlingly good gewürztraminer and top-class chardonnay and sauvignon blanc. The vineyard's stony soil reflects the rays of the sun onto the ripening grapes, which is one of the reasons Alan has had such success with syrah—most parts of the country are too cool for it to ripen. ✉ Mere Rd., Hastings, ☎ 06/879–9610. ☺ Sat. 11–5, Sun. 11–4.

If you are traveling with children, spend a couple of hours at **Fantasyland** (✉ Grove Rd., ☎ 06/876–9856). Admission is $3, and it's open 9–5. Disney World it is not, but you'll please the kids with miniature golf, go-cart riding, and a variety of play equipment. The 30-acre park is a fine place for a picnic lunch.

Dining and Lodging

$$$ ✗ **Piccolo's.** This bright and airy restaurant in a restored villa has rapidly gained a reputation as one of the best in the region. Nicky Smith runs the front of the house, while her partner, Tony, fronting the stoves, turns out dishes that have won a lot of favor with locals. Chicken breast is baked in a corn husk, lamb brains are turned into kebabs, and squid and octopus get together in the form of Asian-style dumplings. Sides include couscous, greens with Chinese oyster sauce, grilled vegetables, and braised courgettes (zucchini). The wine list is nicely focused. ✉ Nelson St. and Lyndon Rd., Hastings, ☎ 06/878–1188. AE, DC, MC, V. Licensed or BYOB. Closed Sun.–Mon. No lunch.

$$–$$$ ✗ **Corn Exchange.** Big and buzzy, this eatery once was a storehouse for local produce. A wood-fired pizza oven, moved here from Auckland's Cin Cin on Quay, dominates the kitchen. Beyond pizza, try the likes of oven-roasted lamb on a honeyed pumpkin cake or cervena venison with a bourbon-based reduction sauce. Choose local labels or wine from outside the region. ✉ 118 Maraekakohoe Rd., Hastings, ☎ 06/870–8333. AE, DC, MC, V.

$$ ✗ **Brookfields Winery Restaurant.** Run in cooperation with the winery, this pleasant spot offers a splendid selection of Joel Marquet's French- and Italian-inspired dishes that taste perfect alongside a glass of Brookfields wine. ✉ Brookfields Rd., Meeanee, ☎ 06/834–4615. AE, DC, MC, V. No lunch Mon.-Wed. Dinner by arrangement only.

✕ **Rose & Shamrock.** The developers of this Irish pub were so keen on authenticity, they sent their architect on a three-week tour of Ireland. The result is like a transplant from Dublin. Beers, wines, and spirits mix with good, honest pub fare like T-bone steak and a generous seafood platter. Hints of restaurant style creep in with dishes like crumbed chicken breasts with apricot sauce. ⊠ *Napier Rd., Havelock North,* ☎ *06/877–2999. AE, DC, MC, V.*

$$$$ ✕🗗 **Mangapapa Lodge.** The beautifully restored Mangapapa Lodge
★ was once the home of the Wattie family, which started a fruit-picking business that is now one of New Zealand's giants. Each room is in the style, and with the furniture, of a particular country—the Austrian room, for example, has a large four-poster bed decorated with Austrian folk art. Owners Guenter and Shirley Engels are wine and food enthusiasts, and dinners at the lodge are open to house guests and casual diners. Recent dishes have included a summer salad of Hawke's Bay smoked chicken with a Parmesan biscuit and Cajun-spiced Hawke's Bay lamb rump on polenta. ⊠ *466 Napier Rd., Havelock North,* ☎ *06/878– 3234,* 🗠 *06/878–1214. 9 rooms. AE, DC, MC, V. Jun.–Sept.*

$$$ 🗗 **Hawthorne Country Lodge.** In a former life Jeanette Kelly was the
★ Auckland-based publicist for Taupo's Huka Lodge, so she knows a thing or two about the hospitality business. She and husband Peter restored this charming house and planted its extensive gardens. A hearty breakfast featuring local produce is included in the tariff, and Jeanette—a competent cook as well as a friendly and relaxed hostess—will prepare other meals by arrangement. Dinners can also be arranged with local wine makers. ⊠ *420 State Hwy. 2, Hastings South,* ☎ *06/878–0035,* 🗠 *06/878–0035. 5 rooms. BP. AE, DC, MC, V.*

Napier and Hawke's Bay A to Z

Arriving and Departing

BY BUS
Newmans (☎ 09/309–9738) and **InterCity** (☎ 09/358–4085) both operate daily bus services between Napier and Auckland, Rotorua, and Wellington. Once in Napier you can book on either operation at the visitor information center.

BY CAR
The main route between Napier and the north is Highway 5. Driving time from Taupo is 2½ hours. Highway 2 is the main route heading south. Driving time to Wellington is five hours.

BY PLANE
Air New Zealand (☎ 06/835–3288) has several flights daily between Napier and Auckland, Wellington, and Christchurch.

BY TRAIN
Bay Express leaves Napier at 2:20 daily for Wellington, arriving in the capital at 7:45 PM. It leaves Wellington for Napier at 8 AM, arriving Napier at 1:20. If you are traveling to South Island, you will probably have to overnight in Wellington before joining the Cook Strait ferry. Bookings can be made for both the train and the ferry at Napier's visitor information center (⊠ Marine Parade, ☎ 06/834–1911).

Contacts and Resources

EMERGENCIES
Dial 111 for **fire, police, and ambulance** services.

GUIDED TOURS
The **Art Deco Trust** has an excellent and informative guided walking tour of Napier. The 2-km (1-mi) walk takes 2½ hours and includes slide and video presentations. Or take the Trust's self-guided Art Deco

Walk; booklets are available at its shop. ⊠ *Art Deco Shop, 163 Tennyson St.* ☞ *$7.* ☉ *Tour late Dec.–Feb., Wed. and weekends at 2.*

Bay Tours has a four-hour tour of area wineries. It offers a chance to sample some of the boutique wines unavailable to independent travelers. If you are traveling south by rail, the company has a tour that connects with the train to Wellington. ⊠ *Napier Visitor Information Centre, Marine Parade,* ☎ *06/843–6953.* ☞ *$30.* ☉ *Tour daily at 1.*

VISITOR INFORMATION

Napier Visitor Information Centre. ⊠ *Marine Parade, Napier,* ☎ *06/834–4161,* FAX *06/835–7219.* ☉ *Weekdays 8:30–5, weekends 9–5.*

GISBORNE AND EASTLAND

Traveling to Eastland takes you well away from the tourist track in North Island. For some people, that is reason enough to make the trip. Once here, you will find rugged coastline, accessible beaches, dense forests, gentle nature trails, and small, predominantly Maori communities. Eastland provides one of the closest links with the nation's earliest past. Kaiti Beach, near the city of Gisborne, is where the *waka* (long canoe) *Horouta* landed, and nearby Titirangi was named by the first Maori settlers in remembrance of their mountain in Hawaiki, their Polynesian island of origin. Kaiti Beach is where Captain Cook set foot in 1769—the first European landing in New Zealand.

Gisborne's warm climate and fertile soil make the region one of New Zealand's most successful wine areas. Often overshadowed by Hawke's Bay (and its formidable PR machine), Gisborne has 7,000 acres under vine, and it is the country's largest supplier of chardonnay grapes. It has in fact been dubbed the chardonnay capital of New Zealand, which makes that the variety to concentrate on if you go tasting.

Gisborne

🕉 *210 km (130 mi) northeast of Napier, 500 km (310 mi) southeast of Auckland.*

Gisborne is the easternmost city in New Zealand, and it is the first in the world to see the new day's sunrise. The Maori name for the Gisborne district is Tairawhiti (tye-ra-*fee*-tee)—the coast upon which the sun shines across the water. Although the city (population 30,000) is hardly large, you will need a day or so to get around town properly. Most of the historical sights and other attractions are too spread out to explore them all by foot, and you'll need a car to get into the spectacular countryside nearby.

The **Museum and Arts Centre,** with its Maori and Pakeha artifacts and an extensive photographic collection, provides a good introduction to the region's Maori and colonial history. It also has changing exhibits of local and national artists' work. ⊠ *18 Stout St.,* ☎ *06/867–3832.* ☞ *Free.* ☉ *Weekdays 10–4, weekends 1:30–4.*

Cook Landing Site National Historic Reserve has deep historical significance for New Zealanders, but not so much to keep an international visitor amused. At Kaiti Beach, across the river southeast of the city center, it is marked by a statue of Captain James Cook, who first set foot on New Zealand soil here on October 9, 1769. The beach itself, at low tide, attracts interesting bird life. ⊠ *Esplanade on south end of Turanganui River.*

The **Titirangi Domain** on Kaiti Hill has excellent views of Gisborne, Poverty Bay, and the surrounding rural areas. Titirangi was the site of an extensive pa (fortified village), the origins of which can be traced back at least 24 Maori generations. The **Titirangi Recreational Reserve,** part of the domain, is a pleasant place for a picnic or a walk among native trees. The domain is south of Turanganui River. Pass the harbor and turn right into Esplanade, then left into Crawford Road, right into Queens Drive, and follow it to several lookout points in the Domain.

Te Poho o Rawiri Meeting House is one of the largest Maori marae in New Zealand, and the interior has excellent traditional carving. On the side of the hill stands the Toko Toro Tapu Church. Ask permission to explore both sites from the **Visitor Information Centre** (☞ Contacts and Resources *in* Gisborne and Eastland A to Z, *below*) in town. ⊠ *Kaiti Hill,* ☎ *06/867–2835.* ☜ *Small donation suggested.*

Matawhero Wines is a Gisborne original—both in style and longevity. Gewürztraminer is a specialty for owner Denis Irwin, but you can also taste chenin blanc, chardonnay, cabernet-merlot blends, and pinot noir, often from earlier vintages. The vineyard is southwest of Gisborne; follow State Highway 35 out of town. ⊠ *Riverpoint Rd., Gisborne,* ☎ *06/868–8366,* FAX *06/867–9856.* ☉ *Spring–fall, weekdays 11–4, weekends 11–5; winter, weekdays 11–4, Sat. 11–5.*

Millton Vineyard has an attractive garden area, making it a logical place to sit with a picnic lunch and sip some barrel-fermented chardonnay. The award-winning Opou Riesling is also recommended. James and Annie Millton grow their grapes organically and biodynamically, following the precepts of philosopher Rudolf Steiner. ⊠ *Papatu Rd., Manutuke, Gisborne,* ☎ *06/862–8680,* FAX *06/862–8869.* ☉ *Summer, daily 10–5; winter, by appointment.*

OFF THE
BEATEN PATH

Eastwoodhill Arboretum found its inspiration not in the native trees of New Zealand but in English gardens—not an uncommon phenomenon. William Douglas Cook returned home from a trip to England in 1910 and began planting 160 acres. Only first-rate material was collected for the plantings, and the result today is a stunning collection of over 500 genera of trees from around the world. Eastwoodhill is a place of seasonal change seldom seen in New Zealand. In spring and summer daffodils mass yellow, magnolias bloom in clouds of pink and white, and cherries, crab apples, wisteria, and azalea all add to the spectacle. In autumn and winter leaves of yellow, rust, and scarlet cover the ground. As in other New Zealand gardens, the rapid growth of nonnative trees make them outstanding features, well worth a couple hours' enjoyment. The main tracks in the park can be walked in about 45 minutes. Maps and self-guided tour booklets are available. Eastwoodhill can be reached by driving west from Gisborne center on Highway 2 toward Napier and turning at the rotary into the Ngatapa-Rere Road before leaving town. Follow it 35 km (22 mi) to the arboretum. ⊠ *Ngatapa-Rere Rd.,* ☎ *06/863–9800,* FAX *06/863–9081.* ☜ *$5.* ☉ *Daily 9–5.*

Dining and Lodging

$$$ ✕ **Café Villagio.** This casual and relaxed café/restaurant in a converted
★   house is a Gisborne favorite. Walking past an aromatic lavender hedge is a heady preface for tastes of grilled salmon kebabs on a salad of potatoes, feta cheese and lentils, or sautéed lamb sweetbreads with mushrooms and polenta. Center your meal on local tarakihi fish, panfried and paired with an olive-spiked potato mash, or pork stuffed with prunes and served with a honey and ginger sauce. The wine list is very local, the service cheerful. ⊠ *M57 Ballance St., Gisborne,* ☎ *06/868–1611,* FAX *06/868–6855. AE, DC, MC, V. Sept.–Apr., no dinner Sun.–Tues.; May–Aug., no lunch Sat.–Mon., no dinner Sun.–Tues.*

$$$ ✗ **Pete's on the Beach.** Score a table at the window overlooking the wide Pacific, and you'll happy indeed to have chosen this Gisborne institution. There's a reasonable emphasis on seafood, but not as much as you'd expect from Pete's location. The style is unadventurous but flavorsome, and the view really does make up for any shortcomings. The fish of the day is usually a good bet, or if you're feeling carnivorous, look for mint-marinated lamb rump or a Cajun-dusted T-bone. ✉ *Marine Parade, Medway Beach, Gisborne,* ☎ *06/867–5861. AE, DC, MC, V. No lunch.*

$$–$$$ ✗ **Wharf Café/Landfall Restaurant.** Standing on opposite ends of a former storage shed on the Gisborne wharf, these two eateries are the work of the entrepreneurial John Thorpe. The Wharf Café is the more casual of the two, with hot and cold running snacks, a buffet table, and pizzas, along with dishes like fig-stuffed chicken breasts and a sort of carbonara-like fettuccine with mushrooms. Landfall ups the ante with grilled pear with Waimata blue cheese and crayfish and zucchini rolls with ginger and sprouts. After the meal, check out The Works, a Thorpe-run operation a couple of hundred yards away—go for tastings of wine and cheese that that John and his brother Rick make. ✉ *60 The Esplanade, Gisborne,* ☎ *06/868–4876 for Wharf Café, 06/ 867–2034 for Landfall. AE, DC, MC, V.*

$ ✗ **Verve Café.** This funky little middle-of-town coffee bar is a popular stop for backpackers from around the world. The decor is eclectic, the reading matter interesting, and the food simple and tasty—seafood chowder reliable, salads generous, and cakes suitably decadent. Best of all, the coffee's terrific—and if the bush has got you starved for technology, sip a hot one while you surf the Internet. ✉ *121 Gladstone Rd., Gisborne,* ☎ *06/868–9095. AE, DC, MC, V.*

$$$$ ✗⌸ **Katoa Country Lodge.** The gardens around this country home are the first things to impress. The next is the hospitality of hosts Zona and Charles Averill, which a quick glance at the visitors' book will confirm. You can join the Averills for dinner (most choose to) or eat alone—either way this is a great place to relax and sample New Zealand wine and delicious country cuisine. Wineries are easy to get to, and farm walks, cross-country horse riding, even expeditions to see freshwater eels are among the lodge's farm-related activities. Evenings you can relax in the sitting room—and contemplate, if not play, the Mason and Hamlin organ. Furniture and fittings in the rooms tend to wear classic British creams, greens, and burgundies. Rates include meals, predinner drinks, and wine at dinner. ✉ *Taurau Valley Rd., Manutuke, Gisborne,* ☎ *06/862–8764,* ⒻⓍ *06/862–8764. 6 rooms. V.*

$$$–$$$$ ✗⌸ **Acton Estate.** Lisa and Andrew Tauber's transformation of Acton into one of the finest boutique lodges in the country included finding its dining room table, once in residence at Lupbrook Hall in England, at a Sydney auction house and rescuing a writing desk and chair for one room from a schooner built in 1902. Rooms vary in size and price; two have bathrooms down the hall. There is a charming cottage at the back of the main house; the Grand Master Room has a French cherrywood bed covered in luxurious Italian linen. Hosts James (who doubles as chef) and Jenni (who covers the rest) Reddington add their friendly and efficient touches. Even though the four-course evening meal is not included in the tariff (breakfast *is*), Acton is still priced below other comparable lodges around the country. ✉ *577 Back Ormond Rd., Gisborne,* ☎ *06/867-9999,* ⒻⓍ *06/867-1116. 7 rooms. Tennis court, billiards. BP. AE, DC, MC, V.*

$$ ✗⌸ **Waiatai Valley Farmstays.** Sophia Ross's Cordon Bleu training makes Waiatai stand apart from the usual Kiwi homestay. She can deliver anything from Thai red curry chicken to lamb shanks Romarin over to the farm cottage across the road from where she lives with farmer

husband John. If you want to sample local seafood, or bantam eggs from the farm, just ask. Rooms have large windows looking out to the farm, wooden bedsteads with white bedspreads, wooden chests of draws, wardrobe space, and kitchen facilities—plain, perhaps, but with fantastic sunrises and sunsets. This is a working farm, so sheep come right up to the balcony. Local bird life abounds, and trout fishing and bushwalks are all easily accessible. Lunch and dinner are available for an additional cost. ⊠ *Pirinoa Station, 418 Waiatai Valley Rd., R.D. 6, Wairoa,* ☎ *06/837–7552,* ℻ *06/837–7552. 1 cottage. BP. No credit cards.*

$$ 🏠 **Tunanui Station Cottages.** This is about as far away from what you're used to as you can get. Tunanui Station is a 3,000-acre sheep and cattle station, and the road here from Gisborne winds through Eastland's hill country before it takes you past some of the most spectacular coastal views in the country. You can stay in a 90-year-old restored cottage or a farmhouse. The cottage has more historic charm, including a lovely kauri table in the hallway, made by a local craftsman, and rimu tongue-and-groove flooring. The farmhouse has more room and better views over the peninsula. Both are self-catering, so bring food for cooking on site. You can also arrange to have breakfast and dinner at extra cost at the owners' nearby home. ⊠ *Tunanui Rd., Opoutama, Mahia,* ☎ *06/837–5790,* ℻ *06/837–5797. 3-bedroom cottage, 4-bedroom farmhouse. No credit cards.*

Outdoor Activities and Sports

FISHING

Albacore, yellowfin tuna, mako sharks, and marlin are all prized catches off the East Cape from January to April. Fishing operators include **Tolaga Bay East Cape Charters** (☎ 06/862–6715), whose skipper, Bert Lee, has had more than 35 years' experience in recreational fishing, and **Coastline Charters** (☎ 06/863–9801).

JET BOATING

Motu River Jet Boat Tours (☎ 07/315–8107) combines the thrills and spills of speeding along the river with the opportunity to learn about the ecology and history of the region. The trip lasts about two hours and costs $60.

MOUNTAIN BIKING

Mountain Bike Adventures (☎ 07/315–5577) has an escorted day tour on the Old Motu Coach Road, including two hours of downhill riding through the Meremere Scenic Reserve and Urutawa State Forest. The $70 price tag includes bikes and lunch, and a support vehicle follows riders. The company also has "single track" tours on narrow, winding trails through dense bush.

Gisborne–Opotiki Loop

Soak in the beauty and remoteness of Eastland driving the loop between Gisborne and Opotiki, the northwest anchor of the East Cape. Rolling green hills drop into wide crescent beaches or rock-strewn coves. Small towns appear here and there along the route, only to fade into the surrounding landscape. It is one of the country's ultimate roads less traveled. Some scenic highlights are **Anaura Bay,** with rocky headlands, a long beach, and offshore islands; it is between **Tolaga Bay** and **Tokomaru Bay,** two former shipping towns. Tolaga Bay has an incredibly long wharf stretching over a beach into the sea, and Cooks Cove Walkway is a pleasant amble through the countryside past a rock arch. In **Tikitiki** farther up the coast, an Anglican Church is full of carved Maori panels and beams. Tikitiki has a gas station.

East of the small town of **Te Araroa,** which has the oldest pohutukawa (po-hoo-too-*ka*-wa) tree in the country, the coast is about as remote as you could imagine. At the tip of the cape (21 km, or 13 mi, from Te Araroa), the **East Cape Lighthouse** and fantastic views are a long steep climb from the beach. **Hicks Bay** has another long beach. Back toward Opotiki, **Whanarua** (fahn-ah-*roo*-ah) **Bay** is one of the most beautiful on the East Cape, with isolated beaches ideal for a picnic and a swim. Farther on, there is an intricately carved Maori marae (meeting house) called Tukaki in **Te Kaha.**

If you plan to take your time along the way, inquire at the **Gisborne–Eastland Visitor Information Centre** (☞ Contacts and Resources *in* Gisborne and Eastland A to Z, *below*) about lodging. There are motel accommodations at various points on the cape. Driving time alone on the loop—about 330 km (205 mi)—is about five hours without stops.

Urewera National Park

㊲ *125 km (78 mi) west of Gisborne.*

Urewera National Park is a vast, remote region of forests and lakes straddling the Huiarau Range. The park's outstanding feature is the glorious **Lake Waikaremoana** (sea of rippling waters), a forest-girded lake with good swimming, boating, fishing, and walks. The lake is circled by a 50-km (31-mi) walking track; the three- to four-day walk is popular, and in the summer months the lakeside tramping huts are often heavily used. There are many other short walks nearby. The one-hour Lake Waikareiti Track is especially recommended. For information, contact the Department of Conservation Field Centre at Aniwaniwa, on the eastern arm of Lake Waikaremoana (⊠ Aniwaniwa, Private Bag, Wairoa, ☎ 06/837–3803). The motor camp on the lakeshore has cabins, chalets, and motel units. In summer a launch operates sightseeing and fishing trips from the motor camp.

Gisborne and Eastland A to Z

Arriving and Departing

BY CAR

Gisborne is a long way from almost anywhere, though the coastal and bush scenery along the way makes the drive wholly worthwhile. The most direct route from the north is to follow State Highway 2 around the Bay of Plenty (☞ Chapter 2) to Opotiki, Eastland's northern gateway, then continue to Gisborne through the Waioeka Gorge Scenic Reserve. The drive from Auckland to Gisborne takes seven hours. South from Gisborne, you will pass through Wairoa, about 90 minutes away, before passing Napier, Hawke's Bay, and Wairarapa on the way to Wellington, about 7½ hours by car.

BY PLANE

Air New Zealand Link (☎ 06/867–9490) flies daily to Gisborne from Auckland and Wellington.

Contacts and Resources

GUIDED TOURS

Country Helicopters Gisborne has heli-fishing excursions, wine tours, and a "white knuckle" trip. Shorter trips around Gisborne and its beaches cost $60. ☎ *06/868–8911.*

Roy and Lesley Cranswick's **Nomad Off-Road Tours** go way off the beaten track on four-wheel-drive trips on the Tarndale Slip, formed by the largest movement of earth in the southern hemisphere. Trips in-

volve river crossings and working on farms and logging sites, if desired.
✉ *6 Hunter St., Gisborne,* ☎ *06/868–4187.*

VISITOR INFORMATION
The **Gisborne–Eastland Visitor Information Centre** is easily identifiable
by the Canadian totem pole next door. ✉ *209 Grey St., Gisborne,* ☎
06/868–6139, FAX *06/868–6138.* ☉ *Daily 9–5:30.*

NEW PLYMOUTH AND TARANAKI

On a clear winter day, with a cover of snow, Mt. Taranaki (its Maori
name, Mt. Egmont is its English moniker) towers above its flat rural
surroundings and seems to draw the sky right down to the sea. No less
astonishing in other seasons, the solitary peak is similar in appearance
to Japan's Mt. Fuji. It is the icon of the Taranaki region, and the
province has shaped itself around the mountain. Northeast of Taranaki,
the provincial seat of New Plymouth huddles between the monolith
and a rugged coastline, while smaller towns dot the road that circles
the mountain's base. For visitors, Mt. Taranaki is often the center of
attention. You can hike up it and around it, ski on it (for a short period), stay the night on it, and dine at restaurants on its flanks.

The Taranaki region is one of the most successful agricultural areas in
the country because of layers of volcanic ash that have created superb
free-draining topsoil, and a mountainous coastal position that ensures
abundant rainfall. What serves farmers serves gardeners as well. Some
of the country's most magnificent gardens grow in the rich local soil,
and the annual Rhododendron Festival held late in the year celebrates
the area's horticultural excellence.

Taranaki has plenty of other ground-level delights, too. By the water's
edge you can surf, swim, and fish, and several museums delve into
Taranaki history, which is particularly rich on the subject of the Maori.
You could take in most of the area in a couple of days, but that will
keep you on the run. Just getting from place to place around the mountain takes time. Most people use New Plymouth as a base, though Stratford and Hawera also have comfortable, if basic, accommodations.

The weather is constantly in flux—locals say that if you can't see
Egmont it's raining, and if you can it's going to rain. Day in and day
out, this meteorological mix makes for stunning contrasts of sun and
cloud on and around the mountain. The changing aspects of the volcano, combined with the Maori legends of Mt. Taranaki—how as a
lover he had fought with other peaks for a woman who didn't learn
of his affection until too late, after he retired with his wounds to where
he stands today—can lead a traveler to wax poetical:

This fondness of heart—
Will you come back tomorrow,
my Taranaki?

New Plymouth

❸❽ *375 km (235 mi) south of Auckland, 190 km (120 mi) southwest of*
Waitomo.

New Plymouth is a center both for one of New Zealand's most productive dairy regions and the nation's gas and oil industries. This natural wealth means that even when New Zealand's economy is in hard
times, the people of New Plymouth retain a sense of optimism. Prior
to the arrival of Europeans, several Maori *pa* (fortified villages) were
in the vicinity. In the mid-1800s, Maori-European land disputes racked

Taranaki, and open war broke out in New Plymouth in 1860. Formal peace between the government and Maori was made in 1881, after which New Plymouth began to form its current identity.

While you're in New Plymouth, you will always have the impression that nature is beckoning—either the looming mountain or the nearby sea. The city itself doesn't have as much to offer as the surrounding countryside, but take time to explore its serene parkland, and the museum if you have a rainy morning.

If you're driving to Taranaki from the north, the Awakino Gorge on Highway 3 between Mahoenui and the coast is breathtaking. Sheep have worn trails that seem to hang on the sides of precipitous green hills that are broken here and there with marvelous limestone outcrops. The other thing to look for coming this way is the view of Mt. Egmont as soon as you hit the coast—it is nothing short of awesome.

Pukekura Park and the connected **Brooklands Park** are the main reasons to stay in New Plymouth proper. You could easily spend half a day in the parks, especially if you're botanically inclined. Pukekura has water running throughout, and the view from the park's teahouse across the boating lake, with Mt. Egmont as a backdrop, is one of New Zealand's finest. You can hire rowboats to explore the small islands and nooks and crannies of the main lake. The park also has a fernery—caverns carved out of the hillside that connect through fern-cloaked tunnels—and botanical display houses. The fern and flowering plant collections are some of the most extensive in the country.

Brooklands was once a great estate. During the land wars of the 1860s, local Maori burned down the manor house, and the brick fireplace is all that remains of it, standing alone in the sweeping lawns among trees. Planted in the second half of the 19th century, giant copper beeches, pines, walnuts, and oaks will amaze you with their great presence. The Monterey pine, magnolia soulangeana, ginkgo, and native karaka and kohekohe are all the largest of their kind in New Zealand. Take a walk along the outskirts of the park on tracks leading through native, subtropical bush that are popular with local runners. This area has been relatively untouched for the last few thousand years, and 1,500-year-old trees are not uncommon. A puriri tree near the Somerset Street entrance is believed to be more than 2,000 years old.

Other features of Brooklands are **the Gables,** a colonial hospital built in 1847, which now serves as an art gallery and medical museum. The adjacent zoo is an old-fashioned example of how to keep birds and animals, but it is still a favorite of children. Brooklands has a rhododendron dell and a bowl used for a variety of entertainment throughout the year. ⊠ *Liardet St., Brooklands Rd.,* ☎ *06/759–6060.* ☜ *Free.* ☉ *Daily dawn–dusk; teahouse July–May, Wed.–Mon. dawn–dusk; display houses daily 10–noon and 1–4; tour by appointment.*

Taranaki Museum, founded in 1847, is the second oldest in New Zealand. The museum cares for a large number of *Taonga* (Maori treasures) that are associated with various *iwi* (tribes). Also of interest is a diverse collection of colonial items, many of which date to the earliest years of European settlement. ⊠ *Ariki and Egmont Sts.,* ☎ *06/ 758–9583.* ☜ *Free.* ☉ *Weekdays 10:30–4:30, weekends 1–5.*

The Queen Elizabeth II National Trust is a publicly funded organization established to conserve privately held native landscapes. The two New Zealand gardens in the trust are in Taranaki: in New Plymouth, **Tupare,** and south of the mountain in Kaponga, **Hollard Gardens** (☞ Kaponga, *below*).

Complete with Tudor-style houses, Tupare is truly an English-style garden. Built in 1927, the estate of Sir Russell and Lady Matthews sits on a steep hillside that plunges down to the rushing Waiwhakaiho (why-fah-kye-ho) River. Russell Matthews, a roading contractor, cleverly enlisted his crew during the off-season to build the impressive terraces, garden walls, and pools that define Tupare. Many varieties of maple trees have been planted, along with a grand tulip tree, cherries and magnolias, and a stand of native rimu pine. There are numerous rhododendrons and azaleas, to be expected in Taranaki, with underplantings of helebores, daffodils, and bluebells, creating a glorious floral vision in spring. Tupare is also noted for its autumnal foliage display. ⊠ *487 Manorei Rd., New Plymouth,* ☎ *06/758–6480.* ⊡ *$5.* ⊘ *Daily 9– 5. Some paths may be closed in winter for maintenance.*

Stately **Mt. Egmont** rises 8,309 ft right out of the sea, and if you spend any more than a few hours in the vicinity, it is difficult not to be drawn toward it. The lower reaches are cloaked in magical subtropical forests; above the tree line lower vegetation allows you to look out over the paddocks and seascape below. The three main roads to the mountain turn off State Highway 3 and are all well signposted. The first, as you drive south from New Plymouth, leads to the **North Egmont Visitor Centre.** Displays at the center are looking tired and outdated, but it's still worth dropping in to learn something about the mountain and its lush vegetation. North Egmont is the starting point for several walks, and it has a cafeteria. The second road up the mountain takes you to the **Mountain House** and, a little farther on **Stratford Plateau,** the mountain's ski field. Here you will find more walks of various durations. The third road takes you to the southernmost **Dawson Falls Visitor Centre,** which also has displays about the mountain and five popular walks of varying difficulty taking 1–2½ hours.

If you are serious about getting out and striding, consider taking from three to five days to walk around the entire mountain. The circuit is well signposted, and there are accommodation huts along the way, the cost for which is usually $8 for adults per night. You can also ascend the summit of Mt. Egmont quite easily in summer, and a variety of other intermediate options are available.

To get a shadowy feeling for part of the Maori past in New Plymouth, pay a visit to **Koru Pa,** the former stronghold of the Nga Mahanga a Tairi *hapu* (subtribe) of the Taranaki iwi. The bush has taken it back in large measure, but you can still make out the main defensive ditch and stonewalled terraces that drop a considerable way from the highest part of the pa, where chiefs lived, down to the Oakura River. Part of the reserve has a picnic site. Take Route 45 out of New Plymouth and turn left onto Wairau Road. Take it to Surrey Hills Road, where another left will take you to the pa site. ⊠ *Surrey Hills Rd.*

On the western outskirts of New Plymouth, the world-renowned ★ **Pukeiti Rhododendron Trust** scenically spreads over 900 acres of lush native rain forest adjacent to Egmont National Park on the northwest slope of the mountain. The Pukeiti (poo-kay-*ee*-tee) collection of 2,500 hybrid and species rhododendrons is the largest in New Zealand. Many of these varieties were first grown here, like the giant winter-blooming *R. protistum var. giganteum* Pukeiti, collected from seed in 1953 and now standing 15 ft tall—or the beautiful Lemon Lodge and Spring Honey hybrids that bloom in spring. Kyawi, a large red rhodie, is the very last to bloom, in April (autumn).

Rhododendrons aside, there are many other rare and special plants to enjoy at Pukeiti. All winter long the Himalayan daphnes fragrance the pathways. Spring- to summer-growing candelabra primroses can reach up to 4 ft, and for a month around Christmas spectacular 8-ft Himalayan cardiocrinum lilies bear heavenly scented 12-inch white trumpet flowers. If you're not an avid gardener, walking the paths that wind throughout the vast gardens and surrounding native bush is also a delight. Pukeiti is a wonderful bird habitat, so keep your eyes and ears open for them, too. ⊠ *Carrington Rd., 20 km (12½ mi) southwest of New Plymouth center,* ☎ *06/752–4141,* ℻ *06/752–4151.* ☜ *$6.* ☉ *Daily 9–5. Closed Dec. 25.*

Dining and Lodging

$$$ ✕ **The Orangery.** The decor and surroundings have been modeled on a 16th-century Tuscan landscape, complete with citrus trees and a fountain. Start with marinated baby squid stuffed with a paua (black abalone) and coriander farci and served on a bed of chili tomatoes, then turn to main courses such as seafood paella or cervena (venison) steaks with a tamarillo (tree-tomato) sauce. And do leave room for dessert. ⊠ *Courtney and Leach Sts., New Plymouth,* ☎ *06/758–0589. AE, DC, MC, V.*

$$–$$$ ✕ **André L'Escargot Restaurant and Bar.** Considered by longtime locals to be the finest restaurant in New Plymouth, L'Escargot focuses on classic southern French preparations, serving lighter world-beat dishes as well. Dine inside New Plymouth's oldest commercial building on such delights as a warm salad of quail with roasted garlic cloves, or osso buco, or veal in a sherry, cream, and mushroom sauce, or a traditional *pissaladiére* tart of onions, aubergine, capsicum (bell pepper), olives, and anchovies. Desserts return to Europe for inspiration. ⊠ *37–43 Brougham St., New Plymouth,* ☎ *06/758–4812. AE, DC, MC, V.*

$$–$$$ ✕ **Steps Restaurant.** The thoroughly pleasant old-house atmosphere
★ here will get you out of the travel-meal rut while you're in Taranaki. Lunchtimes are thoroughly relaxed, with down-home, friendly service and hearty vegetarian dishes. Evenings are more upscale, the welcome is just as genuine, and you can tuck into grilled goat cheese with a mini-isalad and panfried fish with rosemary and lemon risotto. ⊠ *37 Gover St.,* ☎ *06/758–3393. MC, V. Licensed or BYOB. Closed Sun.–Mon.*

$–$$ ✕ **Macfarlane's Caffe.** One of the new generation of New Zealand restaurants—friendly, ambitious, casual, and looking around the world for influences—Macfarlane's does its best to liven up the dining scene in the town of Inglewood, midway between New Plymouth and Stratford. Yogurt and granola or traditional farm-style breakfasts, lunches of Caesar salad or attractively assembled sandwiches, and at dinner panfried salmon, variations on the char-grilled steak theme, and pasta, pizza, and burgers are persuasively prepared and pleasantly delivered. New Zealand wine and beer are in abundance. ⊠ *Kelly and Matai Sts., Inglewood,* ☎ *06/756–6665. AE, MC, V. No dinner Sun.–Wed.*

$$ 🏨 **Devon Hotel.** This hotel has standard, comfortable rooms and enough flexibility to cater to families. It's easy to find, close to the city, and has a friendly atmosphere to match its family-managed status. Hotel guests may use facilities at a nearby health club. ⊠ *390 Devon St. E, New Plymouth,* ☎ *06/759–9099,* ℻ *06/758—2229. 100 rooms with bath and shower. Restaurant, bar, pool. AE, DC, MC, V.*

$$ 🏨 **Henwood House.** This century-old B&B occupies a homestead that has been completely refurbished and refined by architect Graeme Axten and his wife, Lynne. The two play the role of charming hosts to the likes of the British high commissioner in New Zealand (who recommends the place, if you'd like to know), but the rates make Henwood House accessible not only to heads of state. There is a variety of rooms, including one with a balcony and fireplace. The property is 6 km (4 mi) from town, and it is extremely peaceful. Breakfast is served in the country-style kitchen each morning, and you'll find it easy to relax in the rather grand guest lounge evenings. ⊠ *122 Henwood House, New Plymouth,* ☎ *06/755–1212. 5 rooms, 3 with shower, 2 with shared bath. BP. MC, V.*

Outdoor Activities and Sports

BEACHES

Some of the coastal waters can be quite wild, so it's wise to swim at patrolled beaches. **Fitzroy Beach** and **East End Beach** both have lifeguards in summer and are easily accessible from New Plymouth. **Ngamotu Beach,** along Ocean View Parade, is calm and suitable for young children. Fitzroy and East End are both popular with surfers, as is **Back Beach.**

BOATING

★ **Happy Chaddy's Charters**' launch starts with the guide announcing, "Hold on to your knickers, because we're about to take off"—then the old English lifeboat rocks back and forth in its shed (with you on-board), slides down its rails, and hits the sea with a spray of water. The trip lasts an hour, during which time you'll see seals and get a close-up view of the Sugar Loaf Islands just offshore from New Plymouth. ⊠ *Ocean View Parade, New Plymouth,* ☎ *06/758–9133.* ▣ *$20, chartered fishing trip $10 per person (minimum 8 people).*

Stratford

39 *41 km (27 mi) southeast of New Plymouth.*

The town of Stratford itself is remarkable for its ordinariness. A stroll down its main drag—with its shops and food stores—will give you a local sense of New Zealand's agricultural life. Above town on the mountain there are excellent hiking trails, and in the valley to the east are some of the country's most interesting private gardens.

★ Of all the gardens in New Zealand, the one you'll most likely want to return to is **Aramaunga,** whether to see the garden itself or Gwyn Masters, its presiding sage and sprightly creator. A garden is surely a reflection of its maker, and Mrs. Masters has over the last 50 years transformed a farm paddock into a garden with a personality to match her own. At Aramaunga, which means the "path between the mountains," you'll see her enthusiasm, intelligence, and generosity of spirit everywhere. Most visitors comment on the wisteria, from the century-old specimen on the front of the cottage to others cleverly grown as standards or encouraged to climb into the treetops along with various clematis species to throw bursts of color where it is least expected.

The very act of walking through the garden is a delight—through discreet passageways, onto open lawns, around bends, always following the contours of the land. The garden constantly changes as you progress, heightening your sense of anticipation. Beds are filled with masses of color and form that mix beautifully: rhododendrons (ask to see the true red Gwynneth Masters hybrid that she developed from seed), azalea mollis, magnolias, cherries, and Japanese maples, along with interesting pottery and herbaceous plants that include lots of self-seeded columbine (she can't bring herself to pull out any of these charmers). Eventually, the path arrives in front of a stream, which was dammed years ago to form a pond that reflects along its edges golden bog primula, white libertia, purple iris, and lavender wisteria shrubs. Bridges crossing the pond connect with woodland on the opposite shore, where a glorious view back across the water, gardens, and cottage bring to mind Gwyn Masters's affinity for Claude Monet's garden at Giverny: his passion for color and relaxed form. Like Monet, Mrs. Masters is always creating things in her garden—creating beauty just like a painter. Aramaunga is open to the public by appointment; there is a small entry fee. ☎ 06/765–7600.

Dining and Lodging

$$–$$$ ✕🏠 **Mountain House Motor Lodge.** From the restaurant where some of New Zealand's most unique meals are carefully prepared to motel-style rooms that have no more to recommend them than their cleanliness and their location on the eastern flank of Mt. Taranaki, the Mountain House simply is what it is. (Keith and Bertha Anderson originally created the more polished Swiss chalet–style Dawson Falls Lodge, then moved here to be closer to town.) Dinner is a marriage of Bertha (*ber*-ta) Anderson's Swiss upbringing and delicious New Zealand produce. From the sea, creamed local paua (black abalone), or delicately smoked freshwater eel that may be the best you've ever tasted, or seasonal whitebait fritters make great starters—especially appropriate with a Marlborough Riesling. Moving to heartier main courses, lamb or lean cervena venison call for pinot noir, or cabernet-merlot if you like reds with a bit of grunt. Apple strudel and cream is a wonderful way to wrap up the alpine meal. If you do stay at the motor lodge, the most spacious rooms, 4 through 8, stand apart from the main building. Trails from the building ascend or branch out on the lower reaches of the mountain; in winter a T-bar lift from the lodge takes you to the base of the snowfields. ⊠ *Pembroke Rd., Box 303, Stratford,* ☎ ℻ *06/765–6100, 0800/657–100. 10 rooms. Restaurant, bar. AE, DC, MC, V.*

$$ 🏠 **Te Popo.** A delight for flora- and fauna-philes, this was once the abode of artist Janet Marshall, who was particularly fond of painting birds. Her husband, Graham, planted deciduous trees among the natives to attract numerous varieties of birds to the property. New owners Lori and Bruce Ellis have converted part of the late-'70s, mushroom-color, Spanish-style homestead on the property to guest lodgings, creating a very peaceful environment. Tuis, wood pigeons, bellbirds, and fantails still visit the gardens year-round—you'll also see them in some of Janet's paintings. Rooms themselves have plenty of natural light, and the colorful furnishings work well with the outside surrounds. Rates include breakfast; dinner is available by separate arrangement. Te Popo is a 15-minute drive from Stratford town on good country roads. You can visit the gardens separately ($3), but it's well worth staying the night. ⊠ *636 Stanley Rd., Midhirst, R.D. 24, Stratford,* ☎ *06/762–8775,* ℻ *06/762-8775. 2 rooms with shower. BP. MC, V.*

Kaponga

18 km (11 mi) west of Stratford.

The reasons to come to Kaponga, unless you're just driving through on your way around the mountain, are Dawson Falls, which is the southern entrance to Mount Egmont National Park, and the magnificent Hollard Gardens. In the long light of a sunny afternoon, the view of Mt. Taranaki from Opunake Road is inspiring.

★ Surrounded by dairy farms, **Hollard Gardens** was conceived in 1927 when Bernard and Rose Hollard sectioned off a piece of their land and started building the impressive collection of plants now under the care of the Queen Elizabeth II National Trust. The 14-acre garden was created in two stages: The old garden, dating from 1927, is a woodland area with narrow, winding paths, intensely planted with rhododendrons, azaleas, camellias, and other related plants. It is an intimate area with great character. The new garden was established in 1982. Its broad lawns, paths, and large mixed borders contain a comprehensive blend of exotics and natives. Brochures at the information shelter detail two self-guided walking tours and help locate some of the treasures.

Look in the Moon Bed for the rare epaulette tree and the native, yellow-flowering kawhai (*kah*-fye), which attracts tuneful bellbirds and tuis. The grand, golden totara foliage on Rabbit Ridge is stunning in winter, and the 70-year-old passion vine draped on tawa trees has bright orange fruit in autumn. Both are on the Bush Walk. The main season for flowering is from September through March. ⊠ *Upper Manaia Rd. off Opunake Rd., Kaponga,* ☎ *06/764–6544.* ⊡ *$5.* ☉ *Daily 9–5. Closed Dec. 25.*

Dining and Lodging

$$$ ✕⊞ **Dawson Falls Lodge.** The most delightful accommodation in the region, with a touch of eccentricity, Dawson Falls has been styled on a Swiss alpine lodge. All rooms have Swiss decor, each with its own character and touches. It stands about halfway up Mt. Egmont, so the air is very fresh, and the loudest noises you'll hear are those of the local bird population. Request a room with a view up the mountain. The restaurant is good, but the lodge itself is the star. ⊠ *Manaia Rd. off Opunake Rd. from Stratford,* ☎ *06/765–5457. 11 rooms, 2 with bath, all with shower. Restaurant, bar, lounge. AE, DC, MC, V.*

Hawera

40 *29 km (18 mi) south of Stratford.*

Tawhiti Museum is a labor of love for Nigel Ogle, who bought an old cheese factory in 1976 and proceeded to fill it up with life-size figures from Taranaki's past. He creates the fiberglass figures from molds of local people, giving them a far more lifelike look than those in other museums. You may get a chance to watch Nigel at work, or discuss regional history with him. On the first Sunday of each month, the Tawhiti Bush Railway drives back to historical logging operations in Taranaki, where other figures are used to illustrate the life of the times. Take Onhangai Road southeast out of Normanby, or Tawhiti Road northeast out of Hawera, and continue 4 km (2½ mi) to the museum. ⊠ *7 Ohangai Rd., Hawera,* ☎ *06/278–6837.* ⊡ *$5.* ☉ *Sept.–May, Fri.–Mon. 10–4; June–Aug., Sun. 10–4.*

Just up the road from Tawhiti Museum, **Turuturumokai Pa** is one of the most impressive Maori citadels in the province. Defense ditches and walls ring the former village, and the top is pocked with storage pits. This pa is an astonishing piece of earthwork. ⊠ *Turuturu Rd. near Ohangai Rd., Hawera.* ⊡ *Free.* ☉ *Dawn–dusk.*

Taranaki A to Z

Arriving and Departing

BY BUS

New Plymouth is served daily by **Newmans** (☎ 09/309–9738) and **InterCity** (☎ 09/358–4085) from Auckland, Wellington, and other cities.

BY CAR

New Plymouth looks well out of the way on the map, but it is only 4½ hours from Auckland, a little farther from Wellington. From the north, head to Te Kuiti near Waitomo caves, then simply continue on State Highway 3. To leave Taranaki, take State Highway 3 south to the next main center, Wanganui. Staying on Highway 3, keep traveling to Sanson, where you have the option of following State Highway 1 down the west coast to Wellington, or heading east through Palmerston North, the Manawatu Gorge, and on to the Wairarapa region.

BY PLANE

Air New Zealand (☎ 09/379–0861) operates flights seven times daily between Auckland and New Plymouth and five times daily into Wellington.

Contacts and Resources

CAR RENTALS

AA Host Southern Cross Rental Cars. ✉ *49–55 Powderham St., New Plymouth,* ☎ *06/758–1955.*

GUIDED TOURS

Taranaki Scenic Flights' most popular tour is to the snowcapped summit of Mt. Egmont (Taranaki). You can also take a trip along the coastline, around the city, or out to the Maui offshore gas field. ✉ *New Plymouth Airport,* ☎ *06/755–0500,* FAX *06/755–1478.*

LATE-NIGHT PHARMACY

Bruce Laird Pharmacy. ✉ *68 Vivian St.,* ☎ *06/758–8263.* ◷ *Daily 8:30–8:30.*

VISITOR INFORMATION

New Plymouth Information Centre. ✉ *Leach and Liardet Sts., New Plymouth,* ☎ *06/759–6080,* FAX *06/758-1395.* ◷ *Weekdays 8:30—5, weekends 10–3.*

Stratford Information Centre. ✉ *Broadway and Miranda Sts., Stratford,* ☎ *06/765–6708,* FAX *06/769–6073.* ◷ *Oct.–Mar., weekends 10–3, Mon. 10–2; Apr.–Sept., Sat. 10–3, Mon. 10–2.*

WELLINGTON

New Zealand's capital city is indeed named for the then-duke of Wellington, ultimate conqueror of Napoléon at Waterloo in 1815. And it was English pioneers, having purchased land from the New Zealand Company, who settled here. In 1840, shortly after the signing of the Treaty of Waitangi, Auckland was chosen as the site for the national capital. But prosperous and influential South Island gold miners waged a campaign for a more central capital, and by 1865 they managed to have the seat of government moved to Wellington.

This city of 407,000, squeezed against the sea by peaks that rear up nearly 3,000 ft, works its way up the surrounding hills from the western shores of Port Nicholson. Behind the city, suburbs full of quaint timber houses hunker on the sides of precipitous slopes. The air currents funneled through Cook Strait, the 17-km-wide (11-mi-wide) channel separating North and South islands, give the city a feisty climate. Windy Wellington is a nickname that springs readily to the lips of most New Zealanders who don't live here. Although the city's reputation for climatic vigor is exaggerated, it's no accident that one of its landmarks is an experimental, wind-powered generator that overlooks the suburb of Brooklyn.

Exploring Wellington

A Good Walk

Wellington is an easy city to get around on foot, although some of its tangles of streets can get confusing. Much the best shopping lies south of there in Victoria Street and in the Manners and Cuba Street pedestrian malls. The following walking tour includes city views, formal gardens, literary history, some fine examples of 19th-century architecture, and the seat of government. Allow about three hours.

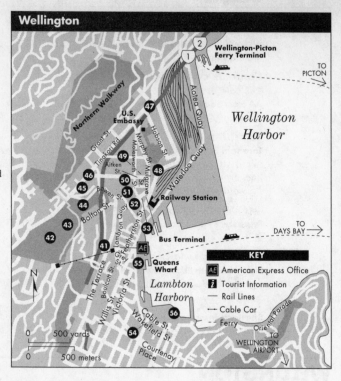

Begin at the **Kelburn Cable Car** ㊶ terminus in Cable Car Lane off Lambton Quay, opposite Grey Street. It's a good way to get up and see the city's layout—and end up walking down many of the hills instead of up them.

Leave the Kelburn Terminal and take the Northern Walkway, following the arrow that points to St. Mary Street. This path skirts the edge of the **Wellington Botanic Garden** ㊷ with city views on one side and the domes of the Dominion Observatory on the other. As you round this hilltop, you'll see an immense green hill with transmission towers on top; this is Tinakori Hill, known to the Maoris as Ahumairangi—"sloping down from the sky." Continue along the path, which becomes quite steep as it plunges toward the **Lady Norwood Rose Garden** ㊸, with more than 100 rose cultivars spilling out their blossoms and fragrance between November and the end of April.

Tear yourself away from the roses and walk to the right around the enclosed Anderson Park, following the sign to Bolton Street Memorial Park. At the end of this short road, detour to the monument on the right. The **John Seddon Memorial** ㊹ is dedicated to the remarkable turn-of-the-century prime minister. Close to the memorial a track zigzags down the hill beneath a stand of pohutukawa trees. At the bottom, cross Bowen Street, walk downhill, take the path to your left, and climb narrow old **Ascot Street** ㊺, with its wonderful old city cottages. At the top of the rise, stop for breath on a bench that has been thoughtfully provided in the shady courtyard.

Turn right into **Tinakori Road** ㊻. Another fact of early life in Wellington is illustrated by **No. 306,** the pasta shop. Pressed for want of level ground, the citizens of early Wellington tended to build tall, narrow houses. This example—one room wide and five stories high—took things to extremes. Just below the house, make a short detour to see the three

CHASE

Flying to France on Friday? Get Francs from Chase on Thursday. Call Currency To Go at 935-9935 for overnight delivery.

CHASE CURRENCY TO GO 935-9935

Or pounds for London. Or Deutschmarks for Düsseldorf. Or any of 75 foreign currencies. Call **Chase Currency To Go℠ at 935-9935** in area codes 212, 718, 914, 516 and Rochester, N.Y.; all other area codes call 1-800-935-9935. We'll deliver directly to your door.* Overnight. And there are no exchange fees. Let Chase make your trip an easier one.

CHASE. The right relationship is everything.℠

With guidebooks for every kind of travel—from weekend getaways to island hopping to adventures abroad—it's easy to understand why smart travelers go with **Fodor's**.

At bookstores everywhere.
www.fodors.com

Smart

superbly kept timber houses side by side in Upton Terrace. Behind a green fence a few steps farther down Tinakori Road is **Premier House,** the official residence of the prime minister until 1935, when the new Labour government, caught up in the reforming zeal of socialism, turned it into a dental clinic.

Continue down a relatively drab part of Tinakori Road to No. 25, just beyond the Hobson Street Bridge. This is the **Katherine Mansfield House** ㊼, where the celebrated writer was born (as Kathleen Beauchamp) and lived the first five years of her life.

The next section of the walk passes architecture of a more public ilk. Turning back along Tinakori Road to the Hobson Street overpass, and on the far side of the motorway, turn right to walk through the elms of Katherine Mansfield Memorial Park. Turn left around the rather stern compound of the U.S. Embassy, and walk down Murphy Street, which becomes Mulgrave Street, to **Old St. Paul's Cathedral** ㊽, one of the country's wooden Gothic Revival gems. Continue down Mulgrave Street and turn right at Archives House into Aitken Street. The modern building on the right is the **National Library** ㊾, housing the nation's largest collection of books. Cross Molesworth Street and walk through the gate to the various **Parliament Buildings** ㊿ on the far side. Left of Parliament House, the **Executive Office Building** (51), alias the Beehive, is the strange-looking office space for government officials.

Walk down the hill from the Beehive to the **Cenotaph** (52), the memorial to New Zealanders killed in battle—these were soldiers who oftentimes fought for the British Commonwealth when no immediate threat was posed to the safety of the New Zealand islands themselves. Across the road from the Cenotaph are the tremendous wooden **Original Government Buildings** (53).

The wide street curving behind the bronze lions is Lambton Quay. As its name suggests, this was once Wellington's waterfront. All the land between your feet and the present-day shoreline has been reclaimed. From this point, the shops of the city center are within easy walking distance along Lambton Quay.

Sights to See

㊺ **Ascot Street.** The tiny, doll-like cottages along Ascot were built in the 1870s, and this remains the finest example of a 19th-century streetscape in Wellington. There is a bench at the top end of the street that has been thoughtfully provided in the shady courtyard if you need to catch your breath. ✉ *Off Glenmore and Tinakori Sts. north of Wellington Botanic Garden.*

(52) **Cenotaph.** New Zealand has a proud and distinguished military record, and this memorial honors citizens killed in battle. "Few Americans appreciate the tremendous sacrifices made by New Zealanders in the last two world wars," James A. Michener wrote in *Return to Paradise.* "Among the allies, she had the highest percentage of men in arms—much higher than the United States—the greatest percentage overseas, and the largest percentage killed." ✉ *Bowen St. and Lambton Quay.*

★ **City Gallery.** Whether it's the latest exhibition of New Zealand's avant-garde artists, an international collection visiting the gallery, the Open City film series, or just the gallery's café, there are plenty of reasons to put Wellington's eyes-and-ears-on-the-arts into your schedule. It is an excellent representation of New Zealand's thoughtful, contemporary cultural set—something that you won't see much of in the countryside. The gallery has no permanent collection, so everything here is transitory. You may be in town when a show of local painters is on the walls or a Max Ernst exhibition. The film series plays everything from John Huston to New Zealand documentaries scored with music played by the National Symphony Orchestra. ✉ *Civic Sq., Wakefield St., Box 2199,* ☎ *04/801–3952,* 🖷 *04/801–3950.* 💴 *$4–10, depending on the exhibit.* 🕙 *Daily 11–5.*

54 **Civic Square.** Wellington's newish Civic Square is one symbol of the cultural vitality of Wellington and the interest currently invested in it. Reminiscent of an Italian piazza, it is a delightful sanctuary from the traffic and wind, with its outdoor cafés. The **City Gallery,** perhaps the nation's finest art space, the Library, and the concert venue Town Hall are all just steps apart. Architect Ian Athfield's steel nikau palms are a marvel. ✉ *Wakefield, Victoria, and Harris Sts.*

51 **Executive Office Building.** It would be difficult to imagine a more complete contrast in architectural styles than that of Parliament House and the Executive Office Building. Known for obvious reasons as the Beehive—not that it produces anything sweet—it contains the offices of government ministers and their staffs. ✉ *Molesworth St.*

44 **John Seddon Memorial.** This monument is dedicated to the colorful and popular liberal politician who served as prime minister from 1893 to 1906. Under Seddon's leadership, New Zealand became the first country to give women voting rights and to pay its citizens an old-age pension. ✉ *Bolton Street Memorial Park, northeast end of Wellington Botanic Garden.*

47 **Katherine Mansfield House.** Here at 25 Tinakori Road the writer, *née* Kathleen Beauchamp, came into the world (1888) and lived the first five years of her life. Mansfield left to pursue her career in the wider world of Europe when she was 20, but many of her short stories are set in Wellington. A year before her death in 1923, she wrote, "New Zealand is in my very bones. What wouldn't I give to have a look at it!" The house, which has been restored as a typical Victorian family home, contains furnishings, photographs, videos, and tapes that elucidate Mansfield's life and times. ✉ *25 Tinakori Rd., Thorndon,* ☎ 🖷 *04/473–7268.* 💴 *$4.* 🕙 *Daily 10–4.*

41 **Kelburn Cable Car.** The Swiss-built funicular railway makes a short but sharp climb to Kelburn Terminal, from which there are great views across parks and city buildings to Port Nicholson. Sit on the left side during the six-minute journey for the best scenery. ✉ *Lambton Quay at Grey St.,* ☎ *04/472–2199.* 💴 *$1.50 one way, $2.50 return.* 🕙 *Departures about every 10 mins, weekdays 7 AM–10 PM, weekends 9 AM–10 PM.*

★ **43** **Lady Norwood Rose Garden.** On a fine summer day you couldn't find a better place to go for a sniff and a smile. The rose garden is in fact the most popular part of the ☞ **Wellington Botanic Garden.** Situated on a plateau, the formal circular layout consists of 106 beds, each planted with a single variety of modern and traditional shrubs. Climbing roses cover a brick-and-timber colonnade on the perimeter. Adjacent to the rose beds, the Begonia House conservatory is filled with tender plants and has a teahouse serving light meals. ✉ *North end of Wellington Botanic Garden, Tinakori Rd. (for carpark),* ☎ *04/801–3071.* 💴 *Small charge.* 🕙 *Begonia House daily 10–4, main garden open 24 hrs.*

55 **Maritime Museum.** The handsome Harbour Board Building is full of paintings, figureheads, nautical apparatuses, and fine scale models of ships, including the *Wahine,* which sank in Cook Strait in 1968 with the loss of 51 lives. Most displays belong to the old-fashioned, glass-cabinet school of museum design. ✉ *Queens Wharf Events Centre,* ☎ *04/472–8904.* 💴 *$2.* 🕙 *Weekdays 9:30–4, weekends 1–4:30.*

49 **National Library.** This modern building houses the nation's largest collection of books, as well as the remarkable Alexander Turnbull Library. The latter, named after the noted bibliophile who founded it, contains an extensive Pacific history section, including accounts of every important European voyage of discovery since Magellan. A collection of sketches of New Zealand made by early visitors is displayed in changing exhibitions. ⊠ *Molesworth and Aitken Sts.,* ☎ *04/474–3000.* ☉ *Weekdays 9–5, Sat. 9–1.*

48 **Old St. Paul's Cathedral.** Consecrated in 1866, the church is a splendid example of the English Gothic Revival style executed in wood. Even the trusses supporting the roof transcend their mundane function with splendid craftsmanship. The hexagonal oak pulpit was a gift from the widow of Prime Minister Richard Seddon, in memory of her husband. ⊠ *Mulgrave St., Thorndon,* ☎ *04/473–6722.* ☉ *Mon.–Sat. 10–4:30, Sun. 1–4:30.*

53 **Original Government Buildings.** This second-largest wooden structure in the world is now home to Victoria University's law faculty. You can explore the inside of the building between 9 and 5. ⊠ *Lambton Quay.*

NEED A
BREAK?

Reds Espresso Café. Using a little trend appeal to lure you in from the street, coffee culture and tasty morning and afternoon fare will make you want to linger here awhile, snacking on savory muffins, or an avocado and brie roll, or a turkey sandwich. These are merely appetizers for Reds' apple cake, dark rich chocolate cake, croissant cake bread pudding, and fantastic espresso. Stop here to pick up a bite to take aboard the ferry to South Island if you're heading that way. ⊠ *49 Willis St.,* ☎ *04/473–3558. MC, V.*

50 **Parliament Buildings.** At a cost of more than $150 million over four years, Parliament Buildings have been painstakingly restored. The pink Gothic Revival structure on the right is the General Assembly Library, a soaring, graceful building compared with the ponderous gray bulk of the Parliament House next door. The layout of the House of Representatives, where legislation is presented, debated, and either passed or rejected by majority vote, is a copy of the British Houses of Parliament at Westminster, right down to the Speaker's mace and the dispatch boxes. Tours of the building explain the parliamentary process in detail. ⊠ *Molesworth St.,* ☎ *04/471–9999.* 🎫 *Free.* ☉ *Tours depart daily at varying times.*

☝ **56** **Te Papa–Museum of New Zealand.** Opened early in 1998, this museum quickly exceeded all expectations by attracting more visitors—250,000 in its first month—than anything else in New Zealand. This is partly because of the lack of modern, interactive museums elsewhere in the country, but also because Te Papa is such a good introduction to the country's people, cultures, landforms, flora, and fauna—with exhibits that make you feel an earthquake by standing in a house that rocks and shakes, or that take you into a marae (Maori meeting house) where a *powhiri* (Maori greeting involving song and speeches) welcomes you. You can also explore an outdoor forest area with moa (the extinct, ostrichlike native bird) bones and glowworms or delve into the stories of New Zealand's early European migrants. In the Time Warp area, a sort-of theme park where most activities have additional fees, you can simulate a bungee jump ($6), a trip back to the ancient Gondwanaland supercontinent ($8), or leap three generations ahead to Wellington in 2055 ($8). Four discovery centers allow children to weave, hear storytelling, and learn a bit of Maori through song. Eateries in the complex come with an impeccable pedigree, having been set up by a team of top chefs. ⊠ *Cable St., Wellington,* ☎ *04/381–7000.* 🎫 *Free; some exhibits cost up to $8.* ⊙ *Daily 10–6, Thurs. to 9 PM.*

46 **Tinakori Road.** The lack of suitable local stone combined with the collapse of most of Wellington's brick buildings in the earthquake of 1848 ensured the almost exclusive use of timber for building here in the second half of the 19th century. Most carpenters of the period had learned their skills as cabinetmakers and shipwrights in Europe, and the sturdy houses in this street are a tribute to their craftsmanship. Two notables are the tall and narrow Number 306 and Premier House just up the road from 306. From the Botanic Garden, follow Glenmore Road northeast until it turns into Tinakori Road around ☞ **Ascot Street.**

★ **42** **Wellington Botanic Garden.** In the hills overlooking downtown, this urban delight has scenery as varied as its terrain. Woodland gardens under native and exotic trees fill the valleys, water-loving plants line a pond and mountain streams, dry craggy slopes are studded with succulents and rock-loving plants, and lawns spread over flatter sections with beds of bright seasonal bulbs and annuals. The lovely ☞ **Lady Norwood Rose Garden** is in the northeast part of the garden. **Cater Observatory,** the only one of its kind in New Zealand, has public displays and programs, among which Public Nights is a great opportunity for those from the northern hemisphere to learn about the southern night sky. Also at the north end of the garden, the **Bolton Street Memorial Park** is one of the earliest cemeteries in the country, dating from 1840. It's a pleasant place to admire mature trees and antique roses. If you don't want to walk the hill up to the garden, the ☞ **Kelburn Cable Car** can take you. ⊠ *Tinakori Rd. (for carpark), many entrances surround gardens,* ☎ *04/801–3071.* 🎫 *Small charge.* ⊙ *Weekdays 9–4, weekends 10–4. Public Nights mid-Dec.–Jan., Tues. and Sat. at 7; Feb.–early Dec., Tues. and Sat. at 6.*

Around Wellington

★ **Moss Green Garden.** Set in the steep, bush-clad hills along the Akatarawa River, Moss Green makes for a superb day trip from the capital for serious gardeners and those venturing off the beaten path. Some 9 ft of rain fall here annually, and the land and vegetation have evolved to flourish under these conditions, as have Bob and Jo Munro. With great horticultural skill and intelligence, they plant accordingly, boldly using indigenous plants and unusual exotics from the Himalayas, North America, and Europe. Where possible, Jo has planted broad perennial borders (both Munros are English born, and styles of their native land do appear), and Bob has built bridges and ponds and is completing a fern walk through a section of their 40 acres of unspoiled bush. The Munros have also placed copper sentinels, stone tables and chairs, and large ceramic vessels throughout the garden—pieces that they created in their other lives as nonhorticultural artists. These are every bit as intriguing as the garden itself.

There are two approaches to the garden, both via Akatarawa Road an hour north of Wellington: From the east follow Highway 2 from the city to Upper Hutt, where Akatarawa Road climbs into the valley to Moss Green. There are wonderful old trestle bridges as you near the garden. From the west take Akatarawa Road from Highway 1 in Waikanae. You'll climb it over the pass, dropping down to the garden from above. This approach is not for the faint of heart, as it may be the narrowest, most precipitous road on North Island—watch closely for oncoming cars! Whichever way you come, the reward of a trip to Moss Green is a unique garden in a natural setting where the gardeners after more than 25 years are still amazed by so many shades of green. Visitors are welcome to picnic on the grounds. ⊠ *2420 Akatarawa Rd.,*

Upper Hutt, ☎ 04/526–7531, ℻ 04/526–7507. ✆ $5. ☉ Aug.–Apr., Wed.–Mon. 10–5; June and July, by appointment.

★ **Otari Native Botanic Garden.** Anyone with even the slightest interest in native New Zealand flora should pick up picnic provisions and spend an afternoon at Otari, just outside the city. Devoted to gathering and preserving indigenous plants, Otari's collection is the largest of its kind. With clearly marked bushwalks and landscape demonstration gardens, it aims to educate and thereby ensure the survival of New Zealand's unique and diverse plant life. While in the garden, you'll learn to dissect the forest, from the various *blechnum* ferns underfoot to the tallest emerent trees towering overhead—the rimu, kahikatea (ka-hee-ka-tee-ah), and northern rata—and everything in between. Look and listen for the native birds that flock to this haven: the bellbird (korimako), gray duck (parera), fantail (piwakawaka), New Zealand wood pigeon (kereru), silvereye (tauhou), and tui, among others. Cultivated borders highlight everything from Wellington coast plants to hebe cultivars to grasses and alpine rock garden plants. ⊠ *Wilton Rd., Wilton; take the No. 14 Wilton bus from downtown (20 mins), ☎ 04/475–3245. ✆ Free. ☉ Daily dawn–dusk.*

Southward Museum. This is in fact the largest collection of vintage and veteran cars in the southern hemisphere, with more than 250 vehicles: among them Bugattis, a Hispano-Suiza, one of only 17 Davis three-wheelers ever made, a De Lorean, a gull-wing 1955 Mercedes 300SL, gangster Micky Cohen's armor-plated 1950 Cadillac, and a Cadillac once owned by Marlene Dietrich. The motorcycle collection, which has a number of early Harley-Davidsons and Indians, a Brough Superior, and a Vincent V-twin, is almost as impressive. The museum is just off Highway 1, a 45-minute drive north of Wellington. ⊠ *Otaihanga Rd., Paraparaumu, ☎ 04/297–1221. ✆ $5. ☉ Daily 9–4:30.*

Dining

Wellington restaurants have a more cosmopolitan feel than those in other urban centers—maybe it's result of the capital city's diplomatic population. Wellington has loads of every sort of eatery, from ethnic cafés, hole-in-the-wall coffee bars, wine bars, and brasseries to velvety restaurants where you'll find yourself speaking in hushed tones.

City Center

$$$$ ✕ **Logan Brown.** This temple to gastronomy in a former bank building won oohs and aahs for its opulent decor before the food earned its own reputation. East-West combos include kumara (sweet potato) and peas in samosa pastry, and a rare fillet of hare garnished with Japanese shiitake mushrooms. Salmon is char-grilled and served with pureed fennel, while crayfish (clawless lobster) is adorned with only a lime aioli, allowing its own flavor to shine. The wine list includes many rare imports, plus the very best from New Zealand. ⊠ *Cuba St. at Vivian St., ☎ 04/801–5114. AE, DC, MC, V. No lunch weekends.*

$–$$$$ ✕ **Petit Lyon.** Singular is the catchword for this Wellington institution.
★ Or perhaps it should be plural, as you can choose from three levels and styles of eating—an oyster bar, a dining room, and a salon. Diners call the shots in the inexpensive and hugely successful oyster bar: Select a basic ingredient—seafood, meat, or poultry—then decide on the cooking method and the accompanying sauce and vegetables. The dining room serves a range of the sometimes outrageous but always challenging dishes for which chef/owners Ian Garner and Kent Baddeley have become famous. Examples? Think about wild duck legs baked in late-harvest Riesling with apricots and cognac, served over wild rice flavored with fresh vanilla pods—or a fillet of water buffalo with

white and black sesame seeds and pink and green peppercorns. The salon presents a six-course "surprise" menu at $150 or $250 per person, including wine. ⊠ *33 Vivian St.,* ☎ *04/384–9402. Reservations essential for salon. Jacket required. AE, DC, MC, V. Closed Sun. No lunch Sat. in dining room or salon.*

$$$ ✕ **Boulcott Street Bistro.** Serious foodies flock to this long-established bistro in a historic house for modern interpretations of French country classics. Owner/chef Chris Green makes a terrine from ham hock and duck livers, panfries field mushrooms with truffle oil, and tops paua fritters with crème fraîche and watercress. Serious winter fare includes braised oxtail with mashed potatoes and a traditional cassoulet. Not that it's all French—Asian influences surface in dishes like Szechuan tuna, served rare, and green-shell mussels in a red curry paste. ⊠ *99 Boulcott St.,* ☎ *04/499–4199. AE, DC, MC, V. No lunch weekends.*

$$$ ✕ **Brasserie Flipp.** Style, polish, and subdued lighting make Flipp a fash-
★   ionable choice among Wellington's sophisticates. Sensibly innovative dishes have included grilled fish with olive-oil-roasted potatoes, caramelized shallots, and anchovy butter; tartare of cervena (venison) with slow-roasted tomatoes, arugula, and shaved Parmesan; and a Muslim chicken curry with coconut *sambal.* The wine list has a good selection of New Zealand wine and token bottles from just about everywhere else. ⊠ *RSA Bldg., 103 Ghuznee St., Wellington,* ☎ *04/ 385–9493. AE, DC, MC, V.*

$$$ ✕ **Castro's.** It's been a butcher's shop and a delicatessen—now it's a contemporary NZ café with a pretty serious kitchen. The pasta is mostly made on the premises, and it is sensitively dressed. Duck is roasted Asian style with honey and star anise, and squab is fired up with a generous dollop of chili jam. Castro's also puts more thought into its soups than most places around town. If the paddle crab and capsicum (bell pepper) combo is listed, don't miss it. Bonus points for the excellent coffee. ⊠ *12 Marjoribanks St.,* ☎ *04/384–8733. AE, DC, MC, V.*

$$$ ✕ **Dockside and Shed Five.** These separate restaurants in separate buildings are listed together because they are both in a redeveloped waterfront warehouse—both specialize in seafood. Look for char-grilled salmon fillet with buckwheat noodles and a ginger and mint salad at Shed Five, and char-grilled grouper fillet with green olive *tapenade* and warm scallopini and red onion salad at Dockside. ⊠ *Dockside:* ⊠ *Shed 3, Queens Wharf, Jervois Quay,* ☎ *04/499–9900. AE, DC, MC, V.* ⊠ *Shed Five:* ⊠ *Shed 5, Queens Wharf, Jervois Quay,* ☎ *04/499–9069. AE, DC, MC, V.*

$$$ ✕ **Roxburgh Bistro.** This bustling bistro has been around for a while,
★   but in recent times it's become one of the city's hot spots. Chef/owner Mark Limacher has a way with offal dishes. If the lamb tongues are on, order them pronto—the chef braises them in serious stock with herbs and spices for six hours, so they're melt-in-the-mouth tender. And this is one of few restaurants in the country to make a thing of turkey— look for turkey tenderloins in Parmesan batter, served with hummus, red pepper salsa, capers, and raisin gravy. Commendably, individual local cheeses are offered rather than the ubiquitous mixed cheese board. The wine list is serious and well priced. ⊠ *18 Marjoribanks St.,* ☎ *04/385– 7577. AE, DC, MC, V. No lunch Sat. Closed Sun.–Mon.*

$$$ ✕ **White House.** Chef Paul Hoather's cooking gets the vote from a num-
★   ber of Wellington foodies as the best in town. The restaurant occupies a cute cottage that dates from the 1870s, but the food is pure 1990s. Try the garlic-marinated poussin (spring chicken) or any of the adventurous ravioli combos—prawns and scallops were blended into a filling on a recent menu. Desserts are well worth saving space for and often include fresh berries grown just up the coast. ⊠ *270 Willis St.,* ☎ *04/385–8555. AE, MC, DC, V.*

$$-$$$ ✕ **Café Paradiso.** A place to see and be seen, this corner site in Courtney Place has long been an in-crowd favorite. The food is Pacific Rim at its best. Recent offerings have included pork loin rubbed with cumin and served with a pineapple- and coriander-scented reduction sauce and Moroccan-flavored chicken breast with cashew-spiked couscous and preserved lemon. ⊠ *20 Courtney Pl.,* ☎ *04/384–2675. AE, DC, MC, V.* ☺ *No lunch weekends.*

$ ✕ **Dixon Street Gourmet Deli.** This city-center delicatessen stocks a fine
★ range of taste treats. There are home-baked breads and bagels, an international choice of meats, cheeses, pickles, and preserves, plus local smoked fish, green-shell mussels—everything you need for a superior picnic. If you prefer to dine in, you can do that, too—the deli has a licensed café attached. ⊠ *45–47 Dixon St.,* ☎ *04/384–2436. MC, V.*

$ ✕ **The Lido.** This bustling corner café across from the tourist information center is a pleasant, funky place that turns out inspired savory and sweet muffins, pasta dishes, vegetarian food, and yummy desserts—at breakfast, lunch, and dinner. The café stays open past midnight; and you can sit indoors or out when weather permits. ⊠ *Victoria and Wakefield Sts.,* ☎ *04/499–6666. Reservations not accepted. No credit cards.*

Wellington Suburbs

$$$ ✕ **Tinakori Bistro.** This popular shop-front bistro has a modern, French-influenced menu and a long-standing reputation for reliability. Entrées are mostly seafood oriented, and main courses lean toward the hearty—char-grilled Scotch fillet with béarnaise sauce and potato mash and an oven-roasted herbed loin of lamb with roasted mushrooms, parsnips, and a garlic, kumara (sweet potato), and roasted onion cake have appeared on recent menus. ⊠ *328 Tinakori Rd., Thorndon,* ☎ *04/499–0567. AE, MC, V. Licensed and BYOB. No lunch weekends.*

Lodging

Lodging in Wellington is peculiarly polarized, with elegant and expensive hotels on one end, homestays on the other, and nothing in between.

City Center

$$$$ ⛶ **Parkroyal Wellington.** If you are looking for the luxury, facilities,
★ and glamour that only a large international hotel can deliver, this is the best in town—possibly the best in the country. Guest rooms are decorated in sea greens and blues with blond wood furnishings, and bathrooms are comfortably appointed. Bureau rooms have a desk and a queen-size bed instead of two doubles. Request a room with ocean views. Service by the young staff is excellent throughout the hotel. The Parkroyal is in the city center, within walking distance of shops, restaurants, and the central business district. The Panama Street Brasserie is a favorite breakfast spot for the city's power brokers, and the refined upstairs Kimble Bent's restaurant is superb. ⊠ *Featherston and Grey Sts., Wellington,* ☎ *04/72–2722,* ℻ *04/472–4724. 232 rooms with bath. 2 restaurants, 2 bars, indoor pool, outdoor pool, sauna, exercise room, laundry. AE, DC, MC, V.*

$$$ ⛶ **City Life Wellington.** This contemporary all-suite hotel has an excellent location, right in the middle of the city. Added to this its spacious rooms and reasonable rates, and you've got one of the best value lodgings in town. Guests have a wide selection of studios and one-, two-, and three-bedroom suites with cream and white carpets and walls enlivened by Asian-style area rugs. Facilities, including self-catering kitchens, are similar—the main difference between rooms is their size. The hotel is popular with businesspeople visiting Wellington and has a security system in the elevator restricting access to floors, and washer and dryer plus dishwasher (though the rooms are also serviced)

in all suites. If you don't want to cook your own dinner, the hotel is handy to many restaurants, and the nearby Paris Restaurant provides room service if you don't want to leave your suite. Despite the location, you don't get street noise in the rooms. ✉ *300 Lambton Quay, The Terrace, Wellington,* ☎ *04/472–8588,* ℻ *04/473–8588. 65 rooms with bath and shower. Exercise room. AE, DC, MC, V.*

$$$ ⌂ **Shepherds Arms Hotel.** New Zealand's oldest hotel, this was once the coach terminus for the Thorndon/Karori area. Now the Shepherds Arms has been taken back close to its original state by the current owner—and given its original name. Four-poster beds, deep-blue carpets, and burgundy curtains all add to the charm of the hotel. Its only failing is that in keeping with the time it was first built, the rooms are fairly small (especially the three single rooms, which share a bathroom). Head down to the bar after 5 and mix with locals as they come in for a drink after a busy day at the office. Old photos on the wall show what Wellington looked like in the hotel's early days. The Shepherds Arms is extremely popular, especially on weeknights, so reserve well in advance. By Wellington standards it is a bit out of town—about four minutes' walk to the Parliament Buildings and about 10 to the main shopping district. ✉ *285 Tinakori Rd., Thorndon, Wellington,* ☎ *04/ 472–1320,* ℻ *04/472–0523. 12 rooms, 5 with bath and shower, 4 with shower only. Restaurant, bar. AE, DC, MC, V.*

$ ⌂ **Halswell Lodge.** Rooms at this hotel on the edge of the city center are compact and functional, but each has en-suite facilities and a reasonable standard of comfort. The surroundings offer a wide choice of restaurants. Rooms at the front are affected by street noise during the daytime. ✉ *21 Kent Terr., Wellington,* ☎ *04/385–0196,* ℻ *04/385– 0503. 19 rooms with bath. AE, DC, MC, V.*

Wellington Suburbs

$ ⌂ **Tinakori Lodge.** In a historic suburb overlooking the city, this lodge offers atmospheric bed-and-breakfast accommodations in tranquil surroundings. The rooms, which can sleep up to three, are simply furnished but comfortable. The city center is a 10-minute walk, and there are several restaurants in the vicinity. The owners are extremely friendly and helpful. Children are accommodated by arrangement. ✉ *182 Tinakori Rd., Thorndon,* ☎ *04/473–3478,* ℻ *04/472–5554. 10 rooms share 3 baths. BP. AE, DC, MC, V.*

Nightlife and the Arts

For a current listing of cultural events in Wellington, check the *Capital Times, City Voice,* or *Wellington Evening Post.*

The Arts

Wellington is the home of the **New Zealand Ballet Company** and the **New Zealand Symphony Orchestra.** The main venues for the performing arts are the **Michael Fowler Centre** and **Town Hall** (✉ Civic Sq., Wakefield St., ☎ 04/801–4242) for theater and music both classical and contemporary, and the **St. James Theatre** (✉ Manners St., ☎ 04/802–6910) and the **Opera House** (✉ Courtenay Pl., ☎ 04/ 385–0832) for drama, ballet, and opera. **Tiketek** (☎ 04/385–0832) sells tickets for local performances.

The **Downstage Theatre** holds frequent performances of stage classics. ✉ *Hannah Playhouse, Courtenay Pl. and Cambridge Terr.,* ☎ *04/384– 9639.*

Nightlife

The most vigorous sign of life after dark in Wellington is found in bars. On the ground floor of the Parkroyal Hotel at the corner of Grey and

Featherston streets, the **Arizona Bar** (☎ 04/495–7867) is packed on Friday and Saturday nights, as is the nearby **Malthouse**, at 47 Willis Street (☎ 04/499–4355). The best place to catch rock music is **Bar Bodega** (✉ 286 Willis St., ☎ 04/384–8212) or **St John's Bar** (✉ 5–9 Cable St., ☎ 04/384–3700).

Two hot, hot, *hot* Wellington bars are the Grand and CO2. The well-lived-in **Grand** (✉ 69–71 Courtenay Pl., ☎ 04/80–7800), once a brewery and then a distillery, has exposed brick walls, timber floors, and four levels with everything from a 400-person main bar to a garden bar to a 10-table poolroom. **CO2** (✉ 28 Blair St., ☎ 04/38–1064) is smallish and, true to its name, serves only sparkling wine. This brave philosophy has taken off like a popping cork. Thirty-six brands are sold by the glass, and serious bar food makes much use of local seafood like whitebait and crayfish.

Wellington A to Z

Arriving and Departing

BY BUS

InterCity buses (☎ 04/495–2443) arrive and depart from Wellington Railway Station. The terminal for **Newmans** buses (☎ 04/499–3261) is the InterIslander Ferry Terminal, 3 km (2 mi) from the city center.

BY CAR

The main access to the city is via the Wellington Urban Motorway, an extension of National Highway 1, which links the city center with all towns and cities to the north.

BY FERRY

The **InterIsland Line** (☎ 0800/802–802) runs vehicle and passenger ferries between Wellington and the South Island port of Picton. The one-way adult fare is $38 during school holidays, $30 at other times. Children ages 4–14 who are with their parents and in a vehicle travel free of charge; otherwise, they pay half price. The fare for a medium-size sedan is $150 during school holidays, $114 at other times. (Most rental agencies have North Island–South Island transfer programs for their vehicles: Leave one car off in Wellington and pick another one up in Picton on the same contract. It is common practice, quickly and easily done.) The crossing takes about three hours and can be very rough. There are at least two departures in each direction every day, and bookings should be made in advance, particularly during holiday periods. The ferry terminal is about 3 km (2 mi) from the city. A free bus leaves Platform 9 at the Wellington Railway Station for the ferry terminal 35 minutes before sailings.

BY PLANE

Wellington International Airport lies about 8 km (5 mi) from the city. **Super Shuttle** (☎ 04/387–8787) operates a 10-seater bus between the airport and any address in the city ($8 for one person, $10 for two). The bus meets all incoming flights; tickets are available from the driver.

BY TRAIN

The **Wellington Railway Station** (☎ 04/498–3000) is on Bunny Street, 1½ km (about 1 mi) from the city center.

Getting Around

BY BICYCLE

If the sun is shining and the wind is still, a bicycle is an ideal way to explore the city and its surrounding bays. **Penny Farthing Cycles** (✉ 89 Courtenay Pl., ☎ 04/385–2772) hires out mountain bikes for $25 per day or $140 per week, including helmet.

BY BUS

Wellington's public bus network is known as **Ridewell.** For trips around the inner city, the fare is $1. **Daytripper** tickets ($5), allowing unlimited travel for one adult and two children, are available from bus drivers after 9 AM. For maps and timetables, contact the information center (⊠ 142–146 Wakefield St., ☎ 04/801–7000).

Contacts and Resources

EMBASSIES AND HIGH COMMISSIONS

Australian High Commission. ⊠ 72–78 Hobson St., Thorndon, ☎ 04/473–6411. ☉ Weekdays 8:45–12:15.

British High Commission. ⊠ 44 Hill St., ☎ 04/472–6049. ☉ Weekdays 9:30–noon and 2–3:30.

Canadian High Commission. ⊠ 61 Molesworth St., Thorndon, ☎ 04/473–9577. ☉ Weekdays 8:30–4:30.

United States Embassy. ⊠ 29 Fitzherbert Terr., Thorndon, ☎ 04/472–2068. ☉ Weekdays 10–noon and 2–4.

GUIDED TOURS

Harbour Capital Bus Tours' Coastline Tour takes in attractions in the city center and along the Miramar Peninsula to the east. The 2¾-hour tour departs at 1:30 PM from the Visitor Information Centre at Victoria and Wakefield streets. ☎ 04/499–1282. 🖃 $21.

Westpac Trust Ferry, a commuter service between the city and Days Bay, on the east side of Port Nicholson, is one of the best-value tours in the city. On the way to Days Bay you can stop at Somes Island, formerly a quarantine station that is an unusual picnic spot on a summer afternoon. Days Bay itself has a seaside village atmosphere, local crafts shops, and great views of Wellington. Weekdays the catamaran departs from Queens Wharf at 6:15, 7:20, 8:20, noon, 2, 4:15, 5:30, and 6:30; weekends, at 10:15, noon, 2, 3:45, and 5. The direct trip takes 25 minutes. ⊠ Queens Wharf, ☎ 04/499–1273. 🖃 Round-trip $14.

Wally Hammond, a tour operator with a great anecdotal knowledge and a fund of stories about the city, offers a 2½-hour minibus tour of the city and Marine Drive. This can be combined with a half-day Kapiti Coast Tour, during which Southward Car Museum is visited. Tours depart from Travel World, Mercer and Victoria streets, at 10 and 2. Passengers can be picked up at their city hotels at no extra cost. ☎ 04/472–0869. 🖃 City tour $20, combined tour $70.

EMERGENCIES

Dial 111 for **fire, police, or ambulance** services.

Wellington Hospital. ⊠ Riddiford St., Newtown, ☎ 04/385–5999.

The After-Hours Pharmacy. ⊠ 17 Adelaide Rd., Newtown, ☎ 04/385–8810. ☉ Weekdays 5 AM–11 PM, Sat. 9 AM–11 PM, Sun. 10–10.

TRAVEL AGENCIES

American Express Travel Service. ⊠ 203 Lambton Quay, ☎ 04/473–1221.

Thomas Cook. ⊠ 108 Lambton Quay, ☎ 04/473–5167.

VISITOR INFORMATION

Wellington Visitor Information Centre. ⊠ Civic Administration Bldg., Victoria and Wakefield Sts., ☎ 04/801–4000. ☉ Daily 8:30–5:30.

THE WAIRARAPA

Wellington residents call the Rimutaka Range to the north of the city "the Hill," and for years it has been both a physical and psychological barrier that has allowed the Wairarapa region to develop at its own pace, in its own style. The hill has also kept tour buses away, and as a result landscapes such as the Pinnacles—cliff faces carved by the wind into shapes reminiscent of a cathedral—are uncrowded and easy to reach. There are great hikes and walks in the area. Times are changing quickly, however. An expanding wine trail in the southern Wairarapa is drawing visitors in increasing numbers, as well as city dwellers who want to move into the region for a lifestyle change. Meanwhile, the Wairarapa is still a place to discover—yet another delightful corner of New Zealand that can make you agonize over where to spend your time in the countryside.

Martinborough

57 *70 km (44 mi) north of Wellington.*

Martinborough is the hub of the Wairarapa's wine industry, and as a result this small town is attracting interest from developers keen to cash in on growing tourist numbers. So far changes have been tasteful, with people refurbishing historic places and opening their homes as B&Bs. The town gets its name from founder John Martin, who planned the streets in a Union Jack pattern stretching out from a square that remains the center of activity. Most restaurants and shops are on or close to the square.

Local records indicate that grapes have been raised in the region since the turn of the century. The present industry only dates back to 1979, and the popularity of **Martinborough wine** has grown tremendously since the mid- to late 1980s. That said, many local producers have small outputs, which means that some local varieties can be scarce everywhere but here, and prices tend to be higher than in other New Zealand wine regions. A number of the wineries are within a 10-minute walk of town, and there is a wine-trail horse-carriage tour as well. As in Hawke's Bay, red grape varieties seem to have the best go in the area's soil, with pinot noir being the most exceptional. Keep in mind that from year to year, any given winery's varieties may change depending on grape quality. Here is a short list of the best of the region's wineries:

Dry River (⌂ Puruatanga Rd., ☎ 06/306–9388) is possibly the country's hottest small (read: tiny) producer, whose ultraselectively produced vintages sell out immediately on release. Bringing home a bottle of its gewürztraminer or pinot noir would be a coup. Call ahead for an appointment. **Ata Rangi Vineyard** (⌂ Puruatanga Rd., ☎ 06/306–9570) makes exceptional chardonnay, pinot noir, and Célèbre (a cabernet-merlot-shiraz blend), again in small quantities. Tastings are held October–April, daily 11–5. **Martinborough Vineyard** (⌂ Princess St., ☎ 06/306–9955), open daily 11–5, is a larger but equally superior regional winery—actually the first to convince the world of the Wairarapa's pinot noir potential. Martinborough's chardonnay is also very fine. **Palliser Estate** (⌂ Kitchener St., ☎ 06/306–9019) has come out with some of the best local whites. Its straight sauvignon blanc and late-harvest Riesling are distinguished wines. Palliser is open daily 10–6.

OFF THE
BEATEN PATH

For an excursion that definitely isn't in tourist brochures, visit **Ruakokopatuna Glow Worm Caves.** You'll walk right through a cave following a freshwater stream, so expect to get wet feet, and take a torch

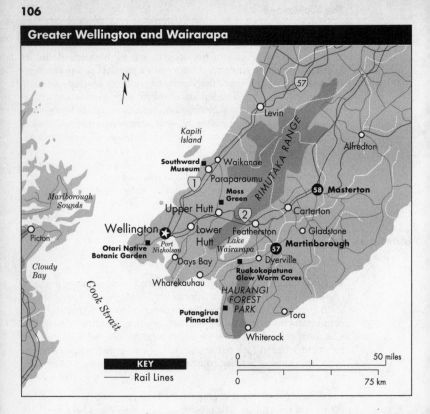

(flashlight). The glowworm display here is not quite as impressive as the one at Waitomo in the King Country, but the sense of adventure is much greater—nobody will tell you to duck when you're approaching a low-hanging rock, so be careful. Once you have found a cluster of glow-worms, turn your torch off for the best display, then switch it on again as you walk deeper into the cave. And keep in mind that as you stay in the cave longer, your eyes will adjust to the darkness, allowing you to see more lights. Take Lake Ferry Road south from Martinborough 7 km (4½ mi), turn left on Dyerville Road, and drive another 8 km (5 km) to a sign for the caves. Entrance is free, and it is best to call ahead for permission before you go. ☎ 06/306-9393.

The **Putangirua Pinnacles Scenic Reserve** near the bottom of North Island at Cape Palliser is protected from the hordes by its relative isolation. The big attractions are the spectacular rocks, which have been carved in the cliffs along a stony riverbank by badlands-type erosion. An hour-long walk from the carpark will take you to incredible views. If you're feeling adventurous, there is a bushwalk involving some steep climbs and won-derful vistas of the coast, as far off as South Island on a clear day. The Pinnacles are an hour's drive from Martinborough on good roads. Take Lake Ferry Road south out of town for 25 km (16 mi), turn left at the sign for Cape Palliser, and drive 15 km (9 mi) to Te Kopi, from which signs point to the reserve.

Dining and Lodging

$$$ ✕▥ **Martinborough Hotel.** This restored 1890s bed-and-breakfast hotel
★ is right in Martinborough's town square. The attractive Martinborough Bistro on site has a garden bar serving local wine, where you can enjoy a game of petanque (the French game *boules*) with other guests while sipping a glass of chardonnay. At dinner whitebait fritters (in season)

are served with lemon and dill mayonnaise, and the seared tuna is paired with an avocado and tomato salsa. Veal shanks are boned and sit on a mushroom and green pea risotto, and the cervena (venison) medallions are matched with a red onion and potato tart. Rooms have historic atmosphere, each decorated uniquely with area rugs and a mix of antique and contemporary furnishings, such as four-poster beds and writing tables. Some bathrooms have claw-foot tubs, and upstairs rooms open onto a veranda. ⊠ *33 Strassbourg St.,* ☎ *06/306–9350. 10 rooms with bath. Restaurant, 2 bars. BP. AE, DC, MC, V.*

Masterton

🟢 *40 km (25 mi) north of Martinborough, 230 km (144 mi) south of Napier.*

Masterton is Wairarapa's major population center, but you will find little of interest beyond its suitability as an exploring base. If you're traveling with children, **Queen Elizabeth Park** has a large playground, a rather outdated aviary, miniature golf, a miniature railway, and a small aquarium.

There are enjoyable bushwalks in beautiful forests laced with streams at **Tararua National Park,** which also has picnic facilities. The Mt. Holdsworth area at the east end of the park is particularly popular for tramping. To get there, turn off State Highway 2 onto Norfolk Road, 2 km (1 mi) south of Masterton.

For nature lovers, **Mount Bruce National Wildlife Centre** is a unique, well-managed wildlife park. The center provides rare glimpses of New Zealand's endangered species, including the takahe, a flightless bird thought to be extinct until it was rediscovered in 1948. The Campbell Island teal, shore plover, saddleback, stitchbird, kokako, and kiwi are all remarkable species, and you can take a look at New Zealand's living dinosaur, the tuatara. There are also trails to walk through native bush, and a tearoom. ⊠ *State Hwy. 2, 30 km (19 mi) north of Masterton,* ☎ *06/375–8004.* 🎫 *$6.* ☉ *Daily 9:30–4. Closed Dec. 25.*

Dining and Lodging

$$$$ ✕🏨 **Wharekauhau.** An hour's drive from Masterton on the rugged coast
★ at Palliser Bay, this Edwardian-style homestead set on a 5,000-acre working sheep station is luxury lashed by nature. On a hot summer afternoon this is one of the most peaceful places on earth; on a windy, wet morning it's like something out of *Wuthering Heights.* The public areas are in the homestead, which retains the feeling of a family lodge (owners Bill and Annette Shaw and their children still have a lot to do with the resort). Guest rooms are fashioned after staff quarters, with a style and comfort that farmworkers, of course, never had. Each room has a king-size bed, a small patio, an open fireplace, and cordless phones. On the farm you can take in the workings of the sheep station and walk around the gloriously remote coastline. Trout fishing is also an option, as are tours to the seal colony at Palliser Bay. And if you don't feel like driving, come by helicopter or arrange for a chauffeur. Rates include breakfast, dinner, and predinner drinks. ⊠ *Western Lake Rd., Palliser Bay, R.D. 3, Featherston,* ☎ *06/307–7581,* 𝖥𝖠𝖷 *06/307–7799. 20 rooms. Pool, tennis courts, fishing. AE, DC, MC, V.*

$$$ ✕🏨 **Copthorne Resort Solway Park.** Masterton's largest hotel is popular with both conference groups and families because of the range of on-site extras, such as tennis and squash facilities, children's play equipment, and indoor games. Rooms are standard but comfortable. There is a choice of restaurants, and the regular buffet meal provides reliable New Zealand–style fare. ⊠ *High St. S, Masterton,* ☎ *06/377–*

5129, FAX 06/378–2913. 102 hotel rooms, 5 motel units. 2 restaurants, bar, pool. AE, DC, MC, V.

Wairarapa A to Z

Arriving and Departing

BY CAR

A car is almost essential for getting around the Wairarapa. State Highway 2 runs through the region from north and south, between Napier and Wellington. From Wellington, you'll drive through Upper Hutt, over the Rimutaka Range, then into the gateway town of Featherston. Highway 53 will take you to Martinborough; Masterton is farther north along State Highway 2. The journey from Wellington to Martinborough takes 1½ hours; Masterton is another half hour. From Napier, Masterton is about three hours.

Contacts and Resources

GUIDED TOURS

The **Horse and Carriage Establishment** runs tours around the vineyards. The company also has twilight carriage drives, mystery tours, and horse and carriage hire for any specific journey. ⊠ *Martinborough,* ☎ *025/477–852.*

VISITOR INFORMATION

Tourism Wairarapa. ⊠ *5 Dixon St., Masterton,* ☎ *06/378–7373,* FAX *06/378–7042.* ☼ *Weekdays 8:30—5:30, weekends 9–4.*

4 Upper South Island

Natural wonders never cease—not on South Island. Nor do the opportunities for adventure: sea-kayaking, glacier hiking, trekking, fishing, mountain biking, rafting, and rock climbing. If you'd rather have an easier feast for your senses, fly over brilliant glaciers and snowy peaks, watch whales from on deck, and taste some of Marlborough's and Nelson's delicious wines. Add New Zealand hospitality, and you can't go wrong.

THE CLOSE PASSAGE across Cook Strait separates North
Island from South Island, but the difference between
the two is far greater than the distance suggests.
Whether you're seeing South Island from aboard a ferry as it noses
through the rocky entrance to Marlborough Sounds or through the window of a plane bound for Christchurch, the immediate impression is
that the landscape has turned feral: The mellow, green beauty of North
Island has given way to jagged snowcapped mountains and rivers that
charge down from the heights and sprawl across vast, rocky shingle
beds. South Island has been carved by ice and water, a process still rapidly
occurring. Locals will tell you that you haven't seen rain until you've
been drenched by a storm on the West Coast, where annual precipitation is ambitiously measured in meters.

The top half of South Island is a fair introduction to the contrasts of
New Zealand's less populated island. The Marlborough Province occupies the northeast corner, where the inlets of Marlborough Sounds
flow around verdant peninsulas and sandy coves. Inland from the
sounds is the country's newest land under vine, where since the mid-
'70s a burgeoning wine culture has developed. An abundance of other
fruit is grown in the area as well. Marlborough is relatively dry, beautifully sunny, and in summer the inland plains look something like the
American West, with mountains rising out of grassy flats. Throughout Upper South Island, you'll notice commercial foresting of the
hills—Californian *Pinus radiata* (Monterey pine) mature rapidly in New
Zealand soil. Their 25-year harvest cycle is one of the shortest in the
world, a fact duly noted by Japanese lumber concerns.

The northwest corner of the island, the Nelson region, is a sporting
paradise with a mild climate that allows a year-round array of outdoor
activities. Sun-drenched Nelson is the area's gateway, a vibrant town
with wholesome restaurants, an interesting flock of local craftspeople,
and an abundance of their wares. To the west of the city, Abel Tasman
National Park, like the Marlborough Sounds across the island, is
ringed with spectacular coastal waters—of a nearly indescribable
blue—studded with rock outcrops guarding coves and sands that are
sea-kayakers', trekkers', beachcombers', and sunbathers' dreams. The
area is literally surrounded by great national parks and hiking tracks,
such as the newly opened Kahurangi National Park, Nelson Lakes National Park, and the Heaphy Track, one of the country's great walks.

After the gentler climate of Marlborough and Nelson, the wild grandeur
of the West Coast comes as a surprise. This is Mother Nature with her
hair down, flaying the coastline with huge seas and drenching rains
and littering its beaches with evocative pieces of bleached driftwood.
When it rains, you'll feel like you're inside a fish bowl; then the sun
bursts out, and you'd swear you're in paradise. It is a country that has
created a special breed of people, and the rough-hewn and powerfully
independent locals—known to the rest of the country as coasters—occupy a special place in New Zealand folklore.

These three regions, which ring the north and west coasts of South Island, offer an immense variety of scenery, from the siren seascapes of
Marlborough Sounds and rocky Kaikoura, to the mellow river valleys
of Golden Bay and Abel Tasman National Park, to the West Coast's
colliding rain forests and glaciers, where the Southern Alps soar to 12,000
ft within 32 km (20 mi) of the shore.

Note: For more information on bicycling, fishing, hiking, and sea-kayaking in Upper South Island, *see* Chapter 6.

Pleasures and Pastimes

Dining

For seafood, game, and fresh fruit and vegetables, the top of the South Island is hard to beat. In Marlborough check out at least one winery restaurant—there's no better way to ensure that your meal suits what you're drinking. Salmon and green-shell mussels are both farmed in the pristine Marlborough Sounds, and local crops—besides grapes—include cherries (delicious!) and garlic. In Kaikoura try crayfish (clawless lobster). The region is in fact named after the delicacy, and you'll find it in restaurants or in makeshift caravans and roadside sheds. While in the West Coast make sure you try whitebait fritters. And be aware that restaurants and cafés around the glaciers can be quick to close their doors at night. Be there by 8:30, or you may go hungry.

CATEGORY	COST*
$$$$	over $45
$$$	$35–$45
$$	$25–$35
$	under $25

*per person, excluding drinks, service, and general sales tax (GST, 12.5%)

Lodging

North Islanders might disagree, but you may find New Zealand's friendliest people in the rural areas of South Island. And the best way to get to know them is to stay with them. Bed-and-breakfasts, farmstays, and homestays, all a variation on the same theme, abound in South Island in some spectacular coastal or mountain settings. Your hosts will feed you great breakfasts and help with advice on where to eat and what to do locally. Other choices include luxury lodges and standard, inexpensive motel rooms—there are plenty of the latter.

CATEGORY	COST*
$$$$	over $200
$$$	$125–$200
$$	$80–$125
$	under $80

*All prices are for a standard double room, excluding general sales tax (GST, 12.5%).

Mountains and Glaciers

South Island is piled high with mountains. The massive Southern Alps mountain chain virtually slices the island lengthwise, and many outlying ranges spring up farther north. Most of the mountains are easily accessible. You can walk on and around them, ski, or catch a helicopter to land on a glacier and tramp around. Much of the skiing in the upper half of South Island is reasonably challenging for intermediate skiers—the more advanced should look farther south.

Trekking and climbing are as challenging as you care to make them. Department of Conservation tracks and huts are spread around the region, and you can get details on hundreds of hikes from department offices or information centers. Even if you just want to take a casual, scenic walk, the opportunities are endless. In some places, such as the Kaikoura Coastal Track, pioneering farmers have banded together to create farm-to-farm hiking trails. These take you through otherwise inaccessible mountains, bush, or coastal areas.

Wildlife and Wilderness

The West Coast is the habitat for some very interesting creatures. South by Lake Moeraki, fiordland crested penguins and New Zealand fur seals are abundant, and bird life up and down the coast is fascinating. On the other side of the island, the Kaikoura Coast is still a sleepy and uncrowded region where you can get as close to whales, dolphins, and seals as possible in their environment.

South Island's West Coast has a rugged beauty that can be inviting in one instance and almost threatening the next. You can wake up to the sun shining off tall, snowcapped mountains, then a couple of hours later the mist and rain can swirl around the peaks and give them an entirely different complexion. Because of changing conditions, check local conditions before you head into some of the world's most dramatic mountain, bush, and coastal scenery.

Wine

In a little more than 20 years, Marlborough has established a solid international reputation. Because of the region's unique growing conditions, grapes come off the vines bursting with flavor. It's an exciting feistiness that many American connoisseurs consider too unbridled—but the wine is delicious, and you should seriously consider bringing a few bottles home. And at any of the these small boutique wineries, it's quite likely you'll share your first taste of their labors with the wine makers themselves.

Exploring Upper South Island

Most people come to Marlborough and Nelson on the ferry to Picton, the northern entrance to South Island. From here the choices open up before you. In four days you can see much of the northernmost part of the island. To undertake a walk on the Queen Charlotte, Abel Tasman, or Heaphy tracks, you'll need more time. For the West Coast three days is a bare minimum—it takes a half day just to get there.

Great Itineraries

Numbers in the text correspond to numbers in the margin and on the Upper South Island map.

IF YOU HAVE 2 DAYS

Spend a day touring the wineries in and around ⛨ **Blenheim** ④. On the second day head down to ⛨ **Kaikoura** ⑤, stopping at the **Awatere Valley Gardens** or **Winterhome** on the way to crayfish town before continuing to Christchurch. You could otherwise head straight from the ferry to ⛨ **Nelson** ⑥, taking the first day in town and the second in Abel Tasman National Park or in Nelson's wineries and craft shops.

IF YOU HAVE 4 DAYS

With four days you confront the kind of either/or conundrum that makes trip planning for South Island difficult: See the top of the island—the wineries of ⛨ **Blenheim** ④, relaxing ⛨ **Nelson** ⑥, the beautiful beaches and forests of ⛨ **Abel Tasman National Park** ⑪, perhaps all four days hiking one of Abel Tasman's tracks or the **Queen Charlotte Track** in the Marlborough Sounds—or head straight for the coastal rock formations, glaciers, and wildlife of the **West Coast.**

IF YOU HAVE 7 DAYS

You *could* try to cover three of the major areas in this chapter—Marlborough, Nelson, and the West Coast, or Marlborough, Nelson, and Kaikoura, but allowing three or four days for two areas is a better plan. Spend a day or two at the wineries, a day or two on the Marlborough Sounds sea-kayaking or walking, perhaps swinging through **Havelock** ③ on the way to or from the beautiful Kenepuru and Pelorus sounds, then head to ⛨ **Nelson** ⑥ or the **West Coast.**

Or spend the first three days in and around Nelson, looking at arts and crafts, tasting wine, and taking in ⛨ **Abel Tasman National Park** ⑪

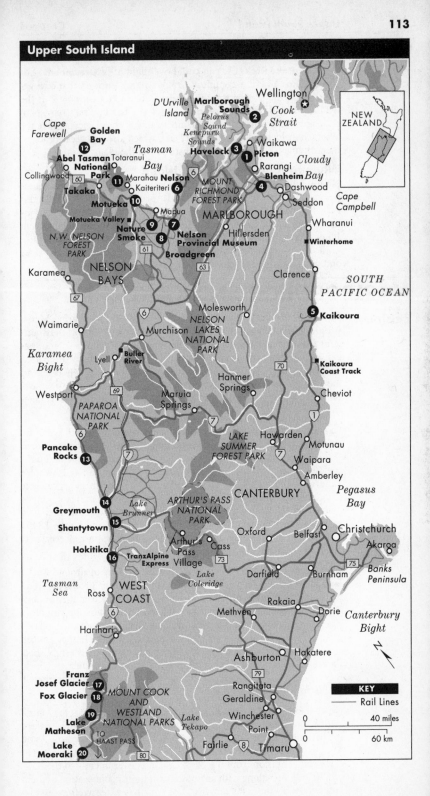

NEW ZEALAND

Wellington

Cook Strait

D'Urville Island

Marlborough Sounds ②

Pelorus Sound

Kenepuru Sounds

Cape Farewell

Golden Bay

⑫ **Abel Tasman National Park**

Tasman Bay

Totaranui

Collingwood 60

⑪ Marahau

Takaka

Kaiteriteri

Motueka

⑩

Motueka Valley ■

Nelson ⑥

⑨ **Nature Smoke** ⑦

Broadgreen

N.W. NELSON FOREST PARK

⑧

61

Mapua

Nelson Provincial Museum

MOUNT RICHMOND FOREST PARK

Havelock ③ **Picton** ①

Waikawa

Rarangi

Blenheim ④ Dashwood

Seddon

MARLBOROUGH

Hillersden

63

Cloudy Bay

Cape Campbell

Wharanui

■ Winterhome

Karamea

67

Waimarie

Karamea Bight

Westport

NELSON BAYS

6

Murchison

NELSON LAKES NATIONAL PARK

Molesworth

Clarence

SOUTH PACIFIC OCEAN

⑤ **Kaikoura**

Lyell ■ **Buller River**

69

Maruia Springs

Hanmer Springs

70

■ Kaikoura Coast Track

Cheviot

PAPAROA NATIONAL PARK

Pancake Rocks ⑬

6

7

7

LAKE SUMMER FOREST PARK

Hawarden

1

Motunau

Waipara

Amberley

Pegasus Bay

Greymouth ⑭

Lake Brunner

Shantytown ⑮

Hokitika ⑯

TranzAlpine Express

ARTHUR'S PASS NATIONAL PARK

Arthur's Pass Village

Cass

73

Lake Coleridge

CANTERBURY

Oxford

Belfast

Darfield

Burnham

75

Christchurch

Akaroa

Banks Peninsula

Tasman Sea

Ross

WEST COAST

6

Harihari

Rakaia

Methven

Ashburton

Dorie

Hakatere

Canterbury Bight

Franz Josef Glacier ⑰

Fox Glacier ⑱

MOUNT COOK AND WESTLAND NATIONAL PARKS

79

Rangitata

Geraldine

Lake Matheson ⑲

Lake Tekapo

Winchester

TO HAAST PASS

Lake Moeraki ⑳

80

Fairlie

8

Point

Timaru

KEY

— Rail Lines

0 ———— 40 miles

0 ———— 60 km

and **Golden Bay–Takaka** ⑫, then head to the West Coast. On the way down, stop at the town of Punakaiki for the coastal phenomenon called **Pancake Rocks** ⑬. You could overnight at ⚇ **Greymouth** ⑭ or ⚇ **Hokitika** ⑯ before continuing to Westland National Park to get yourself on the ⚇ **Franz Josef Glacier** ⑰ or ⚇ **Fox Glacier** ⑱. If the wildlife around ⚇ **Lake Moeraki** ⑳ lures you to the West Coast, plan to spend two or three days there after a day at the glaciers. Leave the West Coast by heading south to Haast, which also has great beaches, then driving to Wanaka or Queenstown via the Haast Pass.

When to Tour Upper South Island

Nelson and Marlborough are pleasant year-round, but beach activities are best from December to mid-April. Between December and early February is the busiest time on walking tracks, with New Zealanders setting out on their own holidays. Snow covers the mountains from June through October, which is a beautiful sight from seaside Kaikoura. The pleasures of winter weather around the glaciers—clear skies and no snow at sea level—are so far a well-kept local secret.

MARLBOROUGH AND KAIKOURA

By Stu Freeman, Stephen Wolf, and Mere Wetere

The Marlborough Sounds were originally settled by seafaring Maori people, who in their day kept to the coastal areas, living off the abundant fruits of the sea. It's no wonder they didn't venture inland, because these coastal areas are spectacular. The Maori named the area Te Tau Ihu o Te Waka a Maui (the prow of Maui's canoe), as legend has it that from his canoe Maui fished up North Island with the jawbone of a whale. Consequently North Island is called Te Ika a Maui—the fish of Maui.

Captain James Cook met the Maori settlers around 1770, when he stopped in the sounds to repair his ships and take on fresh provisions. Whalers later set up shop in Queen Charlotte Sound, but it wasn't until the 1840s that Pakeha (Europeans) came to the Wairau and Awatere valleys around Blenheim. Thirty years later, the unwittingly prescient Charles Empson and David Herd began planting red muscatel grapes among local sheep and grain farms. Their modest viticultural torch was rekindled in the next century by the Freeth family, and by the 1940s Marlborough wineries were producing constantia, port, sherry, and Madeira most successfully.

At the same time, commercial wineries were growing up around Auckland and Hawke's Bay. But the volume of their grape production didn't meet their needs. In the mid-1970s the North Island Montana company planted vines in Marlborough to increase the supply of New Zealand grapes. Other vintners followed suit, and within a decade today's major players—like Hunters, whose founder, Ernie Hunter, almost single-handedly launched the Marlborough name—had established the region's international reputation. There are now 39 wineries, which is New Zealand's single largest area under vine, and local growers sell grapes to wine makers outside the area.

Down the coast from Blenheim, Kaikoura is another area that the Maori settled, the predominant tribe being Ngai Tahu. True to their seafaring heritage, they are active in today's whale-watching interests. As of March 1998, Ngai Tahu is one of the first major Maori tribes to receive compensation from the New Zealand government—to the tune of $70 million—along with an apology for unjust confiscation of their lands, forests, and fishing areas. The tribe has extensive interests in tourism, fishing, and horticulture. Kaikoura's name is its original significance for the Maori—"to eat crayfish." These clean-tasting, clawless lobsters are a delight, and there aren't better reasons to come to Kaikoura than to eat *kaikoura* and to take in the refreshing ocean air.

Picton

❶ *29 km (18 mi) north of Blenheim, 110 km (69 mi) east of Nelson.*

The maritime township of Picton lies at the head of Queen Charlotte Sound and is the arrival point for ferries from North Island, as well as a growing number of international cruise ships. It plays a major role in providing services and transport by water taxi to a multitude of remote communities in the 200 square mi of islands, peninsulas, and waterways that make up the Marlborough Sounds Maritime Park. With such an expansive watery environment, it is not surprising that Picton is a yachting mecca and has two sizeable marinas, at Picton Harbour and at the adjacent Waikawa Bay. Along with the port of Havelock, these make up the second-largest marina complex in New Zealand.

There's plenty to do in the township, with craft markets during summer, historical sights to see, and walking tracks to scenic lookouts over the sounds. The township wraps around the harbor and is easy to traverse on foot. It has a good number of restaurants—seafood gets top billing—within easy reach of relatively reasonable inns.

❷ Picton is the base for cruising in the **Marlborough Sounds,** the labyrinth of waterways that was formed when the rising sea invaded a series of river valleys at the northern tip of the South Island. Backed by forested hills that at times rise almost vertically from the water, the sounds are a wild, majestic place edged with tiny beaches and rocky coves and studded with islands where such native wildlife as gannets and the primitive tuatara lizard have remained undisturbed by introduced species. Maori legend says the sounds were formed when a great warrior and navigator called Kupe fought with a giant octopus. Its thrashings separated the surrounding mountains, and its tentacles also became parts of the sunken valleys. These waterways are the country's second favorite for boating after the Bay of Islands, but for their isolation and rugged grandeur they are in a class of their own.

Much of the area around Picton is a national park, and it has changed little since Captain Cook found refuge here in the 1770s. There are rudimentary roads on the long fingers of land jutting into the sounds, but the most convenient access is invariably by water. One of the best ways to discover the area is by hitching a ride in Havelock aboard the *Pelorus Mail Boat,* which delivers mail and supplies to outlying settlements scattered around Pelorus Sound (☞ Guided Tours *in* Marlborough and Kaikoura A to Z, *below*).

To get your feet on the ground in and around the sounds, you can take any number of hikes on the **Queen Charlotte Track.** Starting northwest of Picton, the trail stretches 67 km (42 mi) south to north, playing hide-and-seek with the sounds along the way. Tramp through lush native forests filled with bird life, and stop here and there for a swim or to pick up shells on the shore. Unlike tracks such as the Abel Tasman in Golden Bay, there are no Department of Conservation huts to stay in, just a few points on the way for camping. There are other types of accommodation on the walk, however, from backpacking options to lodges, resorts, and homestays (☞ Lodging, *below*). Boats such as the *Cougar Line* can drop you off at various places for one- to four-day walks (guided or unguided), or you can kayak parts of it (☞ Guided Tours *in* Marlborough and Kaikoura A to Z, *below*).

For local and Queen Charlotte Track information, contact the **Picton Visitor Information Centre** (⊠ Picton Foreshore, ☎ 03/573–7477, 𝔽𝔸𝕏 03/573–5021).

Dining and Lodging

$$$ ✕ **Marlborough Terranean.** Murals, murals, murals—they're all around you at Lothar and Tracy Greiner's Mediterranean-leaning (hence the name) restaurant. Seafood chowder is always a good bet, as is carpaccio of sliced raw beef fillet with extra-virgin olive oil, lemon juice, and Parmesan. That Italian classic, saltimbocca—a schnitzel of milk-fed veal (hard to find in NZ) topped with smoked ham in a sauce with white wine, cream, and sage—is a big seller, and there are three preparations of fresh Marlborough fish. The decisions continue on the dessert list, with a choice of five accompaniments for homemade chocolate mousse— what joy! ⊠ *31 High St.,* ☎ *03/573–7122. AE, DC, MC, V.*

$ ✕ **Expresso House.** This relative newcomer to picturesque Picton has rapidly established a reputation for quality and unbelievably good value. Open sandwiches like spicy chicken on rye bread with lemon-caper sauce, regularly changing soups (Thai fish chowder is great), and salad bowls that might include smoked salmon or chicken satay rule the day. At night matters get more serious—bistrolike even—with a rare-baked beef fillet, or salmon oven-baked and topped with a dill cream sauce. Save room for the homemade desserts. ⊠ *58 Auckland St.,* ☎ *03/573–7112. MC, V.*

$$$ ✕▥ **Craglee Lodge.** On a hillside overlooking the emerald waters of the Bay of Many Coves, this three-level complex is a perfect place to unwind. It's swathed in pungas (tree ferns) and native bush and serenaded by bellbirds and tuis. Marilyn and Gary Lowe serve healthy fare from the sea and the region's produce. All of the comfortable, contemporary rooms open onto balconies and look over the bay. Two challenging tracks from the lodge are worth climbing for two reasons: the stunning views from Kenepuru Saddle and Marilyn's great packed lunch. You can also rent kayaks and dinghies, and fishing trips can be arranged. Take a 45-minute *Cougar Line* water taxi ride, possibly accompanied by dolphins, to get to this remote spot. Rates include three meals. ⊠ *Bay of Many Coves, Queen Charlotte Sound, Private Bag 407, Picton,* ☎ *03/579–9223,* 𝔽𝔸𝕏 *03/579–9923. 5 rooms, 2 with bath. Restaurant, lounge. AE, DC, MC, V.*

$$ ▥ **House of Glenora.** One of Picton's oldest houses, built in the 1860s for the town's first magistrate, is a stylish combination of homestay, weaving school, and gallery, in which you'll find exquisite examples of Birgite Armstrong's natural fiber garments. This gracious, smoke-free home, with a large, sunny veranda overlooking sprawling gardens and views toward the harbor, has all but one of its five rooms upstairs. They're spacious and inviting, each with its own color theme. Swedish born Birgite and her Australian husband, Neale, have used native woods such as kauri and rimu extensively in restoring Glenora in styles old and new. Breakfast is included in the rates, and there is a common lounge for guests. ⊠ *22 Broadway, Picton,* ☎ *03/573–6966,* 𝔽𝔸𝕏 *03/573–7735. 5 rooms, 2 with bath. Shop. MC, V.*

$$ ✕▥ **Punga Cove Resort.** This sanctuary in the Queen Charlotte Sound was carved out of the bush. From its crossroads on the Queen Charlotte Track—go for a steep hike to the south onto ridges that overlook the sounds—there are serene vistas of Camp Bay and Endeavour Inlet. If you only want to come for an evening meal, you can dine indoors or out on seared scallops and baby squid dressed with brandy and hazelnuts on Thai noodles, or poached salmon fillet on an herbed crab cake served with roasted red pepper aioli, or a hardier panfried venison with wild mushrooms, fresh herbs, and a blueberry sauce. The A-frame

chalets tucked into the bush, all with en suites and some with cooking facilities, are sunny retreats at a reasonable rate. More luxurious options are the self-contained chalets: large, tastefully decorated, and with two bedrooms with king-size beds, as well as a barbecue and ample wraparound decking. Budget accommodations with shared facilities are also available. You can rent kayaks and dinghies on site, fishing trips can be arranged, and there is a small grocery market. Access is quickest by the *Cougar Line* water taxi, 45 minutes from Picton. Otherwise, a two-hour-plus drive winds along Queen Charlotte Sound Drive to the turnoff at Link Water, where you come through the spectacular scenery of the Kenepuru Sound via some 15 km (10 mi) of gravel road—this is wonderfully off the beaten track. ✉ *Punga Cove, Endeavour Inlet, Queen Charlotte Sound, Rural Bag 408, Picton,* ☎ *03/579–8561 or 0800/809–697,* 🖷 *03/579–8080. 2 luxury chalets with bath, 11 smaller chalets with en suites. Restaurant, bar, pool, sauna. AE, DC, MC, V.*

En Route To take the long way to Blenheim (☞ *below*), **Port Underwood Road** is yet another unbelievably scenic road in a country full of unbelievably scenic roads. There are picnic areas north of Waikawa before you reach the eastern coastal bays, and a couple more near Rarangi. Get on Waikawa Road north out of Picton and continue through the town of Waikawa, then turn south at Opihi Bay. You could also pick up the road driving north out of Rarangi.

Heading west out of Picton toward the town of Havelock (☞ *below*), **Queen Charlotte Drive** rises spectacularly along the edge of Queen Charlotte Sound. It cuts across the base of the peninsula that separates this from Pelorus Sound, then drops into a coastal plain before coming to Havelock. Beyond town the road winds through forested river valleys before it rounds the eastern side of Tasman Bay and reaches Nelson. To start the drive from the InterIslander ferry terminal in Picton, turn right after leaving the carpark and follow the signs.

About a third of the way to Havelock, **Governor's Bay** is a gorgeous spot for a picnic, a stroll along the forested shore, or a swim in season. Watch for seabirds, and, if the sun is dipping in and out of the clouds, the changes in the colors of the bay.

Havelock

❸ *35 km (22 mi) west of Picton.*

Arguably the green-shell mussel capital of the world, Havelock is at the head of the **Kenepuru and Pelorus sounds,** and trips around the sounds on the *Pelorus Mail Boat* depart here. Locals will forgive you for thinking you've seen what the Marlborough Sounds are all about after crossing from North Island to South Island on the ferry—that's just a foretaste of better things to come. Small, seaside Havelock (pop. 400) is good to potter around in, looking at crafts and tucking into some of those mussels.

Dining

$ ✕ **Mussel Boys Restaurant.** Outside, mussels are playing rugby on the roof. Inside, mussels are served two ways—steamed for three minutes in the whole shell (steamers) and on the half shell (flats). Delicately enhancing the mussel's flavor is a choice of light sauces in which the mussels are steamed, like white wine, garlic and fresh herbs, or coconut, chili, and coriander, or even basil, parsley, and pesto with tomato and Parmesan cheese. So delighted was one visitor that he remarked, "When are you coming to San Francisco?" Look for Framingham's 1997 Sauvignon Blanc—a superb complement. In winter the Boys closes at 8 PM. ✉ *73 Main Rd., Havelock,* ☎ *03/574–2824. AE, DC, MC, V.*

Blenheim

❹ *29 km (18 mi) south of Picton, 120 km (73 mi) southeast of Nelson, 129 km (80 mi) north of Kaikoura.*

Locals pronounce it *blennum,* and most people come to Blenheim for one reason—wine. Marlborough vies with the city of Nelson for the highest total sunshine hours in New Zealand, and this plentiful yet not intense sun affords local grapes a long, slow ripening period. That combined with stony soil that reflects heat onto the ripening bunches and relatively low rainfall is the key to the audacious flavors of the area's grapes. Whites reign supreme. Cabernet sauvignon has mostly been pulled out following disappointing results, although both merlot and pinot noir show promise.

In 1973 the Montana company sent two Californian wine authorities to investigate local grape-growing potential. Both were impressed with what they found. It was the locals who were skeptical—until they tasted the first wines produced.

There is no reason to race around to all the wineries here—if you do, chances are good that your taste buds won't serve you very well by the time you get to the 39th tasting room. Those mentioned below are among the country's notables, but you won't go wrong if you stop at any of the vineyards around Blenheim. More than half of the wine bottled here is exported, particularly to the United Kingdom, so if you're coming from the United States, you have some great discoveries ahead of you.

The streets where most wineries are located are arranged more or less in a grid, which makes getting around relatively straightforward. Pick up a map of the Marlborough wine region at the **Blenheim Visitor Information Centre** (☎ 03/578–9904, ᖴᴬˣ 03/578–6084) in the Forum on Queen Street in the center of Blenheim.

Allan Scott Wines. Allan Scott helped plant the Stoneleigh vineyard for Corbans before launching his own label in 1990. Now he makes well-respected sauvignon blanc, chardonnay, and Riesling and is dabbling with red varieties. The tasting room is adjacent to a pleasant indoor-outdoor restaurant. ⊠ *Jackson's Rd. (R.D. 3), Blenheim,* ☎ *03/572–9054,* ᖴᴬˣ *03/572–9053.* ☉ *Daily, summer 9–4:30, winter, daily 10–4:30. Restaurant daily, evenings Oct.–Mar.*

Gillan Estate Wines. Entrepreneurial Blenheim residents Toni and Terry Gillan have launched a shopping center, a hotel, and this well-regarded wine company since they moved to town a few years ago. *Méthode champenoise* sparkling wine is their specialty, but their wine maker, Sam Weaver, also crafts very good sauvignon blanc and enjoyable chardonnay and merlot. The wine is made under contract off-site, but the pleasant tasting room is well worth visiting, not least for the tasty tapas prepared to partner the wine. ⊠ *Rapaura Rd. (R.D. 3), Blenheim,* ☎ *03/572–9979,* ᖴᴬˣ *03/572–9980.* ☉ *Daily.*

Hunter's Wines. Expatriate Irishman Ernie Hunter's marketing skills thrust Marlborough into the international spotlight, and the company he founded continues to be a leader. Tragically, he died in a car accident at the age of 37. Energetic Jane Hunter, his wife, took the reins and has masterfully shaped Hunter's reputation—which should be no surprise, since she has a long family history of wine making. Expect consistently strong sauvignon blanc—the oak-aged version is particularly good—tangy and delightfully herbal. Chardonnay will have very subtle oak flavors and intense fruit. There is usually an Estate White and an Estate Red, sometimes a vivacious gewürztraminer and maybe even a rosé. The winery also has a worthy restaurant (☞ Dining, *below*). ⊠ *Rapaura Rd., Blenheim,* ☎ *03/572–8489,* fax *03/572– 8457.* ☉ *Mon.–Sat. 9:30–4:30, Sun. 10–4.*

Cloudy Bay Vineyards. From the start, Kevin Judd has produced first-class sauvignon blanc, and an equally impressive chardonnay was added to the portfolio soon afterward. That was the intention of Australia's Cape Mentelle Vineyards when they got Cloudy Bay up and running in 1985. The winery's sauvignon blanc is one of New Zealand's best, with crisp, well-balanced fruit. Drink it young. Chardonnay is more complex and better suited to two or three years in the cellar and to drinking with more flavorful food—smoked salmon, for example— without being too oaky. The star, however, may be Cloudy Bay's Pelorus sparkling wine, a wonderfully creamy, savory yet crisp Méthode Champenoise. Very intriguing. ⊠ *Jackson's Rd., Blenheim,* ☎ *03/ 572–8914,* fax *03/572–8065.* ☉ *Daily 10–4:30; tours by appointment.*

Corbans Marlborough Winery. The Stoneleigh name is the one to look for at Corbans; it is one of the best-known names in stores overseas these days. So you may have already tasted Stoneleigh's Sauvignon Blanc at home, but it's likely that you haven't tried the Riesling, which is strikingly clear, full, and smooth. ⊠ *Jackson's Rd., Blenheim,* ☎ *03/572– 8198,* fax *03/572–8199.* ☉ *Daily 10–4:30; tours by appointment.*

Vavasour Wines. An almost instant hit among Marlborough's mid-'80s start-ups, the small, extremely conscientious wine-making operation at Vavasour produces sensitively balanced whites and reds. Based on the quality of a given year's harvest, grapes will be used either for Reserve vintages available in limited quantities or the medium price-range Dashwood label. Vavasour is in its own microclimate, in the Awatere Valley south of Blenheim. The viticulturist and wine maker focus on the finesse of smaller grape yields. You won't taste as many varieties here, but what you taste will be interesting and very well crafted. ⊠ *Redwood Pass Rd., Awatere Valley, 20 km (12 mi) south of Blenheim,* ☎ *03/575–7481,* fax *03/575–7240.* ☉ *Oct.–Mar., daily 10–4; Apr.– Sept., Mon.–Sat. 10–4; tours by appointment.*

Wairau River Wines. Phil and Chris Rose were the first contract grape growers in Marlborough. Now they produce a small range of wines under their own label. The tasting room is made from mud bricks; it also serves as a restaurant, concentrating on local produce. Try the multi-award-winning sauvignon blanc, then move on to the elegant chardonnay and, if it's available, the startlingly good, sweet Riesling, made in some years from grapes infected with the mold the French call the "noble rot." ⊠ *Rapaura Rd. and State Hwy. 6, Blenheim,* ☎ *03/572–9800,* fax *03/572–9885.* ☉ *Daily 10–5.*

Awatere Valley Gardens. Spend an afternoon strolling in three delightful gardens a short drive south of Blenheim. Because the summer of 1997– 98 in New Zealand was visited by what many called the drought of the century, you'll appreciate the tenacity and labor that made these gardens' survival possible. All have splendid herbaceous borders, as well as their own individual characteristics. At **Alton Downs,** take in the results of Alistair and Gaye Elliot's love of heritage roses, such as the French Alberic Babier, propagated around 1850, and their 200-ft oak walk. **Richmond Brook** has belonged to one family since 1848, so Yvonne Richmond's garden has many mighty trees, among them a magnificent sequoia standing next to the equally impressive homestead. An antique fruit tree orchard is underplanted with a carpet of daffodils in spring, and there is an ornamental pond in which potted blue Louisiana irises flourish. Carolyn and Joe Ferraby's **Barewood** has beautiful terraced borders blooming pink, blue, apricot, and white surrounding their century-old cottage. A sizable potager (kitchen garden) filled with ornamental vegetables and herbs is hedged with hornbeam and pathed with old bricks. A 100-year-old cob house on the property was the original home of Mr. Ferraby's ancestors. Carolyn now uses it as a shop, where she sells plants and garden accessories. ✉ *Alton Downs, Awatere Valley Rd., 5 km (3 mi) west of State Hwy. 1,* ☎ *03/575–7414,* FAX *03/5757111.* ✉ *Richmond Brook, Marama Rd., outside Seddon, 13 km (8 mi) west of State Hwy. 1,* ☎ *03/575–7506,* FAX *03/575–7506.* ✉ *Barewood, Marama Rd., outside Seddon, 18 km (11 mi) west of State Hwy. 1,* ☎ *03/575–7432,* FAX *03/545–7436.* 🖾 *$4 per person per garden.* ☉ *By appointment.*

Dining and Lodging

$$$ ✕ **d'Urville Wine Bar and Brasserie.** On the ground floor of Hotel d'Urville (☞ *below*), this restaurant serves everything from a cup of coffee to a delightful dinner. The setting is unusual and tasteful, and the food, cooked by a recent New Zealand Chef of the Year, is excellent. The seafood chowder is chock-full of piscatorial goodies, and the scallops are perfectly cooked—which means just barely. Best of all are the Marlborough Sounds mussels. The kitchen steams them open in herb-laced white wine and serves them with black beans and chili. ✉ *52 Queen St., Blenheim,* ☎ *03/577–9945. AE, DC, MC, V.*

$$$ ✕ **Rocco's.** This might not be the top Italian restaurant in the country, but chef/owner Piero Rocco makes sure it's the most fun. A mad-keen fisherman, Piero was once fined for catching the fish he put on his menu—crazy, but he didn't have a commercial fishing license. Now he buys his seafood, and it's still quite good. He also makes his own pasta and prosciutto ham, and he's particularly proud of his grilled scampi with garlic and parsley butter. Ask his advice about which Marlborough wine to choose—he's fanatical about the local product. If he joins your table, watch out for his grappa—it's dangerous! ✉ *5 Dodson St., Blenheim,* ☎ *03/578–6940, AE, DC, MC, V.*

$$–$$$ ✕ **Bellafico Caffé & Wine Bar.** Brunch, lunch, dinner—take your pick, they're all superb here. Start the day with fresh fruit on crunchy granola, or savory waffles with sliced banana, maple syrup, and crispy bacon. Later, choose a pizza—with chorizo, olives, tomato, and basil, for one—or share a meze platter with smoked beef, gherkins, *tapenade*, pickles, and cheese. At night the house-smoked wild venison starter makes a break from all that farmed cervena (venison), and if you're a serious meat lover, you can follow that with sautéed pork medallions on a bed of red cabbage with orange and walnut marmalade. Noncarnivore? Vegetarians are taken just as seriously with dishes like vegetable curry (famous locally) and pumpkin ravioli with a creamy mushroom sauce. ✉ *17 Maxwell Rd., Blenheim,* ☎ *03/577–6072, AE, DC, MC, V.*

$$ ✕ **Hunter's Vineyard Restaurant.** Dining at a vineyard is a great way
★ to appreciate just how seriously New Zealand wine makers consider food when creating their wine. Local produce is the star at this pleasant indoor/outdoor eatery. Marlborough green-shell mussels with Thai green curry sauce are a good match for Hunter's Sauvignon Blanc or Gewürztraminer; salmon steak with dill yogurt sauce and potatoes will go better with chardonnay. Local venison with a juniper and coriander sauce and sirloin of beef with fresh herb and garlic butter may tempt you to try one of the Hunter's reds. They're leaner and greener than North Island reds, but they do seem appropriate with local food. ✉ *Rapaura Rd., Blenheim,* ☎ *03/572–8803. AE, DC, MC, V.*

$ ✕ **Paddy Barry's Bar and Restaurant.** Locals come here for a chat and a beer, and the menu is casual, straightforward, and well priced. In other words, it's a good place to come down from traveler's stomach and overenthusiastic gourmandizing. A plate of battered and fried seafood is very reasonable, a pleasure alongside a well-poured Guinness. You'll find Guinness *in* the food, too, in the form of a beef 'n' Guinness hot pot, one of three on offer. ✉ *51 Scott St., Blenheim,* ☎ *03/578–7470. AE, DC, MC, V.*

$$$ ✕🏨 **The Marlborough.** The Art Deco–inspired furnishings throughout this attractive, contemporary luxury hotel are enhanced by a color scheme that seems to emulate the region's ripening produce, its brilliant sun, and the blue-green waters of the Marlborough Sounds. Standard rooms have queen-size beds, deluxe rooms and suites have high rimu (native pine) ceilings and super-king-size beds. Suites also have whirlpool baths. The hotel is on the edge of town, opposite the Wairau River on the road to Nelson. ✉ *20 Nelson St., Blenheim,* ☎ *03/577–7333,* 🄵🄰🄷 *03/577–7337. 22 deluxe rooms, 2 standard rooms, 4 suites. Restaurant, bar. AE, DC, MC, V.*

$$$$ 🏨 **Hotel d'Urville.** Every room is indeed unique in this modern bou-
★ tique hotel in the old Public Trust building. You could choose the Raja Room, where silk saris are draped over the main bed and there are various brass ornaments and a carved Javanese day bed—or an African theme, or the sensory trip of the Colour Room. One room matches the overall theme of the hotel and is based on the exploits of Dumont d'Urville, who made voyages to the Pacific and the Antarctic in the 1820s and 1830s. The hotel is built around the Public Trust's original vault, which now serves as a public area for guests. The hotel also has a very good restaurant (☞ *above*). ✉ *52 Queen St., Blenheim,* ☎ *03/577–9945,* 🄵🄰🄷 *03/577–9946. 9 rooms, 3 with bath, 6 with shower only. Restaurant, bar. AE, DC, MC, V.*

$$$$ 🏨 **Timara Lodge.** Taking a relaxing stroll around the well-tended gar-
★ dens, rowing about the lodge's pond, enjoying a drink inside in the library, or tasting some of the finest meals in the country along with appropriate glasses of local wine around a magnificent oak table—Timara Lodge offers one of the most luxurious experiences on South Island. Built in 1923 as a rural getaway, the lodge is a marvel of craftsmanship and the use of native timber. Downstairs, beautifully constructed rooms and furnishings speak of the quiet elegance of times past. In rooms, bedsteads swollen with comfortable linens stand alongside well-chosen antiques. Jeremy and Suzie Jones preside over the lodge, with Jeremy turning out masterful dishes that focus on the freshness of local ingredients: fruits and greens, scallops (with roe in season), salmon, venison, or tender racks of lamb. Wine tours, trout fishing, sea-kayaking, golf, skiing, even whale-watching (an hour and a half away in Kaikoura) can be arranged for you. The hefty per-person price includes breakfast, dinner, and cocktails. ✉ *R.D. 2, Dog Point Rd., Blenheim,* ☎ *03/572–8276,* 🄵🄰🄷 *03/572–9191. 4 rooms. AE, DC, MC, V.*

$$–$$$ 🏨 **Le Grys Vineyard Homestay.** If wine has brought you to Marlborough, consider starting the day in your own cottage in the heart of a vineyard. Waterfall Lodge is a self-contained mud-block cottage with a brook running past, literally surrounded by the Le Grys vineyard's sauvignon blanc, pinot noir, and chardonnay grapes. The main bedroom has a canopied queen-size bed, and you don't even have to leave the cottage for breakfast, as it arrives in a hamper at the front door. You can also stay in the spacious ranch-style homestead, with its wraparound verandas and sophisticated touches, with hosts John and Jennifer Joslin, who built the house and cottage. Their first Le Grys Sauvignon Blanc was bottled in 1996, and the first pinot noir should be ready by the time you arrive. Rates include breakfast, and the hosts can arrange trout fishing, horse trekking, boating on the sounds, and scenic flights. The homestay is 12 km west of Blenheim in Renwick; two minutes west of town you'll see Conders Bend Road on the left.

⊠ *Conders Bend Rd., Renwick,* ☎ *03/572–9490,* ⨳ *03/572–9491.*
1 room, 1 cottage . MC, V.

Fishing

For information on stream fishing in the Nelson Lakes district and deep-
sea fishing out of Picton, *see* Chapter 6.

En Route   Susan Macfarlane is on the mark when she says that there is no other
garden in New Zealand quite like her **Winterhome.** There are the dry
limestone soil and an abundance of sunshine that lend a Mediterranean
air to this land. But it is with a strong sense of design and drama that
Susan and her husband, Richard, have moved beyond the cottage-gar-
den phenomenon so popular today. Winterhome is virtually a study in
the rules of traditional garden design and its emphasis on structure.
Straight lines and geometric patterns provide clear boundaries for the
plantings. The palette is restrained, and the effect is unified and rhyth-
mic. A large, sunken garden is hedged with dwarf boxwood and filled
solely with fragrant, white Margaret Merril roses. A broad pathway takes
you past sweeps of lavender boldly punctuated by evergreen spires. High
brick walls enclose spaces and provide a sense of intimacy and safety.
Benches are exactly where you want them: in a cool spot at the end of
a long pathway or overlooking the Pacific. Views are always considered at Winterhome and somehow made more enticing for having been
framed with aesthetic control, be it by greenery or perhaps the span of
an arched gateway. Winterhome is midway between Blenheim and
Kaikoura. ⊠ *State Hwy. 1, Kekerengu,* ☎ *03/575–8674,* ⨳ *03/575–
8620.* 🔳 *Small entry fee.* ☉ *Late Oct.–Easter, daily 10–4.*

The Store. Susan and Richard Macfarlane of **Winterhome** have literally branched out and built a one-stop store and café below their gardens at Kekerengu, on the main highway between Blenheim and
Kaikoura. Its dramatic setting at the edge of the Pacific Ocean—which
is literally pounding at your feet—makes it a great place to relish
cooked crayfish and a glass of wine or to stop for a light meal, lunch,
or dinner. ⊠ *State Hwy. 1, Kekerengu,* ☎ *03/575–8600.*

Kaikoura

❺   *129 km (81 mi) south of Blenheim, 182 km (114 mi) north of
Christchurch.*

The town of Kaikoura sits on a rocky protrusion on the east coast, backed
by an impressive mountainous upthrust. There is plenty of local crayfish to be had at roadside stalls, which is an excellent reason to come
here, but an even better one is sighting the sperm whales that frequent
the coast in greater numbers than anywhere else on earth. The sperm
whale, the largest toothed mammal, can reach a length of 60 ft and a
weight of 70 tons. The reason for the whales' concentration in this area
is the abundance of squid—among other species the giant squid of seafaring lore—which is their main food. Scientists speculate that the
whales use a form of sonar to find the squid, which they then bom-
bard with deep, powerful sound waves generated in the massive cav-
ities in the fronts of their heads. Their hunting is all the more remarkable
considering that much of it is done at great depths, in darkness. The
whales' food sources swim in the trench just off the continental shelf,
barely a half mile off Kaikoura. You are most likely to see the whales
between October and August.

Fyffe House is Kaikoura's oldest surviving building, erected soon after
Robert Fyffe's whaling station was established in 1842. Built on whale-
bone piles, the house provides a look at what life was like when peo-

ple aimed at whales with harpoons rather than cameras. ⊠ *62 Avoca St., Kaikoura,* ☎ *03/319–5835.* 🎫 *$3.50.* ☉ *Daily 10–5.*

The Kaikoura Peninsula has two **walks**—not to be confused with the Kaikoura Coast Track (☞ Outdoor Activities and Sports, *below*)— that are particularly worthwhile, considering the town's spectacular coastal scenery: the cliff-top walk, from which you can look over seal colonies, and the longer shoreline walk that takes you much closer to the colonies. Consult the information center about tides to avoid getting flooded out of certain parts of the walks. ⊠ *Walks start at the end of Fyffe Quay.*

On the first Saturday of October the town celebrates its annual **Seafest,** during which the best of this coastal area's food, wine, and beer are served up while top New Zealand entertainers perform on an outdoor stage. Tickets are available from the **Kaikoura Information and Tourism Centre** (☞ Visitor Information *in* Marlborough and Kaikoura A to Z, *below*).

Dining and Lodging

$$$ ✕ **White Morph Restaurant.** Set in what was once the first bank of Kaikoura, White Morph has historic elegance. Locally made gilded mirrors and marine art adorn the walls, but the best scenes are the seaside views from the front windows. Crayfish features strongly on the menu; also look for other local fish and dishes like sesame-coated lamb racks, Kobe-style (marbled Japanese) beef with kumara- (sweet potato-) and-poppy-seed *rösti,* and marinated chicken in a Thai-style chili sauce. ⊠ *92–94 the Esplanade,* ☎ *03/319–5676. AE, DC, MC, V.*

$$ ✕ **The Craypot.** This casual and modern café relies strongly, as the name suggests, on the local delicacy. It's expensive, but it's also the best in the country. Other types of seafood also figure large on the menu, and there are also steak, chicken, and lamb dishes. The homemade desserts are worth leaving a space for. In summer there is outdoor dining; in winter an open fire roars at night. ⊠ *70 West End Rd.,* ☎ *03/319–6027. AE, DC, MC, V.*

$ ✕ **Hislops Café.** Homey and wholesome Hislops is a few minutes' drive north of town and well worth the trip for breakfast, lunch, or dinner, especially when the sun happens to be streaming in the windows. In the morning you'll find tasty eggs and bacon, and a real treat in the freshly baked whole-grain bread served with marmalade or honey. There are also tasty muffins, both sweet and savory. Lunches and dinners are all based on organic whole foods used with imagination and style. On fine days eat outside on the veranda. ⊠ *Main Hwy.,* ☎ *03/319–6971. MC, V.*

$$ 🏠 **Old Convent.** Some old habits are hard to shake. At this 1912 former French convent, it's easy to imagine a once-austere cluster of robed nuns rustling silently about their day. In fact, French architect and chef Marc Launay and wife Wendy have infused a warm and welcoming touch and added creature comforts that its former residents would have eschewed, at the same time preserving essential aspects of the convent. They've cleverly combined what must have been small adjoining studies and mediation rooms for the nuns. The two large queen bedrooms have great views of the Kaikoura Ranges. The guest lounge used to be a chapel and still has its cathedral ceiling, and there is an ornate wrought-iron stairwell that winds down from the chapel to a reception area. The heart of this sprawling bed-and-breakfast has to be the French restaurant where many guests get together around large rimu wooden tables in the morning or during dinner (rates include breakfast; dinner is $40 per person). The convent is a few minutes' drive out of town. ⊠ *Mt. Fyffe Rd.,* ☎ FAX *03/319–6603. 11 rooms, 4 with shared bath. Restaurant, croquet, bicycles. AE, MC, V.*

$$ ☷ **White Morph Motor Inn.** A waterfront view is hard to ignore in most places—even more so on the rugged coast of Kaikoura. This contemporary motel-style inn is in a great spot just opposite the beach, and its two foremost suites get the best views of the sea. Of the 19 self-contained units 12 are studios, four are luxury suites with king-size beds and double spa baths, and three others are two-bedroom apartments with lounges and kitchens downstairs and two bedrooms upstairs. Upstairs rooms have decks from which you can enjoy views of the magnificent Kaikoura Ranges, and downstairs units have courtyards. You can book local activities from here, and the inn's restaurant (☞ *above*) is in a historic building next door. ✉ *92–94 the Esplanade, Kaikoura,* ☎ *03/319–5014,* ℻ *03/319–5015. 12 rooms, 4 suites, and 3 apartments. AE, DC, MC, V.*

$ ☷ **Beachfront Bed and Breakfast.** The big attraction here is the beachside location and the sea views—which are best in upstairs rooms. Sit on the balcony and enjoy a crayfish tail and a bottle of wine while you take in the sea air. It's that feeling of contentment that enticed owner Glynn Beets, after being away from New Zealand for 20 years, to fall in love with the top end of South Island. Glynn also loves cooking and happily prepares breakfast to suit your preferences. All rooms are spacious and comfortable; three doubles upstairs have en suites, the twin downstairs a separate shower and toilet. In part because of reasonable prices, this is always the first bed-and-breakfast in town to sell out—phone well ahead to book a room. ✉ *78 the Esplanade,* ☎ *03/319–5890,* ℻ *03/319–5895. 4 rooms with shower. MC, V.*

Outdoor Activities and Sports

Whale-watching and swimming with dolphins and/or seals are both extremely popular in December and January, so either avoid Kaikoura at those times or book well in advance. To keep your feet on terra firma, the three-day Kaikoura Coast Track is a great way to see a spectacular mix of rugged coastline, pioneering farms, and mountain scenery.

HIKING

The Kaikoura Coast Track. The descendants of two Scottish pioneering families—the Caverhills and Macfarlanes, who settled the huge 57,000-acre Hawkswood Range in 1860—have opened up their farms and homes to travelers. This three-day walk combines uncrowded hiking—10 people at a time maximum—and farm hospitality. Take binoculars to search out sea life like whales and dolphins.

Warm, clean cottages with kitchens and hot baths or showers are at the end of each day's hike. You can arrange a meal with your hosts on weekdays or buy fresh farm produce to prepare yourself. Breakfast and lunches are also available. The first night is at Hawkswood in the historic sheep station setting of the **Staging Post,** where host J. D. Macfarlane has a passion for Shakespeare and old stagecoaches. Accommodations are in rustic mud-brick or log cabins. A challenging five- to six-hour walk the next day will take you to **Ngaroma,** Heather and Bruce Macfarlane's 3,000-acre sheep and cattle farm. **The Loft** has a large lounge with a log fire and rooms that each sleep up to four people. Day two's hike is along the beach, passing an ancient buried forest before heading across farmland to an area of regenerating bush. Around the dinner table at **Medina,** where you'll spend the third night in either **Te Whare** or the **Garden Cottage** (better for couples), you might meet David Handyside's father, Miles, who settled the 1,600-acre sheep and cattle farm in 1945. The third day, a demanding four- to five-hour walk, takes you over the 2,000-ft-plus Mt. Wilson, with its breathtaking views of the Waiau River and the Kaikoura Ranges.

The fee for walking the track is $90 per person, and a guided walk can be arranged ($100 per person per day). If you opt to have all meals included and need bedding, the total cost is $81 per person per day. Bookings are essential. The track is a ¾-hour drive south of Kaikoura and a 1½-hour drive north of Christchurch on State Highway 1. ⊠ *Medina, R.D. Parnassus, North Canterbury,* ☎ *03/319–2715,* ℻ *03/319–2724.* ☉ *Oct.–Apr.*

SWIMMING WITH DOLPHINS AND SEALS

Top Spot Seal Swims (☎ 03/319–5540) has two trips daily November–April, $35 per person. **Graeme's Seal Swims,** a shore-based operation, has three trips daily November–April, $35 per person. **Dolphin Mary Charters** (☎ 03/319–6777) has dolphin swims at 6 AM, 9 AM, and 12:30 PM from October to April. The cost is $80 per person.

WHALE-WATCHING

Whale Watch™ Kaikoura Ltd. Whale Watch is owned by the Ngai Tahu *iwi* (tribe). Since arriving in the Kaikoura area in AD 850, the Ngai Tahu, the predominant South Island Maori iwi, claim to have lived and worked based on a philosophy of sustainable management and sensible use of natural resources. Having worked these waters since 1987, Whale Watch skippers can recognize individual whales and adjust operations, such as the boat's proximity to the whale, accordingly. Allow 3½ hours for the whole experience, 2½ hours on the water.

Book in advance: 7 to 10 days November–April, 3 to 4 days at other times. Trips depend on the weather, and should you miss seeing a whale, which is rare, you will get up to an 80% refund of your fare. Take motion-sickness pills if you suspect you'll need them: Even in calm weather, the sea around Kaikoura often has a sizable swell. ⊠ *The Whaleway Station, Box 89, Kaikoura,* ☎ *03/319-6767 or 0800/655–121 (toll-free),* ℻ *03/319–6545.* ▨ *$95. AE, DC, MC, V.*

Wings Over Whales. If you'd rather get above the action, take a 30-minute whale-spotting flight. Your aircraft, a nine-seater Islander or a 14-seater GAF Nomad N24A, will be smoothly and skillfully piloted to circle above, affording a bird's-eye view of the giant sperm whales' immensity. While searching for other whales' telltale water spouts, pilot and copilot provide informative commentary on the creatures' habits. The trick is to stay glued to your window—which isn't hard because at least half the time, with the plane banked in an almost perpetual circle, gravity ensures that your face is just about stuck to it. ⊠ *Peketa Airfield, State Hwy. 1, Kaikoura,* ☎ *03/319–6580 or 0800/226–269 toll-free,* ℻ *03/319–6668.* ▨ *$85. AE, DC, MC, V.*

By dint of interactive digital imagery—to wit a photo of you superimposed onto a whale's tail—**Whale Watch Photography** prints clever color photos and postcards. It takes about five minutes to shoot and process the photos. ⊠ *The Whaleway Station, Box 89, Kaikoura,* ☎ *0800/655–121, ext. 823.*

Marlborough and Kaikoura A to Z

Arriving and Departing

BY BUS

InterCity (☎ 03/379–9020) runs daily between Christchurch and Kaikoura.

BY FERRY

InterIsland Line (☎ 0800/802–802) runs vehicle and passenger ferries between Wellington and Picton. The one-way adult fare is $46. The fare for a medium-size sedan is $165 during school holidays, $116 at other times. The crossing takes about three hours and can be very rough. InterIsland's slightly more expensive fast ferry *The Lynx* does the journey in half the time when it runs from November until April. There are at least two departures in each direction every day, and bookings should be made in advance, particularly during holiday periods. The ferry docks in Picton at the town wharf.

BY PLANE

The very scenic flight from Wellington to Picton takes about a half hour. **Air New Zealand Link** (☎ 09/357–3000) has 10 departures to and from Wellington daily. From Wellington, **Soundsair** (☎ 0800/505–005) serves Picton ($45) and Blenheim ($65).

Getting Around

BY BOAT

See Guided Tours, *below.*

BY CAR

Blenheim is a 25-minute drive from the ferry terminal in Picton and a two-hour drive from Nelson to the west and Kaikoura to the south.

Contacts and Resources

CAR RENTAL

Most rental agencies have North Island–South Island transfer programs for their vehicles: Leave one car off in Wellington and pick another one up in Picton on the same contract. It is common practice, quickly and easily done. If you initiate a rental in Picton, the following agencies are represented at the ferry terminal: **Avis** (☎ 03/573–6363), **Budget** (☎ 03/573–6009), and **Hertz** (☎ 03/573–7224).

EMERGENCIES

Dial 111 for **fire, police, or ambulance** services.

GUIDED TOURS

Action in Marlborough. To see the glorious Marlborough Sounds, try a two- or four-day fully catered and guided inn-to-inn walk on the **Queen Charlotte Track.** The four-day walk includes all land and water transport, comfortable accommodations in three Sounds Resorts—Punga Cove Resort (☞ Picton Lodging, *above*), Furneaux Lodge, and the Portage. Experienced guides ensure that you are well informed on the area's rich natural and human history. Advance bookings are essential. The company also guides hikes along the Kaikoura Coastal Track. ✉ *59 Lakings Rd., Blenheim.* ☎ FAX *03/578–4531 or 0800/266–266.* 🕮 *2-day: $375 per person; 4-day`$799.*

The Pelorus Mail Boat, **Adventurer,** a small launch that makes a day-long trip ferrying mail and supplies around Pelorus Sound, is one of the best ways to discover the waterway and meet its residents. The boat leaves from Havelock, west of Picton, Monday, Wednesday, Thursday, and Saturday at 11:15 and returns in the late afternoon. The trip costs $54 per person. ✉ *For reservations,* ☞ *Beachcomber Cruises, below. You can also make bookings at the Havelock Outdoor Centre,* ✉ *65A Main Rd., Havelock,* ☎ FAX *03/574–2114.* 🕮 *$66.*

Beachcomber Cruises can take you to and from any point on the Queen Charlotte Walkway for unguided day or longer unguided walks. Boats depart at 10:15 and 2:15 and charge around $30. ✉ *Beachcomber Pier, Town Wharf, Box 12, Picton,* ☎ *03/573–6175,* FAX *03/573–6176.*

The **Cougar Line** runs scheduled trips through the Queen Charlotte Sounds four times daily, dropping passengers (sightseers included) at accommodations, private homes, or other points. A Queen Charlotte drop-off and pickup service costs $43 for multiday hikes, $40 for day hikes that end at Furneaux Lodge. Water taxi service to area lodges costs from $12 to $30, depending on distances. ⊠ *Picton Wharf*, ☎ *03/573–7925 or 0800/504–090*, FAX *03/573–7926*.

Mussel Farm Cruises will take you into the largely untouched Kenepuru and Pelorus sounds, which are part of the labyrinth of waterways comprising the Marlborough Sounds. The world's largest production of green-shell mussels is done in the sounds, and guide Ed Knowles runs a daily four-hour cruise to visit farms where the mussels are at varying stages of development. You can even get in and swim with them. The 40-ft MV *Mavis* is a 1919 kauri-wood launch. ⊠ *Havelock Outdoor Centre, 65a Main Rd., Havelock*, ☎ FAX *03/574–2114.* 🖴 *$45.*

Marlborough Sounds Adventure Company has one- and four-day guided kayak tours of the sounds, as well as kayak rentals for experienced paddlers. The cost is $80 for a one-day guided tour, $475 for a three-day guided tour, including water transportation, food, and camping equipment. A kayak rental costs $40 per person per day. The company also guides trampers on the Queen Charlotte Walkway on three-day ($550) or four-day ($795) trips. ⊠ *The Waterfront, London Quay, Picton*, ☎ *03/573–6078*, FAX *03/573–8827.*

Secrets of Marlborough (⊠ Awatere Valley, Blenheim, ☎ 03/575–7525) has a selection of tours that focus on gardens, wine, local scenery, and other local interests.

VISITOR INFORMATION

Blenheim Visitor Information Centre. ⊠ *The Forum, Queen St.,* ☎ *03/578–9904*, FAX *03/578–6084.* ☼ *Daily 8:30–5:30*

Kaikoura Information and Tourism Centre. ⊠ *West End,* ☎ *03/319–5641*, FAX *03/319–6819.*

Picton Visitor Information Centre. ⊠ *The Foreshore,* ☎ *03/573–7477*, FAX *03/573–5021.*

NELSON AND THE NORTHWEST

Set on the broad curve of its bay with views of the Tasman Mountains on the far side, and with a sunny and agreeable climate, Nelson makes a strong case for itself as one of the top areas in New Zealand for year-round adventure. To the west, the sandy crescents of Abel Tasman National Park and Golden Bay beckon with their seaside charms. To the south, mellow river valleys and the peaks and glacial lakes of Nelson Lakes National Park are a pristine wonderland for hiking, mountaineering, and cross-country skiing. Beyond those geographic splendors, Nelson has more hours of sunlight than any major city in the country. New Zealanders are well aware of these attractions, and in December and January the city is swamped with vacationers. Apart from this brief burst of activity, you can expect to have the roads and beaches mostly to yourself.

Nelson

❻ *116 km (73 mi) west of Blenheim.*

Relaxed, hospitable, and easy to explore on foot, Nelson has a way of making you feel like you should stay longer than you are, no matter how long you're here. Local craftspeople weave wool into clothing and blankets and make pots and jewelry that fill up shops throughout the area. You can make your way around the mostly two-story town in a day, poking into shops and stopping at cafés, but two days is a practical minimum, especially if you need to get yourself back together in the midst of a busy itinerary. Use Nelson as a base for a variety of activities within an hour's drive of the town itself.

To get your bearings in town, the **Visitor Information Center** is on the corner of Trafalgar and Halifax streets. The heart of town is farther up Trafalgar Street, between two parallel roads, Bridge Street and Hardy Street. These areas are fringed with shops, some of them with walk-through access back on to Trafalgar Street. A Saturday crafts market is held at the Montgomery carpark. There are a few shops in Nile Street and Selwyn Place, but the majority are in Trafalgar, Hardy, and Bridge streets. For a dose of greenery, the **Queens Gardens** are on Bridge Street between Collingwood and Tasman.

Suter Art Gallery exhibits both historical and contemporary art. It is the easiest way to see work from an area that has long attracted painters, potters, woodworkers, and other artists. Many of them come for the scenery, the lifestyle, and the clay, with Nelson considered the ceramics center of New Zealand as a result. In recent years the gallery has increased its emphasis on painting and sculpture. Exhibits change every three or four weeks. ⊠ *Queens Gardens, Bridge St.,* ☎ *03/548–4699,* ℻ *03/548–1236.* ✐ *$2.* ☼ *Daily 10:30–4:30.*

Nelson's iffy architectural contribution is **Christ Church Cathedral,** which sits on a hilltop surrounded by gardens. Work on the church began in 1925 and dragged on for the next 40 years. During construction the design was altered to withstand earthquakes, and despite its promising location at the end of Trafalgar Street, it looks like a building designed by a committee.

Despite its tiny size, **Neudorf Vineyard** has established a big reputation for chardonnay, and Riesling, sauvignon blanc, sémillon, and pinot noir are also highly regarded. Owners Tim and Judy Finn are enthusiastic about their region's attributes and will talk at length about local food and wine. Platters of bread and cheese are available at the cellar door. The top wines wear the Moutere designation on the label. ⊠ *Neudorf Rd., Upper Moutere,* ☎ *03/543–2643,* ℻ *03/543–29550.* ☼ *Sept–end of May, daily 10–5.*

Seifrieds Vineyard is a 15-minute drive from Nelson's main center, on the way to Motueka, and is the best-known winery in the region by far. Hermann Seifried was one of the region's wine-making pioneers, having established his vineyard in 1974. Dry red wine had been produced at a small vineyard in the area from 1918, but it was hardly what you'll find today. Hermann produces fine sauvignon blanc, chardonnay, and especially Riesling. There is a restaurant attached to the tasting room. ⊠ *Redwood Rd., Appleby,* ☎ *03/544–5599,* ℻ *03/544–5522.* ☼ *Daily 11–5.*

Dining and Lodging

$$$ ✕ **Walnut Café.** This classy café, 15 minutes from Nelson city, is undoubtedly one of the best around. The food is imaginative, and the chef makes good use of local produce. Various salads of baby greens served with Nelson seafood are invariably delicious, and braised pork belly is sensational in winter. Nelson wines are a strong feature on the list. ⊠ *251 Queen St., Richmond,* ☎ *03/544–6187. AE, DC, MC, V.*

$$–$$$ ✕ **The Boat Shed.** The name is no flight of marketing fancy—this is a genuine boat shed, jutting into the bay. Chef Luke McCann has a nice Asian-influenced touch. His green-shell mussels are steamed, Chinese style, with ginger, garlic, and a hint of five-spice powder; paddle crabs from nearby Golden Bay are wok-steamed with black beans and ginger. Crayfish from holding tanks can be simply steamed, or smeared with herb butter and grilled. ⊠ *350 Wakefield Quay, Nelson,* ☎ *03/546–9783. AE, DC, MC, V. Licensed and BYOB.*

$$ ✕ **Appleman's.** Long established as one of Nelson's best restaurants,
★ Appleman's startled the locals by moving to Richmond, 20 minutes out of town, early in 1997. John Appleman is a skilled cook and loves working with local seafood. Look for Golden Bay whelks and crabs and Nelson Bay scallops and Motueka crabs, all prepared in often-traditional but always-flavorsome ways. ⊠ *294 Queen St., Richmond,* ☎ *03/544–0610. AE, DC, MC, V. No lunch.*

$$ ✕ **Broccoli Row.** This friendly, self-styled fish and vegetarian restau-
★ rant is highly regarded for its presentation and innovative cooking. The small menu caters to varied appetites with dishes such as grilled scallops with rosemary, salmon fillet stuffed with ratatouille, asparagus and Brie tart with tomato-basil sauce, a tapas platter, Caesar salad, and seafood chowder with garlic focaccia. The Mediterranean-style courtyard is the place to eat when the sun is shining. ⊠ *5 Buxton Sq., Nelson,* ☎ *03/548–9621. AE, DC, MC, V. Closed Sun.*

$$$ ▦ **Cambria House.** Built for a sea captain, this 1860 house has been
★ sympathetically modernized to offer B&B accommodations with personality and a dash of luxury. The furnishings mix antiques and floral-print fabrics, and the rooms are very comfortable. Each has an en-suite bathroom with shower; two have a shower and separate bathtub. The house is in a quiet street within easy walking distance of the center of Nelson. Rates include breakfast. Children are not accommodated. ⊠ *7 Cambria St., Nelson,* ☎ *03/548–4681,* ℻ *03/546–6649. 7 rooms with bath. MC, V.*

$$$ ▦ **Cathedral Inn.** Well-traveled hosts Suzie and Jim Tohill have turned this 1878 heart-of-Nelson deanery into a beautiful manor somewhere between a small hotel and a welcoming and luxurious bed-and-breakfast. From the outside the it appears almost Mediterranean—the front courtyard has turquoise and terra-cotta colors—but inside you'll find appealing, period-style wallpapers and solid colonial-style furniture made from native rimu and kauri wood, as well as wrought-iron or brass bedsteads. Rooms have hair dryers, robes, and tea- and coffee-making facilities. Breakfast in the large drawing room around the recycled matai wood table is a gracious affair. The inn is a short walk through Christ Church Cathedral's garden to shops and restaurants. ⊠ *369 Trafalgar St. S, Nelson,* ☎ *03/548–7369,* ℻ *03/548–0369. 7 rooms with bath. AE, D, MC, V.*

$$$ ▦ **Mapledurham.** This colonial-style homestead in the nearby town of Richmond, presided over by Deborah and Giles Grigg, is as friendly and comfortable a place as you'll find in the Nelson area. The hosts are ever ready with suggestions about local activities and restaurants, and the garden around the house and fresh flowers in your room make it a pleasant place to come to at the end of the day. Take advantage of the private trellised courtyard covered in vines at the back of the garden or the shade of the home's spacious veranda. Incredible full breakfasts make for a lavish start in the morning. ⊠ *8 Edward St., Richmond,* ☎ ℻ *03/544–4210. 3 rooms, 2 with bath. Boccie, croquet. MC, V.*

$$ ▦ **Aloha Lodge.** A stone's throw from Tahunanui Beach, this modern bed-and-breakfast has luxury accommodations at a reasonable price. The design of the lodge is Asian, even in its garden, landscaped using the principles of the Chinese design philosophy *feng shui.* An ample breakfast is served in the outer courtyard or the spacious dining room. Hosts John and Linda Bergman are always willing to help out with information on the area's activities and sights. Aloha Lodge is in Tahunanui, about a five-minute drive from Nelson via Haven Road. ⊠ *19 Beach Rd., Tahunanui,* ☎ *03/546–4000,* ℻ *03/546–4420. 17 rooms and 4 suites. AE, DC, MC, V.*

Outdoor Activities and Sports

There is hiking and sea-kayaking aplenty in the glorious forest-and-coastal Abel Tasman National Park west of Nelson (☞ Abel Tasman National Park, *below*). For information on stream fishing in the Nelson Lakes district, *see* Chapter 6.

Shopping

There are crafts shops in various parts of town, and a stroll will take you past many of them. Throughout the region their are more than 300 full-time artists who work in many media: ceramics, glassblowing, woodturning, fiber, sculpture, and painting. Not surprisingly there are 16 arts-and-crafts trails to follow, for which there is a brochure at the information center. There is also a colorful Saturday-morning crafts market. If you are going to be in town in September, call ahead to find out when the **New Zealand Wearable Art Awards** will be held. At this extravaganza—the brainchild of Nelson resident Susie Moncrieff—entries from around the world are eye-opening; some are quite inspired.

Fibre Spectrum. The work of numerous craftswomen is well represented here—everything from sweaters, wraps, hats, throws, and rugs to interesting baskets woven with twigs. ⊠ *280 Trafalgar St.,* ☎ *03/548–1939 or 03/546–7738.*

Jens Hansen Workshop. Hansen's skilled craftspeople create thoughtfully designed, well-made jewelry. Contemporary pieces are handmade at the workshop-showroom, and many are set with local stones and shells. ⊠ *320 Trafalgar Sq.,* ☎ *03/548–0640.*

Hoglund Art Glass Blowing Studio. From the collectible family of penguins to the bold and innovative large platters and vases, the Hoglund touch is unmistakable. Ola and Marie Hoglunds' designs are in keeping with a growing trend in Pacific-feel art—bold colors and inspiration from New Zealand's environment, with origins in the clean designs of their native Scandinavia. ⊠ *Lansdowne Rd., Richmond,* ☎ *03/544–6500,* ℻ *03 /544–9935.*

Around Nelson

❼ The **Nelson Provincial Museum** is on the grounds of **Isel Park** and has a small but outstanding collection of Maori carvings. The museum also has a number of artifacts relating to the so-called Maungatapu murders, grisly goldfields killings committed near Nelson in 1866.

Isel House, near the Nelson Provincial Museum, was built for Thomas Marsden, one of the region's prosperous pioneers. It was Marsden who laid out the magnificent gardens surrounding the house, which include a towering California redwood and a 140-ft Monterey pine. The house itself contains the Marsden family's impressive porcelain and furniture.

To get to the Isel Park from Nelson, follow Rutherford Street out of town—the street was named for the eminent nuclear physicist Ernest Rutherford, who was born and raised nearby. On the outskirts of the city, take the right fork onto Waimea Road and continue as it becomes Main Road. Turn left into Marsden Road, where a sign points to the park. ⊠ *Isel Park, Stoke, 7 km (4½ mi) south of Nelson,* ☎ *03/547–9740.* 🎟 *Isel Park $2, Isel House $2.50.* ☉ *Isel Park Tues.–Fri. 10–4, weekends 2–5; Isel House Sept.–May, weekends 2–4.*

❽ **Broadgreen** is a fine example of a Victorian cob house. Cob houses, made from straw and horsehair bonded together with mud and clay, are commonly found in the southern English county of Devon, where many of Nelson's pioneers originated. The house is furnished as it might have been in the 1850s, with patchwork quilts and kauri furniture. ⊠ *276 Nayland Rd., Stoke,* ☎ *03/546–0283.* ☒ *$2.* ☉ *Nov.–Apr., Tues.–Fri. 10:30–4:30, weekends 1:30–4:30; May–Oct., Wed. and weekends 2–4:30.*

★ ❾ It might be hard to resist stopping at **Nature Smoke,** operated by Vivienne and Tom Fox, who buy their fish right off local boats, fillet it, marinate it according to a secret recipe, smoke it—and offer samples. Especially if you're headed south, you won't find a better lunch along the way than a slab of smoked snapper or albacore tuna with a loaf of crusty bread from the bakery in Motueka and apples from one of the roadside orchard stalls. Nature Smoke is in Mapua Port on the wharf in a blue corrugated-iron building. ⊠ *Mapua Wharf,* ☎ *03/540–2280.* ☉ *Daily 9–5:30; extended hrs in summer.*

En Route West of Mapua, on the way to Motueka, Highway 60 loops around quiet little sea coves that, for all but the warmest months of the year, mirror the snow-frosted peaks on the far shore. The tall vines along the roadside are hops, used in the making of beer.

Motueka

❿ *50 km (31 mi) west of Nelson.*

Motueka (mo-too-*eh*-ka) is an agricultural center—tobacco, hops, kiwifruit, and apples are among its staples. South of town, the Motueka River valley is known for trout fishing, rafting, and its sporting lodges. About 15 km (9 mi) northeast of town on the edge of the national park, **Kaiteriteri Beach** is one of New Zealand's best-known beaches, famous for its golden sand and great for a swim.

Dining and Lodging

$$$$ ✕▥ **Motueka River Lodge.** One of New Zealand's exclusive fishing retreats, this lodge offers tranquillity, marvelous scenery, and a superb standard of comfort. Owned and operated by former Londoner, adman, and publisher Mick Mason and Cordon Bleu–trained Fionna Mason, the lodge is on 80 acres of the Motueka Valley bordering the Motueka River, with magnificent mountain views. The interior of the rustic house is accented with antiques collected around the world. You can hike and raft nearby, but the lodge's specialty is fishing, especially dry fly-fishing for brown trout in the wild river country, which can be reached only by helicopter. The activities are restricted outside the October–April fishing season. Rates include all meals. ⊠ *Motueka Valley Rd., Motueka,* ☎ ℻ *03/526–8668. 5 rooms with bath. Hot tub, tennis court, fishing. AE, DC, MC, V.*

$$$ ✕▥ **Doone Cottage.** This serene 100-year-old country homestay is set in a pretty part of the Motueka River valley, within easy reach of five trout streams. Hosts Stan and Glen Davenport are a relaxed, hospitable couple who have lived in this valley for many years. Rooms are comfortable and crowded with family memorabilia. Dinners are likely to feature organically grown vegetables, fruit, and local meat. Children are not accommodated. Doone Cottage is a 20-minute drive from Motueka. ⊠ *R.D. 1, Motueka,* ☎ ℻ *03/526–8740. 3 rooms. MC, V.*

Boating and Rafting

Ultimate Descents Rafting Adventure Company. Don Allardice, one of New Zealand's leading white-water adventurers, guides on the Buller (Grade 3–4) or the Karamea (Grade 5) rivers. Choose from half-day, full-day, or multiday trips. Full-day rates run around $105. ⊠ *Box 208, Motueka,* ☎ *03/528–6363 or 0800/748–377,* ℻ *03/528–6792.*

Rapid River Adventure Rafting has rafting trips down the Gowan or Buller rivers (both Grade 3–4). Choose from a half-day, full-day, or two-day trip. Full-day trips cost $105. ⊠ *Box 996, Nelson,* ☎ *03/545– 0332,* FAX *03/545–7076.*

En Route   If you don't head out to Abel Tasman National Park and Golden Bay and are headed toward the West Coast, turn south onto Highway 61 at the Rothmans Clock Tower in Motueka, following the sign to Murchison. The road snakes through **Motueka Valley** alongside the Motueka River, which is edged with poplars and yellow gorse, with the green valley walls pressing close alongside. If this river could talk, it would probably scream, "Trout!" After the town of Tapawera, turn south on State Highway 6 and continue to the West Coast.

Abel Tasman National Park

77 km (48 mi) northwest of Motueka, 110 km (69 mi) northwest of Nelson.

Beyond the town of Motueka, Highway 60 passes close to Kaiteriteri ⓫ Beach, then turns inland to skirt **Abel Tasman National Park.** Its coastline is a succession of idyllic beaches backed by a rugged hinterland of native beech forests, granite gorges, and waterfalls. The cove and inlets at **Anchorage**, to mention one part of the park, are spectacular.

Abel Tasman has a number of walking trails, from both Totaranui at its north end and Marahau in the south. The most popular is the two- to three-day **Coastal Track**, open year-round. Launches of **Abel Tasman National Park Enterprises** (☞ Hiking, *below*) will drop off and pick up hikers from several points along the track. A popular way to explore the clear waters and rock-strewn coastline is by sea kayak(☞ Outdoor Activities and Sports, *below*). The main accommodations base for the national park is **Motueka** (☞ *above*) and Marahau (☞ Dining and Lodging, *below*).

Dining and Lodging

$$ ✕🏠 **Awaroa Lodge & Cafe.** Relax in an idyllic part of the spectacular Abel Tasman National Park—Awaroa Bay, surrounded by native bush and just two minutes' walk to the beach. You can choose from standard doubles with shared facilities or fully self-contained chalets. Much of the wood used to build and to finish the interiors has been recycled from the surrounding bush, and the modern furniture suits the setting. The attached restaurant, with its chunky wooden furnishings and open adobe fireplace, serves hearty vegetarian fare (and some meat) with most produce grown organically on the property. ⊠ *Awaroa Bay, Abel Tasman National Park, Motueka,* ☎ FAX *03/528–8758. 7 rooms with bath, 6 with shared bath. Restaurant. AE, DC, MC, V.*

$$ 🏠 **Abel Tasman Marahau Lodge.** With Abel Tasman National Park 200 yards in one direction and the Marahau beach 200 yards in the other, this location is hard to resist. The boutique lodge has spacious fully self-contained chalets, clustered in groups of two or four with native gardens between them. Units are finished in natural wood and have high cathedral ceilings, clean-lined wooden furniture, New Zealand wool carpets, queen- or king-size beds, and balconies from which to take in the park's natural beauty. The lodge has a communal kitchen, and staff can make reservations for local sea-kayaking, horse trekking, and swimming with seals. ⊠ *Marahau, R.D. 2, Motueka,* ☎ *03/527–8250,* FAX *03/527–8258. 8 rooms with bath. Whirlpool, sauna. DC, M, V.*

Outdoor Activities and Sports

HIKING

Bushwalk in the park on your own—it's called freedom walking—or opt for a guided walk. The **Department of Conservation Field Centre** (✉ 1 Commercial St., Takaka, ☎ 03/525–9136) provides trail maps.

Abel Tasman National Park Enterprises guides two-, three-, and four-day treks along the southern half of the Abel Tasman Track. This is one of the most popular trails in the country, particularly in summer. Spend nights in comfortable lodges; during the day explore the coastline and forests of the national park. One day of the four-day trip is spent sea-kayaking. Walkers carry only a light day pack, and all meals are provided. The guided walks are graded as easy. ✉ *265 High St., Motueka,* ☎ *03/528–7801 or 0800/223–582,* FAX *03/528–6087. 3 days per person $625–$800; 5 days per person $895–$1,100, includes meals, transport, accommodations.*

SEA-KAYAKING

Abel Tasman Kayaks has one- and two-person kayaks for hire at Marahau, at the south end of Abel Tasman National Park, which gives paddlers ready access to beaches and campsites that are often inaccessible to hikers. The company does not rent to solo kayakers, and a minimum two-day rental is required. The cost is $95 per day for a double kayak. Guided kayak tours cost from $90 per person per day. ✉ *Marahau, R.D. 2, Motueka,* ☎ *03/527–8022,* FAX *03/527–8031.*

Ocean River Adventure Company has a variety of guided sea-kayaking trips in Abel Tasman National Park, lasting from one to five days. Guided trips cost from $90 per person per day, freedom rentals from $95 for a double kayak with a two-day minimum rental. ✉ *Marahau, R.D. 2, Motueka,* ☎ *03/527–8266,* FAX *03/527–8006.*

Golden Bay–Takaka

⓬ *55 km (35 mi) north west of Motueka; 110 km (70 mi) west of Nelson.* The gorgeous stretch of coastline that begins at the town of Takaka is known, deservedly, as **Golden Bay.** Alternating sandy and rocky shores curve up to the sands of Farewell Spit, the arcing prong that encloses the bay. Dutch navigator Abel Tasman anchored here briefly just a few days before Christmas 1642. His visit ended tragically when four of his crew were killed by Maori. Bitterly disappointed, Tasman named the place Moordenaers, or Murderers' Bay, and sailed away without ever setting foot on New Zealand soil. If you have time to explore it, Golden Bay is a delight—a sunny 40-km (25-mi) crescent with a relaxed crew of locals who firmly believe they live in paradise.

Eight kilometers west of Takaka is **Waikoropupu Springs,** known as Pupu Springs. This is the largest spring system in New Zealand, and clear cold water bubbles into the Waikoropupu Valley after traveling underground from its source at the nearby Takaka River. Dated tourist brochures still available in the area show people swimming in the springs, but this is now frowned upon—alas—because of the impact it has on the delicate flora within the springs. It's best to leave the swimming costume in the car and take a leisurely stroll around the valley on the 90-minute Pupu Walkway. Take your time and go quietly—the better to spot tuis, bellbirds, wood pigeons, and other bird life.

Less well known but no less fascinating is **the Labyrinth,** a system of twisting tunnels and gullies carved into the rocks by long-receded river systems. The phenomenon went unnoticed for years and until recently was simply part of grazing land. Now the delightfully eccentric and totally enthusiastic Dave Whittaker has proclaimed himself to be "keeper of the rocks" and has opened the place to the public. You will find rocks shaped like crocodiles and other reptiles, plus a natural maze. Dave has hidden a few gnomes and other fairy tale creatures around the park, which is great for kids. A troll bridge, an Asian garden, and a picnic site are other features. ⊠ *Off Abel Tasman Dr.,* ☎ *03/525–8434.* ☉ *12:30–5.* ⊠ *$5.*

Beaches

Golden Bay has miles of swimming beaches. **Paton's Rock** is one of the best near Takaka. Check the tides before taking the 10-minute drive from town, as swimming is best with a full tide. Farther out, less suitable for swimming, but spectacular for its coastal landscapes is **Wharariki Beach.** You'll find massive sand dunes, and among these you're likely to come across fur seals sunbathing. They are, of course, wild seals, and if you get too close to them, they might charge or even bite. Keep a 15-ft distance. To get here, drive past Collingwood and follow the signs. Go as far as the road will take you, then walk over farmland on a well-defined track for 20 minutes.

Lodging

$$ ⊞ **Anatoki Lodge.** These spacious, contemporary chalets are close to Takaka center. Owners Ian and Rosemary Douglas can help point out the main attractions and best places to eat in the area. Soft furnishings are covered in deep blue, burgundy, and forest green fabrics, and cooked or Continental breakfast can be delivered to your chalet. ⊠ *87 Commercial St., Takaka,* ☎ *03/525–8047,* ℻ *03/525–8433. 5 studios, 4 1-bedrooms, 1 2-bedroom. Indoor pool. AE, DC, MC, V.*

Outdoor Activities and Sports

FISHING

For information on deep-sea fishing in Golden Bay out of Takaka, *see* Adventure Vacations, Chapter 6.

KAHURANGI NATIONAL PARK

The wild Kahurangi National Park has a diversity of walks and treks. This vast patch of land includes in its compass great fern-clad forests, rivers, rolling hills, snowcapped mountains, and beaches pounded by West Coast surf. The most famous walk is the **Heaphy Track.** It is known primarily as a "free walk"—a slight misnomer in that trekkers need to pay a nominal fee to camp or use huts ($6–$12) during the four- to six-day experience. It is best to purchase these tickets in advance from information centers at Nelson, Motueka, or Takaka. Tickets in hand, all you really need to do is get to the track and start walking toward Karamea on the West Coast. Huts along the way have gas cooking and heating facilities, water, and toilets. You'll need to carry your own food and bedding. And be prepared for weather of all kinds at all times of year—bring rain gear and warm clothing even in summer (and insect repellent for the sand flies!). The east entrance to the park is 35 km (23 mi) west of Takaka, south of the town of Collingwood.

The **Department of Conservation Field Centre** (⊠ 1 Commercial St., Takaka, ☎ 03/525–9136) provides local trail maps.

If you feel like having some expert company on hikes around the national park, **Kahurangi Guided Walks** (☎ 03/525–7177) runs easy one-day treks ($60) on routes known to locals but virtually untouched by visitors. One goes to a remote historic hut, known as Chaffey Cottage, where a couple lived for 40 years. A more strenuous, two-day walk ($170) goes to the rarely visited Boulder Lake.

Kahurangi National Park Bus and Charter Services (☎ 03/525– 9434 or 025/451–434) offers transport to the track from Takaka on demand

for $90 (drop-off and pickup). From Nelson, **Intercity** runs buses at
7:30 AM each day. ☎ *03/548–1539.* ⚑ *$31.*

HORSE TREKKING

Cape Farewell Horse Treks has a range of treks, from trips around a farm
yard for kids to overnighters down the West Coast. In between is the
very popular 2½-hour swimming trek, during which you ride bareback
into the sea. For great views, ask about the Pillar Point Light trek. Book
ahead in summer. ⊠ *Wharariki Beach Rd., Puponga,* ☎ *03/524–8031.*

Nelson and the Northwest A to Z

Arriving and Departing

BY BUS

InterCity buses are readily available to Nelson from the ferry terminal
in Picton. From Nelson, InterCity runs the length of both the west and
east coasts daily (reservations from Nelson, ☎ 03/548–1539).

BY CAR

Nelson is about a two-hour drive from the ferry in Picton. The distance is 145 km (90 mi), but the winding roads don't allow for fast
open-road driving.

From Nelson, Highway 6 runs southwest to the West Coast, down the
coast to the glaciers, then over the Haast Pass to Wanaka and Queenstown. If you're going to the West Coast, allow at least seven hours for
the 458-km (284-mi) journey from Nelson to Franz Josef. The same ap-
plies if you plan to drive from Nelson to Christchurch, 424 km (265 mi)
to the southeast, whether you drive through the mountains of Nelson
Lakes National Park or through Blenheim and Kaikoura down the coast.

BY PLANE

Air New Zealand (☎ 03/546–9300) and **Ansett New Zealand** (☎ 04/
471–1044) link Nelson with Christchurch, Queenstown, Dunedin, the
West Coast town of Hokitika, and all major cities on North Island.
Nelson Airport is 10 km (6 mi) south of the city. **Super Shuttle**'s (☎
03/547–5782) buses meet all incoming flights; the cost is $8 to the city
for one passenger, $5 each for two. Taxi fare is about $14.

Contacts and Resources

CAR RENTAL

Avis (⊠ Airport, ☎ 03/547–2727), **Budget** (⊠ 74 Trafalgar St., ☎ 03/
546–9255), and **Hertz** (⊠ Trent Dr., ☎ 03/547–2299).

EMERGENCIES

Dial 111 for **fire, police, or ambulance** services.

GUIDED TOURS

The **Scenic Mail Run** is a five-hour tour aboard the bus that delivers
the mail and supplies to isolated farming communities around Cape
Farewell, at the tip of Golden Bay. The tour includes lunch on a 2,500-
acre grazing property. The eight-seater bus departs from the Collingwood post office on Golden Bay. ⊠ *Collingwood Bus Services,
Collingwood,* ☎ *03/524–8188.* ⚑ *$30.* ☽ *Tour weekdays at 9:30.*

Abel Tasman National Park Enterprises runs boats along the majestic shoreline of the park. A popular option is to leave the boat at Bark
Bay on the outward voyage, take a two-hour walk through forests,
and reboard the boat at Torrent Bay. The 6½-hour cruise departs daily
from Kaiteriteri, a one-hour drive northwest of Nelson, at 9 AM. A
bus connection from Nelson leaves the Visitor Information Centre
at 7:35 AM. A cruise/flight option is also available. Buy a take-out
lunch at Motueka—supplies on board are basic. ⊠ *Old Cedarman*

House, Main Rd., Riwaka, ☎ *03/528–7801.* 🚢 *Cruise from Kaiteriteri $42, cruise-flight from Nelson $112, Nelson–Kaiteriteri round-trip bus $17.*

Nelson Day Tours has trips around the city and its immediate district, as well as going farther afield to Motueka and Kaiteriteri Beach and south to Nelson Lakes National Park. ✉ *258 Rutherford St., Nelson,* ☎ *03/545–1055,* 📠 *03/546–9170.*

VISITOR INFORMATION
Nelson Visitor Information Centre. ✉ *Trafalgar and Halifax Sts.,* ☎ *03/548–2304.* ⏱ *Daily 9–5.*

THE WEST COAST

Southwest of Nelson, the wild West Coast region is virtually a land unto itself. The mystical Pancake Rocks and blowholes around Punakaiki (poon-ah-*kye*-kee) set the scene for the rugged, sometimes forlorn landscape to the south. Early Pakeha (European) settlers lived a hardscrabble life, digging for gold and farming where they could, constantly washed by the "Wet Coast" rains. The towns along the way don't have much of interest in their own right, but they are good bases from which to explore the coast, mountains, lakes, and forests of the region.

At the glacier towns of Franz Josef and Fox, the unique combination of soaring mountains and voluminous precipitation mean that the massive valleys of ice descend straight into rain forests—interestingly enough a combination also found on the southwest coast of South America. South of the glaciers, the road follows the seacoast, where fur seals and fiordland crested penguins inhabit fantastical beaches and forests. On sunny days the Tasman Sea along the stretch between Lake Moeraki and Haast takes on a transcendent shade of blue.

For all its beauty, this is not the most hospitable of New Zealand's provinces. The people are friendly and welcoming, but the landscape and weather can make things difficult if you don't have an adventurous streak. Locals pride themselves on their ability to coexist with the wild, primeval landscape on their doorstep. Be prepared for rain, fog, and cold nights, all of which can get your spirits down. The meteorological mix can, unfortunately, mean that the glacier flight that you planned at Franz Josef or Fox won't fly the day that you're there. If you do end up here on a rainy "wet coast" day, keep in mind that you might wake up the next morning to have brilliant sunshine lighting up the region's glorious scenery.

En Route   If you're driving to the West Coast from Nelson or Motueka, the road beyond Murchison parallels the broad **Buller River** as it carves a deep gorge from the jagged mountain peaks. Nineteen kilometers (12 miles) south of Murchison, the **Newtown Hotel**, no longer licensed, teeters on the brink of the gorge, surrounded by a wild junkyard of obsolete farm machinery. The Buller once carried a fabulous cargo of gold, but you'll have to use your imagination to reconstruct the days when places such as Lyell, 34 km (21 mi) past Murchison, were bustling mining towns. **Hawk's Crag**, where the highway passes beneath a rock overhang with the river wheeling alongside, is the scenic climax of the trip along the Buller. Before the town of Westport, turn left to continue along Highway 6. You are now entering the West Coast region.

Punakaiki

269 km (168 mi) southeast of Nelson.

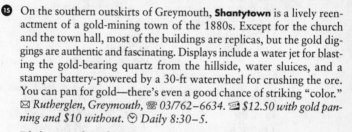

Punakaiki is just a small collection of shops at first glance. In fact, the big attraction is not the town. From the visitor center, an easy 10-minute walk leads to a fantastic maze of limestone rocks stacked high above the sea. These are the surreal **Pancake Rocks,** the outstanding feature of the surrounding **Paparoa National Park** (☎ 03/731–1895, FAX 03/731–1888). At high tide, a blowhole spouts a thundering geyser of spray. Aoraki (Mt. Cook) is sometimes visible to the south.

Greymouth

44 km (28 mi) south of Punakaiki.

The town of Greymouth (said like the anatomical feature) is aptly named—it's a rather dispirited strip of motels and timber mills. But the **Jade Boulder Gallery** is a great place to pick up a distinctive souvenir. The gallery exhibits the work of Ian Boustridge, one of the country's most accomplished sculptors of greenstone, the jade that is highly prized by the Maori. Earrings start at about $10, and sculpture can cost anything up to $35,000. You'll find that the stone can manifest itself in a number of colors, including deep blues, rusts, even cream, depending on what minerals and conditions have worked their magic. ⊠ *1 Guiness St., Greymouth,* ☎ *03/768–0700.* ☉ *Daily 8–5.*

On the southern outskirts of Greymouth, **Shantytown** is a lively reenactment of a gold-mining town of the 1880s. Except for the church and the town hall, most of the buildings are replicas, but the gold diggings are authentic and fascinating. Displays include a water jet for blasting the gold-bearing quartz from the hillside, water sluices, and a stamper battery-powered by a 30-ft waterwheel for crushing the ore. You can pan for gold—there's even a good chance of striking "color." ⊠ *Rutherglen, Greymouth,* ☎ *03/762–6634.* 🎫 *$12.50 with gold panning and $10 without.* ☉ *Daily 8:30–5.*

Dining and Lodging

$$$$ ✕🏨 **Lake Brunner Sporting Lodge.** Set on the southern shore of Lake
★ Brunner, a 40-minute drive southeast of Greymouth, this sprawling lodge, first established in 1868, has excellent fishing, a variety of activities, and a high level of comfort at a price that is relatively low by the standards of New Zealand's elite lodges. Rooms are large and well equipped, with the emphasis on comfort rather than opulence. The best rooms are at the front of the villa, overlooking the lake. The lodge is known for its clear-water stalking, since brown trout can be easily seen in the clear waters of the surrounding rivers. Fly-fishing is the primary method used but fine spin fishing is also available at certain times of the year, and the lodge follows a catch-and-release policy. Hiking, boating, mountain biking, bird-watching, and nature tours are also available. If you get a chance to walk through the Carew Reserve—the lodge is surrounded by untouched forests—at the back of the lodge, do so with hostess Marian van der Goes. Her knowledge of the rain forest will open your eyes to things you would otherwise miss, such as native orchids nestled in the boughs of high branches. Rates include all meals. ⊠ *Mitchells, R.D. 1, Kumara, Westland,* ☎ FAX *03/738–0163, 12 en-suite rooms. Fishing, mountain bikes, library. AE, DC, MC, V. Closed Aug.–Sept.*

$$ 🏨 **Ashley Motor Inn.** This motor inn has modern, comfortable rooms, though Greymouth and its surroundings, compared with other parts of the West Coast, have little to justify an overnight stop. ⊠ *70 Tasman St., Greymouth,* ☎ *03/768–5135,* FAX *03/768–0319. 60 rooms with bath. Restaurant, bar, pool, hot tub, sauna, coin laundry. AE, DC, MC, V.*

Hokitika

16 *41 km (26 mi) south of Greymouth.*

Hokitika won't exactly wow you, but if you're finding the drive down to the glaciers a bit long, it is a convenient stopover for the night. There are crafts shops in town if you have time for browsing or a few local bushwalks, and the beach is littered with some very interesting driftwood. If you happen to get into town in the middle of a rainstorm, it might seem bleak.

One annual Hokitika event worth stopping for is the **Wildfoods Festival,** where you'll find a plethora of gourmet bushtucker (food from the bush) from the West Coast's natural food sources. Bite into such delectables as huhu grubs (they look like large maggots), worm sushi, whitebait patties (far more mainstream), and snail caviar, and wash it all down with gorse wine, moonshine, or Monteith's bitter beer. The mid-March fest attracts crowds of up to 13,500, four times the local population. Entertainment includes lively performances by members of the Hokitika Live Poets Society at the tree stump by Billy Tea Hut (where else). It can get rowdy at night at the barn dance, which seems to spill through the town. Of course, a good dump of West Coast rain will quiet things down—until the next year. Take your gum boots.

Lodging

$–$$ 🏨 **Teichelmann's Central Bed & Breakfast.** Named for Ebenezer Teichelmann, the surgeon-mountaineer-conservationist who built the original part of the house, this is the most comfortable place in town. The place has been a bed-and-breakfast for 25 years, and its genteel atmosphere has a lot to do with hosts Russell Wenn and Julie Collier, who are happy to make suggestions for local activities. Furnishings are a combination of antique and country cottage style, using plenty of native wood. At breakfast serve yourself fruit and cereals from the Southland beech-wood sideboard. And the rimu bookcase is full of literature about the area. ⊠ *20 Hamilton St.,* ☎ *03/755–8232.* 🕾 *03/755–8239. 4 rooms with bath, 2 with shared bath. BP. AE, MC, V.*

Franz Josef and Fox Glaciers

17 18 *Franz Josef is 146 km (91 mi) south of Hokitika; Fox is 24 km (15 mi) south of Franz Josef.*

The north end of **Westland National Park** begins at the Franz Josef glacier field. These glaciers—New Zealanders say "glassy-urs"—are formed by the massive precipitation of the West Coast—up to 300 inches per annum—which descends as snow on the névé, or head, of the glacier. The snow is compressed into ice, which actually flows downhill under its own weight. There are more than 60 glaciers in the park; the most famous and accessible are at **Franz Josef** and **Fox.** There are parking areas outside the towns of Franz Josef and Fox from which you can walk about 30 minutes to reach the glaciers' terminal faces. Both parking lots can be terrorized by keas (*kee*-ahs)—mountain parrots—which specialize in destroying the rubber molding around car windows. Keas are harmless to humans, and a coating of insect repellent around the window frames should safeguard your vehicle.

Trails from the parking lots wind across the rocky valley floor to the glacier faces, where a tormented vocabulary of squeaks, creaks, groans, and gurgles can be heard as the glacier creeps down the mountainside at an average rate of up to 3 ft per day. Care must be taken here, since rocks and chunks of ice frequently drop from the melting face.

These being New Zealand glaciers, there is much to do besides admire them. You can fly over them in helicopters or planes and land on the stable névé, or hike on them with guides. Remember that these structures are dynamic and always in motion—an ice cave that was visible yesterday might today be smashed under tons of ice that used to be just uphill of it. Likewise some of the fascinating formations that you see on the surface of the glacier were fairly recently at the very bottom of it higher up in the valley. It pays not to be in or on anything that is about to collapse, and guides know where to avoid such dangers.

Flights are often best made early in the morning, when visibility tends to be best. Fox Glacier is slightly larger and longer than Franz Josef, but you'll miss nothing important if you see only one. Both glaciers have separate townships, and if you are spending the night, Franz Josef is marginally preferable.

Seasons around the glaciers are an interesting thing. Summer is of course warmer and by far the busiest season. But there is a lot more rain and fog that can nix flightseeing and hiking plans. In winter snow doesn't fall at sea level in Franz Josef or Fox. Winter is in fact a well-kept secret. Skies are clearer, which means fewer canceled flights and glacier hikes and more of the dazzling sunshine that makes views of the mountains so spectacular both from the towns and at elevations.

⑲ Outside the town of Fox Glacier, **Lake Matheson** has one of the country's most famous views. A walking trail winds along the lakeshore, and the snowcapped peaks of Aoraki and Mt. Tasman are reflected in the water. Allow at least an hour for the complete walk to the "view of views." The best time is early morning, before the mirrorlike reflections are fractured by the wind. From town, turn toward the sea where a sign points to Gillespies Beach, then turn right again to reach the lake.

Dining and Lodging

$$ ✕ **Blue Ice Café.** You'll welcome an alternative both in cuisine and decor to the steak-and-chips joints so common on the West Coast. Along with pizza and a light menu of salads, lasagna, and the like, you'll find greenshell mussels, pork ribs, rack of lamb, and cervena (venison). Coffee and desserts such as hot kumara (sweet potato) custard pudding or fudge cake are delicious. With a 2 AM license, Blue Ice buzzes long into the night in the tourist season. ⊠ *South end of Main Rd., Franz Josef,* ☎ *03/752–0707. MC, V.*

$$$ ✕🏨 **Franz Josef Glacier Hotels.** The largest hotel in the glacier region, this motor-inn-style complex at the north end of Franz Josef village offers rooms a cut above the average in size and furnishings. Be sure to ask for a room with glacier views—particularly stunning as the sun rises over the Southern Alps and lights up the glaciers. Larger suites with upgraded facilities are also available, and the hotel has a choice of three restaurants. ⊠ *State Hwy. 6, Franz Josef,* ☎ *03/752–0729 or 0800/ 228–228,* FAX *03/752–0709. 147 rooms with bath. 3 restaurants, 3 bars, 2 hot tubs, coin laundry. AE, DC, MC, V.*

Outdoor Activities and Sports

FISHING

For information on fishing around Franz Josef and Fox, *see* Chapter 6.

ON AND ABOVE THE GLACIERS

The walks to the glacier heads mentioned above are the easiest and most basic ways to experience the glaciers. Walks mentioned below are the most reasonable of all guided glacier trips, and seeing the ice formations up close—the shapes created by the glaciers' movement and the streams of water running through them—is unforgettable.

Flying over the glaciers is also quite thrilling, and that thrill comes at considerable expense. The ultimate combination is to fly by fixed-wing plane or helicopter to the top or middle of the glacier and get out and walk on it. Fixed-wing landings on the snow atop the ice fields are fabulously scenic, but you have only 10 minutes out of the plane. Heli-hikes give you the most time on the ice, two to three hours of snaking up and down right in the middle of a stable part of the glacier. If you've never flown in a helicopter, the experience can be nearly heart-stopping. It is exactly what you'd imagine flying on a magic carpet would be like, the way the pull of the rotors lifts you up and into the glacial valleys. As you make your way to a landing spot, the pilot banks the helicopter so that the only things between you and the mass of ice below you are a sheet of glass and centrifugal force. It's a wild ride.

Alpine Guides Fox Glacier has half- or full-day guided walks on Fox Glacier, the only safe way to experience the ethereal beauty of the ice caves, pinnacles, and crevasses on top of the glaciers. The 3½- to 4-hour walk travels about 2 km (1 mi) up the glacier. The climb requires some fitness. Arguably the best option is to heli-hike, combining a helicopter flight onto and off Fox Glacier and walking for two hours on the ice with a guide. ⊠ *Box 38, Fox Glacier,* ☎ *03/751–0825,* ℻ *03/ 751–0857.* ☎ *½-day $39, full-day $55, heli-hikes $165.* ☉ *Tour daily at 9:30 and 2.*

The **Helicopter Line** operates several scenic flights over the glaciers from heliports at Franz Josef and Fox. The shortest is the 20-minute flight over Franz Josef Glacier ($125 per person); the longest is a 40-minute flight that includes a landing on the head of the glacier and a circuit of Aoraki and Mt. Tasman ($245). Two-and-a-half-hour heli-hikes are yet another option ($175). ⊠ *Main St., Box 45, Franz Josef,* ☎ *03/ 752–0767 or 0800/807–767,* ℻ *03/752–0769.*

Mount Cook Lines Ski Plane has fixed-wing skiplanes that fly over the glaciers. Landings amid craggy peaks in the high-altitude snowfields are otherworldly. The 40-minute ($160) and one-hour ($210) flights both cover Fox and Franz Josef glaciers; the longer one includes a circuit of Aoraki and lands on Tasman Glacier. ⊠ *Franz Josef,* ☎ *03/752– 0714 Franz Josef, 0800/800–737 Fox .*

Lake Moeraki

⑳ *90 km (56 mi) south of Fox Glacier, 30 km (19 mi) north of Haast.*

Lake Moeraki itself sits in the midst of Westland National Park. There isn't a town here; it's the site of a thoughtfully designed wilderness lodge (☞ *below*). The immediate area's public access is **Monro Beach.** The 45-minute walk to the beach takes you through spectacular, fern-filled native forest to a truly remarkable beach: Rock clusters jut out of incredibly blue waters, and rivers and streams flow over the sand into the Tasman Sea. You might arrive at a time when spunky little fiordland crested penguins are in transit from the sea to their stream- or hill-side nests. Early morning and late afternoon are good but not sure bets to find them.

A mile south of the trail entrance on the beach is a seal colony, which you will smell before you see it. If you venture that way, be sure to keep about 16½ ft (5 m) away from the seals (the legal distance), and don't block their path to the sea. A spooked seal will bowl you over on its lurch for the water and may even bite, so be extremely respectful of their space. Sculpted dark gray rocks also litter the beach to the south, and seals like to lie behind them and among them, so look carefully before you cross in front of these rocks.

Monro Beach is an utter dream, not least if you collect driftwood or rocks. On the road a mile or so south of it, there is a lookout over the rock stacks at **Knights Point.** Farther south still, between Moeraki and Haast, the walkways and beach at **Ship Creek** are another stop for ferny forests and rugged coastline. Sand flies here can be voracious. Bring insect repellent and hope for a windy day!

En Route Beyond Lake Moeraki, Highway 6 continues along the south coast to Haast, where it turns inland to Wanaka and Queenstown. The driving time between Moeraki and Wanaka is about five hours.

Dining and Lodging

$$$ ✕🏠 **Wilderness Lodge Lake Moeraki.** The natural splendor of the sur-
★ roundings at Lake Moeraki is the equal of any on the West Coast. The lodge lies along a river flowing out of the lake, north of the town of Haast. Fiordland crested penguins—the rarest on earth—nest along streams and on hills above the beach. On-staff naturalists' will take you to see fur seals and, if he's around, the giant elephant seal whom they call Humphrey. They will also take you along while they feed local eels in the morning. Canoes and kayaks are available for paddling the lake, and forest trails from the lodge, some of which lead to the beach, echo with the sound of rushing streams and birdcalls. After a day outdoors, you'll eat local produce and drink New Zealand wine at dinner. There are also glowworm and night-sky walks, on which guides point out the enchanting constellations of the southern hemisphere. Dr. Gerry McSweeney, a leading voice in New Zealand's conservation movement, runs the lodge with the intention of demonstrating that tourism was an economic alternative to logging in the forests of South Westland. Rates include full breakfast and dinner, short guided nature activities, and the use of canoes and mountain bikes. Longer guided hikes, fishing guides, lunch, and dinner drinks come at extra charge. ✉ *Private Bag, Hokitika,* ☎ ℻ *03/750–0881. 20 rooms with bath. Beach, boating, fishing, laundry service. AE, DC, MC, V.*

Fishing

For information on deep-sea fishing out of Haast, *see* Chapter 6.

West Coast A to Z

Arriving and Departing

BY BUS

InterCity buses run the length of the West Coast daily (reservations from Nelson, ☎ 03/548–1539; Greymouth, ☎ 03/768–5101; Franz Josef, ☎ 03/752–0164).

BY CAR

The north end of the West Coast is roughly a four-hour drive from Nelson or a five- to six-hour drive over Arthur's Pass from Christchurch, the very top of which is harrowing to say the least (Hokitika and Greymouth are about 256 km/166 mi, from Christchurch).

BY TRAIN

The West Coast in general is poorly served by the rail network, but one glowing exception is the **TranzAlpine Express** (☎ 800/802–802), which ranks as one of the world's great rail journeys. This passenger train crosses the Southern Alps between Christchurch and Greymouth, winding through beech forests and mountains that are covered by snow for most of the year. The bridges and tunnels along this line, including the 8-km (5-mi) Otira Tunnel, represent a prodigious feat of engineering. The train is modern and comfortable, with panoramic windows as well as dining and bar service. The train departs Christchurch daily at 9 AM and arrives in Greymouth at 1:25 PM; the return train departs Greymouth at 2:25 PM and arrives at Christchurch at 6:35 PM. The one-way fare is $76; round-trip $99.

Contacts and Resources

EMERGENCIES
Dial 111 for **fire, police, or ambulance** services.

VISITOR INFORMATION
Franz Josef Glacier Visitor Information Centre. ⊠ *State Hwy. 6, Franz Josef,* ☎ *03/752–0796.* ☉ *Daily 8–4:30.*

Greymouth Visitor Information Centre. ⊠ *Regent Theatre Bldg., McKay and Herbert Sts.,* ☎ *03/768–5101.* ☉ *Weekdays 9–5.*

5 Christchurch and Lower South Island

This is it—picture-postcard New Zealand, where the country's tallest mountains are reflected in crystal-clear lakes and sheer rock faces tower above the fjords. The choice of activity is yours. You can enjoy some of the world's most dramatic views in complete peace and quiet or leap—literally, if you'd like—from one adrenaline rush to the next.

AS THE KEA FLIES, it's only 130 km (80 mi) from the eastern shores of South Island to its highest peak, 12,283-ft Aoraki (Mt. Cook). As many as 60 glaciers of varying size are locked in the Southern Alps, slowly grinding their way down to lower altitudes, where they melt into running rivers of uncanny blue-green hues. Aoraki National Park is a World Heritage Area, and the alpine region around it contains the Tasman Glacier, New Zealand's longest.

The wide open Canterbury Plains separate the mountains from the ocean. This is some of New Zealand's finest pastureland, and the higher reaches of the Canterbury are sheep station territory, where life and lore mingle in South Island's cowboy country. This is the territory where young Samuel Butler dreamed up the satirical *Erewhon*—the word is an anagram of "nowhere." The station he lived on is now on a horse-trekking route.

Trekking is one of the things that Southland does best. The southwest corner of the island, where glaciers over millennia have cut the Alps into stone walls dropping sheer into fjords, is laced with walking tracks that take you into the heart of wild Fiordland National Park. The Milford Track is the best known—it has been called the finest walk in the world since a headline to that effect appeared in the London *Spectator* in 1908. If you're not keen on walking all the way to the Milford Sound, drive in and hop on a boat and take in the sights and sounds from on deck.

Christchurch was built on the fortunes made from the Canterbury region's sheep runs. People call it the most English city outside England, which may owe something to the grand but unworkable settlement scheme of devout Tory John Robert Godley. His fears of the collapse of religion and civility in the mid-19th century may have had something to do with establishing the earthy gentility that makes the city such a pleasant foil for the wilds of South Island.

Gold, on the other hand, fueled Dunedin's glory days. Following the Central Otago strike of 1861 thousands of tons of gold were shipped out of the city's port, but not before some of it went into building some of New Zealand's finest buildings in the city. Southwest of Dunedin, hanging off the bottom of South Island, Stewart Island is virtually a study in remoteness. Commercial fishing settlements give way to bushland that the kiwi—so rare elsewhere in the country—still haunts. Expansive views across the Foveaux Strait from time to time alight with the *aurora australis,* the spectacular southern hemisphere equivalent of the northern lights.

South Island is without doubt the wilder of the country's two largest islands. Beyond the well-defined tourist routes, its beech forests, lakes, trout streams, and mountain trails are a paradise for hikers, anglers, and anyone who enjoys a good dose of fresh air.

Note: For more information on bicycling, cross-country skiing, fishing, hiking, horse trekking, rafting, and sailing in lower South Island, *see* Chapter 6.

Pleasures and Pastimes

Dining

Christchurch has a fairly wide range of eateries, from cosmopolitan restaurants to earthy vegetarian cafés. The region also boasts a thriving wine industry. **Giesen Wine Estate** (⊠ Burnham School Rd., ☎ FAX 03/347–6729) is the biggest in town and well worth visiting. In the Waipara district, 40 minutes or so from the city center, see **Pegasus Bay** (⊠ Stockgrove Rd., Amberley, ☎ FAX 03/314–6869), run by the Donaldson family.

The small fishing town of Bluff is known for two reasons in New Zealand—it is the southernmost tip of the South Island, and it gives its name to an oyster. The Bluff oyster is one of the country's great delicacies, so pick up a dozen fresh ones from a fish shop if you can, or try them in a restaurant. As for Dunedin and Queenstown, you'll find a good variety of eateries because of the former's student population and the latter's influx of international visitors.

Hiking

South Island's southwestern wilderness areas are the stuff of legendary tramping. The Milford Track, the Kepler, the Routeburn, the Hollyford—it doesn't get any better than these. Mountains, fjords, waterfalls, rain forests—you'll see it all.

Jumping

Don't worry, New Zealanders aren't going to pressure you into jumping off a bridge with an elastic cord tied to your ankles. But if you have an overwhelming desire to bungee, this is the place to do it. The cost of the jump usually includes a "been there–done that" T-shirt and even a video of your daredevil act.

Lodging

No matter where you stay in Christchurch, you're sure to find some of the best lodging in New Zealand, from luxury hotels to very fine B&Bs. The rest of lower South Island is blessed with great views, and you will always be able to find a place to stay overlooking a lake, river, or mountainous landscape. If you can forego luxury, basic but comfortable cabins can often be found in the most beautiful places. Farmstays are often set on lush green grasslands with snowcapped mountains as a backdrop.

Skiing

South Island's best-known ski areas are here—use Wanaka as a base for Treble Cone and Cadrona, and Queenstown serves Coronet Peak and the Remarkables. For the biggest thrill, go heli-skiing in areas otherwise unreachable.

Exploring Christchurch and Lower South Island

Great Itineraries

Touring the lower half of South Island requires making difficult choices. Do you want to walk the Milford Track, or does the remote Stewart Island appeal more? Will you go away disappointed if you miss Queenstown, the adventure capital, or would you just as soon station yourself in the snowy reaches of Aoraki? The Otago Peninsula has its own spectacular scenery, interesting wildlife, and the charming city of Dunedin. And then there is Christchurch and side trips from the city to the precipitous Banks Peninsula.

To literally see it all would take a good three weeks, if you intend to do it justice and stay sane. Short of that, treat each of these areas as two- to three-day segments, mix them up to suit your fancy, and take into account travel time of three to five hours between each.

Numbers in the text correspond to points of interest on the Canterbury Region and the Southern Alps; Christchurch; and Southland, Otago, and Stewart Island maps.

The Canterbury Region and the Southern Alps

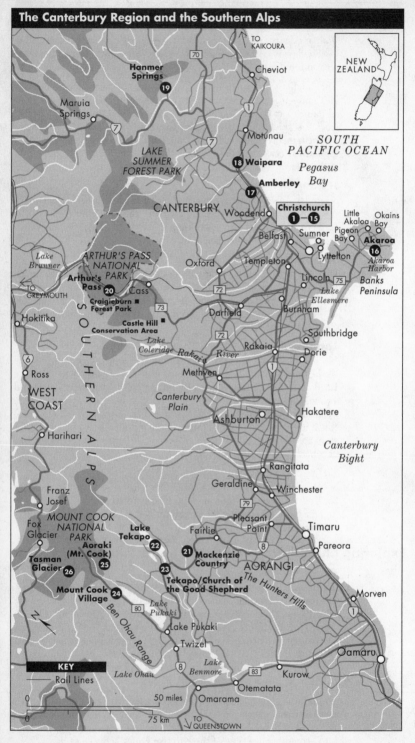

TO KAIKOURA

Cheviot

Hanmer Springs **19**

Maruia Springs

LAKE SUMMER FOREST PARK

Motunau

SOUTH PACIFIC OCEAN

Waipara **18**

Pegasus Bay

Amberley **17**

CANTERBURY

Woodend

Christchurch **1** — **15**

Little Akaloa

Okains Bay

Belfash

Sumner

Pigeon Bay

Akaroa **16**

Oxford

Templeton

Lyttelton

Akaroa Harbor

Lake Brunner

ARTHUR'S PASS NATIONAL PARK

Arthur's Pass **20**

Cass

Lincoln

Banks Peninsula

TO GREYMOUTH

Craigieburn Forest Park

Castle Hill Conservation Area

Darfield

Burnham

Lake Ellesmere

Hokitika

Lake Coleridge

Rakaia River

Rakaia

Southbridge

Dorie

Ross

WEST COAST

Methven

Canterbury Plain

Ashburton

Hakatere

Harihari

Canterbury Bight

Franz Josef

Rangitata

Fox Glacier

MOUNT COOK NATIONAL PARK

Geraldine

Winchester

Tasman Glacier **26**

Lake Tekapo **22**

Aoraki (Mt. Cook) **25**

Fairlie

Pleasant Point

Timaru

Pareora

21 Mackenzie Country

AORANGI

Tekapo/Church of the Good Shepherd **23**

The Hunters Hills

Mount Cook Village **24**

Lake Pukaki

Morven

Ben Ohau Range

Lake Pukaki

Twizel

Oamaru

Lake Ohau

Lake Benmore

Kurow

KEY

Rail Lines

0   50 miles

0   75 km

Otematata

Omarama

TO QUEENSTOWN

NEW ZEALAND

IF YOU HAVE 3 DAYS

Spend the first or last day in **Christchurch,** strolling through the beautiful **Botanic Gardens** ⑤, poking around the **Arts Centre** ⑧, perhaps heading out to **Mona Vale** ⑫ for afternoon tea. Then choose whether to fly to **Aoraki** ㉕ or to **Queenstown** ㉘ or to **Stewart Island** ㊳–㊴ for two days. If you pick Aoraki, explore some of South Canterbury one day, making sure to stop at **Lake Tekapo** ㉒, and take in the view from inside the **Church of the Good Shepherd** ㉓. You could spend the night there or on Mt. Cook. On the next day take a flight over the mountain or onto the **Tasman Glacier** ㉖, followed by a walk into the Hooker Valley or up Mt. Sebastopol.

IF YOU HAVE 5 DAYS

Spend two days in **Christchurch,** using the second to see the **International Antarctic Centre** ⑩ or ride the **Christchurch Gondola** ⑭. You could otherwise take the whole day and go to the town of **Akaroa** ⑯ on the Banks Peninsula, drive up the summit of the volcanic dome, then take a road down to one of the bays on the other side of the peninsula. On the third day fly to **Queenstown** ㉘. Depending on how active you are, you could easily spend three days here throwing yourself off a bridge, heli-skiing, jet-boat riding, white-water rafting, and taking a steamer trip on Lake Wakatipu. Leave some time to relax and take in the stunning views from the **Skyline Gondola** ㉙ as well. On the fourth day head to **Milford Sound** ㉜ to take in the amazing spectacle of sheer cliffs, deep water, and dense native bush. You could spend a day in **Wanaka** ㉗, stopping in at **Stuart Landsborough's Puzzle Museum** and/or taking a half- or full-day hike in the area. From here you could easily tack on a trip to the stunning West Coast (☞ Chapter 4), driving over the scenic Haast Pass to get there.

IF YOU HAVE 8 DAYS

With eight days you have the luxury of taking your time. You could spend four of them on the **Milford** or the **Kepler** Track, a couple more in **Queenstown** ㉘ and a couple more in **Christchurch** ①–⑮ or **Dunedin** ㉝. Or you could feel like you're skirting the edge of the earth by driving to Dunedin to explore the fascinating Otago Peninsula and view its wildlife, **Larnach Castle** ㉞, and **Taiaroa Head** ㉟, then continuing to the southernmost **Stewart Island** ㊳–㊴, where you can spend four days doing some serious bushwalking and looking for kiwi birds in the wild. You could combine two or three days in Christchurch with two or three in Dunedin and the same on Stewart Island. Or just go alpine and spend all of your time around Aoraki, Wanaka, and Queenstown.

When to Tour Christchurch and Lower South Island

Because of the Alps, this is the part of New Zealand that gets cold with a capital C in winter, so if you're coming for warm weather stay away between May and September. For skiing, snowboarding, and so forth, this is *the* time to come. From July through September you can be assured of snow around Queenstown and Wanaka, where the ski scene is pretty lively. In the height of summer—from December into February—popular places like Queenstown can get so crowded that they lose the relaxed, laid-back atmosphere New Zealand is famous for. If you hold off until April or May, leaves turn yellow and red, and the nearby mountains have a smattering of early season snow. You'll have the Alps more to yourself, and some lodgings offer bargains.

CHRISTCHURCH

Christchurch is something of a paradox—a city under the grand delusion that it is somewhere in southern England. The drive from the airport into town takes you through pristine suburbs of houses lapped by seas of flowers and past playing fields where children flail at one another's legs with hockey sticks. The heart of this pancake-flat city is dominated by church spires, its streets are named Durham, Gloucester, and Hereford, and instead of the usual boulder-leaping New Zealand torrents, there bubbles, between banks lined with willows and oaks, the narrow River Avon, suitable only for punting. The inner city is compact and so easy to explore by foot that there is little need to follow a preset walking tour. Just pick a sight or two, like Cathedral Square or the Arts Centre, and set out—you won't have very far to go. Outside the city boundaries, there are a number of special-interest museums and activities about 20 minutes away by car. There are also side trips from Christchurch into the Canterbury Plains countryside and to the Akaroa Peninsula, the remnant of an ancient volcanic dome whose steep, grassy walls drop to the sea.

With a population approaching 300,000, Christchurch is the largest South Island city and the only one with an international airport. It is also the forward supply depot for the main U.S. Antarctic base at McMurdo Sound, and if you come in by plane, you are likely to see the giant U.S. Air Force transport planes of Operation Deep Freeze parked on the tarmac at Christchurch International Airport.

Exploring Christchurch

❹ Antigua Boatshed. Built for the Christchurch Boating Club, this is the only boat shed that remains of the half dozen that once stood along the Avon. Canoes may be rented for short river trips. ⊠ *Rolleston Ave.,* ☎ *03/366–5885.* 🎫 *Single canoe $5 per hr, double canoe $10 per hr.* ☉ *Daily 9:30–4:30.*

★ ❽ Arts Centre. Why Canterbury University gave up its former quarters seems a mystery. The collection of Gothic Revival stone buildings it used to inhabit represents some of New Zealand's finest architecture. In the college days of Ernest Rutherford (1871–1937), the university's most illustrious pupil, classes were of course held in what is now the Arts Centre. Just past the information desk inside is what is known as Rutherford's Den, the modest stone chamber where the eminent physicist conducted experiments in what was at the time a new field, radioactivity. It was Rutherford who first succeeded in splitting the atom, a crucial step in the harnessing of atomic power. In 1908 Rutherford's work earned him the Nobel prize—not for physics but for chemistry.

The Arts Centre houses diverse galleries, shops, theaters, and crafts studios. It is also an excellent place to stop for food, coffee, or a glass of wine if you are walking from the Cathedral Square to the Canterbury Museum—there are three cafés and a wine bar. There is also a **Saturday and Sunday Market,** where you'll find handmade items of clothing and crafts that you may want to bring home with you. For a $5 guided tour of the center led by the "town crier"—Hear ye, hear ye—you should meet at the clock tower at 11 or 2, Monday–Friday. ⊠ *Worcester St. between Montreal St. and Rolleston Ave.,* ☎ *03/366–0989.* ☉ *Shops and galleries daily 10–4:30, with extended hrs in the summer. Tours by arrangement (☎ 03/366–0980).*

NEED A   The Arts Centre has four eateries in its stone buildings and quadrangles.
BREAK?   Housed in a mock-Tudor building, **Dux de Lux** is an upbeat, popular

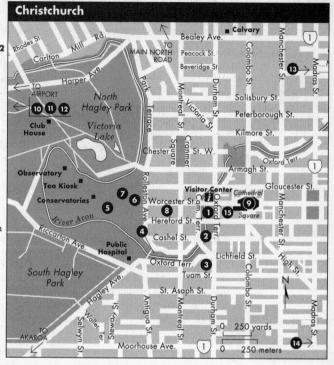

Christchurch

cafeteria-style restaurant. The blackboard menu offers vegetarian items and seafood: quiches, crepes, sandwiches, pies, fresh vegetable juices, and a range of crisp salads and breads. The courtyard is a great spot on a sunny day, especially with a beer from the brewery next door. And at night the brewery bustles with twenty- and thirtysomethings. The **Boulevard Bakehouse** is great for coffee and a sweet, there is a café half a block down from the Bakehouse, and the **Annies Restaurant and Wine Bar** is the most refined of the four, a very pleasant place to taste New Zealand wine alongside bistro fare. All but the wine bar have outdoor seating in season. ⊠ *41 Hereford St., near Montreal St.,* ☎ *03/ 366–6919. No credit cards.*

2 Bridge of Remembrance. Arching over the Avon, this bridge was built in memory of the soldiers who crossed the river here from King Edward Barracks, just down Cashel Street, on their way to the battlefields of Europe during the First World War. ⊠ *Avon River at Cashel St.*

6 Canterbury Museum. If you're used to sophisticated international museums, this one, like many in New Zealand, won't exactly twirl your buttons. In case you do come, expect to see a reconstruction of an early Christchurch streetscape and the display of Maori artifacts. The Hall of Antarctic Discovery charts the links between the city and the U.S. bases on the frozen continent from the days of Captain Scott; Christchurch is still used as a forward supply depot for U.S. Antarctic bases. The museum stands at the east end of the **Christchurch Botanic Gardens** (☞ *below*). ⊠ *Rolleston Ave. and Worcester St.,* ☎ *03/366–8379.* ☒ *Donation requested.* ☉ *Daily 9:30–4:30.*

1 Captain Robert Falcon Scott statue. "Scott of the Antarctic" (1868–1912), who visited Christchurch on his two Antarctic expeditions, is just across Worcester Street from the information center. The statue was sculpted by his widow, Kathleen Lady Kennett, and inscribed with his last words, written as he and his party lay dying in a blizzard on their return journey from the South Pole. ⊠ *Worcester Blvd. and Oxford Terr.*

★ ❺ **Christchurch Botanic Gardens.** Your introduction to the garden will probably begin just beyond the ☞ **Robert McDougal Gallery** at the remarkable 310-ft herbaceous border, which should clue you in to the scale of things to come. These superb gardens are known for the magnificent trees that were planted in the 19th century. Many are the largest specimens found in the country—or even in their native lands. Pick up the Historic Tree Walk brochure for a self-guided who's who tour of the tree world. There are a number of specialty gardens to visit, as well. In spring spend time in the woodlands, carpeted in daffodils, in the rock garden, or at the primrose garden. In summer the rose garden is a demonstration of every conceivable way to grow these beauties, and the annual plantings and water garden call out for attention now as well. In autumn that magnificent perennial border and the herb garden continue to amaze. And as the weather cools, the hips of species roses begin to redden, putting on yet another display. Spend time in the conservatories to discover tropical plants, cacti, and ferns on days when you'd rather not be outside. Any time of the year, be sure to go to the New Zealand plants area, because seeing plant life that you won't find in other countries is one of the best reasons to come here. A small information center has displays, books, and plant information. ⊠ *Rolleston Ave.,* ☎ *03/366–1701.* 🎫 *Free.* ☉ *Daily 7 AM–dusk, conservatories daily 10:15–4.*

❾ **Christchurch Cathedral.** The city's dominating landmark was begun in 1864, 14 years after the arrival of the Canterbury Pilgrims, but it wasn't consecrated until 1904. Carvings inside commemorate the work of the Anglican missionaries, including Tamihana Te Rauparaha, the son of a fierce and, for the settlers, troublesome Maori chief. Free guided tours begin daily at 11 and 2. For a view across the city to the Southern Alps, climb the 133 steps to the top of the bell tower. The cathedral is known for its boys' choir, which can be heard singing evensong at 4:30 Friday, except during school holidays. It is in **Cathedral Square,** the city's focal point, which functions as a bus terminal and a venue for an arts-and-crafts market, food stalls, and street musicians.

If it's close to 1 PM when you emerge from the cathedral, look for the bearded gentleman with long hair, who's easy to spot because of the crowd that instantly forms around him. This is the **Wizard,** who offers funny and irreverent dissertations on just about any controversial subject—especially religion, politics, sex, and women's issues. Originally a freelance soapbox orator, the Wizard (whose real name is Ian Channel) became so popular that he is now employed by the city council—one of his frequent targets. Don't be too disappointed if he's not around; his appearances have become less frequent in recent years, and he doesn't come out in winter, between May and October. ⊠ *Cathedral Sq.* 🎫 *Tower $2.50.* ☉ *Daily 8:30 AM–9 PM.*

❿ **Christchurch Gondola.** East of the city in the Port Hills, the gondola is the best vantage point from which to overlook Christchurch, the Canterbury Plains, and Lyttleton Harbour. At the top, you can wander through the **Time Tunnel,** which gives a brief history of the region and finishes with an audiovisual about present-day Canterbury. Best of all, sit with a drink at the Red Rock Cafe and watch the sunset. Remember to ride the tram with your back to the mountain for the best views. If you don't have a car, free shuttles leave regularly from the visitor center. ⊠ *10 Bridle Path Rd., Heathcote,* ☎ *03/384–4914.* 🎫 *$12; $9 after 5 PM.* ☉ *Mon.–Sat. 10 AM–12:45 AM, Sun. 10 AM–11:45 PM.*

❿ International Antarctic Centre. Ever since Scott wintered his dogs at nearby Quail Island in preparation for his ill-fated South Pole expedition of 1912, Christchurch has maintained a close connection with the frozen continent. Dedicated to the past, present, and future of Antarctic exploration, this complex includes intriguing interactive displays, in which you can feel firsthand the −5°F Antarctic conditions, for example, as well as photographs and exhibits showing the sophisticated clothing and hardware that modern-day scientists use to carry out their work at the Antarctic bases. The audiovisual show is superb. The exhibition is within walking distance of the airport—you can also catch a free shuttle from there—and about a 20-minute drive from central Christchurch. There is also a café and bar and an Antarctic shop with a variety of mementos to take home. ⊠ *Orchard Rd.,* ☎ *03/358–9896.* ☞ *$14.* ☉ *Oct.–Mar., daily 9–8; Apr.–Sept., daily 9–5:30.*

⓬ Mona Vale. One of Christchurch's great historic homesteads, the turn-of-the-century, riverside Mona Vale makes for a lovely outing from the city. Come for lunch or Devonshire tea and make believe that your estate lies along the Avon as you stroll under the stately trees and through the well-tended fuchsia, dahlia, herb, and iris gardens. Stop to smell the many roses, then move on to the fernery and lily pond. If the mood really takes you, go for a punt ride (a gondola-like boat) and contemplate your travels from the water. ⊠ *63 Fendalton Rd., 1 7/10 km (1 mi) from city center,* ☎ *03/348–9659 or 03/348–9666.* ☞ *Free.* ☉ *Grounds Oct.–Mar., daily 8–7:30; Apr.–Sept., daily 8:30–5:30; morning and afternoon tea Sun.–Fri.; smorgasbord lunch Sun. (reservations essential).*

⓭ Nga Hau E Wha National Marae. This Maori culture center provides a rare chance to gain insight into South Island Maori culture. Its name means "marae (meeting house) of the four winds," where people from all points of the compass meet and are welcome. Guides explain elements of Maori culture, history, and protocol. If you visit by night, you are challenged in a traditional, fearsome Maori way, before pressing noses as part of the welcoming ceremony. You also eat a *hangi* (traditional Maori feast) and view Maori action songs. Bookings are essential for the evening meal and performance, and the price includes round-trip transport from the city. ⊠ *250 Pages Rd.,* ☎ *03/388–7685.* ☞ *Tour $5.50, hangi meal and cultural performance $55.* ☉ *Tour daily at 11 and 2, hangi and performance daily at 7.*

⓫ Orana Park Wildlife Trust. This slice of the African plains in Canterbury is home to endangered species such as cheetah and white rhino. Animals have plenty of room to roam, which happily doesn't leave you with those feelings of pity that traditional zoos sometimes inflict. Orana also has native reptiles and birds and is a particularly good place to see the elusive tuatara, a reptilian relic of prehistoric New Zealand. The park also has a twilight safari experience (reservations essential) from early December to February. Orana is 25 minutes from the city center, in the same general direction as the airport and the International Antarctic Centre. ⊠ *McLeans Island Rd., Harewood,* ☎ *03/359–7109.* ☞ *$12, twilight safari (including barbecue) $35.* ☉ *Daily 10–5:30, last admission 4:30; twilight safari begins 5:45.*

❼ Robert McDougal Art Gallery. You're likely to see some of the city's more innovative shows here, along with works by 19th-century New Zealand artists and an international collection of painting and sculpture, including two Rodins. It is behind the Christchurch Museum next to the Botanic Gardens. ⊠ *Rolleston Ave.,* ☎ *03/365–0915.* ☞ *Free.* ☉ *Daily 10–4:30.*

❸ St. Michael and All Saints Anglican Church. St. Michael's dates from the city's earliest days. Christchurch was founded in 1850 by the Canterbury Association, a group of leading British churchmen, politicians, and peers who envisioned a settlement that would serve as a model of industry and ideals, governed by the principles of the Anglican faith. The first settlers the association sent out were known as the Canterbury Pilgrims, and their churches were focal points for the whole community. Built in 1872, the white-timber St. Michael's is an outstanding building. One of the bells in the wooden belfry came from England aboard one of four ships that carried the Canterbury Pilgrims. ⊠ *Oxford Terr. and Durham St.* ☺ *Daily noon–2.*

❶❺ Southern Encounter–Aquarium of Discovery. Fish and divers in the heart of Christchurch? This giant aquarium has an enormous variety of New Zealand fish species—from rocky tidal-pool creatures to those from lakes, rivers, and the briny deep. In some displays you can actually touch the critters—if you want to. Watch divers feed giant eels or carpet sharks, cod, skates, and other rarely seen deep-water fish. There's also a historic gold-mining town and a fishing lodge where you can learn fly tying from an expert. ⊠ *Cathedral Square, Christchurch,* ☎ *03/377–3474,* FAX *03/377–9196.* ⊟ *$12.50.* ☺ *Nov.–Mar., daily 9–9; Apr.–Oct., daily 9–6.*

OFF THE
BEATEN PATH

GETHSEMANE GARDENS – Set high overlooking Pegasus Bay in suburban Sumner, Gethsemane isn't quite like your local garden center back home. It is, as you might guess from the name, a born-again Christian garden, and the benefit the plants receive from the tonic of spirituality seems clear. The nursery, with its extensive display gardens, has the largest, most colorful disease- and pest-free plants going. As you approach, take note of the 90-ft-long fence work that spells GETHSEMANE. Inside, four meticulous knot gardens form a Star of David, Star of Bethlehem, and two parallel Jerusalem crosses. The Rosery is filled with fragrant old-fashioned roses and more lettering: The path work spells JESUS. The potager, an ornamental vegetable garden, has as its centerpiece a life-size *pietà* covered by a trellised structure supporting a forbidding crown-of-thorns plant. The plant people among you may be too amazed by the lushness of the gardens to notice any symbolism. Perhaps, then, you should end your visit to Gethsemane at the small chapel, where you can pray to have plants of your own like these. The garden is a 20-minute drive east of central Christchurch. ⊠ *33 Revelation Dr., at top of Clifton Terr., Sumner,* ☎ *03/326–5848.* ⊟ *$2.* ☺ *Daily 9–5.*

Dining

$$$$ ✕ **Thornley's.** Local culinary icon Peter Thornley worked in a couple of London hot spots before returning to launch French Farm, on the Akaroa Peninsula. Now he's back city-side, and his restaurant is widely regarded as the best in town. Peter likes well-focused flavors, so his tomato soup, for example, contains very little besides the star ingredient—and the taste is sublime. Pink-cooked lamb is served alongside aubergine (eggplant) from a wood-fired oven, and crab meat from Golden Bay, near Nelson, sits atop slivered scallops drizzled with gazpacho sauce. The wine list concentrates on New Zealand, but top bottles from other countries are available. ⊠ *Worcester St. at Oxford Terr.,* ☎ *03/366–2400. Reservations essential. AE, DC, MC, V.*

$$$ ✕ **Le Bon Bolli.** Phillip Kraal's eccentrically decorated eatery—think ancient Rome crossed with Provence—tries to be all things to all foodies and comes close to succeeding. À la carte selections include a terrine of cervena with bell peppers, braised ox cheeks, tagliatelle of oysters with

salmon caviar, and an assortment of fresh fish poached in vintage Chablis. There is also a French-style tasting menu ($95 per person). ⊠ *Montreal and Worcester Sts.*, ☎ *03/374–9035. AE, DC, MC, V.*

$$ ✕ **Azure.** Tasty food and a casual atmosphere attract both the local business set and visitors to town to this relatively new café-style restaurant. Apart from blackboard specials—often the best dishes of the day— also look for the salmon and vegetable lasagna with squid ink pasta. Wide floors, large windows, and a choice of indoor and outdoor dining give Azure a light and breezy feeling and make it a great place for lunch. ⊠ *128 Oxford Terr.*, ☎ *03/365–6088. AE, DC, MC, V.*

$$ ✕ **Bardellis.** The name says it all—a bar, a deli, and an Italian accent. Stylish and medium loud, this is where Christchurch's younger set comes for honest food and good New Zealand wine by the glass or bottle. Typical dishes are grilled chicken breast on a sourdough bun, Thai seafood curry, and seared salmon on a potato galette. Vegetarians, look for the likes of pumpkin and peanut ravioli, or egg noodles tossed with greens, cashews, mixed sprouts, and capsicums (bell peppers). This is a good choice for casual outdoor eating on a warm summer evening. ⊠ *98 Cashel Mall*, ☎ *03/353–0001. AE, DC, MC, V.*

$$ ✕ **Espresso 124.** This smart, modern restaurant is a good bet for mid-
★ morning coffee or midnight snacks—it has a high-energy atmosphere generated by the stylish crowd that frequents it. Simplicity is the key on a menu that features thin-crust pizza, char-grilled steak, lamb shank, and seafood. The river and the heart of the city are both close. Part of the operation is a lunchtime deli, with inexpensive sandwiches, focaccia, pasta, and savory pies. Dine indoors or out; there is live jazz some nights. ⊠ *124 Oxford Terr.*, ☎ *03/365–0547. AE, DC, MC, V.*

$ ✕ **Main Street Café and Bar.** If you lived in Christchurch and liked hearty
★ vegetarian cooking, you'd probably end up at this bohemian storefront haunt once a week with a good friend. Pumpkin and kumara (native sweet potato) balls with peanut sauce are rich and yummy, and daily soups or a choice of three mixed salads with a piece of homemade bread will help you get out of a vacation-food rut. Espresso is great, and desserts are phenomenally delicious. Main Street is open for all meals (counter service only), and there's plenty of seating at old wooden tables in a few rooms downstairs, upstairs, and outside. The bar next door has a selection of beers from around the world. ⊠ *840 Colombo St., at Salisbury St.*, ☎ *03/365–0421. AE, DC, MC, V.*

Lodging

$$$$ 🏨 **Charlotte Jane.** Go on spoil yourself and let hosts Moira and
★ Siegfried Lindlbauer do the same at this magnificent 1891 villa, once a girls' school, now a luxurious bed-and-breakfast. Inside and out, the house speaks for itself—a stunning Victorian veranda, a stained-glassed window above the entrance depicting the *Charlotte Rose* (one of the first four ships to bring settlers to Christchurch in 1850), crystal chandeliers from Austria, a native kauri- and rimu-wood staircase, ivory damask curtains, English-tile bathrooms, a rimu-paneled dining room, and period furniture throughout every one of the 10 beautiful guest rooms. The gardens combine natives like cabbage and kauri trees with camellias and lots of old roses. Suites have large spa baths, and the Honeymoon Suite has a great hand-carved Elizabethan mahogany four-poster bed. The finishing touches of fine cooking, gourmet breakfasts, superb hosting, and being just minutes from the city are all here, adding to the welcoming atmosphere. ⊠ *110 Papanui Rd.*, ☎ *03/355–1028,* 𝙵𝙰𝚇 *03/355–8882. 10 rooms with bath. In-room VCRs, no smoking rooms, laundry service. AE, DC, MC, V.*

$$$$ ⊞ **Millennium.** The 1996 Millennium is the most stylish of a new crop of Christchurch hotels, with an interesting mix of European and Asian touches in the public areas. In rooms Italian lamps stand beside Oriental ginger jars, and the designer has chosen strong classical blues and golds, with sophisticated results. The primary advantage is being in the middle of the city at Cathedral Square. And because of the wonders of double-glazed windows, you can enjoy the view but not have to put up with the noise. ⊠ *14 Cathedral Sq.,* ☎ *03/365-1111 or 800/35-8888,* ℻ *03/365-7676. 179 rooms with bath. Restaurant, bar, health club, sauna, business services, valet parking. AE, DC, MC, V.*

$$$$ ⊞ **Parkroyal Christchurch.** This plush hotel, in a prime location over-
★   looking Victoria Square and the river, added a touch of glamour to the city's accommodations scene when it opened in 1988. The rooms are large and luxurious, colored in rich tones of burgundy, gold, and blue. In summer the best views are from rooms overlooking Victoria Square, but in the winter popularity switches to those with views of the snow-capped Alps to the west. The hotel is especially well equipped with restaurants and bars. A pianist plays in the glass-roof atrium—the heart of this hotel—at lunch or in the evening. The Canterbury Tales restaurant, which specializes in innovative New Zealand cookery, and the Japanese restaurant, Yamagen, which has *teppan yaki* and traditional fare, are among the city's finest. ⊠ *Kilmore and Durham Sts.,* ☎ *03/365-7799,* ℻ *03/365-0082. 296 rooms with bath. 3 restaurants, 3 bars, sauna, exercise room, bicycles, car rental. AE, DC, MC, V.*

$$$ ⊞ **Centra.** A hotel with business travelers at heart, the Centra has some of the most interesting rooms in town. In this converted bank building, guests stay in what once were offices—rooms' shapes and sizes are anything but standard. The hotel is in the central business district, just a minute or two walk from Cathedral Square and close to Victoria Square. The Streetside Bar is arguably the best place in Christchurch to have a gin and tonic, to watch Christchurch's working population go by on a weekday, or to mix with them in the evening. ⊠ *Cashel and High Sts.,* ☎ *03/365-8888,* ℻ *03/365-8822. 201 rooms with bath. Restaurant, bar, health club, business services. AE, DC, MC, V.*

$$$ ⊞ **Copthorne Durham Street.** Opposite the Christchurch Casino and five minutes' walk from Cathedral Square, this is perfectly located to make the most of the inner city of Christchurch. Most of the spacious rooms have views over the city toward the Port Hills or to the mountains in the west. Furnishings are tasteful and modern. ⊠ *Durham and Kilmore Sts.,* ☎ *03/365-4699,* ℻ *03/366-6302. 161 rooms, 19 suites. Restaurant, bar, refrigerators, room service, sauna, exercise room, baby-sitting, free parking. DC, MC.*

$$ ⊞ **Riverview Lodge.** This grand Edwardian house overlooking the Avon
★   is one of the finest bed-and-breakfasts in Christchurch. With interesting native timber in details throughout the house—such as solid kauri stairs and doors—it offers superbly comfortable, historic accommodations and a tasty breakfast at about the same price as a motel room. Upstairs, the Turret Room is spacious and interesting, but the large room on the side is also bright, with interesting woodwork and its own bathroom, with a deep claw-foot tub and an original copper cistern. Ernst Wipperfuerth is an amiable, offbeat host, and don't hesitate to ask him about dining or exploring suggestions. Children are accommodated by prior arrangement. The city center is a pleasant (and safe at night) 15-minute walk along the river, which allows you to leave the car behind. ⊠ *361 Cambridge Terr.,* ☎ ℻ *03/365-2860. 4 rooms with bath. Boating, bicycles. BP. MC, V.*

$$ ⊞ **Turret House.** Built in 1905 as a family home for a retired farmer, this lodge has comfortable, well-maintained rooms and a friendly

atmosphere that makes it another standout among Christchurch's bed-and-breakfast accommodations. All rooms are furnished differently, and prices vary accordingly. For a couple, the medium-size rooms offer a good combination of space and value. Current managers Patrick and Justine Dougherty are retired farmers from Central Otago. If you happen to be interested in rugby, the couple are both keen on the sport—and happy to fill you in on the latest. Despite its location close to a major intersection, noise is not a problem. ✉ *435 Durham St.,* ☎ *03/365–3900. 8 rooms with bath. BP. AE, DC, MC, V.*

Nightlife

Christchurch's after-dark action doesn't match the range of activities available during the day, but that doesn't mean you have to tuck into bed as soon as the sun goes down. A recent addition to the city is the **Christchurch Casino,** which has blackjack, roulette, baccarat, gaming machines, and other ways to try your luck. It is the only casino on South Island. Dress is smart-casual or better, and you will be turned away at the door if you arrive in jeans. ✉ *30 Victoria St.,* ☎ *03/365–9999.* ☉ *Mon.–Wed. 11 AM–3 AM, Thurs. 11 AM–Mon. 3 AM.*

For dancing into the wee hours, your best bet is the **Ministry,** modeled on the concept of the European club the Ministry of Sound. The club attracts a fairly young crowd, so if you're feeling a bit gray, it does have a front bar where the music is not so loud. ✉ *90 Lichfield St.,* ☎ *03/379–2910.* ▣ *$6.* ☉ *Wed.–Sun. 9 PM–7 AM.*

Bar Particular has a café and club with a sizable dance floor and drag shows Saturday at half-past midnight. ✉ *Colombo and Lichfield Sts.,* ☎ *03/3650781.* ☉ *Café: Tues.–Sat. 6 PM–1 AM; club: Wed.–Sat. 9 PM–2 AM.*

Outdoor Activities and Sports

Bicycling
Pacific Cycle Tours has a seven-day, 386-km (241-mi, some of it off-road) escorted bicycle tour from Christchurch—riding over Arthur's Pass on the TranzAlpine Express, then cycling up the West Coast, over to Kaikoura, and back down to Christchurch. Mountain bikes, the train trip, midrange accommodations, and breakfast and lunch are included, as is a backup bus. ✉ *17 Trent St., Christchurch,* ☎ *03/389–0583,* 🗎 *03/389–0498.* ▣ *$1,575.*

Fishing
For information on trout and salmon fishing in Rakaia in the Canterbury region, *see* Adventure Vacations, Chapter 6.

Horse Trekking
Around Christchurch, the Canterbury Plains and encircling mountain ranges provide a dramatic setting for riding. *See* Adventure Vacations, Chapter 6, for operators and trip information.

Shopping

The best **Arts Centre** shopping is at the **Saturday- and Sunday-morning craft market,** which has various Kiwi goods, including handmade sweaters and woolens, that you might want to take home with you. Inside the Arts Centre buildings, the **Galleria** consists of a dozen shops and studios for artisans and crafts workers, from potters to weavers to some very good jewelry makers. The quality of work varies considerably from shop to shop, but this is one of the few places where many crafts workers are represented under one roof. Most shops, including a bookstore, are open from 10 to 4; some are closed weekends. Most do not take credit cards. ⊠ *Worcester St.,* ☎ *03/379–7573.*

Bivouac sells a complete range of outdoor gear and maps. ⊠ *76 Cashel St.,* ☎ *03/366–3197.*

Johnson Grocer–Leight & Co. If you happen to spot this old-time grocer on Colombo Street on your own, good for you. If not, stop in at tiny Number 787 between Kilmore and Peterborough, which is chockablock with food products from the world over—toffee, fudge, and bread and cheese for a picnic—with a British emphasis, of course. Leight & Co. has been in the hands of only two owners since 1911, the current one since 1950. ⊠ *787 Colombo St.,* ☎ *03/366–3027.*

Christchurch A to Z

Arriving and Departing

BY BUS AND TRAIN
Mount Cook Landline (☎ 03/343–8085) and **InterCity** (☎ 03/377–0951) operate daily bus services between Christchurch and Dunedin, Mt. Cook, Nelson, and Queenstown. InterCity also operates a daily **TranzAlpine Express** train to Arthur's Pass Village and Greymouth. The **Super Shuttle** (☎ 03/365–5655) also goes to Arthur's Pass Village and Greymouth from Christchurch.

BY CAR
Highway 1 links Christchurch with Kaikoura and Blenheim in the north and Dunedin in the south. Driving time for the 330-km (205-mi) journey between Christchurch and Mount Cook Village is five hours; between Christchurch and Dunedin, 5½ hours.

BY PLANE
Ansett New Zealand (☎ 03/371–1146) and **Air New Zealand** (☎ 03/379–5200) link Christchurch with cities on both North and South islands. **Mount Cook Airlines** (☎ 03/379–0690) flies from Christchurch to Queenstown, Aoraki, and Te Anau. **Christchurch Airport** is 10 km (6 mi) northwest of the city. **Super Shuttle** buses (☎ 03/361–5655) meet all incoming flights and charge $7 per passenger to city hotels. **CAN-RIDE** buses operate between the airport and Cathedral Square from 6 AM to 11 PM daily. The fare is $2.70. A **taxi** to the city costs about $15.

Getting Around
The city of Christchurch is flat and compact, and the best way to explore it is on foot.

BY BICYCLE
Trailblazers (⊠ 96 Worcester St., ☎ 03/366–6033) hires out mountain bikes for $25 per day. The shop is open weekdays 9–5:30 and weekends 10–4.

BY BUS OR TRAM
The historical **Christchurch Tramway** (☎ 03/366–7830) serves as an attraction in its own right and doubles as a way to get around when those feet tire. A city circuit takes in Cathedral Square, Worcester Boulevard, Rolleston Avenue, Armagh Street, and New Regent Street. It stops close to all major attractions, including the Arts Centre, Botanic Gardens, and Canterbury Museum. A one-hour ticket costs $5; a full-day pass costs $10. You'll have no need to use the confusing bus system unless you are actually heading out of town.

Contacts and Resources

EMERGENCIES
Dial 111 for **fire, police, or ambulance** services.

Guided walking tours ($8) of the city depart daily at 10 and 2 from the Christchurch–Canterbury Visitor Information Centre (☞ Visitor Information, *below*) and from the red-and-black booth in Cathedral Square. It takes about two hours.

Punting on the Avon is perfectly suited to the pace of Christchurch. You can hire punts with expert boatmen at the Worcester Street Bridge, near the corner of Oxford Terrace, from 10 to 6 in summer and from 10 to 4 the rest of the year. A 20-minute trip costs $10.

Anne and Brian Lucas' **Canterbury Trails, Ltd.** (⊠ 5 Dannys Lane, Cashmere, Christchurch, ☎ 03/337–1185, FAX 03/337–5085) run day tours from Christchurch to Akaroa (which can include farm visits and harbor cruises), Arthurs Pass National Park, and Hanmer Springs. Generous lunches come with New Zealand wine; prices range from $320 to $375 per couple. There are also nine-day wilderness-and-luxury-lodge trips for $3,930 per person.

The **Gray Line** (☎ 03/343–3874) runs a half-day Morning Sights tour ($26) and a full-day tour of Akaroa ($54). All tours leave from the Christchurch Visitor Information Centre daily at 9.

Christchurch–Canterbury Visitor Information Centre. ⊠ *Worcester Blvd. and Oxford Terr., Christchurch,* ☎ *03/379–9629.* ☉ *Weekdays 8:30–5, weekends 8:30–4.*

SIDE TRIPS FROM CHRISTCHURCH

Depending on where you're headed for the rest of your New Zealand getaway, brief jaunts from Christchurch can add much to your experience of the area. The Banks Peninsula, east of the city, is additional proof that you can find scenic delights no matter what corner of the country you turn to. Looking north, consider stopping in Amberley or Waipara if you're en route to or from Kaikoura. Hanmer Springs' thermal baths are good for a relaxing soak. Plan an entire day for either of these side trips.

Akaroa and the Banks Peninsula

⑯ *82 km (50 mi) east of Christchurch.*

Bearing the shape of a long-dormant volcanic cone, the Banks Peninsula—that nub that juts into the Pacific southeast of Christchurch—has a wonderful coastline indented with small bays where sheep graze almost to the water's edge. Its main source of fame is the town of Akaroa, which was chosen as the site for a French colony in 1838. The first French settlers arrived in 1840 only to find that the British had already established sovereignty over New Zealand by the Treaty of Waitangi. Less than 10 years later, the French abandoned their attempt at colonization, but the settlers remained and gradually intermarried with the local English community. Apart from the street names and a few surnames, there is little sign of a French connection anymore, but the village has a splendid setting, and on a sunny day it makes a marvelous trip from Christchurch. A half day will get you to and from Akaroa, including a drive up to the edge of the former volcanic dome, but take a full day if you want to do other exploring of the peninsula.

The best way to get the feel of Akaroa is to stroll along the waterfront from the lighthouse to Jubilee Park. The focus of historic interest is the **Akaroa Museum,** which has a display of Maori greenstones and embroidery and dolls dating from the days of the French settlement. The museum includes Langlois-Eteveneaux House, the two-room cottage of an early French settler, which bears the imprint of his homeland in its architecture. ⊠ *Rues Lavaud and Balguerie,* ☎ *03/304–7614.* ☒ *$2.50.* ☉ *Daily 10:30–4:30.*

The picture-book **Church of St. Patrick,** near the museum, was built in 1864 to replace two previous Catholic churches—the first destroyed by fire, the second by tempest. ⊠ *Rue Pompallier.* ☉ *Daily 8–5.*

The contrast of the rim of the old volcanic cone and the coves below is striking, and an afternoon driving to the summit, around it, then dropping into one of the coves leaves you with a feeling like you've found your own corner of the world. **Okains Bay** is one of five bays on the peninsula to go to for that. A small settlement lies at the bottom of a road that winds down from the summit and ends at a beach sheltered by tall headlands. There's a cave in the rocks on the right and a path above it that leads to the remnants of a pier, now just a cluster of tilting pilings in the water. A stream lets out into the bay on the left side of the beach. Sheep paddocks rise a couple of hundred feet on either side of the sand, cradling it in green. There's a small general store that doubles as a post office back in the village, as well as a tiny old church to poke your head into if you're curious.

Another way to get to the feel of the peninsula is to have an afternoon cold one with locals at **Hilltop Tavern.** ⊠ *Hwy. 75 at Summit Rd.*

Dining and Lodging
In Akaroa, eat at **L'hotel** (☎ 03/304–7559), where the ambience is old-world and the food a mix of traditional and contemporary. Nearby, **French Farm** (☎ ☎ 03/304–5784) is a vineyard with an attached restaurant.

$$$ 🏠 **Oinako Lodge.** Surrounded by a garden and greenery a five-minute walk from the town and harbor of Akaroa, this charming Victorian manor house still has its original ornamented plaster ceilings and marble fireplaces. The name *Oinako* is Maori for "place of Nako," believed to be a Maori chief from the area. You'll find fresh flowers in the spacious and pleasantly decorated rooms; some have balconies. There are books, music, and a piano in the guest lounge. Children are accommodated by prior arrangement. Hosts Judith and Trevor Jackson will ensure you find peace and quiet in this seaside retreat. ⊠ *99 Beach Rd., Akaroa,* ☎ *03/304–8787. 6 rooms with bath. Guest lounge and dining room. BP. AE, DC, MC, V.*

Hiking
The 35-km (22-mi) **Banks Peninsula Track** crosses beautiful coastal terrain. From Akaroa you hike over headlands, and past several bays, waterfalls, and seal and penguin colonies, and you might see Hector's dolphins at sea. Two-day ($60) and four-day ($100) tramps are available between October 15 and May 15. Overnight in cabins with fully equipped kitchens, which you might share with other hikers. Rates include lodging, transport from Akaroa to the first hut, landowners' fees, and a booklet describing the features of the track. ⊠ *Box 50, Akaroa,* ☎ *03/304–7612.*

Arriving and Departing
BY CAR
The main route to Akaroa is Highway 75, which leaves the southwest corner of Christchurch as Lincoln Road. The 82-km (50-mi) drive takes about 90 minutes.

Guided Tours

Akaroa Tours (☎ 03/379–9629) has a shuttle between the Christchurch Visitor Information Centre and Akaroa; buses depart Christchurch weekdays at 10:30 and 4, Saturday at noon, and Sunday at noon and 6:45; buses depart Akaroa weekdays at 8:20 and 2:20, weekends at 10:30 (round-trip $30).

Amberley

⑰ *50 km (31 mi) north of Christchurch.*

Passing through the small township of Amberley, about 40 minutes north of Christchurch, could be uneventful if it weren't for a great café and bar that serve delicious local food and wine.

Dining and Lodging

$$ ✕ **Norwester Café & Bar.** Cultured dining in a rural places is one of life's great pleasures. Try an ostrich-egg frittata, an Italian omelet filled with kumara (sweet potato), spinach, and spring onions and served with a tomato and rocket (arugula) salad for brunch or lunch. After 5 PM you can order the fish of the day, panfried and served with grilled bananas, coriander, and lime salsa and steamed jasmine rice. A great complement is Waipara Springs' Riesling. ⊠ *95 Main North Rd., Amberley,* ☎ *03/314–9411. AE, DC, MC, V.*

$$$ ⬚ **Old Glenmark Vicarage Country Inn.** History abounds in this former Anglican vicarage, built in 1906 along with the nearby church. Painstakingly restored by Malcolm and Penny Pester, this typical New Zealand villa has a handcrafted kauri-wood foyer so arresting that it makes you want to reach out and touch it. You can almost hear the sounds of the large garden parties once held here in the 1920s and '30s as you recline in the cool shade of the veranda. Most of the country-style decor is Penny's work—the front room is a sumptuous favorite for couples. Produce from the area is served at breakfast, with former-chef Malcolm turning out the croissants and breads. You can play croquet on the grounds. ⊠ *161 Church Rd., R.D. 3, Amberley,* ☎ FAX *03/ 314–6775. 4 rooms with bath. Croquet. BP. AE, DC, MC, V.*

Waipara

⑱ *57 km (35 mi) north of Christchurch.*

The attractive rural township of Waipara is about 45 minutes north of Christchurch heading toward Kaikoura. The area was once renowned for its profusion of moa (the enormous extinct flightless bird) bones. It used to be dotted with swamps—perhaps the reason the Maori named it Waipara, meaning "muddy water"—into which hundreds of moa tumbled over the centuries.

These days the town is better known for its excellent chardonnays and Rieslings, such as those of **Waipara Springs Winery,** where you'll be able to sample Riesling, sauvignon blanc, chardonnay, cabernet sauvignon, and pinot noir. Opened in 1990, its Australian wine maker Kym Rayner has been making wines in New Zealand for 15 years, and in northern mid-Canterbury since 1992. You can also taste the wine and try their produce in the winery's restaurant, open daily 11–5. ⊠ *Omihi Rd., State Hwy. 1, Waipara,* ☎ FAX *03/314–6777.*

Waipara is a departure point for the **Weka Pass Railway,** which drives through farmlands and interesting rock formations in a train pulled by a vintage locomotive. It runs the first and third weekends of the month and public holidays. ⊠ *McKenzies Rd.,* ☎ *03/389–4078.* ⊠ *$12.*

Hanmer Springs

⑲ *120 km (75 mi) north of Christchurch.*

Long before Europeans arrived in New Zealand, Maori travelers knew the Hanmer Springs area as Waitapu (sacred water). Early settlers didn't take long to discover these thermal springs, which bubble out into a serene alpine environment, just a two-hour drive from Christchurch. More than 100 years ago European visitors would "take the water" for medicinal purposes, but nowadays you will find it far more pleasant to lie back and relax in the water than to drink the stuff. The **Hanmer Springs Thermal Reserve** remains the number one reason to visit the area and now consists of seven thermal pools, a freshwater 25-meter pool, and a toddlers' pool. The reserve also has massage, a sauna and steam room, a fitness center, and a licensed restaurant. Unfortunately, the facility, nicely built though it is, is more a functional than an aesthetic retreat—it looks more like a town pool than a scenic spa. ⊠ *Amuri Ave., Hanmer Springs,* ☎ *03/315–7511.* ⌧ *$6, private pool $10 per person (minimum 2 people), sauna $6 per ½-hr.* ⊙ *Daily 10–9.*

The forest around Hanmer Springs, planted by convict labor in the early 1900s, has a distinctly European look. You'll find European larch, Austrian pine, European alder, and other varieties. The information center has maps and fact sheets detailing several walks.

Arriving and Departing

BY CAR
From Christchurch follow Highway 1 north to Highway 7 at Waipara, 57 km (35 mi) from the city. The drive then continues through the small town of Culverden, where Highway 7A turns toward Hanmer Springs, which is well signposted.

Visitor Information

Hurunui Visitor Information Centre. ⊠ *Off Amuri Rd. next to Hanmer Springs Thermal Reserve,* ☎ *03/315–7128.* ⊙ *Daily 10–5.*

THE SOUTHERN ALPS

The Canterbury Plains, which ring Christchurch and act as a brief transition between the South Pacific and the soaring New Zealand Alps, are the country's finest sheep pastures, as well as its largest area of flat land. But although this may be sheep—and horse-trekking—heaven, the drive south along the plain is mundane by New Zealand standards until you leave Highway 1 and head toward the Southern Alps. By contrast, the drive to Arthur's Pass quickly takes you up into the hills, and Route 73 is a good way to get to Westland and the glaciers at Fox and Franz Josef, but it would be the long way to Queenstown.

Arthur's Pass

⑳ *153 km (96 mi) northwest of Christchurch.*

Arthur's Pass National Park is another of New Zealand's spectacular alpine regions, and hiking opportunities abound. On the way to the pass, the **Castle Hill Conservation Area** is littered with interesting rock formations. There is a parking area on the left several miles past Lake Lyndon. Along with Craigieburn Forest Park, Castle Hill gets less rainfall than Arthur's Pass National Park. Craigieburn itself has wonderful beech and fern forests.

Arthur's Pass National Park has plenty of half- and full-day hikes and 11 backcountry tracks with overnight huts for backpacking amid local natural wonders: waterfalls, gorges, alpine wildflowers and higher-altitude grasslands, and stunning snowcapped peaks.

The pass is the major midisland transit to the West Coast. The west side of the pass is unbelievably steep—be aware that this may be the most hair-raising paved road you'll ever drive. The village of Arthur's Pass itself isn't much to speak of, and in foul weather it looks rather forlorn. There are a restaurant and a store for basic food supplies.

Lodging

$$$ ☒ **Wilderness Lodge Arthur's Pass.** That pot of gold at the end of the rainbow is in fact a Southern Alps lodge surrounded by spectacular peaks, beech forests, tawny tussock grassland, rare plants, unique bird life, serene lakes, and wild rivers. Ecologist Dr. Gerry McSweeney's second back-to-nature hotel-lodge (the other is Wilderness Lodge Lake Moeraki, Chapter 4) is a 6,000-acre sheep farm in a valley called *Te Ko Awa a Aniwaniwa* (Valley of the Mother of Rainbows) by its first Maori visitors. From a hillside perch it overlooks the huge meandering Waimakariri River, which has carved a gaping swath through the pass. By taking trips to nearby lakes, limestone caves, and desert landscapes—and from evening talks and slide shows—staying here constitutes a superb short course in rare, high-country ecology and sheep farming. All meals are included in the rates; some guided trips and all drinks are not. ☒ *130 km (81 mi) west of Christchurch on State Highway 73 (Box 33, Arthur's Pass 8190), Canterbury,* ☎ *03/318–9246,* ℻ *03/318–9245, 20 rooms. Lounge, library, boating, fishing, laundry service. AE, DC, MC, V. Closed June.*

Aoraki (Mt. Cook)

330 km (205 mi) southwest of Christchurch.

㉑ You will know you have reached the **Mackenzie Country** after you cross Burkes Pass, and the woodland is suddenly replaced by high-country tussock grassland, which is dotted with lupines in the summer months. The area is named for James ("Jock") Mckenzie (the man is Mckenzie, but the region that took his name is *Mackenzie*), one of the most intriguing and enigmatic figures in New Zealand history. Mckenzie was a Scot who may or may not have stolen the thousand sheep that were found with him in these secluded upland pastures in 1855. Arrested, tried, and convicted, he made several escapes from jail before he was granted a free pardon nine months after his trial—and disappeared from the pages of history. Regardless of his innocence or guilt, there can be no doubt that Mckenzie was a master bushman and herdsman.

These days farmers are battling tens of thousands of rabbits whose nibbling and digging is eroding valuable soil easily blown away by strong local winds—you'll see the damage these beguiling bunnies have done when you're out hiking. Like possums, these European-introduced animals reproduce unchecked in an environment with no natural predators. In early 1998 one Mackenzie Country farmer, sick of waiting for the government to do something about the plague, took matters into his own hands and illegally released a homemade version of the deadly rabbit calicivirus disease (RCD) with dramatic results—RCD killed an estimated 90% of the local rabbit population. Evidence of RCD has since been found in rabbits on North Island as well.

㉒ Approaching the snowy peaks of the Southern Alps, the long, narrow expanse of **Lake Tekapo** is one of the most photographed sights in New Zealand. Its extraordinary milky-turquoise color comes from rock flour—rock ground by glacial action and held in a soupy suspension.
㉓ On the east side of the lakeside power station is the tiny **Church of the**

Good Shepherd, which strikes a dignified note of piety in these majestic surroundings. A nearby memorial commemorates the sheepdogs of the area. Before fences were erected around their runs, shepherds would tether dogs at strategic points to stop their sheep from straying. As you drive into the small town, you'll notice a knot of glitzy Asian restaurants with tour buses parked outside. It's rather an off-putting image if you've come for peace and quiet, but it's relatively easy to keep the township at your back and your eyes turned on the lake and mountains—and get a tasty meal when you'd like one.

㉔ **Mount Cook Village** (pop. 300), consists of a visitor center, a grocery store, and a couple of hotels. The national park surrounds the village. Aoraki National Park includes 22 peaks that top the 10,000-ft mark, **㉕** the tallest of which is **Aoraki (Mt. Cook)**—at approximately 12,283 ft, it is the highest peak between Papua New Guinea and the Andes. The mountain's Maori name is Aoraki, after one of three brothers who were the sons of Rakinui, the sky father. Their canoe was caught on a reef and frozen, forming South Island. In these parts, South Island's oldest Maori name is Te Waka O Aoraki—Aoraki's canoe—and the highest peak is Aoraki, himself frozen by the south wind, then turned to stone. The officially recognized name of this mountain and many other South Island places will return to their original Maori names as part of a 1998 settlement between the government and the major South Island Maori tribe, Ngai Tahu.

Aoraki was dramatically first scaled in 1894 by three New Zealanders—Fyfe, Graham, and Clarke—just after it was announced that an English climber and an Italian mountain guide were about to attempt the summit. In a frantic surge of national pride, the New Zealand trio resolved to beat them to it, which they did on Christmas Day. The mountain is still considered a difficult ascent. In the summer of 1991 a chunk of it broke away, but fortunately there were no climbers in the path of the massive avalanches. High Peak, the summit of the mountain, is now about 66 ft lower, but its altered form makes for a much more difficult ascent.

If the sun is shining, the views are spectacular, and even unambitious walks are inspiring. If the cloud ceiling is low, however, you may wonder why you came—and the mountain weather is notoriously changeable. Because a lengthy detour is required to reach Mount Cook Village, it is advisable to contact the **Visitor Information Centre** (☎ 03/435–1818) to check weather conditions. The center is open daily 8–5.

Radiating from the Mt. Cook visitor center is a network of **hiking trails** offering walks of varying difficulty, from the 10-minute Bowen Track to the 5½-hour climb to the 4,818-ft summit of Mt. Sebastopol. Particularly recommended is the walk along the Hooker Valley, a two- to four-hour round-trip. There are frequent ranger-guided walks from the visitor center, with informative talks on flora, fauna, and geology.

A unique hands-on educational experience is to take a half-hour hike to the 2-square-km (¾-square-mi) **Terminal Lake of the Tasman Glacier.** Fed by the glacier and the Murchison River, the lake was only formed in the last 10 years, due to the retreat of the glacier. Experienced guides Kylie Wakelin and Brent Shears (☞ Guided Tours *in* Southern Alps A to Z, *below*) have sound knowledge of the glacier and can take you by boat to explore some of the large floating icebergs that have calved (fallen away) from the Tasman Glacier. It's an eerie experience skimming across the milky-white water and closing in on icebergs—even riding *through* where they have melted—to touch rocks caught in the ice that have never before been felt by human hands.

The other main activity at Mt. Cook is **flightseeing.** From the airfield at Mount Cook Village, helicopters and fixed-wing aircraft make spectacular scenic flights across the Southern Alps. One of the most exciting is the one-hour trip aboard the ski planes that touch down on the ㉖ **Tasman Glacier** after a dazzling scenic flight. The 10-minute stop on the glacier doesn't allow time for much more than a snapshot, but the sensation is tremendous. The moving tongue of ice beneath your feet—one of the largest glaciers outside the Himalayas—is 29 km (18 mi) long and up to 2,000 ft thick in places. The intensity of light on the glacier can be dazzling, and sunglasses are a must. Generally, the best time for flights is early morning. During winter the planes drop skiers on the glacier at 10,000 ft, and they ski down through 13 km (8 mi) of powder snow and fantastic ice formations. With guides, this run is suitable even for intermediate skiers. Ski-plane flights cost about $195 for adults; helicopter flights range from $140 to $270. Ski planes are flown by **Mount Cook Line** (☎ 03/435–1848), helicopters by the **Helicopter Line** (☎ 03/435–1801). **Alpine Guides Ltd.** (⊠ Box 20, Mount Cook, ☎ 03/435–1834) can assist with guides for all treks and ski trips in the national park.

Glacier Explorers leave from the Hermitage Hotel or Mount Cook YHA for tours of Tasman Glacier and its lake. ⊠ *Box 18, Mount Cook,* ☎ *03/435–1809 or 03/435–1820.* 🎫 *$60.* ☉ *Oct.–May.*

Dining

$$$ ✗ **Panorama Room.** You couldn't ask for a better view—floor-to-ceiling windows that put you right at nature's feet. The menu changes seasonally and includes whitebait fritters or crayfish, which you can order as sashimi or broiled with herb and garlic butter. The less expensive ($$) Alpine restaurant also belongs to the Hermitage (☞ Lodging, *below*). ⊠ *Mount Cook Village,* ☎ *03/435–1809. Reservations essential. Jacket required. AE, DC, MC, V. Closed Apr.–Sept. No lunch.*

Lodging

Lodging at Mount Cook Village is controlled by a single company that operates four hotels here. There is also a comfortable YHA Hostel in town with standard dormitory and private double or twin accommodations. Or look to the surrounding high-country's farmstays or motels next to Lake Tekapo.

MT. COOK VILLAGE

$$$$ 🏨 **The Hermitage.** Famed for its stupendous mountain views, this rambling hotel is the luxury option at Mount Cook Village. Generally speaking, the layout and ambience of the hotel do not match its surroundings, and you might find it disappointing. It is fair to note that strict laws govern any major changes to the historic hotel's structure. Things such as the colors used on exterior walls and roofs must be either brown or green. Extensive refurbishment is planned but yet to get underway. Still, you're not going to wake up every day staring at such a stunning view or to the sound of keas (those large, cheeky mountain parrots) fighting it out in the carpark. ⊠ *Mount Cook Village,* ☎ *03/435–1809,* FAX *03/435–1879. 104 rooms with bath. 2 restaurants, bar, café, sauna, shops. AE, DC, MC, V.*

$$ 🏨 **Mount Cook Motels.** A great option for a group or family, these self-contained apartments can accommodate up to six people comfortably. Furniture is far from plush—some effort has been made to brighten up these rather plain green and brown apartments with plaid bedspreads and boldly patterned curtains. Some rooms have 1970s-style wood paneling half way up the wall. The option of cooking your own meals makes for something of a bargain in this mountain village. ⊠ *Mount Cook*

Village, ☎ *03/435–1809 or 0800/686–800 (in N.Z. only),* FAX *03/435–1879. 12 units. AE, DC, MC, V.*

$ 🛏 **Mount Cook YHA Hostel.** This friendly, well-equipped, well-located alternative is open all day and has facilities for guests with disabilities. Call ahead to reserve space; it fills up in summer. Although the majority of the accommodations are dormitory style, there are two doubles and five twins at reasonable rates. ⊠ *Bowen at Kitchener Dr.,* ☎ *03/435–1820. 70 beds in 16 rooms with shared showers. Kitchen, sauna, TV/video room, laundry, shop. DC, MC, V.*

LAKE TEKAPO AND VICINITY

$$$$ 🛏 **Lilybank Lodge.** This remote hunting lodge is built of off-white South Island Oamaru stone and recycled rimu timber. It is part of a thriving deer farm nestled in magnificent surrounds between two rivers—the MacCauley and the Godley—a 45-minute drive from Lake Tekapo, but you'll have to call hosts Wynsome Adams and Gerard Oldolthof before you leave to get you across the rushing river. Mounted animal trophies hang on public area walls. Rooms have recycled timber furniture, plush duvets, and bathrooms with rimu vanities and black-and-white tiles. In the lodge rustic stone pillars punctuate the dining room, lounge, and sunroom. Rates include all meals; alcoholic drinks, telephone calls, and laundry are extra. ⊠ *Box 60, Lake Tekapo,* ☎ *03/680–6522,* FAX *03/680–6838. 8 suites with bath. Horseback riding, fishing. AE, DC, MC, V.*

$$ 🛏 **The Chalet.** The Chalet's six fully self-contained apartments face the turquoise waters of Lake Tekapo. The best are those with spacious living rooms and lake views. Each unit has individuality—the clown room has rag rugs spread over timber floors and a collection of clowns. Some of the other rooms are studios with kitchens open on a single room, others might have a stone fireplace and beamed cathedral ceiling or large lounge rooms with sliding-glass doors giving on the lake. Two of the studios have no appreciable views. The hosts can coordinate hunting, fishing, and nature tours. Lake Tekapo Services, a grocery store in town, is a five-minute walk away. ⊠ *Pioneer Dr., Box 2, Lake Tekapo,* ☎ FAX *03/680–6774,* ☎ *0800/843–242 (in N.Z. only). 6 units with bath. Hiking, fishing, laundry service. MC, V.*

$$ 🛏 **Holbrook Station.** A high-country sheep station running 9,500 Merino sheep on 35,000 acres that climb in parts as high as 6,500 ft, Holbrook lets you feel like you can play at farming while on holiday. The station rents out a rustic cottage that is surrounded by a waist-high stone fence and is comfortably fitted inside. A large window in the front lounge room looks out on Mt. Edward. You are welcome to look around the farm, and hosts Lesley and Alister France might be able to arrange involvement in station activities. You can stay on a bed-and-breakfast basis—the meal is served at the main house—or you can prepare your own meals. Lesley will also cook a three-course dinner with wine for $30 per person by arrangement. ⊠ *State Hwy. 8, 12 km (7½ mi) east of Lake Tekapo, Box 4, Fairlee,* ☎ *03/685–8535 or 025/387–974,* FAX *03/658–8534. 3-bedroom cottage. No credit cards.*

Outdoor Activities and Sports

BICYCLING

Exploring South Island on a bicycle is the only way to see it all up close—the range of scenery may be unmatched in all the world. *See* Adventure Vacations, Chapter 6, for operators and trip information.

CLIMBING

Hikes among the mountains of Mt. Cook National Park are spectacular, and the area is also ideal for rock climbing. Experienced climbers and beginners alike can sign up for the appropriate level of **Alpine Guides'**

7- to 10-day mountaineering courses, which begin around $1,600. (⊠ Box 20, Mount Cook, ☎ 03/345–1834).

Pukaki Horsetreks (⊠ Pukaki Canal Rd., Twizel, ☎ 025/280–7353, or 0800/245–549, in N.Z. only) has half-hour to half-day guided trips ($65 per half-day) in winter and half-hour to two-day treks in summer up Mt. Ruataniwha, which overlooks Lake Ohau in the Mackenzie Basin.

Southern Alps A to Z

Arriving and Departing
Buses and the TranzAlpine Express train can also take you there from Christchurch (☞ Arriving and Departing, *below*), and the village of Arthur's Pass has a couple of eateries if you don't bring a picnic. The **Park Visitor Centre** in the village (☎ 03/318–9211) has exceptional information and natural history displays on the park. The center is open daily 8–5.

Arthur's Pass is a 2½- to 3-hour drive from Christchurch.

The 330-km (205-mi) drive from Christchurch straight through to **Mount Cook Village** takes five hours.

Mount Cook Airlines (☎ 03/379–0690) flies from Christchurch to Mt. Cook.

Guided Tours
Glacier Encounters (⊠ Box 18, Mount Cook, ☎ 03/435–1809 or 03/435–1820) has hikes and guided boat trips to Lake Terminal on the Tasman Glacier.

Visitor Information
Mount Cook Visitor Information Centre. ⊠ *Mount Cook Village, ☎ 03/435–1818. ☉ Daily 8–5.*

Lake Tekapo Information. ⊠ *Main Rd., Lake Tekapo, ☎* FAX *03/680–6721. ☉ May–Aug., daily 9–9; Sept.–Apr., daily 10–6.*

Mount Cook–Mackenzie Visitor Information Centre. ⊠ *Wairepo Rd., Twizel, ☎ 03/435–0801 or 0800/435–0801 (in N.Z. only). ☉ Nov.–Apr., daily 8:30–6:30; May–Oct., weekdays 9–5.*

SOUTHLAND

Most of Southland, the western lobe of lower South Island, is taken up by two giant national parks, Fiordland and Mt. Aspiring. Fiordland, the name generally given to the southwest coast, is a majestic wilderness of rocks, ice, and beech forest, where glaciers have carved mile-deep notches into the coast. The scenic climax of this area—and perhaps of the whole country—is Milford Sound. A cruise on the sound is a must. But if you really want to take in the raw grandeur of Fiordland, hike one of the many trails in the area, among them the famous four-day Milford Track, what some call the finest walk in the world. The accommodations base and adventure center for the region is Queenstown.

Wanaka

㉗ *70 km (44 mi) northeast of Queenstown, 87 km (54 mi) south of Haast Pass.*

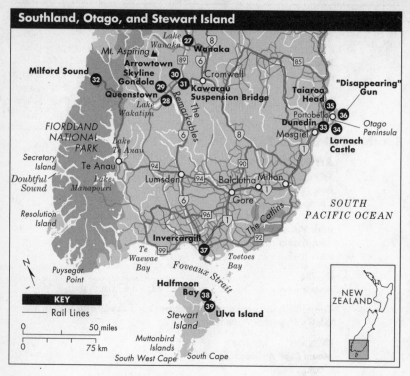

Set on the southern shore of Lake Wanaka, with some of New Zealand's most impressive mountains stretched out behind it, Wanaka is the welcome mat for Mt. Aspiring National Park. It is a favorite of Kiwis on holiday, an alternative of sorts to Queenstown. The region has numerous trekking opportunities, a choice of ski areas, and a diverse selection of other outdoor activities. The town has a couple of unusual man-made attractions as well, if you arrive on a rainy day.

Because of Queenstown's well-established publicity machine, Wanaka has tended to be overlooked by many people in the past. For that reason it manages to retain an almost sleepy-village atmosphere for most of the year. This changes during the December–January summer holidays, and some of the favorite bars and restaurants get lively in the middle of the ski season as well. At those times it certainly pays to book accommodations ahead of time.

Spectacularly sited on the shores of Lake Wanaka, **Rippon Vineyard** is one of the most photographed in the country. Lois and Rolfe Mills planted a "fruit-salad" vineyard in the mid-1970s and spent the next few years sorting out which varieties best suited the region. Now, their portfolio includes Riesling, gewürztraminer, chardonnay, sauvignon blanc, and a particularly fine (but expensive) pinot noir. ⊠ *Mt. Aspiring Rd., Box 175,* ☎ *03/443–8084,* ℻ *03/4431–8034.* ◷ *Dec.–Apr. 11–5 daily, Jul.–Nov. 1:30–4:30. Closed May–Jun..*

On your way into town you'll pass the **New Zealand Fighter Pilots Museum**—a good place to start a joyride flightseeing the region in a Tiger Moth, Pit Special, Harvard, or even a World War II P-51 Mustang, though the latter, at a cost of $2,000, is a little steeper than the $150 Harvard ride. The museum is a tribute to New Zealand fighter pilots, of whom the country contributed more per capita than any other nation in World Wars I and II. A Japanese Oscar MkI is displayed complete with bullet holes from the war. ⊠ *Hwy. 6,* ☎ *03/443–7010,* ₣ₐₓ *03/443–7011.* ⊠ *$6.* ⊙ *Daily 9:30–4.*

Don't make **Stuart Landsborough's Puzzling World** your first stop in Wanaka—you may get hooked trying to solve one of the myriad brain-teasers and not leave until closing. The complex includes the amazing Tumbling Towers and Tilted House, which is on a 15-degree angle (is the water really running uphill?). The maze can be as demanding as you want to make it by setting individual challenges. Most people spend from 30 minutes to one hour in the maze. The place on which to dwell is a section called the Puzzle Centre, which has dozens of people hooked at any given time of day. Just take on the puzzle of your choice, order a cup of coffee, and proceed to get worked up. The place is 2 km (1 mi) east of town—just look for the cartoonlike houses on funny angles. ⊠ *Hwy. 89,* ☎ *03/443–7489.* ⊠ *Puzzle center free; Tilted House and Hologram Hall $3; Tilted House, Hologram Hall, and Maze $6.* ⊙ *Daily 8:30–5:30.*

Dining and Lodging

$$–$$$ ✕ **Wanakai.** Fun, funky surroundings set the scene for an eclectic menu that includes the usual nachos, buffalo potato wedges, and so on. Wanakai also ups the adventure ante with gingered tofu fritters and soy-ginger chicken, and even goes classical with the likes of cervena steaks with a redcurrant and Dijon mustard sauce. Pasta and salads are abundant, and plenty of local wine is served by the glass or bottle. ⊠ *Helwick and Ardmore Sts.,* ☎ *03/443–7795. AE, DC, MC, V.*

$$ ✕ **White House.** Mediterranean and North African influences are evident on the menu of this aptly named eatery. Honest food, served without pretension, is the order of the day—recent listings have included *harissa* chicken and hogget *tagine,* both loaded with Moroccan spices. The atmosphere is casual, with outdoor seating in the summer. Come for lunch or dinner, or just sit with a cuppa—coffee, that is. The home-made ice cream is also a treat. ⊠ *Dunmore and Dungarvon Sts.,* ☎ *03/443–9595. AE, DC, MC, V.*

$$$ 🏠 **Willow Cottage.** Built from stone and cob (a commonly used mix-
★ ture of mud, straw, and horse manure) in the 1870s, this charming white cottage is set on a farm five minutes' drive from Wanaka amid mountains and farmlands. The cottage has been caringly restored by hosts Kate and Roy Summers, who have filled it with period furnishings. One treat is sitting out on the veranda with a glass of wine or coffee; another is having breakfast with the Summerses in their farmhouse. There is also an antiques shop in a converted historic stable on the property. ⊠ *Maxwell Rd., Mt. Barker,* ☎ ₣ₐₓ *03/443–8856. 2 rooms share bath. Coin laundry. AE, DC, MC, V.*

$$ 🏠 **Wanaka Motor Inn.** Close to the lake and 2 km (1 mi) from town, this family-run motor inn has a friendly and casual atmosphere. The rooms' natural color schemes—with timber walls and green carpets—work well with the views. Upstairs rooms have private terraces from which you can enjoy the scenery. Its restaurant and bar are quite cozy. ⊠ *Mt. Aspiring Rd., Wanaka,* ☎ *03/443–8216,* ₣ₐₓ *03/443–9108. 36 rooms with bath. Restaurant, bar. AE, DC, MC, V.*

Outdoor Activities and Sports

FISHING

Locals will tell you that fishing on Lake Wanaka and nearby Lake Hawea is better than the more famed Taupo area. You won't want to enter that argument, but chances are good you'll catch fish if you have the right guide. **Harry Urquhart** (☎ 03/443–1535) has trolling excursions for rainbow trout, brown trout, and quinnat salmon on Lake Hawea, and he has fly-fishing trips as well. **Gerald Telford** (☎

03/443–9257) will take you fly-fishing, including night fishing. For more information on trout fishing around Wanaka, *see* Adventure Vacations, Chapter 6.

WALKING AND TREKKING

You could stay for a week in Wanaka, take a different walk into the bush and mountains each day, and still come nowhere near exhausting all options. If you have time for only one walk, **Mt. Iron** is relatively short and rewarding. A rocky hump carved by glaciers, its summit provides panoramic views of lakes Wanaka and Hawea, plus the peaks of the Harris Mountains and Mt. Aspiring National Park. The access track begins 2 km (1 mi) from Wanaka, and the walk to the top takes 45 minutes. To avoid going over old ground, descend on the alternative route down the steep eastern face.

Mt. Roy is a daylong commitment. A track starts at the base of the mountain, 6 km (4 mi) from Wanaka on the road to Glendhu Bay. The round-trip journey takes about six hours. The track is closed from early October to mid-November.

For information on other local walks, contact the **Department of Conservation** (⊠ Ardmore St., ☎ 03/477–0677).

Queenstown

28 *70 km (44 mi) southeast of Wanaka, 530 km (330 mi) southwest of Christchurch.*

Set on the edge of a glacial lake beneath the sawtooth peaks of the Remarkables, Queenstown is the most popular tourist stop on South Island. Once prized by the Maori as a source of greenstone, the town boomed when gold was discovered in the Shotover, which quickly became famous as "the richest river in the world." Queenstown could easily have become a ghost town when gold gave out—except for its location. With ready access to mountains, lakes, rivers, ski fields, and the glacier-carved coastline of Fiordland National Park, the town has become the adventure capital of New Zealand. Its shop windows are crammed with skis, Polartech, Asolo walking boots, and Marin mountain bikes. Along Shotover Street, travel agents tout white-water rafting, jet boating, caving, trekking, heli-skiing, parachuting, and parapenting (rappelling). New Zealanders' penchant for bizarre adventure sports reaches a climax in Queenstown, and it was here that the sport of leaping off a bridge with a giant rubber band wrapped around the ankles—bungee jumping—took root as a commercial enterprise. Taking its marvelous location for granted, Queenstown is mostly a comfortable, cosmopolitan base for the outdoor activities around it.

Some of the best views of the town and the mountains all around are from the **Queenstown Gardens,** on the peninsula that encloses Queenstown Bay. The **Skyline Gondola** whisks you to the heights of Bob's Peak, 1,425 ft above the lake, for a panoramic view of the town and the Remarkables. You can also walk to the top on the **One Mile Creek Trail.** The summit terminal has a cafeteria, a buffet restaurant, and *Kiwi Magic,* a rather silly 25-minute aerial film that uses stunning effects to provide a tour of the country. The latest addition to the complex is a luge ride—start with the scenic track, then work your way up to the advanced track. If even that isn't exciting enough, you can bungee-jump from the summit terminal (☞ AJ Hackett Bungy *in* Outdoor Activities and Sports, *below*). ⊠ Brecon St., Queenstown, ☎ 03/442–7860, FAX 03/442–6391. ☞ *Gondola $12, Kiwi Magic $7, Luge ride $4.50.* ☉ *Daily 10–10; Kiwi Magic screens every hr on the hr, 11–9.*

Gibbston Valley Wines is the best-known winery in central Otago—the world's southernmost wine-producing region. In 1995 a *cave* (cellar) was blasted out from the side of the hill behind the winery. Wine-tasting tours are held in the cave regularly and are now one of the most interesting aspects of a visit to Gibbston. The showcase wine here is pinot noir, which suits the hot days, cold nights, and the lack of coastal influence. Also available is Riesling, chardonnay, and that classic New Zealand white, sauvignon blanc. The winery also has a restaurant. ⊠ *State Hwy. 6, Gibbston,* ☎ *03/442–6910,* ℻ *03/442–6909.* 🎫 *Wine cave tour and tasting $8.50.* ⊙ *Tasting room daily 10–5; restaurant daily 12–3.*

Chard Farm is dramatically situated on a rare flat spot on the edge of the Kawarau Gorge, not far from Gibbston Valley. The portfolio includes a couple of excellent chardonnays, sauvignon blanc, gewürztraminer, pinot gris, and pinot noir. Production is large by central Otago standards but still tiny in the national scheme of things. ⊠ *Chard Rd., R.D. 1, Gibbston,* ☎ *03/442–6110,* ℻ *03/441–8400.* ⊙ *Daily 11–5.*

Dining and Lodging

$$$ ✕ **Maxum.** Lots of wood and chrome, blue lighting, and chic surroundings set the scene for this new kid on the block, which confidently claims to be the restaurant that will take Queenstown into the new millennium. The menu is eclectic and adventurous—calamari is seared and tossed with feta cheese, olives, and sweet pepper rings; vegetables are char-grilled and mixed with penne pasta; and the oven-roasted beef fillet sits atop candied artichoke hearts. ⊠ *The Mall, Queenstown,* ☎ *03/442–4242. AE, DC, MC, V.*

$$–$$$ ✕ **Gourmet Express.** A popular breakfast spot, this casual diner at the front of a shopping arcade serves pancakes with maple syrup, eggs any way you want, and heart-starting coffee. Gourmet sandwiches and hamburgers and a huge selection of casseroles, grills, salads, and omelets—a good number featuring chili in some shape or form—are available at other times of the day. ⊠ *Bay Centre, Shotover St., Queenstown,* ☎ *03/442–9619. AE, DC, MC, V. BYOB.*

$–$$$ ✕ **Stonewall Café.** At lunch, when this is a casual café, outdoor tables are a good sunny-day choice, but things get a bit flashier (and considerably more expensive) at night, with dishes like Nelson scallops with Danish smoked bacon, char-grilled rib eye of beef, and baked Stewart Island salmon. ⊠ *The Mall, Queenstown,* ☎ *03/442–6429. AE, MC, V. Closed weekends.*

$$ ✕ **Avanti.** This restaurant at the heart of Queenstown serves better-than-average Italian dishes at a far lower price than most in this resort area. Pasta and pizza are prominent on an extensive menu, but so are more substantial meals such as braised lamb shanks and several steak options with Italian-style sauces. Servings are designed for appetites honed on the mountain slopes. ⊠ *The Mall, Queenstown,* ☎ *03/442–8503. AE, DC, MC, V. BYOB.*

$$ ✕ **The Boardwalk.** You might want to eat here just for the view. On ★ the second floor of the steamer wharf building, the restaurant looks over Lake Wakatipu toward the Remarkables. Nothing can quite beat that, but the menu makes a good attempt, and this restaurant has become a favorite with both locals and visitors. Seafood is the specialty, including dishes such as the Provençal classic bouillabaisse, chili squid and prawn *teppan*, and kingfish fillets crusted with lemongrass and ginger. Also look for hearty fare like oven-roasted lamb rump on a pumpkin and parsnip puree. ⊠ *Steamer Wharf, Queenstown,* ☎ *03/442–3630. AE, DC, MC, V.*

$$ ✕ **The Cow.** The pizza and pasta at this tiny, stone-wall restaurant are some of the best-value meals in town, but the place is immensely popular, so be prepared to wait for a table. A roaring fire provides a cozy atmosphere on chilly evenings, but patrons aren't encouraged to linger over dinner, and you may be asked to share your table. ☒ *Cow La., Queenstown,* ☎ *03/442–8588. MC, V. BYOB. No lunch.*

$ ✕ **Remarkable Naff Café.** A 40-year-old Faema coffeemaker takes pride of place on the counter of this coffee shop, and locals say that you don't need to eat after a cup of strong from this place. A cuppa alone may not be *quite* that satisfying, but if you take a piece of banana cake as well, you almost certainly won't feel like lunch for a few hours. Choose from a dozen or more coffees, a few teas, or a hot chocolate and from a small range of cakes and cookies. ☒ *1/62 Shotover St., Queenstown,* ☎ *03/442–8211. No credit cards.*

$$$$ ▦ **Heritage Queenstown.** The newest top-end addition in Queenstown,
★ the Heritage is on Fernhill, a few minutes' walk from the town center. As a result it tends to be a bit more peaceful than other hotels in town, while still having great views of the Remarkables and Lake Wakatipu. The hotel was built almost entirely out of South Island materials, including central Otago schist (stone) and wooden beams from old local railway bridges. Rooms are among the most spacious in town, fitted with writing tables and comfortable sitting areas. There are also three fireplaces with marshmallows on hand for toasting. ☒ *91 Fernhill Rd., Queenstown,* ☎ *03/442–4988,* 𝔽𝔸𝕏 *03/442–4989. 178 rooms with bath. Restaurant, bar, pool, exercise room, hot tub, sauna. AE, DC, MC, V.*

$$$$ ▦ **Millbrook Resort.** A 20-minute drive from Queenstown, this glam-
★ orous resort offers luxurious, self-contained accommodations with special appeal for golfers. Millbrook is an elevated cluster of big, comfortable two-story villas surrounded by an 18-hole golf course that was designed by New Zealand professional Bob Charles. The villas are decorated in country style: pine tables, textured walls, shuttered windows, and a cream-and-cornflower-blue color scheme. Each has a fully equipped kitchen, laundry facilities, a large lounge–dining room, ski closet, and two bedrooms, each with an en-suite bathroom, and the price, all things considered, is a bargain. ☒ *Malaghans Rd., Arrowtown,* ☎ *03/442–1563,* 𝔽𝔸𝕏 *03/442–1145. 56 villas with bath. Restaurant, bar, 18-hole golf course, tennis court. AE, DC, MC, V.*

$$$$ ▦ **Millennium Queenstown.** Providing luxurious accommodations close to town, the Millennium is built at the point where American scientists sighted Venus in 1870. One of the conditions of building the hotel was leaving intact the rock from which the planet was sighted. Of more tangible importance are the comfortable, well-equipped rooms, and the Observatory Restaurant, which adds an international touch to New Zealand fare. ☒ *Franklin Rd. and Stanley St., Queenstown,* ☎ *03/441–8888,* 𝔽𝔸𝕏 *03/441–8889. 220 rooms with bath. Restaurant, bar, sauna, exercise room, baby-sitting. AE, DC, MC, V.*

$$$$ ▦ **Nugget Point.** Poised high above the Shotover River, this stylish re-
★ treat offers one of the finest accommodations in the Queenstown area. Rooms are cozy and luxuriously large, and each has a balcony, a kitchenette, and a bedroom separate from the lounge area. Check out the open-air Jacuzzi perched on the edge of Shotover Valley—great with a glass of champagne and a loved one. The lodge is a 10-minute drive from Queenstown on the road to Coronet Peak, one of the top ski areas in the country. ☒ *Arthurs Point Rd., Queenstown,* ☎ *03/442–7630,* 𝔽𝔸𝕏 *03/442–7308. 35 rooms with bath. Restaurant, bar, pool, sauna, spa, tennis court, squash. AE, DC, MC, V.*

$$$ ▦ **Stone House.** On the hillside overlooking Queenstown and the lake, this handsome, historic cottage has been brought back to life by its enthusiastic owners and is pleasantly decorated in a charming country

style. Breakfasts are large and magnificent. Smoking is not permitted inside the house, and children are not accommodated. Rates include breakfast. ⊠ *47 Hallenstein St., Queenstown,* ☎ ⱻ *03/442–9812. 1 room with bath, 2 with shower. MC, V.*

$$ ⌕ **Trelawn Place.** Perched on the brink of the Shotover Gorge 3 km (2 mi) from Queenstown, this stone-and-timber colonial-style house has homey comforts and million-dollar views. The most popular of the three spacious guest rooms is the blue room, on the ground floor. If you want more privacy and the option of making your own meals, reserve the two-bedroom cottage for a few extra dollars. Rates include breakfast. ⊠ *Box 117, Queenstown,* ☎ *03/442–9160. 4 rooms with bath, 1 cottage with bath. Hot tub. MC, V.*

Outdoor Activities and Sports

BUNGEE JUMPING

AJ Hackett Bungy, the pioneer in the sport, offers two jumps in the area. Kawarau Bridge is the original jump site, 23 km (14 mi) from Queenstown on State Highway 6. Daredevils who graduate from the 143-ft plunge might like to test themselves on the 230-ft Skippers Canyon Bridge. The price is $99 for the Kawarau jump (including T-shirt), and an extra $30 for photos, $39 for a video, or $55 for both photos and video; $120 for Skippers Canyon, including T-shirt and transport. If you want to jump in the dark, Hackett now operates from the gondola terminal in town until 8 PM—the best place to bungee if you're short on time. ⊠ *Box 488, Queenstown,* ☎ *03/442–1177.* ☉ *Winter, daily 8–7; summer, daily 9–8, later in Jan. depending on demand.*

FISHING

For information on trout fishing around Queenstown, *see* Adventure Vacations, Chapter 6.

HIKING

For information on hiking the Milford and Kepler tracks, *see* Hiking *in* the Milford Sound section, *below,* and the Hiking-Tramping section *in* Chapter 6.

HORSE TREKKING

Moonlight Stables has a choice of full- or half-day rides with spectacular views of the mountains and rivers around the Wakatipu-Arrow Basin. Ride across some of the 800 acres of rolling land that make up Doonholme deer farm. Both novice and experienced riders are welcome. Transportation from Queenstown is provided. The company operates a clay-bird shooting range, and you can shoot in combination with the ride. ⊠ *Box 784, Queenstown,* ☎ *03/442–1229.* ☎ *½-day trip $50 per person, $85 including shooting.*

JET-BOAT RIDES

The **Dart River Jet Boat Safari** is a 2½-hour journey 32 km (20 mi) upstream into the ranges of the Mt. Aspiring National Park. This rugged area is one of the most spectacular parts of South Island, and the trip is highly recommended. Buses depart Queenstown daily at 8, 11, and 2 for the 45-minute ride to the boats. ⊠ *Box 76, Queenstown,* ☎ *03/442–9992.* ☎ *$99.* ☉ *Year-round.*

The **Shotover Jet** is the most famous jet-boat ride in the country (and one of the most exciting): a high-speed, heart-stopping adventure on which the boat pirouettes within inches of canyon walls. If you want to stay relatively dry, sit beside the driver. The boats are based at the Shotover Bridge, a 10-minute drive from Queenstown, and depart frequently between 7 AM and 9 PM from December through April, 9:30–4:30 the rest of the year. ⊠ *Shotover River Canyon, Queenstown,* ☎ *03/442–8570.* ☎ *$69.* ☉ *Year-round.*

RAFTING

Kawarau Raft Expeditions runs various half-, full-, and two-day white-water rafting trips in the Queenstown area. The most popular is the Grade-3½ to Grade-5 ride along the Shotover River, an unforgettable journey that ends with the rafts shooting through the 560-ft Oxenbridge Tunnel. ⊠ *35 Shotover St., Queenstown,* ☎ *03/442–9792.* ☞ *$95– $239 per person.* ⊘ *Year-round.*

For something even more physical on the river, **Serious Fun River Surfing** lets you jump on a body board and speed down the rapids that way. It was all started by Jon Imhoof, a backpacker from Hawaii, who now has a team of experienced guides who know their business and make sure surfers are well looked after. You'll enjoy the experience best if you have a reasonable level of fitness. Transport to and from Queenstown hotels is provided. ⊠ *33 Watts Rd., Sunshine Bay, Queenstown,* ☎ *03/442–5262,* ℻ *03/442–5265.* ☞ *$95.* ⊘ *Departure year-round at 10 and 2.*

Arrowtown

30 *22 km (14 mi) northeast of Queenstown, 105 km (66 mi) south of Wanaka.*

Another gold-mining town, Arrowtown lies northeast of Queenstown. It had long been suspected that there was gold along the Arrow River, and when Edward Fox, an American, was seen selling large quantities of the precious metal in nearby Clyde, the hunt was on. Others attempted to follow the wily Fox back to his diggings, but he kept giving his pursuers the slip, on one occasion even abandoning his tent and provisions in the middle of the night. Eventually a large party of prospectors stumbled on Fox and his team of 40 miners. The secret was out, miners rushed to stake their claims, and Arrowtown was born.

After the gold rush ended, the place was just another sleepy rural town until tourism created a new boom. Lodged at the foot of the steep Crown Range, this atmospheric village of weathered timber shop fronts and white- stone churches shaded by ancient sycamores was simply too gorgeous to escape the attention of the tour buses. These days it has become a tourist trap, but a highly photogenic one, especially when autumn gilds the hillsides.

In a less visited part of the town is the former **Chinese settlement.** Chinese miners were common on the goldfields in the late 1860s, but local prejudice forced them to live in their own separate enclave. A number of their huts and Ah Lum's Store, one of the few Chinese goldfield buildings to survive intact, have been preserved. ⊠ *Bush Creek (west end of town).* ☞ *Free.* ⊘ *Daily 9–5.*

31 **Kawarau Suspension Bridge** is where bungee jumpers make their leaps—a spectacle well worth the short detour. As a promotional stunt, the AJ Hackett company once offered a free jump to anyone who would jump nude, but there were so many takers the scheme had to be abandoned. The bridge is on Highway 6, not far from Arrowtown.

Milford Sound

32 *290 km (180 mi) west of Queenstown.*

From Queenstown the road to Milford Sound passes through the town of Te Anau (tay *ah*-no), then winds through deep, stony valleys where waterfalls cascade into mossy beech forests as it enters **Fiordland National Park.** Fiordland, the largest national park in New Zealand, takes its name from the deep sea inlets, or sounds, on its western flank. This is the most rugged part of the country. Parts of the park are so remote that they have never been explored, and visitor activities are mostly confined to a few of the sounds and the walking trails. The nearest services base is the town of Te Anau, which offers a choice of motel, hotel, or motor camp accommodations. Allow at least 2½ hours for the 119-km (74-mi) journey from Te Anau to Milford Sound.

Fiordland's greatest appeal is **Milford Sound,** the sort of overpowering place where poets run out of words, and photographers out of film. Hemmed in by walls of rock that rise from the sea almost sheer up to 4,000 ft, the 16-km-long (10-mi-long) inlet was carved by a succession of glaciers as they gouged a track to the sea. Its dominant feature is the 5,560-ft pinnacle of Mitre Peak, which is capped with snow for all but the warmest months of the year. Opposite the peak, Bowen Falls tumbles 520 ft before exploding into the sea. Milford Sound is also spectacularly wet: The average annual rainfall is around 20 ft. An inch an hour for 12 hours straight isn't uncommon, and two days without rain is reckoned to be a drought. In addition to a raincoat you'll need insect repellent—the sound is renowned for its voracious sand flies.

From the road end, a number of **cruise boats** depart at 11, 1, and 3. If you can, avoid the 1 PM sailing as it costs more than other times and also links with tour buses and is most crowded. The other sailing costs $40. Between mid-December and March it's essential to book ahead. ✉ *Fiordland Travel, Steamer Wharf, Queenstown,* ☎ *03/442–7500.*

There isn't any lodging at Milford Sound, just transportation to and fro. You need to stay in Queenstown or Te Anau and make the trek on the day you plan to come. It is a long drive in and out, so consider letting someone else do it for you. For information on buses and flights to Milford Sound, *see* Southland A to Z, *below.*

Hiking the Milford and Kepler Tracks

If you plan to walk the **Milford Track**—a wholly rewarding, four-day, 54-km (34-mi) bushwalk through Fiordland National Park—understand that it is one of New Zealand's most popular hikes. The track is strictly one-way, and because park authorities control access, you can feel as though you have the wilderness more or less to yourself. Independent and guided groups stay in different overnight huts. Be prepared for rain and snow but also for what many call the finest walk in the world, through a geological wonderland of lush vegetation and fascinating wildlife, past waterfalls, glowworm caves, and trout streams.

If you intend to hike independent of a tour group, call the **Fiordland National Park Visitor Centre** (✉ Box 29, Te Anau, ☎ 03/249–8514, FAX 03/249–8515) well in advance—up to a year if you plan to go in December or January. Freedom walking without a guide requires that you bring your own food, utensils, and bedding. You can fish along the way for trout if you have a license. Going with a guide requires deep pockets (the service costs $1,489) and stamina to carry your pack over the passes, and provides comfortable beds and someone else who does the cooking. Freedom and guided walks begin at Glade Wharf on Lake Te Anau and end with a ferry taking you from Sandfly Point over to the Milford Sound dock. You'll need to take a bus or plane from there to where you'll stay next. For information on guided walks, *see* Hiking *in* Chapter 6.

The 67-km (42-mi) **Kepler Track** forms a loop beginning and ending at the south end of Lake Te Anau. It skirts the lakeshore, climbs up to the bush line, passes limestone bluffs and the Luxmore Caves, and has incredible alpine views and overlooks of South Fiord. There is wonderful bird life along the track, as well. You can camp overnight in huts or use a tent on this three- to four-day tramp, and you'll need to bring food, utensils, and bedding. For information and bookings, call the **Fiord-land National Park Visitor Centre** (⊠ Box 29, Te Anau, ☎ 03/249–8514, ℻ 03/249–8515), open daily 8–8 Dec. 26–Jan.; 8–6 Feb.–Mar. and Oct.–Dec. 24; 9–4:30 Apr.–Sept.

Southland A to Z

Arriving and Departing

BY BUS

From Queenstown, **Mount Cook Landline** (☎ 03/442–7650) runs into Milford Sound. **InterCity** (☎ 03/442–8238) buses go to Nelson via the West Coast glaciers. Both run daily to Christchurch, Mt. Cook, and Dunedin.

BY CAR

Highway 6 enters Queenstown from the West Coast; driving time for the 350-km (220-mi) journey from Franz Josef is eight hours. From Queenstown, Highway 6 continues south to Invercargill—a 190-km (120-mi) distance that takes about three hours to drive. The fastest route from Queenstown to Dunedin is via Highway 6 to Cromwell, south on Highway 8 to Milton, then north along Highway 1, a distance of 280 km (175 mi), which can be covered in five hours.

BY PLANE

Queenstown is linked with Auckland, Christchurch, Rotorua, and Wellington by both **Ansett New Zealand** (☎ 03/442–6161) and **Mount Cook Airlines** (☎ 03/442–7650), which also flies several times daily to Mt. Cook. Mount Cook Airlines also flies into Milford Sound, which is a beautiful flight, weather permitting. Queenstown Airport is 9 km (5½ mi) east of town. The **Johnston's Shuttle Express** (☎ 03/442–3639) meets all incoming flights and charges $6 per person to hotels in town. The taxi fare is about $15.

Contacts and Resources

EMERGENCIES

Dial 111 for **fire, police, and ambulance** services.

GUIDED TOURS

The **Double Decker** (☎ 03/442–6067) is an original London bus that makes a 2½-hour circuit from Queenstown to Arrowtown and the bungee-jumping platform on the Karawau River. Tours ($25) depart Queenstown daily at 10 and 2 from the Mall and the Earnslaw Wharf.

Fiordland Travel has a wide choice of fly-drive tour options to Milford and Doubtful sounds from Queenstown. The cost of a one-day bus tour and cruise on Milford Sound is $132. ⊠ *Steamer Wharf, Queenstown,* ☎ *03/442–7500.*

Outback New Zealand has fascinating safaris into Skippers Canyon (28 km/18 mi north of Queenstown) and farther afield. Owner-operator David Gatward-Ferguson is knowledgeable about the area and is not afraid to debunk some of the local gold rush days' legends. The Skippers trip ends at the Skippers settlement, schoolhouse, and cemetery and includes a morning or afternoon tea at this historic setting. The straightforward tour costs $55, but you can add on helicopter rides, bungee jumping, rafting, and jet boat rides at an extra cost. ⊠ *Box 341, Queenstown,* ☎ *03/442–7386,* ℻ *03442–7346.*

Milford Sound Adventure Tours has a bus-cruise trip to Milford Sound from Te Anau ($80) that includes a cycling option. From the Homer Tunnel, you can leave the bus and coast 13 km (8 mi) down to the sound on mountain bikes. These are smaller and more personal than other tours. ⊠ *Box 134, Te Anau,* ☎ *03/249–7227 or 0800/80–7227 (in N.Z. only).* ⊘ *Tour departs Te Anau daily at 7:30.*

The **TSS *Earnslaw*** is a vintage lake steamer that has been restored to brassy, wood-paneled splendor and put to work cruising Lake Wakatipu from Queenstown. A lunch cruise, an afternoon cruise across the lake to a sheep station, and a dinner cruise are available from July through May. ⊠ *Steamer Wharf, Queenstown,* ☎ *03/442–7500.*

VISITOR INFORMATION

Fiordland National Park Visitor Centre. ⊠ *Box 29, Te Anau,* ☎ *03/249–7921.* ⊘ *Dec. 26–Jan., daily 8–8; Feb.–Mar. and Oct.–Dec. 24, daily 8–6; Apr.–Sept., daily 9–4:30.*

Queenstown Visitor Information Centre. ⊠ *Clocktower Centre, Shotover and Camp Sts.,* ☎ *03/442–4100.* ⊘ *Daily 7–7.*

DUNEDIN AND OTAGO

The province of Otago stretches southeast of Queenstown to the Pacific. Flatter than Southland—as most of the world is—it may look like parts of North Island. Its capital, Dunedin (dun-*ee*-din), is one of the unexpected treasures of New Zealand: a harbor city of steep streets and prim Victorian architecture, with a royal albatross colony on its doorstep. Invercargill is the southern anchor of the province, essentially a farm service community and for most a gateway to Fiordland or a stopover on the way to Stewart Island (☞ *below*).

Dunedin

㉝ *280 km (175 mi) east of Queenstown, 362 km (226 mi) south of Christchurch.*

Clinging to the walls of the natural amphitheater at the west end of Otago Harbour, South Island's second-largest city, with its handsome Victorian townscape, is blessed with inspiring nearby seascapes and wildlife. Its considerable number of university students give the city a vitality far greater than its population of 120,000 might suggest. And its size makes it easy to explore on foot.

Dunedin is the Gaelic name for Edinburgh, and the city's Scottish roots are evident. It was founded in 1848 by settlers of the Free Church of Scotland, a breakaway group from the Presbyterian Church. Today it has the only kilt shop in the country and the only whiskey distillery—and a statue of Scottish poet Robert Burns. The city prospered mightily during the gold rush of the 1860s. For a while it was the largest city in the country, and the riches of the Otago goldfields are reflected in the bricks and mortar of Dunedin, most notably in the Italianate Municipal Chambers building.

Perhaps the most compelling local attraction is the royal albatross colony at Taiaroa Head, the only place on earth where you can see these majestic seabirds with relative ease. Dunedin is also noted for its rhododendrons, which are at their best in October.

The **Octagon** is at the center of town—the city's navel, if you will. The **statue of Robert Burns** sits in front of the cathedral WITH HIS BACK TO THE KIRK AND HIS FACE TO THE PUB, a telling sign to say the least. On Stuart Street at the corner of Dunbar, take notice of the late-Victorian **Law Courts.** Above the Stuart Street entrance stands the figure of Justice, scales in hand but without her customary blindfold (though the low helmet she wears probably has the same effect).

The **Dunedin Railway Station,** a cathedral to the power of steam, is a massive bluestone structure in Flemish Renaissance style, lavishly decorated with heraldic beasts, coats of arms, nymphs, scrolls, a mosaic floor, and even stained-glass windows portraying steaming locomotives. This extravagant building earned its architect, George Troup, the nickname Gingerbread George from the people of Dunedin and a knighthood from the king. The station has far outlived the steam engine and for all its magnificence receives few trains these days. ⊠ *Anzac Ave. at Stuart St.* ⊙ *Daily 7–6.*

The **First Presbyterian Church** on the south side of Moray Place is perhaps the finest example of a Norman Gothic building in the country. The **Early Settlers Museum** preserves an impressive collection of artifacts, from the years when this was a whaling station to the days of the early Scottish settlers to the prosperous gold-rush era of the late-19th century. ⊠ *220 Cumberland St.,* ☎ *03/477–5052.* ⊞ *$4.* ⊙ *Weekdays 10–5, weekends 1–5.*

The 35-room Jacobean-style **Olveston** mansion was built between 1904 and 1906 for David Theomin, a wealthy businessman and patron of the arts, who amassed a handsome collection of antiques and contemporary furnishings. The house and its furnishings are undoubtedly a treasure from an elegant age, but apart from some paintings collected by Theomin's daughter there is very little in it to suggest that it's in New Zealand. Even the oak staircase and balustrade were prefabricated in England. The one-hour guided tour is recommended. ⊠ *42 Royal Terr.,* ☎ *03/477–3320.* ⊞ *$10.* ⊙ *Daily 9–5; tour daily at 9:30, 10:45, noon, 1:30, 2:45, and 4.*

Dining and Lodging

$$$$ ✕ **Bellpepper Blues.** One of the country's most respected chefs, Michael Coughlin uses flair and esoteric ingredients in recipes drawn from the Pacific, the Mediterranean, and the American Midwest. Chicken fillets are seared and served on grilled bacon and mushroom polenta with smoked tomato–chipotle chili essence and red onion relish; duck legs are stuffed with shiitake mushrooms, then pan-roasted with spring vegetables and served on Shanghai noodles with a black bean reduction sauce. The setting, inside a converted pub, is casual and attractive. ⊠ *474 Princes St., Dunedin,* ☎ *03/474–0973. AE, DC, MC, V. Closed Sun. No lunch.*

$$$ ✕ **Ombrello's.** Clever design means diners can eat in a sheltered courtyard between two cottages at this popular eatery. The menu is of the usual Mediterranean-leaning modern New Zealand stripe, presenting dishes like a layered tower of eggplant and capsicum with mozzarella and rocket, or a roasted half chicken on couscous with sweet and sour onions and raisins. Several pasta dishes are also available. ⊠ *10 Clarendon St.,* ☎ *03/477–8773. AE, DC, MC, V. Closed Mon. No dinner Sun.*

$$$ ✕ **Portrait's Restaurant Bar.** Now here's a sleeper—cutting-edge cuisine in the 1960s-holdout Abbey Lodge Motel. But that's just what the talented Helen Mason serves up. Start with the likes of pork and peanut spring rolls sitting atop a Thai salad and drizzled with coriander pesto, or sautéed lamb sweetbreads with shiitake mushrooms and tarragon cream. Move onto baked lemon-and-herb-crusted fish fillets with a tomato and basil sauce, or think about the panfried polenta cake with grilled field mushrooms, zucchini, roasted capsicum, and pesto. The wine list spans the country and has a couple of token Aussies in the red section. ⊠ *900 Cumberland St.,* ☎ *03/477–5380. AE, DC, MC, V. Licensed & BYO. No lunch.*

$$–$$$ ✕ **Abalone.** A superlong bar dominates this quirkily decorated restaurant, but the emphasis is as much on food as ingestion of the more liquid kind. And it's not only the decor that's quirky—recent menus have

seen grilled salmon fillet served with rosemary potatoes and caramelized aubergine, cervena (venison) medallions with a beetroot sauce on crispy noodles, and lamb rumps with ratatouille and a blue cheese crepe. Every dish comes with a wine recommendation. ⊠ *44 Hanover St.,* ☎ *03/477–6877. AE, DC, MC, V. Closed Mon.*

$$ ✕ **Palms Cafe.** Vegetarians are especially well served at this casual, popular restaurant with views over Queens Gardens. The menu changes regularly, and around half of the dishes contain meat. Recent listings have included peppers stuffed with kumara (sweet potato), pineapple, and pine nuts, butternut (squash) with steamed vegetables in a satay sauce, and aubergine (eggplant) and vegetable curry. Carnivores, look for the likes of rib-eye steak with tomato, courgette (zucchini), and bacon, or lamb with rolled-oat crumble. The restaurant has a no-smoking policy. ⊠ *84 Lower High St., Dunedin,* ☎ *03/477–6534. AE, DC, MC, V. BYOB.*

$$$ 🏨 **Cargills Hotel.** In a convenient location close to the city center and many of the city's major sights, this hotel has superior motel-style rooms as well as two-bedroom family suites with spa baths. Furnishings are contemporary, and rooms are spacious; many of them overlook an attractive central courtyard—as does the restaurant, where the contemporary menu includes main dishes like lamb roasted and served on a potato *rösti* with a piquant apple and brandy jus and a quenelle of mint and applesauce. Try these with central Otago favorites like Gibbston Valley's Pinot Noir, Chard Farm's Gewürztraminer, or Rippon's Sauvignon Blanc. ⊠ *678 George St., Dunedin,* ☎ *03/477–7983,* 𝖥𝖠𝖷 *03/477–8098. 50 rooms. Restaurant, bar, room service, free laundry. AE, DC, MC, V.*

$$$ 🏨 **Lisburn House.** This Historic Trust–listed Victorian-Gothic inn,
★ with lovingly tended gardens and many of its 1865 details intact, is a romantic and stately retreat. Outside, original features include decorative Irish brickwork and fish-tail slate roof tiles; inside there are high, molded plaster ceilings, a marble floored foyer, an impressive turn-of-the-century stained-glass entrance, and finely crafted antiques throughout. The three spacious bedrooms are sumptuous affairs, each with beautiful four-poster queen beds and fine linen. You'll have a delicious breakfast on fine china in the stately dining room. ⊠ *15 Lisburn St., Caversham,* ☎ *03/455–8888,* 𝖥𝖠𝖷 *03/455–6758. 3 rooms with bath. Lounge, in-room VCRs. AE, DC, MC, V.*

$ 🏨 **Magnolia House.** Overlooking the city of Dunedin in a prestigious suburb, this gracious B&B offers atmospheric accommodations. The spacious guest rooms are furnished with antiques, and the house is surrounded by a pretty garden that includes native bushland. The house has a no-smoking policy. Rates include breakfast. ⊠ *18 Grendon St., Maori Hill, Dunedin,* ☎ 𝖥𝖠𝖷 *03/467–5999. 1 room with bath, 2 with shared bath. No credit cards.*

Fishing

For information on deep-sea fishing out of Dunedin, *see* Chapter 6.

En Route If you're driving along the coast north of Dunedin, the **Moeraki Boulders** are good to stop and gawk at for a while. These giant spherical rocks are concretions, formed by a gradual buildup of minerals around a central core. Some boulders have sprung open, revealing—no, not alien life forms—interesting calcite crystals. The boulders populate the beach north of the town of Moeraki and south as well at Katiki Beach off Highway 1, about 60 km (37 mi) above Dunedin, or 40 km (25 mi) south of Oamaru.

Otago Peninsula

The main areas of interest on the claw-shape peninsula that extends northeast from Dunedin are the albatross colony and Larnach Castle.

On the return journey to Dunedin, the Highcliff Road, which turns inland at the village of Portobello, is a scenic alternative to the coastal Portobello Road.

㉞ Set high on a hilltop with commanding views from its battlements, **Larnach Castle** is the grand baronial fantasy of William Larnach, an Australian-born businessman and politician. The castle was a vast extravagance even in the free-spending atmosphere of the gold rush. Larnach imported an English craftsman to carve the ceilings, which took 12 years to complete, and the solid marble bath, marble fireplaces, tiles, glass, and even much of the wood came from Europe. The mosaic in the foyer depicts Larnach's family crest and the modest name he gave to his stately pile: the Camp. Larnach rose to a prominent position in the New Zealand government of the late 1800s, but in 1898, beset by a series of financial disasters and possible marital problems, he committed suicide in Parliament House. (According to one romantic version, Larnach's third wife, whom he married at an advanced age, ran off with his eldest son; devastated, Larnach shot himself.) A café in the castle ballroom serves Devonshire teas and light snacks. There are 35 acres of grounds around the castle that include a rhododendron garden, a rain forest garden with kauri, rimu, and totatra trees, statues of *Alice in Wonderland* characters, an herbaceous walk, and a plant shop. ⊠ *Camp Rd.,* ☎ *03/476–1616.* ⊠ *$10.* ⊙ *Daily 9–5.*

㉟ **Taiaroa Head,** the eastern tip of the Otago Peninsula, is the site of a breeding colony of royal albatrosses. Among the largest birds in the world, with a wingspan of up to 10 ft, they can take off only from steep slopes with the help of a strong breeze. Outside of Taiaroa Head and the Chatham Islands to the east, they are found only on windswept islands deep in southern latitudes, remote from human habitation. Under the auspices of the **Trust Bank Royal Albatross Centre,** the colony is open for viewing from October through August, with the greatest number of birds present shortly after the young hatch around the end of January. Between March and September parents leave the fledglings in their nests while they gather food for them. In September the young birds fly away, returning about eight years later to start their own breeding cycle. From the visitor center you go in groups up a steep trail up to the Albatross Observatory, from which you can see the birds through narrow windows. They are only rarely seen in flight. Access to the colony is strictly controlled, and you must book in advance. ⊠ *Taiaroa Head, Dunedin,* ☎ *03/478–0499.* ⊙ *Daily except Christmas Day for tickets, information, shop, and café. Nov.–Mar. 9–dusk; Apr.–Oct. 10–dusk; tours late Nov.–Aug., daily 10:30–4, every half hr in summer, hourly in winter.* ⊠ *1½-hr tour (including fort) $27, 1-hr tour (excluding fort) $22.*

㊱ In the same area as the colony is the **"Disappearing" Gun at Fort Taiaroa,** a 6-inch artillery piece installed during the Russian Scare of 1888. When the gun was fired, the recoil would propel it back into its pit, where it could be reloaded out of the line of enemy fire. The gun has been used in anger only once, when it was fired across the bow of a fishing boat that had failed to observe correct procedures before entering the harbor during World War II. ⊠ *$12.*

If you'd like to observe the world's most endangered penguin in its natural habitat, visit the **Yellow Eyed Penguin Conservation Reserve,** where a network of tunnels have been disguised so you can get up close to this rare and protected species. Experienced guides will interpret the birds' behavior and seasonal habits as you creep through the tunnels—sssh! ⊠ *Harrington Point, 2 Rd., Dunedin,* ☎ *03/478–0286,* FAX *03/478–0257.* ⊠ *$7.50.* ⊙ *Daily 9–5.*

Lodging

$–$$$ ★ ☷ **Larnach Lodge.** It's hard to beat this setting—panoramic sea views, 35 acres of gardens and grounds to stroll in, a castle next door to explore, and astounding luxury theme suites. The Scottish Room is fitted with deep red wallpaper that sets off classic tartan bedcovers and curtains, heavy brass bedsteads, and a Robbie Burns rug. The Enchanted Forest Room's enchanting feature is 1879 William Morris wallpaper. Breakfast is served in the former stables, and lunch or dinner can be arranged at the castle. Affordable rooms with shared facilities ($55) are available in the converted 1871 coach house. ✉ *Camp Rd., Otago Peninsula, Dunedin,* ☎ *03/476–1616,* ℻ *03/476–1574. 12 rooms with bath. AE, DC, MC, V.*

Invercargill

❸ *182 km (115 mi) south of Queenstown; 190 km (120 mi) southwest of Dunedin.*

Originally settled by Scottish immigrants, Invercargill has retained much of its turn-of-the-last-century character, with a broad main avenue and streetscapes with richly embellished buildings. You'll find Italian and English Renaissance styles, Gothic stone tracery, and Romanesque designs in a number of keenly preserved buildings. The city also has botanic gardens, the pyramid-shaped **Southland Museum and Art Gallery,** its chief attraction being a live tuatara—New Zealand's extremely rare, ancient lizard. Take note of the abundance of Jaguars on the road here, a sign of the success of local farming.

Lodging

$$$ ☷ **Homestead Villa Motel.** The Homestead's fully self-contained units are spacious and have contemporary furnishings and decor. All have spa baths. The U-shape motor lodge is a 10-minute walk from the city center and five minutes to Queens Gardens and the Southland Museum and Art Gallery. ✉ *Avenal and Dee Sts.,* ☎ *03/214–0408 or 0800/ 488–588 (in N.Z. only),* ℻ *03/214–0478. 25 units with bath. Kitchenettes, laundry. AE, DC, MC, V.*

En Route The **Southern Scenic Route** is 215 km (135 mi) of mostly tarred road that stretches from Balclutha—south of Dunedin in the scenic Catlins region, known for its stands of native forest and glorious coastline— through Invercargill to Milford Sound in Fiordland.

Dunedin and Otago A to Z

Arriving and Departing

BY BUS

Dunedin is served by **Mount Cook Landline** (☎ 0800/800–287, in N.Z. only, or 03/474–0677) and **InterCity** buses (☎ 0800/664–545, in N.Z. only, or 03/477–8860).

BY CAR

Driving time along the 280 km (175 mi) between Queenstown and Dunedin (via Highway 6 and Highway 1) is four hours. The main route between Dunedin and Invercargill is Highway 1—a 3½-hour drive. A slower, scenic alternative is along the coast, which adds another 90 minutes to the journey.

BY PLANE

Dunedin is linked with all other New Zealand cities by **Ansett New Zealand** (☎ 0800/800–146, in N.Z. only, or 03/477–4146) and **Air New Zealand** (☎ 03/477–5769). **Dunedin Airport** lies 20 km (13 mi) south of the city. **Johnston's Shuttle Express** (☎ 03/476–2519), a shuttle service between the airport and the city, meets all incoming flights and charges $10 per person. Taxi fare to the city is about $30.

Contacts and Resources

EMERGENCIES
Dial 111 for **fire, police, and ambulance** services.

GUIDED TOURS
Another way to get to know about the prolific wildlife of this area is to take a boat trip with **Monarch Wildlife Cruises.** Experienced guides help you identify species and interpret their behavior. The hour-long cruise includes visiting breeding sites of the northern royal albatross, New Zealand fur seals, and three species of shags (cormorants). Depending on the season, you are likely to see sooty shearwaters (mutton birds), blue penguins, variable oyster catchers, and two varieties of gulls. If you are lucky, an albatross will fly over your boat—a spectacular sight with that 6-ft wingspan. ⊠ *Wharf and Fryatt Sts., Dunedin,* ☎ *03/477–4267.* ⊠ *$22.50 for a 1-hr cruise leaving from Wellers Rock.* ☉ *Cruises start at 3:20 and 4:30 in summer, 2:10 and 3:20 in winter.*

Twilight Tours offers various minibus tours of Dunedin and its surroundings, including an afternoon tour that focuses on the albatrosses, penguins, and seals of the Otago Peninsula. The penguin sanctuary is a privately operated venture, and this tour is the only way to see the rare yellow-eyed and little blue penguins. The tour price does not include admission to the albatross colony. Tours depart from the Dunedin Visitor Information Centre. ⊠ *Box 963, Dunedin,* ☎ *03/474–3300.* ⊠ *$46.* ☉ *Tour departs Apr.–Oct., daily at 1:30; Nov.–Mar., daily at 2:30.*

VISITOR INFORMATION
Dunedin Visitor Information Centre. ⊠ *48 the Octagon,* ☎ *03/474–3300,* FAX *03/474–3311.* ☉ *Weekdays 8:30–5, weekends 9–5; extended hrs in summer.*

Invercargill Visitor Information Centre. The center is in the foyer of the Southland Museum and Art Gallery. ⊠ *Victoria Ave., Box 1012,* ☎ *03/214–6243,* FAX *03/218–9753.* ☉ *Weekdays 9–5, weekends 1–5.*

STEWART ISLAND

The third and most southerly of New Zealand's main islands, Stewart Island is separated from South Island by the 24-km (15-mi) Foveaux Strait. Its original Maori name, Te Punga o Te Waka a Maui, means "the anchor stone of Maui's canoe." Maori mythology says the Island's landmass held Maui's canoe secure while he and his crew raised the great fish—the North Island. Today it is more commonly referred to by its other Maori name, Rakiura, which means "the land of the glowing skies"—which refers both to the spectacular sunrises and sunset and to the southern sky's equivalent of the northern lights.

The island covers some 1,700 square km (650 square mi). It measures about 64 km (40 mi) from north to south and about the same distance across at its widest point. On the coastline, sharp cliffs rise from a succession of sheltered bays and beaches. In the interior, forested hills rise gradually toward the west side of the island. Seals and penguins frequent the coast, and the island's prolific bird life includes a number of species rarely seen in any other part of the country. In fact, it is one of the surest places to go to see kiwi birds.

Even by New Zealand standards, Stewart Island is remote, raw, and untouched. Roads total about 20 km (13 mi), and apart from the township of **Oban** at **Halfmoon Bay** on Paterson Inlet, the place is practically uninhabited. The appeal is its seclusion, its relaxed way of life, and—despite a once-busy whaling and lumber-milling industry—its untouched quality.

The smallest playhouse in New Zealand is in Oban. Nikki Davis—self-proclaimed Southland-born lunatic-whose-ego-craves-the-limelight—puts on her one-woman show at the **Gumboot Theatre.** The raving and raved-about *Day in the Life of Stewart Island* parodies four common activities: fishing, paua (abalone) diving, hunting, and the activities of the Stewart Island housewife. In a town that some might mistake for a cultural backwater, this 20-seat theater is small proof that it's alive and fishing. ⊠ *Main Rd.,* ☎ *03/210–1116.* 🖙 *$5.* ☉ *½-hr shows begin running daily at 11 AM.*

㊴ One of the best spots for birding is **Ulva Island,** a one-hour launch trip around the coast from Halfmoon Bay (☞ Guided Tours *in* Stewart Island A to Z, *below*).

Dining and Lodging

$ ✕ **Justcafé.** American Britt Moore has set up shop in paradise. Stop in for great coffee, muffins, quiche, and cold smoked-salmon sandwiches for lunch, or make a reservation for dinner, a set menu based on whatever Stewart Island produce is freshest that day. ⊠ *Main Rd., Oban,* ☎ *03/219–1350. No credit cards.*

$$ 🏠 **Miro Cottage.** Set atop a hill surrounded by bush, this modern, self-contained cottage has room for a family or a group (six maximum) but could equally serve as an intimate hideaway for a couple. Not that you'll be the only inhabitants in this piece of paradise in summer—native birds such as tui, kaka (a native parrot), and the protected kereru (wood pigeon) call the surrounding bush home, too. Your host, Jan Lequesne, will help you settle in and provide information about activities on the island. The cottage is only a three-minute walk from Oban. ⊠ *Box 19,* ☎ 🖷 *03/219–1180. 1 cottage. MC, V.*

$$ 🏠 **The Nest.** Amid the rambling native bush of Halfmoon Bay appears a bed-and-breakfast right out of the English countryside. Built about 1938, it has typical low ceilings, with exposed beams, mullioned windows, and Canadian wood paneling. Lindsay and Lorraine Squires, born and bred Stewart Islanders, have a commercial fishing background, and they'll gladly help out with information on the island. Bedrooms are furnished in period style, and through the diamond-paned leadlight (leaded) windows are views of Halfmoon Bay. There are also a comfortable guest lounge, a patio, and a beautiful garden. ⊠ *Halfmoon Bay,* ☎ 🖷 *03/219–1310. 2 rooms with bath. MC, V.*

$$ 🏠 **Rakiura Motel.** Stewart Island's reputation for hospitality is upheld by host Elaine Hamilton, a fourth-generation islander with a passion for hiking rivaled only by her love for her home. The motel she has managed with her family for 27 years is pretty straightforward, spotless, and comfortable, and it's surrounded by beautiful gardens and native bush. Each unit accommodates up to six people and is fully self-contained, with tea and coffee—you'll just need to bring food. The motel is within easy walking distance of Oban. ⊠ *Horseshoe Bay Rd., Halfmoon Bay,* ☎ *03/219–1096. 5 rooms with bath. MC, V.*

$$ 🏠 **South Sea Hotel.** Right in the heart of Oban overlooking Halfmoon Bay, this waterfront hotel has the air of having heard many a fish story, and its bar is a gathering spot for many island residents. Naturally, seafood is the specialty in the restaurant—try fresh blue cod or the local delicacy, mutton bird. It's not the Ritz, not that that's a Stewart Island ambition, but the staff is welcoming and friendly. ⊠ *Box 25, Oban,* ☎ *03/219–1059,* 🖷 *03/219–1120. AE, MC, V.*

Outdoor Activities

FISHING

For information on deep-sea fishing out of Halfmoon Bay, *see* Chapter 6.

HIKING

A network of walking trails has been established on the northern half of the island, leaving the south as a wilderness area. A popular trek is the **Northern Circuit,** a 10-day walk from Halfmoon Bay that circles the north coast and then cuts through the interior to return to its starting point. The island's climate is notoriously changeable, and walkers should be prepared for rain and mud. For information on walks, contact the **Department of Conservation** (✉ Main Rd., Halfmoon Bay, ☎ 03/219–1218).

SEA-KAYAKING

Stewart Island Sea Kayak Adventures. Some of the best and most remote sea-kayaking abounds around Stewart Island. Paterson Inlet is 100 square km (38 square mi) of bush-clad, sheltered waterways, mostly uninhabited. It has 20 islands, four Department of Conservation huts, and two navigable rivers. ✉ *Innes Dunstan, Innes Backpackers, Argyle St., Oban,* ☎ FAX *03/219–1080.*

Stewart Island A to Z

Arriving and Departing

BY BOAT

Stewart Island Marine (☎ 03/212–7660, FAX 03/212–8377) runs the *Foveaux Express* between the island and Bluff, the port for Invercargill. The one-way fare is $37. Ferries depart Bluff weekdays at 9:30 and 4 between May and August (winter) and from Monday to Saturday at 9:30 and 5 the rest of the year. On Sunday there is a 5 PM departure only (4 PM in winter). The crossing takes one hour.

BY PLANE

Southern Air (☎ 03/218–9129) has several flights daily between Invercargill and Halfmoon Bay. The scenic 20-minute flight costs $120 round-trip. For the best views ask to sit up front with the pilot. There is also direct service from Dunedin to Stewart Island ($180 round-trip). The free baggage allowance is 15 kilograms (33 pounds) per passenger.

Contacts and Resources

EMERGENCIES

Dial 111 for **fire, police, and ambulance** services.

GUIDED TOURS

For information and bookings on fishing trips, kiwi spotting, bird-watching trips to Ulva Island, taxis, water taxis, and boat trips around Paterson Inlet, contact **Oban Taxis & Tours** (✉ Box 180, Stewart Island, ☎ FAX 03/219–1456). The company also hires out motor scooters and dive gear and tanks.

For guided, twilight brown-kiwi spotting, a short hike through native bush, and a boat cruise, contact Phillip and Dianne Smith of **Bravo Adventure Cruises.** The excursion happens on alternate nights. You'll need sturdy footwear and warm clothing. Bring a flashlight. A reasonable level of fitness is required. ☎ FAX 03/219–1144.

VISITOR INFORMATION

Stewart Island Visitor Information Centre. ✉ *Main Rd., Halfmoon Bay,* ☎ *03/219–1218.* ☼ *Weekdays 8–4:30.*

6 Adventure Vacations

Bicycling

Canoeing and Sea-Kayaking

Cross-Country Skiing

Diving

Fishing

Hiking and Tramping

Horse Trekking

Rafting

Sailing

YOU WILL MISS the most vital part of New Zealand if you don't explore the magnificent outdoors. The mountains and forests in this clean, green land are made for hiking and climbing, the rivers for rafting, and the low-traffic roads for bicycling. The rugged coastline looks wonderful from the deck of a small vessel or, even closer to the water, a sea kayak. And this is the country that invented jet-boating.

By David McGonigal, Doug Johansen, and Jan Poole

These activities are commonly split into soft and hard adventures. Hard adventure requires some physical stamina, although you usually don't have to be perfectly fit; in a few cases, prior experience is a prerequisite. In soft adventures the destination is often the adventurous element—you can sit back and enjoy the ride.

With most companies, the adventure guides' knowledge of flora and fauna—and love of the bush—is matched by a level of competence that ensures your safety even in dangerous situations. The safety record of adventure operators is very good. Be aware, however, that most adventure-tour operators require you to sign waivers absolving the company of responsibility in the event of an accident or a problem. Courts normally uphold such waivers except in cases of significant negligence.

You can always choose to travel without a guide, and the material in this chapter complements information in the rest of the book on what to do in different parts of the country. The advantage of going out with a guide is often educational. In unfamiliar territory, you'll learn more about what's around you by having a knowledgeable local by your side than you could traveling on your own.

Bicycling

Cycling is an excellent way to explore a small region, allowing you to cover more ground than on foot and observe far more than you would from the window of a car or bus. Cycling rates as hard adventure because of the amount of exercise you get.

New Zealand's combination of spectacular scenery and quiet roads is ideal for cycling. Traditionally, South Island, with its central alpine spine, has been more popular, but Auckland is where most people arrive, and North Island has enough backroads and curiosities—the Waitomo Caves and the coast beyond, the stunning Coromandel Peninsula, and the hot mud pools of sulfurous Rotorua—to fill days. The average daily riding distance is about 60 km (37 mi), and support vehicles are large enough to accommodate all riders and bikes if circumstances so demand. Rides in South Island extend from the ferry port of Picton to picturesque Queenstown, the center of a thriving adventure day-trip industry. New Zealand Pedaltours operates on both islands, with tours of 9–19 days. New Zealand Backroad Cycle Tours has South Island tours of 4–10 days.

Season: October–March.
Locations: Countrywide.
Cost: From $1,050 including lodging, meals, and support vehicle.
Tour Operators: Adventure Center (⊠ 1311 63rd St., No. 200, Emeryville, CA 94608, ☎ 510/654–1879, FAX 510/654–4200); **New Zealand Backroad Cycle Tours** (⊠ Box 33–153, Christchurch, ☎ 03/332–1222, FAX 03/332–4030). **New Zealand Pedaltours** (⊠ Box 37–575, Parnell, Auckland, ☎ 09/302–0968, FAX 09/302–0967).

Canoeing and Sea-Kayaking

Unlike rafting, where much of the thrill comes from negotiating white water, commercial canoeing involves paddling down gentle stretches of river. Canoeing is soft adventure, as is sea-kayaking, which is excellent in Northland, the Coromandel Peninsula, the top of South Island, Kaikoura, and as far south as Stewart Island.

The tour with Ocean River Adventure Company in the sheltered waters of Abel Tasman National Park provides a waterline view of a beautiful coastline. It allows you to explore otherwise inaccessible golden-sand beaches and remote islands and to meet fur seals on their home surf. When wind conditions permit, paddles give way to small sails, and the kayaks are propelled home by an onshore breeze. Southern Sea Ventures' nine-day trip includes seven days of kayaking on Doubtful Sound in the southwest corner of South Island, with its dramatic fjordland cliffs and cascading waterfalls. Wide river mouths provide forest campsites. The residents of this remote wilderness are bottlenose dolphins and fur seals, which often swim alongside the kayaks.

Season: December–May.
Locations: Northland, the Coromandel Peninsula, Marlborough Sounds, Kaikoura, Abel Tasman National Park, the Southland.
Cost: Around $90 for a one-day tour, $480 for four-day tours.
North Island Tour Operators: Bay of Islands Kayak Co. (⊠ Box 217, Russell, ☏ FAX 09/403–7672); **Mercury Bay Sea Kayaks** (⊠ 17 Arthur St., Whitianga, Coromandel Peninsula, ☏ FAX 07/866–2358).

South Island Tour Operators: Fiordland Wilderness Experience (⊠ 66 Quinton Dr., Te Anau, ☏ 03/249–7700, FAX 03/249–7700); **Marlborough Sounds Adventure Company** (⊠ The Waterfront, Box 195, Picton, ☏ 03/573–6078, FAX 03/573–8827); **Ocean River Adventure Company** (⊠ Main Rd., Marahau Beach, R.D. 2, Motueka, ☏ 03/527–8266, FAX 03/527–8006); **Stewart Island Kayak Adventures** (⊠ Box 32, Stewart Island, ☏ FAX 03/219–1080).

Cross-Country Skiing

Cross-country skiing is arguably the best way to appreciate the winter landscape, and New Zealand's is spectacular. Going cross-country, you'll get away from the downhill hordes and feel like you have the mountains to yourself. Cross-country skiing is hard adventure—the joy of leaving the first tracks across new snow and the pleasure afforded by the unique scenery of the snowfields is tempered by the fatigue that your arms and legs feel at the end of the day. Multiday tours are arranged so that you stay in lodges every night.

Aoraki (Mt. Cook) and its attendant Murchison and Tasman glaciers offer wonderful ski touring, with terrains to suit all skiers. Tours typically commence with a flight to the alpine hut that becomes your base; from there the group sets out each day for skiing and instruction.

Season: July–September.
Locations: Aoraki, South Island.
Cost: $350 for two days, $875 for five days, all inclusive.
Tour Operator: Alpine Recreation Canterbury (⊠ Box 75, Lake Tekapo, 8770, ☏ 03/680–6736, FAX 03/680–6765).

Diving

The Bay of Islands is perhaps New Zealand's best diving location. In the waters around Cape Brett, you can encounter moray eels, stingrays, grouper, and other marine life. Surface water temperatures rarely dip below 60°F. One of the highlights of Bay of Islands diving is the wreck of the Greenpeace vessel *Rainbow Warrior,* which French agents sunk in 1985. It is about two hours from Paihia by dive boat. From September through November, underwater visibility can be affected by a plankton bloom.

The clear waters around New Zealand make for good diving in other areas as well, such as the Coromandel Peninsula where the Mercury and Aldermen islands have interesting marine life. With Hahei Explorer, dive in the newly created marine reserve or right off the coast. Whangamata, with three islands just off the coast, also has very good diving.

Season: Year-round.
Locations: Bay of Islands and the Coromandel Peninsula.
Cost: Around $135 per day.
Tour Operators: Hahei Explorer (⌧ Hahei Beach Rd., Hahei, Coromandel Peninsula, ☎ 07/866–3532 or 025/424–306); **Paihia Dive Hire and Charter** (⌧ Box 210, Paihia, Bay of Islands, ☎ 09/402–7551, FAX 09/402–7110).

Fishing

Fishing means different things to different people. For some it is the simple joy of being away from it all in some remote spot, at a stunning beach, or on a beautifully clear river. For others it's the adrenaline rush when a big one strikes, and the reel starts screaming. Still others say it's just sitting on a wharf or a rock in the sun with a line in hand. Fishing in New Zealand is as good as it gets, so don't pass up an opportunity to drop a line in the water.

Most harbor towns have reasonably priced fishing charters available. They are generally very good at finding fish, and most carry fishing gear you can use if you do not have your own. Inland areas usually have streams, rivers, or lakes with great trout fishing, where guides provide their knowledge of local conditions and techniques. With the aid of a helicopter, you can get into places few people have ever seen.

Freshwater Fishing: Trout and salmon, natives in the northern hemisphere, were introduced into New Zealand in the 1860s and 1880s. Rainbow and brown trout in particular have thrived in the rivers and lakes, providing arguably the best trout fishing in the world. Salmon do not grow to the size that they do in their native habitat, but they still make for good fishing. There is free access to all water. You may have to cross private land to fish certain areas, but a courteous approach for permission is normally well received.

The three methods of catching trout allowed in New Zealand are fly-fishing, spinning or threadlining, and trolling. In certain parts of South Island using small fish, insects, and worms as bait are also allowed. Deep trolling using leader lines and large capacity reels on short spinning rods is widely done on lakes Rotoma, Okataina, and Tarawera around Rotorua and on Lake Taupo, with the most popular lures being tobies, flatfish, and cobras. Streamer flies used for trolling are normally the smelt patterns: Taupo tiger, green smelt, ginger mick, Jack sprat, Parsons glory, and others. Flies, spoons, or wobblers used in conjunction with monofilament and light fly lines on either glass fly rods or spinning rods are popular on all the other lakes.

The lakes in the Rotorua district—Rotorua, Rotoiti, and Tarawera are the largest—produce some of the biggest, best conditioned rainbow trout in the world, which get to trophy size because of an excellent food supply, the absence of competition, and a careful and selective breeding program. In Lake Tarawera, fish from 6 to 10 pounds can be taken, especially in the autumn and winter, when bigger trout move into stream mouths before spawning.

The season around Rotorua runs from October 1 to June 30. In the period between April and June, just before the season closes, flies work very well on beautiful Lake Rotoiti. From December to March fly-fishing is good around the stream mouths on Lake Rotorua. The two best areas are the Ngongotaha Stream and the Kaituna River, using nymph, dry fly, and wet fly. Lake Rotorua remains open for fishing when the streams and rivers surrounding the lake are closed.

Lake Taupo and the surrounding rivers and streams are world renowned for rainbow trout—the lake has the largest yields of trout in New Zealand, an estimated 500 tons. Trolling on Taupo and fishing the rivers flowing into it with a guide are almost surefire ways of catching fish. Wind and weather on the lake, which can change quickly, will determine where you can fish, and going with local knowledge of the conditions on Taupo is essential. The streams and rivers flowing into the lake are open for fly-fishing from October 1 to May 31. The lower reaches of the Tongariro, Tauranga-Taupo, and Waitahanui rivers, and the lake itself, remain open year-round. Lake Waikaremoana in Urewera National Park southeast of Rotorua is arguably North Island's most scenic lake, and its fly-fishing and trolling are excellent.

South Island has excellent rivers with very clear water. Some of them hardly ever see anglers, and that untouched quality is particularly satisfying. South Island's best areas for trout are Marlborough, Westland, Fiordland, Southland, and Otago.

The Canterbury district has some productive waters for trout and salmon—along with the West Coast it is the only part of New Zealand where you can fish for salmon, the quinnat or Pacific chinook salmon introduced from North America. Anglers use large metal spoons and wobblers on long, strong rods. with spinning outfits to fish the Waimakariri, Waitaki, Rakaia, Ashburton, and Rangitata rivers around Christchurch, often catching salmon of 20 to 30 pounds.

Trout fishing is normally tougher than in North Island, with trout being a little smaller on average. But occasionally huge browns are caught. You can catch brown and rainbow trout in South Island lakes using flies, or by wading and spinning around lake edges or at stream mouths.

Saltwater Fishing: No country in the world is better suited than New Zealand for ocean fishing. Its coastline—approximately as long as that of the mainland United States—has an incredible variety of locations, whether you like fishing off rocks, on reefs, surf beaches, islands, or harbors. Big-game fishing is very popular, and anglers have taken many world records over the years. All the big names are here—black, blue, and striped marlin, both yellowfin and bluefin tuna, and sharks like mako, thresher, hammerhead, and bronze whaler.

The most sought-after fish around North Island are snapper (sea bream), kingfish, hapuka (grouper), tarakihi, John Dory, trevally, maomao, and kahawai, to name a few. Many of these also occur around the top of South Island. Otherwise, South Island's main catches are blue cod, butterfish, hake, hoki, ling, moki, parrot fish, pigfish, and trumpeter, which are all excellent eating fish.

Perhaps the most famous angler to fish our waters was adventure novelist Zane Grey, who had his base on Urupukapuka Island in the Bay of Islands. On North Island, the top areas are the Bay of Islands, the nearby Poor Knights Islands, Whangaroa in Northland, the Coromandel Peninsula and its islands, and the Bay of Plenty and White Island off its coast.

Licenses: Different districts in New Zealand for require different licenses. For example, Rotorua is not in the same area as nearby Lake Taupo. So it pays to check at the local fish and tackle store to make sure you are fishing legally. Fees are approximately $50 per year, but at most tackle stores you can purchase daily or weekly licenses. They can also advise you about local conditions, lures, and methods.

Publications: *How to Catch Fish and Where,* by Bill Hohepa, and *New Zealand Fishing News Map Guide,* edited by Sam Mossman, both have good information on salt- and freshwater fishing countrywide.

Season: Generally from October through June in streams and rivers; year-round in lakes and at sea.

Locations: Countrywide.

Cost: Big-game fishing: $800 to $1,200 per day. Saltwater sportfishing: $30 to $50 per half day, depending on how many are on the boat. Heli-fishing: $480 per person, per day. Trolling and fly-fishing for lake trout: from $65 per hour; on rivers and streams from $50 per hour.

North Island Freshwater Operators: Mark Aspinall, (✉ Lake Taupo, ☎ 07/378–4453); **Bryan Colman** (✉ Rotorua, ☎ 07/348–7766); **Mark Draper Fishing & Outdoors** (Mark Draper and Diane Chilcott, ✉ Box 445, Opotiki, Bay of Plenty–East Cape, ☎ FAX 07/315–7434); **Clark Gregor** (✉ Rotorua, ☎ 07/347–1730, FAX 07/347–1313); **Helicopter Line** (Lance Donnelly and Joanne Spencer, ✉ Box 3271, Auckland, ☎ 09/377–4406, FAX 09/377–4597); **Belinda Hewiatt** (✉ Lake Taupo, ☎ 07/378–1471, FAX 07/377–2926); **Chris Jolly Outdoors** (✉ Box 1020, Taupo, ☎ 07/378–0623, FAX 07/378–9458); **Taupo Commercial Launchman's Association** (✉ Box 1386, Taupo, ☎ 07/378–3444, FAX 07/377–2926); **Dennis Ward** (✉ Rotorua, ☎ 07/357–4974).

North Island Saltwater Operators: Bream Bay Charters (Steve and Brenda Martinovich, ✉ 59 Bream Bay Dr., Ruakaka, Northland, ☎ 09/432–7484); **Kerikeri Fish Charters** (Steve Butler, ✉ 23 Mission Rd., Kerikeri, Bay of Islands, ☎ 09/407–7165, FAX 09/407–5465); **Land Based Fishing** (✉ Box 579, Kaitaia, Northland, ☎ 09/409–4592); **Ma Cherie** (John Baker, ✉ Bay of Plenty, ☎ 07/307–0015 or 025/940–324); **Mako Charters** (Graeme McIntosh, ✉ Russell Harbour, ☎ FAX 09/403–7770); **MV** *Taranui* (✉ 17 Pacific Dr., Tairua, Coromandel Peninsula, ☎ 07/864–8511); **Outrigger Charters** (✉ 45 Williams Rd., Paihia, Bay of Islands, ☎ 09/402–6619 or 0800/485–584, FAX 09/402–7273); *Predator* (Bruce and Ann Martin, ✉ Box 120, Paihia, ☎ FAX 09/405–9883); **Sea Spray Charters (N. Z.) Ltd.** (Daryl Edwards, ✉ Box 13060, Tauranga, Bay of Plenty, ☎ 07/572–4241 or 025/477–187); **Seeker** (Ross Mossman, ✉ Hawke's Bay, ☎ 06/835–1397 or 025/442–082); **Te Ra–The Sun** (✉ Whangamata Harbor, Whangamata, Coromandel Peninsula, ☎ 07/865–8681); **Waipounamu Sport Fishing** (John Leins, ✉ Ferry Landing, Whitianga, Coromandel Peninsula, ☎ 07/866–2053, FAX 07/866–5275); **Whangarei Deep Sea Anglers Club** (✉ Box 401, Whangarei, Northland, ☎ 09/434–3818, FAX 09/434–3755).

South Island Freshwater Operators: Alpine Trophies (Dave Hetherington, ✉ Box 34, Fox Glacier, West Coast, ☎ 03/751–0856, FAX 03/751–0857); **Chris Jackson** (✉ Nelson Lakes district, ☎ 03/545–6416); **Fish Fiordland** (Mike Molineux, ✉ R.D. 1, Te Anau, Fiordland, ☎ 03/249–8070); **Fishing & Hunting Services** (Gerald Telford, ✉ 210 Brownston St., Wanaka, Central Otago, ☎ FAX 03/443–9257); **Kamahi Tours** (Bill Hayward, ✉ Box 59, Franz Josef, West Coast, ☎ 03/752–0793, FAX 03/752–0699); **Scott Murray** (✉ Nelson Lakes district, ☎ 03/545–9070); **Rakaia Salmon Safaris** (Geoff Scott and Ray Watts, ✉ The Cedars,

R.D. 14, Rakaia, Canterbury, ☎ 03/302–7444, FAX 03/302–7220); **Southern Lakes Guide Service** (Murry and Margaret Knowles, ✉ Box 84, Te Anau, Fiordland, ☎ 03/249–7565, FAX 03/249–8004); **Western Safaris** (Vern Thompson and Maggie Carlton, ✉ 34 McKerrow St., Te Anau, Fiordland, ☎ 03/249–7226); **Wilderness Fly Fishing N. Z.** (Stephen Couper, ✉ Box 149, Wakatipu, Queenstown, Central Otago, ☎ FAX 03/442–3589).

South Island Saltwater Operators: Haast Fish and Dive (✉ Box 58, Haast, West Coast, ☎ 03/750–0004, FAX 03/750– 0869); **Kenepuru Tours** (Gary and Ellen Orchard, ✉ Kenepuru Sounds, R.D. 2, Picton, Marlborough Sounds, ☎ FAX 03/573–4203); **Miss Portage Charters** (✉ 144 Wailkawa Rd., Picton, Marlborough, ☎ 03/573–7883); **MV *Spirit of Golden Bay 2*** (✉ Golden Bay Charters, Box 206, Takaka, Golden Bay, ☎ FAX 03/525–9135); **Samara Gamefishing Company** (Richard Allen, ✉ Box 5589, Dunedin, Otago, ☎ 03/477–8863, FAX 03/447–7558); **Thorfinn Charters** (Bruce Story, ✉ Box 43, Halfmoon Bay, Stewart Island, ☎ FAX 03/219–1210).

Hiking and Tramping

There isn't a better place on earth for hiking—called tramping here— than New Zealand. If you're looking for short tramps, you may want to head off on your own. For long treks, however, it can be a big help to go with a guide. The New Zealand wilderness is full of such a profusion of interesting flora and fauna that you won't even notice if you're in the country for the first time—unless you have someone along who knows the native bush. Many guides have a humorous streak that can be entertaining as well. Book trips at least three weeks in advance.

Particularly in the peak months of January and February, trails can be crowded enough to detract from the natural experience. One advantage of a guided walk is that companies have their own tent camps or huts, with such luxuries as hot showers—and cooks. For the phobic, it's worth mentioning one very positive feature: New Zealand has no snakes or predatory animals, no poison ivy, poison oak, leeches, or ticks. In South Island, especially on the West Coast, in Central Otago, and in Fiordland, be prepared for voracious sand flies—some call it the state "bird." Pick up insect repellent in New Zealand—their repellent repels their insects.

One of the top areas in North Island for hiking and walking is the rugged Coromandel Peninsula, with 3,000-ft volcanic peaks clothed with semitropical rain forest and some of the best stands of the giant kauri tree, some of which are 45 ft around, and giant tree ferns. There is also gold-mining history on the peninsula, and today the flicker of miners' lamps has given way to the steady green-blue light of millions of glow-worms in the mines and the forest. Kiwi Dundee Adventures, Ltd., has a variety of hiking trips that cover all aspects of the peninsula, as well as New Zealand–wide eco-walks away from the usual tourist spots.

Tongariro National Park in central North Island has hiking with a difference—on and around active volcanoes rising to heights of 10,000 ft, the highest elevation on the island. It is a beautiful region of contrasts: deserts, forests, lakes, mountains, and snow. Sir Edmund Hillary Outdoor Pursuits Centre of New Zealand guides hikes and more strenuous tramping around Ruapehu, as well as other activities at Turangi at the south end of Lake Taupo.

The three- to six-day walks on the beaches and in the forests of the Marlborough Sounds' Queen Charlotte Walkway and in Abel Tasman National Park (in northern South Island) are very popular, relatively easy, and well suited to family groups: Your pack is carried for you, and you stay in lodges. Another option is the Alpine Recreation Canterbury 15-day minibus tour of South Island, with two- to six-hour walks daily along the way. It provides an extensive and scenic cross section, with visits to three World Heritage areas and six national parks and discussions of natural history. Of course, it misses the magic of completing a long single walk.

The most famous New Zealand walk, the Milford Track—a four-day trek through Fiordland National Park—covers a wide variety of terrains, from forests to high passes, lakes, a glowworm grotto, and the spectacle of Milford Sound itself. As the track is strictly one-way (south to north), you rarely encounter other groups and so have the impression that your group is alone in the wild. Independent and escorted walkers stay in different huts about a half day's walk apart. Escorted walkers' huts are serviced and very comfortable; independent walkers' huts are basic, with few facilities. There are other walks in the same area: the Hollyford Track (five days), the Greenstone Valley (three days), and the Routeburn Track (three days). Greenstone and Routeburn together form the Grand Traverse.

If you want to get up close and personal with a mountain, Alpine Guides has a renowned seven-day course on the basics of mountaineering around Aoraki, the highest point in the New Zealand Alps. There is also a 10-day technical course for experienced climbers. New Zealand is the home of Sir Edmund Hillary, who, with Tenzing Norgay, made the first ascent of Mt. Everest, in 1953. The country has a fine mountaineering tradition, and Alpine Guides is its foremost training school.

Season: October–March for high-altitude walks, year-round for others.
Locations: Coromandel Peninsula and Tongariro National Park in North Island, Aoraki and Fiordlands National Park in South Island.
Cost: One- to three-day hikes range from $120 to $895; $1,489 for the six-day escorted Milford Track walk; $2,500 for 13 days. The climbing school costs $1,575 for seven days, including aircraft access, meals, accommodations, and transportation.
Tour Operators: Abel Tasman National Park Enterprises (⌧ 265 High St., Box 351, Motueka, South Island, ☎ 0800/223–582 or 03/528–7801, FAX 03/528–6087); **Alpine Guides** (⌧ Box 20, Mt. Cook, South Island, ☎ 03/435–1834, FAX 03/435–1898); **Alpine Recreation Canterbury** (⌧ Box 75, Lake Tekapo, South Island, ☎ 03/680–6736, FAX 03/680–6765); **Hollyford Tourist and Travel Company** (⌧ Box 94, Wakatipu, Otago, South Island, ☎ 03/442–3760, FAX 03/442–3761); **Kiwi Dundee Adventures, Ltd.** (⌧ Box 198, Whangamata, Coromandel Peninsula, North Island, ☎ 07/865–8809, FAX 07/865–8809); **Marlborough Sounds Adventure Company** (⌧ The Waterfront, Box 195, Picton, South Island, ☎ 03/573–6078, FAX 03/573–8827); **Milford Track Office** (⌧ Box 185, Te Anau, South Island, ☎ 0800/659–255 or 03/249–7411, FAX 03/249–7590); **Routeburn Walk Ltd.** (⌧ Box 568, Queenstown, South Island, ☎ 03/442–8200, FAX 03/442–6072); **Sir Edmund Hillary Outdoor Pursuits Centre of New Zealand** (⌧ Private Bag, Turangi, North Island, ☎ 07/386–5511, FAX 07/386–0204); **World Expeditions** (⌧ 441 Kent St., 3rd floor, Sydney, NSW 2000, ☎ 02/264–3366, FAX 02/261–974).

Horse Trekking

Operators all over New Zealand take people horseback riding along beaches, in native forests, on mountains, up rivers through pine plantations to all sorts of scenic delights. In North Island, Pakiri Beach Horse Rides north of Auckland, Rangihau Ranch and the Ace Hi Ranch in the Coromandel Peninsula, and Taupo Horse Treks at Lake Taupo run trips from several hours to several days.

In South Island, the sweep of the Canterbury Plains around Christchurch—and the surrounding mountain ranges—creates some of New Zealand's most dramatic scenery. One of the best ways to explore the area in some detail is on horseback. Wild Country Equine Adventures has a variety of rides, from a half day with afternoon tea to a three-day excursion including meals and accommodations. Hurunui Horse Treks and Alpine Horse Safaris have similar rides, as well as 8- and 10-day horse treks into remote backcountry in groups of six or fewer, on which you'll stay in rustic huts (without electricity, showers, or flush toilets). The feeling of riding in so much open air, watching the trail stretch to the distant horizon, is unparalleled. Terrain varies from dense scrub to open meadows and alpine passes. In the Nelson area at the top of South Island contact Stonehurst Farm Treks.

Season: October–March.
Locations: Canterbury high country.
Cost: From $90 for a day to $1,200 for 10 days.
Tour Operators: Ace Hi Ranch (⊠ State Hwy. 25, R.D. 1, Whitianga, Coromandel Peninsula, North Island, ☎ FAX 07/866–4897); **Alpine Horse Safaris** (⊠ Waitohi Downs, Hawarden, North Canterbury, South Island, ☎ FAX 03/314–4293); **Hurunui Horse Treks** (⊠ Taihoa Downs, R.D. Hawarden, South Island, ☎ 03/314–4204, FAX 03/314–4204); **Pakiri Beach Horse Rides** (⊠ Rahuikiri Road, R.D. 2, Wellsford, North Island, ☎ FAX 09/422–6275); **Rangihau Ranch** (⊠ Rangihau Road, Coroglen, Coromandel Peninsula, North Island, ☎ 07/866–3875); **Stonehurst Farm Treks** (⊠ R.D. 1, Richmond, South Island, ☎ 03/542–4121, FAX 03/542–3823). **Taupo Horse Treks** (⊠ Karapiti Road, Box 1142, Taupo, North Island, ☎ 07/378–0356, FAX 07/378–3230).

Rafting

The exhilaration of sweeping down into the foam-filled jaws of a rapid is always tinged with fear—white-water rafting is, after all, rather like being tossed into a washing machine. As you drift downriver during the lulls between the white water, it's wonderful to sit back and watch the wilderness unfold, whether it's stately rimu or rata trees overhanging the stream or towering cliffs with rain forest on the surrounding slopes. Rafting means camping by the river at night, drinking tea brewed over a fire, going to sleep with the sound of the stream in the background, and at dawn listening to the country's wonderful bird music. The juxtaposition of action and serenity gives rafting an enduring appeal that leads most who try it to seek out more rivers with more challenges. Rivers here are smaller and trickier than the ones used for commercial rafting in North America, and rafts usually hold only four to six people. Rafting companies provide all equipment—you only need clothing that won't be damaged by water (cameras are carried in waterproof barrels), a sleeping bag (in some cases), and sunscreen. Rafting qualifies as hard adventure.

In North Island, near Rotorua, the Rangitaiki offers exciting Grade-4 rapids and some good scenery. Nearby, the Wairoa offers Grade 5—the highest before a river becomes unraftable—and the Kaituna River has the highest raftable waterfall in the world: a 21-ft free fall. The Tongariro River flows from between the active 10,000-ft volcanic peaks of Tongariro National Park into the south end of Lake Taupo, New Zealand's largest lake. The Tongariro, as well as the mighty Motu River out toward the East Cape, is great for rafting.

In South Island, the great majority of activity centers on Queenstown. The most popular spot here is the upper reaches of the Shotover River beyond tortuous Skippers Canyon. In winter the put-in site for the Shotover is accessible only by helicopter, and wet suits are essential year-round, as the water is very cold. Some of the rapids are Grade 5. The Rangitata River south of Christchurch is fed by an enormous catchment basin, and rafting is serious at all water levels.

The two-day white-water-and-wilderness Danes trip, down the Landsborough River, flows through Aoraki National Park past miles of virgin forest into some very exciting rapids.

Season: Mainly October–May.
Locations: Rotorua, Taupo, the Canterbury, and Queenstown.
Cost: From $80 for one day to $500 for two days (with helicopter set-down), including all equipment (wet suits, helmets, footwear).
Tour Operators: Challenge Rafting (⊠ Box 814, Queenstown, South Island, ☎ 03/442–7318, ℻ 03/441–8563); **Kaituna Cascades** (⊠ Box 2217, Rotorua, North Island ☎ 07/357–5032, ℻ 07/357–4370); **Rangitata Rafts** (⊠ Peel Forest, R.D. 20, South Canterbury, South Island, ☎ 03/696–3735 or 0800/251–251 toll-free in N.Z., ℻ 03/696–3534).

Sailing

Varied coastline and splendid waters have made sailing extremely popular in New Zealand. Admittedly, your role as a passenger on a commercial sailing vessel is hardly strenuous. You are likely to participate in the sailing of the vessel more than you would on a regular cruise line, but for all intents and purposes this is a soft adventure in paradise. The best sailing areas in New Zealand are undoubtedly from the Bay of Islands south to the Coromandel Peninsula and the Bay of Plenty. This coastline has many islands and a wrinkled shoreline that make for wonderful, sheltered sailing. You can take a piloted launch, or if you have the experience, captain a sailboat yourself.

At the bottom of South Island, Southern Heritage Expeditions uses a Finnish-built, 236-ft, 19-cabin, ice-strengthened vessel, the *Akademik Shokalski,* to explore the islands of the southern Pacific Ocean and beyond to Antarctica, with one short voyage each season (November to mid-March) through the deeply indented coastline of Fiordland. In all the areas visited on these programs humans have attempted to occupy the environment. At present, nature is winning it back in the presence of congregations of wildlife, such as the royal albatross, Hookers sea lion, elephant seal, and several penguin species.

Season: Year-round.
Locations: Bay of Islands in North Island, lower South Island.
Cost: Bay of Islands from $415 to $725 per night depending on the craft; Doubtful Sound from $1,300 for five days; Fiordland National Park area from $2,100 for eight days; sub-Antarctic islands of Australia and New Zealand from $4,700 for 16 days.
Tour Operators: Moorings Yacht Charters (⊠ 23B Westhaven Dr., Westhaven, Auckland; mooring address, ⊠ The Jetty, Opua, Bay of Plenty, North Island, ☎ 09/402–7821; ☎ 813/530–5424 reservations in the U.S., ℻ 813/530–9747); **Southern Heritage Expeditions** (⊠ Box 20-219, Christchurch, South Island, ☎ 03/359–7711, ℻ 03/359–3311); **Straycat Day Sailing Charters** (⊠ Doves Bay Rd., Kerikeri, Bay of Islands, North Island, ☎ 09/407–7342 or 025/96–9944).

7 Portraits of New Zealand

New Zealand at a Glance: A Chronology

Flora and Fauna

Books and Videos

NEW ZEALAND AT A GLANCE: A CHRONOLOGY

c. AD 750   The first Polynesians arrive, settling mainly in South Island, where they find the moa, a flightless bird and an important food source, in abundance.

950   Kupe, the Polynesian voyager, names the country Aotearoa, "land of the long white cloud." He returns to his native Hawaiki, believed to be present-day French Polynesia.

1300s   A population explosion in Hawaiki triggers a wave of immigrants who quickly displace the archaic moa hunters.

1642   Abel Tasman of the Dutch East India Company becomes the first European to sight the land—he names his discovery Nieuw Zeeland. But after several of his crew are killed by Maori, he sails away without landing.

1769   Captain James Cook becomes the first European to set foot on New Zealand. He claims it in the name of the British crown.

1790s   Sealers, whalers, and timber cutters arrive, plundering the natural wealth and introducing the Maori to the musket, liquor, and influenza.

1814   The Reverend Samuel Marsden establishes the first mission station, but 11 years pass before the first convert is made.

1832   James Busby is appointed British Resident, charged with protecting the Maori people and fostering British trade.

1840   Captain William Hobson, representing the crown, and Maori chiefs sign the Treaty of Waitangi. In return for the peaceful possession of their land and the rights and privileges of British citizens, the chiefs recognize British sovereignty.

1840–41   The New Zealand Company, an association of British entrepreneurs, establishes settlements at Wanganui, New Plymouth, Nelson, and Wellington.

1852   The British Parliament passes the New Zealand Constitution Act, establishing limited self-government. The country's first gold strike occurs in Coromandel town in the Coromandel Peninsula.

1861   Gold is discovered in the river valleys of central Otago, west of Dunedin.

1860–72   Maori grievances over loss of land trigger the Land Wars in North Island. The Maori win some notable victories, but lack of unity ensures their ultimate defeat. Vast tracts of ancestral land are confiscated from rebel tribes.

1882   The first refrigerated cargo is dispatched to England, giving the country a new source of prosperity—sheep. A century later, there will be 20 sheep for every New Zealander.

1893   Under the Liberal government, New Zealand becomes the first country to give women the vote.

1914   New Zealand enters World War I.

1931   The Hawke's Bay earthquake kills 258 and levels the city of Napier.

1939   New Zealand enters World War II.

1950   New Zealand troops sail for Korea.

1965 Despite public disquiet, troops are sent to Vietnam.

1973 Britain joins the European Economic Community, and New Zealand's loss of this traditional export market is reflected in a crippling balance-of-payments deficit two years later.

1981 Violent antigovernment demonstrations erupt during a tour by a South African rugby team.

1985 The Greenpeace ship *Rainbow Warrior* is sunk by a mine in Auckland Harbour, and a crewman is killed. Two of the French secret service agents responsible are arrested, jailed, transferred to French custody—then soon released.

Sir Paul Reeves is sworn in as the first Maori governor-general.

Relations with the United States sour when the government bans visits by ships carrying nuclear weapons. The U.S. government responds by ejecting New Zealand from the ANZUS alliance.

1989 David Lange resigns as prime minister.

1990 The National Party replaces the Labour Party in government.

1993 The country votes for a major constitutional change, replacing the "first past the post" electoral system inherited from Britain with a "mixed member proportional" (MMP) system. The election sees the National Party clinging to power within a coalition.

1995 New Zealand's *Black Magic* wins the America's Cup yachting regatta. The country goes into party mode over the win, which signals both a sporting triumph and a coming of age technologically.

Mt. Ruapehu in North Island's Tongariro National Park bubbles and sputters, attracting interested onlookers from around the world.

New Zealanders' abhorrence of all things nuclear comes to the fore again with major floating protests against France's resumed nuclear testing in the South Pacific.

1996 Noisy Ruapehu spews debris into the air, covering nearby towns with a few inches of ash.

New Zealand elects its first MMP government, having voted for constitutional change three years earlier. New Zealand First holds the balance of power and goes into government with the National Party.

1997 New Zealand starts to feel the effect of weakening Asian currencies, particularly as numbers of Korean and Japanese tourists fall.

The country goes to the polls for a referendum on a mandatory retirement savings tax and overwhelmingly rejects the idea.

Jenny Shipley replaces Jim Bolger as prime minister, leading the New Zealand First coalition government and becoming the country's first woman PM.

1998 The Government introduces a controversial "work for the dole" scheme, in which people on unemployment benefit are required to work or train 20 hours a week or risk having their income slashed.

As the Asian economic crisis continues to bite, industrial strikes on Australia's waterfront also impact New Zealand's economy. The country's economic fundamentals remain strong, but these outside influences cause the N.Z. dollar to lose value against U.S. currency.

FLORA AND FAUNA

NEW ZEALAND is a fascinating evolutionary case. Its islands are a chip off of the one-time Gonwanaland supercontinent—a vast landmass that consisted of current-day South America, Africa, and Australia that started breaking up some 100 million years ago, well before the evolution of mammals. Since then, floating on its own some 1,200 miles southeast of Australia, this cluster of islands might seem to have developed quietly on its own, away from the hungry predatory jaws of the rest of the world.

But powerful forces of change have been constantly working on New Zealand. Plate tectonics created the rugged, 12,000-plus-ft mountains of South Island. And the Pacific Rim's wild geothermal eruptions left their mark on North Island. For eons volcanic activity has built mountainous cones and laid carpets of ash, making tremendously rich soil for the plant kingdom. The great, rumbling Mt. Ruapehu near Lake Taupo is a living reminder of this subterranean fury.

Global climatic variations haven't spared the islands, either, and on numerous occasions the Antarctic ice cap has edged north from the pole. Glaciers covered South Island and much of North Island, significantly affecting the character of plant life. Some plants adapted, and some couldn't survive. Except for the northern portions of North Island that weren't iced over—interestingly enough the rough extent of New Zealand's glorious kauri trees—after each glacial retreat the country's flora has recolonized the areas previously covered by ice in different ways.

Animals on the islands were, at least until the arrival of humans, almost like living fossils. The only mammal was a tiny bat, and there were no predators until the Maori first came, around AD 700—none, other than hunger. Bird life included the 12-ft flightless moa, which the Maori hunted to extinction. That was easy, because the birds had never before needed to develop evasive behavior to stay alive. The Maori brought dogs and rats, and

Europeans brought deer, possums, goats, trout, and other fauna, some of which were used for their pelts, others for sport. In almost all cases, the exotic fauna have done tremendous damage to the landscape. And the human presence itself has dramatically altered the land. Early Maori farming practices involved burning, which reduced a portion of the forests. When Europeans settled the country, they brought sheep, cattle, and the grasses that their livestock needed to eat. And they cut forests for, among other uses, ship masts. The kauri served this purpose better than any other wood in the world and paid in numbers for that virtue.

None of this makes the forests that cover New Zealand any less exotic, or any less fascinating. Some plants have adapted growth cycles in which the plant completely changes appearance—lancewood is an example—some of them two or three times until they reach maturity. As a result, botanists at one time believed there to be two or three species where in fact there was only one. If you have never been in a rain forest, the sheer density of vegetation in various subtropical areas will be dazzling. There are species here that exist nowhere else on earth. And keep in mind that one-fifth of the country is set aside as parkland. In those wild woods, you will still find no predators, and native species are alive and well, in many cases making comebacks very dramatic indeed.

Here is a short list of plants and animals that you might encounter in New Zealand.

Bellbird. The New Zealand forest has a different sound than any other, and it's this bird and one other, the tui, that make it unique. It's a welcoming, exotic chiming song.

It's a lot easier to get into the grips of a **bush lawyer** plant than out of them. It is a thorny, viny thing that grows in dense forest, climbing in and out of whatever it chooses.

The odd plant clumps fastened to the sides of trees throughout forests are **epiphytes,** not parasites. They grow on the trees but make their own living off water and other airborne particles. Some are orchids, a marvelous sight if you catch them in bloom.

The abundance of **ferns** may be what you most readily associate with the New Zealand bush. Two of the most magnificent are the mamaku and the ponga. The former also goes by the English name black tree fern, and it is the one that grows up to 60 ft tall and is found countrywide, with the exception of the east coast of South Island. The Maori used to cook and eat parts of the plant that are said to taste a bit like applesauce. The ponga is shorter than the mamaku, reaching a height of 30 ft. Its English name, silver tree fern, comes from the color of the undersides of the fronds. Their silvery whiteness illuminates darker parts of the bush. The ponga is the ferny emblem of New Zealand's international sports teams and Air New Zealand.

The **Horoeka** (also called **Lancewood**) tree is one of the freakish New Zealand natives par excellence. In its youth, its long, serrated, almost woody leaves hardly look alive, hanging down from their scrawny trunk. Horoekas inch their way skyward like this for as many as 20 years before maturing, flowering profusely, and bearing black berries.

The towering **kahikatea** (ka-*hee*-ka-*tee*-ah) is the tallest tree in the country, reaching as high as 200 ft with its slender and elegant profile. A mature tree bears a tremendous amount of berries, which Maori climbers used to harvest by ascending 80 branchless ft and more to pluck. These days wood pigeons are the prime consumers of the fruit.

There are still **kauri** trees in Northland and the Coromandel Peninsula that are as many as 1,500 years old, with a girth of at least 30 ft and height upwards of 150 ft. The lower trunks of the trees are branchless, and branches on an old tree begin some 50 ft above the ground. Lumberjacks in the 1800s spared some of these giants, and their presence is awesome. Like so many other native trees, kauris are slow growers—a mere 80-year-old will stand just 30 ft tall. Kauri gum was another valuable item. It doesn't rot, so balls of gum of any age were usable to make varnish and paint. It is now illegal to cut down a kauri, and as a result the trees are making a solid comeback.

Much is said of the formidable South Island **kea** (kee-ah), a mountain parrot, which, because it has been accused of killing sheep, has in the last century barely escaped extinction. Its numbers are significant today, much to the dismay of campers and anyone who lives under a tin roof. Keas love to play, which means anything from ripping tents to shreds to clattering around on metal roofs at all hours to peeling out the rubber gaskets around car windows. They are smart birds, smart enough, perhaps, to delight in taking revenge on those who tried to wipe them out. Observe their behavior keenly; it may be the only way to maintain a sense of humor if harassed.

Don't bet on seeing a **kiwi** in the wild. These nocturnal, bush-loving birds are scarce and shy, their numbers having dwindled with the felling of forests over the last 150 years. Along with the now-extinct giant moa and other species, the kiwi is one of the remarkable New Zealand natives that live nowhere else on earth. If you're keen on seeing one in the feather, plan a trip to Stewart Island and hire a guide to take you on a search, or stop at a wildlife park.

The **manuka** is a small tree shrub found throughout the country in tough impenetrable thickets. Early settlers made a fair tea from the plant until something tastier came along. The tea tree's white or rosy blossoms attract bees in profusion, and they in turn produce the popular, strong-tasting manuka honey that you can find in stores just about everywhere.

The **nikau palm** is one of the country's most exotic-looking trees, growing to a height of about 30 ft. The Maori used different parts of the leaves both for food and for thatch in shelters.

Phormium tenax, also called New Zealand flax, even though it isn't a true flax, has been useful as cordage in traditional and contemporary weaving. It favors damp areas and hillsides. Its thick, spiky, dark green leaves originate from a central saddle and can grow to 6 ft. The telltale flower stalk can reach 15 ft and bears dark red flowers. A number of varieties are ornamental and are very popular in New Zealand gardens.

The **pohutukawa** (po-*hoo*-too-*ka*-wa) tree is a sight both for its gnarly roots that like watery places and its red blossoms, which burst forth toward the end of December—hence its Kiwi name: New Zealand's Christmas tree.

Possums. Currently about 80 million in number, this introduced species is gobbling up New Zealand forests. Try as they may to get rid of them, Kiwis are having a rough go with the tree dwellers. Their nickname, squash 'ems, comes from seeing so many splayed out on roads throughout the country.

Pukeka (poo-*keh*-ka). Effectively the New Zealand chicken, this bird kicks around on farms and roadsides often enough that you're likely to see plenty of them. They're blue, with a red bill, and they stand about 15 inches tall.

Rangiora (rang-ee-*ohr*-ah). You'll get to know this plant better if you remember it as "bushman's friend"—its soft, silvery underside is the forest's best tissue for your underside.

There are a couple of species of **rata**. The northern rata is a parasite, climbing a host tree and eventually cutting off its light and water supplies. The rata and its host wage a long-term struggle, and the rata doesn't always win. The southern rata is a freestanding tree, yielding beautiful red lumber. Rata flowers are a pretty red themselves, resembling the pohutukawa tree's blooms but coming out about a month earlier in November.

If you're in the country in November, you'll see at first more evidence of the **rewarewa** (*re*-wa-*re*-wa) tree in its fallen blossoms on the ground. They are tightly woven magenta bottle-brush-like flowers, with touches of chartreuse and black, that are some of the most enchanting in the country, if in part for their uniqueness.

One of those ingenious New Zealand plants that goes through three stages of being on its way to maturity, the **rimu** red pine is a valuable source of timber. It spends its first stage in life as a delicate treelet, with pale green, weeping branches that look something like an upright moss. It then turns itself into a conical shape before finishing its growth as a soaring, 100-plus-ft wonder with a branchless trunk and a rounded head. Charcoal from rimu was used in traditional Maori tattooing.

Supplejack vines just hang about in the forest, so dense in places that they could make passage next to impossible. You'll often find that their soft, edible tips have been nipped off by the teeth of wild goats that Pakeha (Europeans) introduced. Believe it or not, this is a member of the lily family.

Along with the bellbird, the **tui** is the chanteuse extraordinaire that fills Aotearoa's woods with its magically clear melodies. You may have never thought of birds as actually singing, but you certainly will when you hear a tui.

Wekas (weh-kah) are funny birds. They can appear to be oblivious to what's going on around them as they walk about pecking at this or that, looking bemused. They are flightless rails, and they'll steal your food if you're camping, so hide it away. Generally speaking, they're pleasant to have around, particularly if you're looking for some entertainment.

Wood pigeon. You'll have no trouble figuring out that this is a pigeon, but your jaw will drop at the size—they look like they've been inflated like balloons. They're beautiful birds.

—Stephen Wolf and Barbara Blechman

BOOKS AND VIDEOS

Books

Because of the limited availability of many first-rate books on New Zealand outside the country, there is only so much that you'll be able to read before you go. So leave room in your suitcase for pickup reading once you arrive, and bring something home to make your trip linger longer. One caveat: Because of economies of scale in the New Zealand publishing industry, books tend to be expensive. That's one reason to do some secondhand shopping; another is the stores' usually knowledgeable staff, which can make recommendations.

History. *The Oxford Illustrated History of New Zealand,* edited by Keith Sinclair, provides a comprehensive and highly readable account of the country's social, political, cultural, and economic evolution from the earliest Maori settlements and their world view up to 1989. James Belich's *Making Peoples* looks at New Zealand history from a 1990s perspective, with more emphasis on the Maori view than some earlier publications. *The Colonial New Zealand Wars,* by Tim Ryan and Bill Parham, is a vivid history of the Maori-British battles. Lavishly illustrated with photographs of colonial infantry and drawings of Maori hill forts, flags, and weapons, the book makes far more compelling reading than the dry military history suggested by the title. Another highly readable military-historical book is James Belich's *The New Zealand Wars.* J. C. Beaglehole's *The Discovery of New Zealand* is an authoritative and scholarly analysis of the voyages of discovery, from the first Polynesians to the Europeans of the late 18th century.

Fiction. New Zealand's best-known short story writer is **Katherine Mansfield** (1888–1923), whose early stories were set in and around the city of Wellington, her birthplace. *The Best of Katherine Mansfield* is a fine compilation of stories from five collections. Reading her journals will give you a sense of her passionate romantic side, and as much as she disliked the small-minded provincial qualities of New Zealand, she loved the country deeply.

New Zealand's most distinguished living writer is **Janet Frame.** Her works are numerous, from novels such as her successful *The Carpathians* to a three-part autobiography, which is a lyrical evocation of growing up in small-town New Zealand in the 1920s and 1930s and of the gradual awakening of a writer of great courage. Kiwi filmmaker Jane Campion adapted the middle of it for the screen into *An Angel at My Table.* **Maurice Gee** is another distinguished novelist. His *Plumb* won the James Tait prize for the best novel in Britain when it was published. *Plumb* reaches back to the early 20th century for its story of a renegade parson and his battle with old-world moral pieties. One particularly compelling scene is set in a mining town, where Plumb happens to be the man to hear the last testament of a notorious murderer.

Two of the finest and most exciting writers at work in the country today are **Patricia Grace** and **Witi Ihimaera,** Maori whose story collections and novels are on a par with the best fiction in the U.K. and the States. Grace's stories are beautifully and fluidly related, very much from inside her characters, taking everyday feelings and expanding them into something almost timeless. Look for *The Dream Sleepers and Other Stories* and her novel *Mutuwhenua.* Ihimaera (ee-hee-may-ra) also uses very clear prose and Maori experience. His early novel *Tangi* opens with the death of a father and moves through the 22-year-old son's experience of loss and innocence to his acceptance of his role as a man. Maori elements of the story are fascinating both culturally and emotionally. Also look for his *Bulibasha* and *Nights in the Garden of Spain.*

The most internationally celebrated work of fiction to come from New Zealand in recent years is **Keri Hulme**'s *The Bone People,* winner of the Booker McConnell Prize in 1985. Set on the isolated West Coast of the South Island, this challenging, vital novel weaves Polynesian myth with Christian symbolism and the powerful sense of place that characterizes modern Maori writing. More recently, Alan Duff's *Once Were Warriors* is a frank, uncompromising, and ultimately transcendent look at urban Maori society. Both the novel and the film were real sensations in New Zealand. The sequel, *What Becomes of the Broken Hearted,* and Duff's recently published *Both Sides of the Moon* have also been hugely successful.

Poetry. *100 New Zealand Poems by 100 New Zealand Poets,* edited by New Zealand's current Poet Laureate, Bill Manhire, ranges from the country's earliest poems to the new poets of the 1990s. The final poem in the book is by six year-old Laura Ranger, who went on the publish, at age 10, the outstanding best-seller *Laura's Poems,* which has now sold more than any previous book of New Zealand poetry. Greg O'Brien and Jenny Bornholdt's *My Heart Goes Swimming* is a charming selection of New Zealand love poems. A more wide-ranging and weighty collection is *An Anthology of New Zealand Poetry in English.*

Garden Guides. If you are serious about visiting gardens while in New Zealand, any of the books listed below would be helpful. These are not typically stocked in U.S. bookstores, so make a well-supplied store one of your first stops when you arrive. Hundreds of gardens are listed in Alison McRae's *Garden's to Visit in New Zealand* and Beverly Bridge's *Register of New Zealand Private Gardens Open to the Public, Volume 2.* They both give descriptions of gardens and list addresses, telephone numbers, and visiting times. *The Native Garden,* by Isobel Gabites and Rob Lucas, offers a superb vision of what constitutes a truly New Zealand garden, which of course is dominated by unique indigenous flora. Two other books are more limited in providing information but offer glossy photographs and make good souvenirs: Julian Matthews and Gil Hanly's *New Zealand Town and Country Gardens* and Premier Books's *Glorious New Zealand Gardens.* A superb monthly magazine, *New Zealand Gardener,* highlights several of the country's gardens in each issue. It is available at newspaper shops and bookstores countrywide.

Specialized Guidebooks. Strictly for wine lovers, *The Wines and Vineyards of New Zealand,* by Michael Cooper, is an exhaustive evaluation in words and pictures of every vineyard in the country. For travelers who plan to make hiking a major component of their vacations, *Tramping in New Zealand,* published by Lonely Planet, is an invaluable guide. *A Field Guide to Auckland* is a wonderful introduction to the natural and historic attractions of the Auckland region. It includes an overview of natural and human history and details of over 140 interesting places to visits within easy distance of the city.

Art Books. Three companion volumes—on painting, sculpture, printmaking, photography, ceramics, glass, and jewelry—provide a superb introduction to New Zealand art: *100 New Zealand Paintings, Another 100 New Zealand Artists,* and *100 New Zealand Craft Artists.* Greg O'Brien's *Hotere: Out the Black Window* covers the work of one of the country's most respected artists.

Illustrated Books. *Salute to New Zealand,* edited by Sandra Coney, is a coffee-table book that intersperses lavish photographs with chapters by some of the country's finest contemporary writers. *Wild New Zealand,* published by Reader's Digest, is a pictorial account of the country's landscape, flora, and fauna, supplemented by an informative text with such a wealth of detail that it turns the sensory experience of the landscape into a cerebral one.

Videos

New Zealand's film industry has had a relatively small output, but the quality of its films has been quite high. Jane Campion's *The Piano* (1993) is a prime example, as are her earlier *An Angel at My Table* (1990) and *Sweetie* (1988), which was made in Australia. Roger Donaldson's 1977 thriller *Sleeping Dogs* was the first New Zealand film released in the United States, followed by the equally worthy *Smash Palace* (1982). The tough, urban portrayal of *Once Were Warriors* (1995) is one of the most recent to make it across the Pacific. Its portrait of urban Maori life, unfortunately, makes New Zealand look a little too much like Los Angeles.

INDEX

WHEREVER YOU TRAVEL, *H*ELP IS NEVER FAR AWAY.

From planning your trip to

providing travel assistance along

the way, American Express®

Travel Service Offices are

always there to help

you do more.